D1713772

Dangerous Ground

Dangerous Ground

*Squatters, Statesmen, and
the Antebellum Rupture of
American Democracy*

JOHN SUVAL

OXFORD
UNIVERSITY PRESS

OXFORD
UNIVERSITY PRESS

Oxford University Press is a department of the University of Oxford. It furthers
the University's objective of excellence in research, scholarship, and education
by publishing worldwide. Oxford is a registered trade mark of Oxford University
Press in the UK and certain other countries.

Published in the United States of America by Oxford University Press
198 Madison Avenue, New York, NY 10016, United States of America.

CIP data is on file at the Library of Congress

ISBN 978–0–19–753142–6

DOI: 10.1093/oso/9780197531426.001.0001

1 3 5 7 9 8 6 4 2

Printed by Integrated Books International, United States of America

For Mom, Dad,
and my love Marika

The term "*squatter*" is very ambiguous.

—*Dictionary of Americanisms*, 1848

Squatter Sovereignty. What do those terms mean?

—Abraham Lincoln, 1858

Contents

Acknowledgments

A PROJECT LIKE this incubates with the help of many people.

The study began at the University of Wisconsin-Madison, an institution long at the forefront of scholarship on US public lands and the American West. My advisor, Bill Cronon, is a crucial link to that legacy and has redefined the fields of environmental and western history. It's truly a boon to work with Bill, whose talents as a writer and thinker are matched by his kindness and skills as a mentor. Steve Kantrowitz has been a source of wise, unstinting support and leads the way as an engaged scholar constantly breaking new ground. Susan Johnson has been a generous mentor and model of scholarly excellence. Special thanks to friends and fellow Cronon grads including Brian Hamilton and Rachel Gross who welcomed me into the fold; "Coalition of the Writing" members Brad Baranowski, Skye Doney, Dan Hummel, and Kevin Walters—stalwart companions across the finish line; Leslie Abadie and colleagues who adeptly administer the History Department; Charles L. Cohen, a great teacher; Susan Zaeske, the dynamic Associate Dean for Arts & Humanities; and John Hall and Larry Nesper for their valuable input on this project. Among the joys of studying history at Wisconsin are the interdisciplinary conversations at the Nelson Institute's Center for Culture, History, and Environment (CHE) and proximity to the great Wisconsin Historical Society.

I count myself fortunate to be an editor on the *Papers of Andrew Jackson* and member of the History Department at the University of Tennessee, Knoxville. Tom Coens, Laura-Eve Moss, and Aaron Crawford are the best of colleagues and set standards for excellence in documentary editing. Retired director Dan Feller led this crack team with a sure hand before passing the baton to Michael Woods, an exemplary scholar whom I first met while a doctoral student conducting research at the Stephen A. Douglas Papers. Since that time Michael has been a mentor and friend. UTK's history department, under the leadership of Ernie Freeberg, has been a delightful scholarly home. My thanks to the department and UTK for their support of this project, including the Betsey B. Creekmore Special Collections and University Archives for furnishing images of the Crockett almanacs.

Prior to joining the Jackson Papers I had the good fortune of spending a year as a postdoctoral fellow at the University of Missouri's Kinder Institute on Constitutional Democracy, where historians and political scientists combine to create a uniquely congenial intellectual space. Special thanks to Jeff Pasley, Jay Sexton, Christa Dierksheide, Justin Dyer, Thomas Kane, Allison Smythe, Luke Perez, Rudy Hernandez, and Lawrence Goldman for making my time at Mizzou so enjoyable and productive.

Conducting archival research has been one of the joys of this project. An Alfred M. Landon Historical Research Grant, administered by the Kansas Historical Foundation, helped fund research at the Kansas State Historical Society. I am grateful as well for an Andrew W. Mellon Foundation research fellowship from the Library Company of Philadelphia/Historical Society of Pennsylvania; a Gunther Barth Fellowship from the Bancroft Library; a Donald J. Sterling, Jr. Fellowship from the Oregon Historical Society; and a Robert L. Platzman Memorial Fellowship from the University of Chicago Library. Thanks to the expert archivists at these institutions, as well as those at the National Archives, the Center for Legislative Archives, Library of Congress, California Historical Society, Center for Sacramento History, Indiana State Library, Kenneth Spencer Research Library, and New-York Historical Society. Portions of this book, primarily in Chapter 5, appeared in an earlier form in the Fall 2017 issue of the *Oregon Historical Quarterly*. Thanks to editor Eliza Canty-Jones and staff for their invaluable feedback. My gratitude to Brad Tyer, Renee and David Cerchie, Harry and Vivian Snyder, and Dennis and Louie Austin for providing happy abodes while on the road.

This book has benefited profoundly from the input of talented editors and historians. It's been the privilege of a lifetime working with Susan Ferber and the superb team at Oxford University Press, who have pressed on heroically during challenging pandemic times. Many thanks to Reeve Huston for reading different drafts and offering encouragement and expert guidance; Michael Woods for reading an early version and later draft and sharing trenchant insights that sharpened my arguments; Tom Coens for casting his keen eye over a final draft and suggesting many helpful edits; and the anonymous readers for OUP who provided supremely constructive feedback. Their interventions made this a better book.

My family is a source of unwavering support and love. My thanks and deepest gratitude to Kathy, Geoff, Gregg, Drossy, Johnny, Anna, and Spencer for all the laughter and goodness they bring to the world, and to Moeksie, Monika, and Karl for warmly welcoming me into the Hoffmann clan of the Western Cape. There is no way to adequately express my gratitude to my mother and father for providing a loving home, every opportunity to thrive and, to this day, the best company. Our New York and West Virginia heritage, combined with the family antiques business founded in 1896, have connected me to the past in vivid ways since childhood.

Marika has sustained me every step of the way. She is my sunlight and oxygen, making this life a happy adventure (all the more magical since she brought a little street cat named Knox into our home). She moves through the world with grace, compassion, and cheer. And she built me a desk to finish this book. To her and my parents I dedicate these pages.

Dangerous Ground

Introduction

A TALE OF TWO SQUATTERS

JOHN H. STRINGFELLOW arrived in Kansas soon after Congress opened
the territory to settlement in 1854 and launched a militantly proslavery newspaper that he named, provocatively, the *Squatter Sovereign*. A Virginia-born
Democrat and physician by training, Stringfellow wielded substantial influence in territorial politics and used his publication to frame what was at
stake in key elections. "The Squatters of Kansas will be called upon to decide
whether the government of this Territory shall be given over to the hands of
the Abolitionists and Negro Thieves, or to the true and honest men of the
South," declared one of his newspaper's March 1855 articles. The gangly editor
trusted implicitly that the squatter readers he addressed—white men who
hailed mainly from neighboring Missouri and places throughout the South—
shared his slavery-crusading passions. Just to be sure, though, he peppered
the pages with battle cries like "DEATH TO ALL YANKEES, AND TRAITORS
IN KANSAS!" No doubt he found it gratifying when the squatters of Kansas
elected him to the territorial legislature, where he soon ascended to the post
of House speaker.[1]

Stringfellow was not the only squatter chief in Kansas. His nemesis,
Charles Robinson, had attained prominence as the leader of the Squatter
Riot in Sacramento, a deadly 1850 melee sparked by American settlers in
the aftermath of the US-Mexican War. Surviving a point-blank gunshot,
the bearded, blue-eyed Massachusetts native—also a physician—won a seat
in the California legislature as a champion of squatters' interests. In Kansas,
acquiring land remained his primary focus but for a different purpose. As
agent for the New England Emigrant Aid Company, he smoothed the way
for white settlers from the North to acquire prairie land—much of it still

Dangerous Ground. John Suval, Oxford University Press. © Oxford University Press 2022.
DOI: 10.1093/oso/9780197531426.003.0001

belonging to Native Americans—and establish farms in a bid to make Kansas a free state. A member of the incipient Republican Party and fierce opponent of slavery, Robinson also presided over the splinter Free State government, created in response to voter fraud and rampant thuggery that had placed proslavery men like Stringfellow in positions of power. He would go on to become the first governor of the state of Kansas.

Robinson rejected Stringfellow's brand of squatterism, which he considered a Slave Power ploy to turn Kansas into a stronghold for the ungodly institution. In his eyes, the self-styled squatters fighting for slavery were not genuine settlers but whiskey-swilling, rifle-toting "Border Ruffians" who marched in from Missouri at key junctures to harass free-state partisans and steal elections, and then returned home. Stringfellow, for his part, viewed Robinson and his associates as the true invaders, a pack of holier-than-thou New Englanders backed by rich abolitionists hell-bent on trampling slaveholders' rights. The two men did more than fight a war of words. Throughout 1855 and 1856, they faced off as leaders of dueling governments and, at times, as commanders of warring squatter armies amid the escalating violence of Bleeding Kansas.

Why did men with antithetical ideologies and agendas both self-identify as squatters and claim other squatters as their natural constituents and allies? More puzzling still, why did squatters—figures commonly associated with illicit land grabs—emerge as foot soldiers on the front lines of clashes over slavery that convulsed the nation in the lead-up to the Civil War?

Their outsized influence is surprising given that these controversial settlers had long been fixtures of the frontier West, familiar yet far away from the mainstream of American life. In fact, the very term squatter—defined by Noah Webster as "one that settles on new land without a title"—was an Americanism, first cropping up in the eighteenth century. By the time Stringfellow and Robinson vied to commandeer this identity for their causes, squatters had come to occupy a central and destabilizing position in US political culture. This book tracks how that happened and examines the consequences. Following in squatters' footsteps from 1830 to 1860 imparts novel perspectives on how the United States grew into a continent-spanning juggernaut that afforded upward mobility to a wide spectrum of white males as well as how those territorial conquests fractured the body politic. During this period, the issues of land-claiming and slavery extension became stubbornly intertwined—indeed, the very act of occupying terrain and establishing communities determined whether slavery or freedom would prevail in flashpoints across the West. By transplanting their preferred social systems and agricultural modes, squatters of diverging descriptions became vectors of conflicting visions over America's future.[2]

The heightened visibility and growing clout of white squatters came courtesy of the Jacksonian Democratic Party. Unlike previous generations of statesmen who maligned squatters as outlaws for flouting conventions of titled property and sought to contain them, "the Democracy"—as Jackson's party was known—rose to dominance in the 1830s and 1840s in part by celebrating westward-migrating whites as pioneering yeomen and backing land reforms and hawkish policies that facilitated their acquisition of territory belonging to Native Americans, Mexicans, and rival empires. Once secure in their freeholds in the newly won domains of the West, many of these same squatters supported the Democratic Party, spreading its influence across the land. Such were the dynamics of Squatter Democracy, a force that transformed the political landscape and the actual map of North America in the antebellum era.

"Squatter Democracy" denotes the squatter-statesman alliance that was a defining force in antebellum political culture from 1830 to 1860, central to the rise and rupture of the Democratic Party, the conquests of Manifest Destiny, and the onset of the Civil War. Contemporary actors used the term from time to time in the 1850s after the squatter figure had become highly disruptive to the established political order. For example, an Ohio newspaper aligned with the emerging Republican Party expressed outrage at Democrats including Stephen A. Douglas for what it perceived as their slavery-abetting mishandling of Kansas and their habit of pointing fingers at critics: "To all this wrong, from its inception, the Republicans protested, and Squatter Democracy answered, by bawling out, *Freedom-Shriekers!*" At the same time, ultra-proslavery Democrats also began hurling the term Squatter Democracy as an epithet at Douglas and his supporters. Taking cues from historical usages, this book applies the term to underscore overlooked dynamics that had been gathering force during the previous three decades and exerted a monumental influence on the way Jacksonian political culture cohered and came apart.[3]

Squatter Democracy, or Democratic pro-squatterism, was not a formal movement but rather a marriage of convenience between land-hungry white settlers and a set of influential, opportunistic politicians who recognized that they had much to gain by conspicuously backing efforts to convert the domains of Indians, Mexicans, and European colonists into the private property of those white settlers, who formed their base. Tangible and symbolic elements combined to give Squatter Democracy its strength. In the material realm were the actual frontier settlers who demanded specific policies including preemption, Indian removal, and outright war to acquire land. These measures shared a common thrust: facilitating white American ownership of western terrains at minimal cost to settlers.

Casting conquest as an uplifting enterprise required no small amount of spin. Accordingly, along with the concrete policy pursuits went a constant strain of mythmaking aimed at rebranding squatters from outlaw intruders to virtuous pioneers. Florid paeans to the "hearty pioneer" became a staple of Democratic speech-making and editorializing, drawing their language from settlers' petitions to Congress and amplified in works of popular fiction and art, which increasingly featured squatters as stock characters, further raising their profile in the culture. There was a polemical quality to Democrats' love songs to squatters that dog-whistled a brash message of belonging to partisans while baiting the opposition to cry foul over shameless pandering. Squatter Democracy, thus, was as much a style of politics as it was an agenda-driven coalition. Celebrating frontier settlers and advancing measures to secure their loyalty were two sides of the Squatter Democracy coin.

Pro-squatterism was an engine of Democratic constituency-building and a source of party unity that cut across classes and geographical regions. At its core was a quid pro quo: land for political support. But this alignment of interests also embodied an approach to political economy geared toward empowering white Americans to claim and develop the West while keeping the government's footprint small. Animating the movement was the premise that the continent contained spoils aplenty for white men of all sections and views on slavery—so long as they agreed to let sleeping dogs lie and not argue too stridently for their position. Settlers and their sponsors in government resorted to racist and nationalistic appeals, arguing that land-taking by Anglo-Americans marked a beneficent advance of civilization and republican institutions and that dispossession of Indians, Mexicans, and European colonists was a perfectly acceptable price. Stoking racial and class grievances while delivering tangible spoils in the form of land was a uniquely potent blend in an age of expanding franchise and rapid westward settlement among white Americans.

The heart and soul of this movement was the figure of the squatter, boldly made over by Jacksonians from a disreputable trespasser into a patriotic, pioneering farmer who advanced the national interest by cultivating and populating frontier regions. The trope of the intrepid squatter yeoman accomplished significant ideological work, putting a heroic white face on imperial conquests, reinforcing a sense of class solidarity between elites and the poor, and enabling northern and southern wings of the party to skirt the explosive issue of slavery by rallying behind an expansionist platform framed as simply giving plucky pioneers their due. For opposition Whigs, meanwhile, who favored methodical westward growth and eschewed violent conquest, the squatter symbolized everything they found rapacious, reckless, and uncouth about their rivals. Whig denunciations of squatters were a boon to pro-squatter Democrats who lashed back with charges of elite insensitivity, stoking an us-versus-them mentality. By depicting white squatters as the oppressed, disparaged, and best of all Americans, Democrats fortified their ties with western settlers and justified the conquest of a continent.

White supremacy and patriarchy helped cement the statesmen-squatter alliance. The squatter character conjured by Democratic politicians was a white male yeoman heroically contending against poverty and hostile elements to scratch out a subsistence for his family and fortify his country. It was understood that women—sometimes dubbed "squatteresses"—were integral to the pioneer family household as helpmeets to their husbands and fathers. Meanwhile, actual white squatters and their allies in government sought to prevent free African Americans from owning land and eking out a livelihood even in places that had banned slavery. Those free black farming families that succeeded in establishing themselves in the West did so not only by overcoming the usual hardships and privations of frontier life but also in the face of systematic efforts to exclude them. All the while pro-squatter Democrats looked on Native Americans as dangerous impediments in need of speedy removal, including tribes that had adopted Anglo-American systems of government, private property, and yeoman-style agriculture.[4]

Pro-squatter expansionism was a galvanizing force in Jacksonian politics. Its proponents were powerful Democratic centrists who advanced the party's cardinal principles of egalitarian democracy for white men, aggressive expansion, agrarian development of newly acquired western lands, and, crucially, harmony across sections—a posture that demanded both continued accumulation of new territory to satisfy the ambitions of North and South, and strict neutrality on slavery. In this sense, Squatter Democracy represented a middle way, threading the needle between what historian Sean Wilentz has dubbed the "two distinctive democracies"—a southern "Master Race democracy . . . dedicated to the proposition that white men's equality depended on black enslavement" and a northern democracy "committed to white male democracy and divided over black male participation but hostile to slavery."[5]

A foundational vision of the Democratic Party sprang from the mind of US senator Martin Van Buren of New York who in 1827 conceptualized resurrecting the old Jeffersonian alliance between "planters of the South" and "plain Republicans" of the North. This coalition, which gathered force around the charismatic figure of Andrew Jackson in the 1820s and 1830s, would flourish as long as there were sufficient spoils to satisfy partisans from both sections. To that end, the vast lands of the American West offered ample room for growth. Thomas Hart Benton of Missouri, a staunch ally of Jackson and Van Buren, was the intellectual force behind Democrats' pro-squatter land policies and expansionist agenda, making him a vital progenitor of Squatter Democracy. At the same time, he displayed a degree of frankness and courage that set him apart from the dissembling cadre of politicians that turned Squatter Democracy into a disruptive force in American politics, among them Robert J. Walker of Mississippi, Lewis Cass of Michigan, and Stephen A. Douglas of Illinois. Hailing mainly from the Old Southwest and Old Northwest, these men—allies or disciples of Old Hickory—were strong nationalists adept at suppressing the slavery question in pursuit of party unity and power. The pro-squatter expansionist pitch they helped fashion became a primary script of the Democratic Party, embraced and echoed by partisans in Congress and in statehouses across the land.[6]

The material basis for Squatter Democracy was the abundant territory of North America, which Democrats viewed not as the homelands of Native American peoples or the domains of imperial rivals but as de facto US public lands to be parceled out as private property to white men, preferably those amenable to their politics. This mindset undergirded Democrats' ascendancy and conditioned the claiming of large swaths of the North American West, beginning with the Mississippi Valley in the 1830s and continuing to the Pacific coast in the 1840s. As the country grew in territory, the party gained in strength.

Conquest came at a high cost, though, one paid not only by non-white and non-US peoples dispossessed of their lands, often violently. The same pro-squatter politics that yielded dividends for Democrats in the early years of party-building and set the tone and tempo of territorial expansion grew more precarious as the nation conquered vast domains and tensions over slavery escalated. The US-Mexican War (1846–1848) proved a step too far, laying bare the inner tensions of the Democrats' cross-sectional coalition of planters and plain republicans, forcing to the fore a thorny question: Were squatters genuine yeoman farmers or forerunners of slavery extension? Perceiving the war as a naked land grab by the Slave Power, a number of northern Democrats threatened to withdraw support should the conflict result in any new slave territory. Branded heretics, some joined forces with the burgeoning Free Soil Party, which effectively stole Democrats' squatter-friendly playbook by pushing for free land for poor, non-slaveholding whites. Southerners, meanwhile, grew increasingly shrill in denouncing any barriers to the expansion of slavery.

Confronted with a fracturing party, Democratic leaders including Cass and later Douglas rallied behind the doctrine of popular sovereignty, which authorized settlers themselves, rather than Congress, to determine whether their lands would be slave or free. Proponents framed this solution as a decisive step toward realizing the ideals of republican self-government, but critics on all sides perceived it as a dodge and abdication of leadership. Many southerners—notably Democrats led by John C. Calhoun—were loath to leave slavery's fate to "free-soil adventurers and squatters," particularly when it became clear that the majority of emigrants to the West opposed the institution. Initially, southern elites blasted the doctrine as "squatter sovereignty." However, after it became established policy, they sought to co-opt the squatter to advance the expansionist aspirations of the slaveholding South. Popular sovereignty vested idealized squatters with real authority to resolve the slavery question that had snarled the nation's highest councils. Far from quelling conflict, the policy merely transferred it from Washington to the West, converting flesh-and-blood squatters into proxies on the front lines of battles over slavery that sundered both the Party of Jackson and the country.

Historians have long highlighted the link between westward expansion and intensifying sectional conflicts over the South's "peculiar institution." Few, however, have noted the shadowy figure of the squatter at the forward edge of territorial conquests and clashes over slavery that sparked disunion. This scholarly oversight is surprising given the prominence of the term "squatter sovereignty" in fractious Civil War-era debates over whether new lands would be slave or free. Squatter sovereignty, like Squatter Democracy, was not merely an apt phrase that suddenly appeared in the 1850s but a long-incubating and profoundly unsettling dynamic central to the rise and fall of Jacksonian Democracy and the onset of the Civil War.[7]

Sovereignty—defined by political scientist Daniel Philpott as "supreme authority within a territory"—lies at the heart of the struggles documented here. The combination of authority and territory—an elusive quality of power grounded in a physical place—made sovereignty a principle of the highest importance in a young, rapidly expanding republic. Who had a right to claim western lands and mold the societies that took shape on them? On what basis did those rights stand? And, critically, who had the power to make their claims stick? These questions animated struggles within the US domestic political sphere with its nested loci of power—federal, state, local,

and individual—and its inveterate factionalism driven by parties, geographical sections, and other competing interests. They also played out at the level
of empires, nations, and myriad tribal groups contending for the domains of
the North American West. Not least, they bore upon relations at more inti-
mate scales, as individuals forged lives in frontier regions, bringing disparate
peoples into contact and often conflict. White American squatters became a
disruptive force because they stood at the nexus of authority and territory at
all of these levels, advancing and frustrating competing claims to sovereignty
during a period of aggressive expansion and sociopolitical turmoil. They
came to embody sovereignty, taking the principle from abstraction to incar-
nate fact.[8]

European nations and their colonial spawns rested their sovereign claims
to territory on a variety of justifications, including the "doctrine of discovery" and actual settlement. As rival powers jockeyed for supremacy, the
US flag often followed the squatter. This dynamic accelerated in the 1830s
and 1840s as prominent Jacksonians like Benton, Walker, Cass, and James
K. Polk asserted the nation's "unquestionable" title to contested regions, and
American squatters poured in. Their overwhelming numbers and land-taking
acumen strengthened US assertions of sovereignty over Oregon, Texas, and
other domains. A reverse dynamic often prevailed as well, with the federal
government paving the way for white squatter conquests through heavy-
handed negotiations and outright military force against Native peoples and
adversaries. Sometimes, as in the claiming of Oregon, settlers and the national
state operated in tandem.[9]

A study centered on the antebellum statesmen-squatter alliance and its
effects on US national growth necessarily ventures into the realm of "settler
colonialism" staked out by Australian historian Patrick Wolfe and others.
Wolfe has argued that settler colonialism is a distinct mode of conquest because the drive to permanently occupy territory tends toward the "elimination" rather than exploitation of Native populations. The history chronicled
in this book forms a chapter in the long trajectory of US settler colonialism.
It focuses on a novel effort to harness this force for partisan gain and the
double-edged sword presented by such a quest as squatters proved ungovern-
able, Indians resisted their encroachments, and opposition politicians decried
the foulness of displacing original inhabitants through trickery and force, revealing cross-purposes within the colonizing power.[10]

The rising profile of antebellum American squatters recapitulated
processes that first gave rise to yeoman classes and popular sovereignty itself.
Historian Edmund Morgan argues that the yeoman—the small, independent

landholder—was a pivotal figure in England's long transition from feudal monarchism to a system more akin to republicanism. Amid these changes, English aristocrats in the seventeenth and eighteenth centuries rhapsodized about yeomen as paragons of patriotic virtue and good sense and extended the franchise to these small property owners. Their apparent embrace of "the people" did not spring from high principle, Morgan argues, but out of elites' need to create constituencies and retain power to further their own interests. Morgan underscores the slippery slope that popular sovereignty sits atop, noting that "before we ascribe sovereignty to the people we have to imagine that there is such a thing, something we personify as though it were a single body, capable of thinking, of acting, of making decisions and carrying them out, something quite apart from government, superior to government, and able to alter or remove a government at will." This is where the much-mythologized yeoman proved crucial, because if any character could bear the weight of sovereignty, it was this embodiment of independence, industriousness, and decency.[11]

The virtuous yeoman trope found fertile ground in the United States, where Thomas Jefferson anointed these freeholding farmers as "the chosen people of God" and envisioned them as the anchor of an "Empire of liberty" stretching from ocean to ocean. Like his English ancestors, he lauded yeomen for their autonomy and values and believed they would secure US dominion over the continent. Historian Walter Johnson observes that to Jefferson's mind the "formal sovereignty of the United States . . . would be fulfilled in the shape of a republic of independent, smallholding farmers." But for all their egalitarian rhetoric, Jefferson and allies—not unlike their British peers—understood themselves to be part of a natural elite, born and bred to rule. They expected deference from yeomen.[12]

Andrew Jackson was the first president to break this patrician mold. Though a slaveholding planter himself and member of the Nashville gentry, his hardscrabble youth in the Carolinas and Tennessee, coupled with his renown as an "Indian fighter" and vanquisher of the British in the Battle of New Orleans, made him a hero among backcountry folks who saw something of themselves in him. Jackson ascended to power following the creation of several new western states and as legislatures throughout the nation lowered voting thresholds and extended the franchise to white men across class strata. It was amid this popular turn that the yeoman morphed into the rough-and-tumble squatter. Tributes to this archetypal frontiersman struck a resonant chord—one that evoked a receding Jeffersonian Arcadia blended with backwoods Jacksonian brashness. Where British lords had mainly paid lip service to yeomen and popular sovereignty, Jacksonian Democrats went one crucial step further. Faced with an imploding party, they invested squatters with authority to solve the most vexing problem of the day: slavery's place in America.

Part of what made squatters so controversial was their milieu: the public lands, the seedbed of US development from a string of Atlantic coastal states into a continental power. Squatters' sovereignty as political actors stemmed from their legalized foothold on the rapidly expanding public domain—a position they owed largely to Democratic allies in Washington, DC. Accordingly, this project repositions western lands as a breeding ground of Jacksonian politics. Prompted by their frontier constituents, Democrats in the 1830s took the lead in passing sweeping preemption laws, which forgave squatters their territorial trespasses and enabled them to obtain title retroactively to public land they had illegally occupied. Fiercely opposed by Whig leaders, preemption not only sanctioned squatting but facilitated it, contributing to an era of unprecedented territorial conquests directed by Democrats and spearheaded by squatters. Attending to the dialectical relationship between politicians in the East and squatters in the West—and to the central role of land in their negotiations—allows for fresh assessments of how power flowed in the "Age of Jackson" and the degree to which non-elite white men wielded influence.[13]

Tracking squatters across antebellum America also enriches the historiography of Civil War causation. Generations of scholars portrayed the cataclysm as a clash between incompatible civilizations: a dynamic, industrializing North energized by free labor versus a stagnant, cotton-producing South enervated by the system of chattel slavery. Recent works have called that reading into question, arguing that both sections had an essentially agrarian core. James L. Huston, for example, locates the source of antagonism in incompatible modes of agriculture—the family farm of the North and the slave plantation of the South—both vying for new lands in the West. Despite the differences in their regions' agricultural systems, however, northern and southern Democrats made strikingly similar rhetorical appeals to justify their claims to western lands. It wasn't simply a propaganda war between "two agrarianisms," pitting planter against yeoman, as Henry Nash Smith once argued. It was, in important respects, a contest to define and appropriate the squatter, the Jacksonian incarnation of the yeoman. Democrats had courted a broadening base by heralding this nostalgic embodiment of white agrarian democracy. Rallying behind the squatter enabled them to sidestep the landmine of slavery for years as they unified behind a militantly expansionist agenda that delivered spoils for all. But they got ahead of themselves in their aggressive pursuit of new territory and their coalition blew up, in no small measure because planters and plain republicans held incompatible views on the nature, role, and rights of squatters. Partisans from South and North attempted to appropriate the squatter symbol and imbue it with characteristics favorable to their interests, resulting in the violent scenes that bloodied the plains of Kansas and beyond.[14]

This book explores the testing grounds of Squatter Democracy as this defining force of antebellum political culture emerged and ran its course: the upper and lower Mississippi Valley in the 1830s; the cotton lands of Texas and valleys of Oregon in the 1840s; Gold Rush–era California; and the prairies of Kansas in the 1850s. Throughout, attention returns to Washington, DC, where debates raged whenever Americans staked claims to new western lands. Chapter 1 traces the rise of Squatter Democracy and its role in shaping the Second Party System, pitting Democrats against Whigs, with their diverging constituencies and programs. The discussion offers background on the intersection of land and power from the colonial period through the early American republic to reveal both the continuities and novelties of Jacksonian squatter politics and the sources from which it sprang: populist politicians with a feel for the expanding West, writers at the vanguard of the Democratic revolution, and actual frontier settlers themselves, clamoring for patents to the lands they had claimed.

Chapter 2 examines white supremacy as a cohering force of Squatter Democracy, casting light on the shadow side of the movement's pretensions of benevolence as well as its limitations as an approach to political economy. The lands of the West were manifestly not the exclusive domain of white Americans but rather the homelands of myriad Indian peoples and beacons of opportunity for African Americans, Mexicans, and many others. Yet, as Democrats extended a helping hand to white settlers, they and their frontier constituents closed ranks to force out non-white people wishing to retain or claim territory of their own. Even Native Americans who practiced yeoman farming felt Uncle Sam's relentless squeeze, revealing that Jacksonians' professed love for western farmers ran only skin deep.

Chapter 3 tracks Squatter Democracy as it became, in style and substance, a dominant strain in American politics by the end of the 1830s. Whigs began appropriating the trappings of their rivals' signature brand, first by stoking the legend of one of their own—a colorful congressman from western Tennessee named David Crockett—and then by waging a "log cabin and hard cider" campaign in 1840 that landed western war hero William Henry Harrison in the White House. Whigs then played a leading role in passing the landmark Preemption Act of 1841, which legalized squatting on a mass scale. But

Democrats reclaimed the lost ground in the election of 1844—the focus of Chapter 4—promulgating a hawkish program of expansion led by squatters in Texas and Oregon that sparked conflicts with Mexico and Great Britain. With Polk's victory, Squatter Democracy reached its apex, ushering in an era of unprecedented expansion but also compounding sectional fissures within Democratic ranks.

Chapter 5 examines a crucial turning point as pro-squatterism proved its potency as a force of constituency-building and political economy as well as its capacity to divide even Democrats. American emigrants capitalized on the ideology of Manifest Destiny and settler-friendly land policies to claim Oregon from Great Britain, making US acquisition of that territory a crowning achievement of Squatter Democracy. But the war with Mexico, which broke out at the same time, struck even some of the most ardent expansionists as dangerous overreach. For many northerners, Whig and Democrat alike, the commencement of hostilities confirmed suspicions that proslavery men firmly held the reins of the Democracy. The resulting rise of Free Soilism and the Democrats' knee-jerk response of popular sovereignty converted squatters from dependably Democratic agents of territorial conquests into politically unpredictable arbiters of slavery's future.

Chapter 6 explores the birth of a squatter movement on the Pacific Coast that reflected a widening breach between squatters as debated in Washington and the actual settlers in the West. As Congress clashed over California statehood in 1850—with southerners fixating on the would-be state's antislavery constitution as evidence of "squatter sovereignty" run amok—American settlers rallied under the "Squatter" banner to secure rights to Mexican land. While in important respects fulfilling the promise of Squatter Democracy by extending white American sovereignty over the continent, these squatters were no Democratic pawns. Instead, they inclined toward a free-soil vision of the West and charted an independent course for their cause, making clear that no party held an exclusive monopoly on pro-squatter politics.

By the 1850s, Democrats could not escape the hazards of their squatter-coddling creed. The party had, over the course of the preceding twenty-five years, refashioned these once remote and reviled frontier denizens into a fetish at the heart of their political clan and then vested them with the power to resolve the fraught slavery question. In short, they had unleashed the forces that would wreak havoc in Bleeding Kansas. Chapter 7 explores how competing squatter bands became on-the-ground proxies for antagonistic forces in the national showdown over slavery. Stephen A. Douglas and his allies seeded the field of battle with the Kansas-Nebraska Act of 1854, which repealed the Missouri Compromise and opened the territories to white settlers under the principle of popular sovereignty before Indian titles had been cleared or lands surveyed. Much of the ensuing violence began as land skirmishes but the turf wars quickly spiraled into larger battles between proslavery and free-state squatter factions, revealing how tangled the issues of land and slavery had become. Chapter 8 examines the fallout as the last of the Jacksonian lions attempted to bring peace to Kansas and the country. Old-guard Democrats controlled the White House and top posts in Congress, and they dispatched preeminent pro-squatter statesman Robert J. Walker to Kansas to restore order. Preaching strict neutrality on slavery and arguing that peace would open fields of opportunity for all, Walker clung to popular sovereignty. But guerilla warfare raged on, revealing how uncontrollable the squatter sovereigns had become. The embattled governor's resignation left the Party of Jackson on the brink of collapse, and Kansas and the nation on a war footing.

Chapter 9 analyzes the rupture of the Democracy and the Union. The divided Democrats fielded two candidates for president in 1860—John C. Breckinridge, southern planters' standard-bearer, and Stephen A. Douglas, the favorite of many plain republicans in the North and West. Douglas struggled to shed his association with squatters, but the label stuck to him as both the Breckinridge faction and Lincoln's Republicans lampooned him as a species of "Squatter King" for his unfaltering adherence to popular sovereignty, showing how disruptive the squatter trope had become to the party that had given it life and capitalized on it for so long. The implosion of the Jacksonian political order appeared complete in June 1860 when lame-duck President James Buchanan vetoed the Homestead Act, a policy that in former times would have represented the crowning achievement of Squatter Democracy but instead loomed as a sword of Damocles.

Amid the long tug-of-war over sovereignty, the squatter—once a far-off frontier scourge—transformed from a land-taking agent of Manifest Destiny celebrated and enabled by Democrats into a foot soldier in battles over slavery that rocked the country. The stakes could hardly have been higher as Robinson and Stringfellow rallied their squatter bands to claim the fertile plains of Kansas and the nation's future.

1

Squatter Democracy

THE TOASTS FLOWED freely at William Parker's Mississippi Hotel on October 10, 1830, as Natchez's elite gathered to celebrate the Treaty of Dancing Rabbit Creek, concluded two weeks earlier with the Choctaws, and another recent accord with the Chickasaws. First they raised their glasses to President Andrew Jackson: "He found one half of our territory occupied by a few wandering Indians. He will leave it in the cultivation of thousands of grateful freemen." The next toasts went to the treaties' "able negotiators" and "our departing brethren"—the Choctaws and Chickasaws—"destined where they are going, to learn the right of individual property, and self government." In the giddiness of the moment, the men hoisted their glasses ten more times but amid the good cheer a serious question loomed. Dancing Rabbit Creek opened millions of prime acres of Indian lands to settlement and cultivation. But who would do the cultivating: the enslaved men and women of wealthy cotton planters, or non-slaveholding white farmers of more humble means?[1]

Keynote speaker Robert J. Walker, a lawyer, editor, and prominent Democratic partisan, left no question where he stood. Established planters, he noted, complained that an influx of farmers would compromise their dominant position in the cotton market. Yet such well-to-do men—himself included—stood to gain handsomely from the new lands and therefore had no right to stand in the way of a new generation of cultivators. Besides, he added, planters' wealth came principally from their human property, not their land. Walker turned his attention to the squatters who had already begun settling on the Choctaw Cession and who, in his estimation, merited help from lawmakers to establish farms there. "The hardy pioneer of settlements, the Daniel Boone of the forest, deserves the aid of a paternal government," he intoned. "Would it not be most unjust, that when the emigrant had fixed his new abode in the wilderness, erected his cabins, and commenced his

Dangerous Ground. John Suval, Oxford University Press. © Oxford University Press 2022.
DOI: 10.1093/oso/9780197531426.003.0002

improvements, he should be driven from the home, which he had hoped to secure to himself and his children, by the overbidding of the heartless speculator[?]" Squatters, he continued, were not trespassers on others' land nor simply trailblazing farmers and family men; they were the unsung heroes behind America's growing might. "It is such men as this emigrant, who pushes the bayonet in time of war—upon whose affection the country must repose in the hour of danger, who, tho' poor, is rich in patriotism." In return for their virtue and high sense of duty, Walker proposed granting generous preemption rights to help them acquire the lands they claimed without having to bid for them against speculators at public land sales.[2]

Walker was not the only Democrat singing squatters' praises and preaching compassion toward them. In the North and South, "Jackson men" crooned in the same key. William Leggett, for example, in his 1829 short story "The Squatter," imbued his titular protagonist with noble qualities despite the fact that he had illegally taken up residence on a patch of public land on the Illinois prairie. Traditionally, an eastern intellectual might have portrayed such a man as a criminal trespasser worthy of contempt. But Leggett, an influential New York editor and one of the Democrats' most agile thinkers—who would become an antislavery thorn in the party's side—highlighted his hero's "manliness and intelligence," placing him at the head of a loving family forced by cruel circumstances to scratch out a subsistence living on the margins. If the story had a moral, it was that fate could turn anyone, even the most upstanding American, into a squatter. Therefore these unauthorized settlers deserved respect and sympathy, not disdain.[3]

Leggett and Walker typify the pro-squatter turn among Democrats that would come to exert a defining influence over the party and antebellum politics. Unlike their Jeffersonian forebears who deplored these unauthorized settlers, Jacksonian Democrats worked to remove from squatters the stigma of "intruders" and styled them instead as pioneering yeomen and nation-builders—in a word, "improvers." They also promoted measures that awarded them land patents on favorable terms, spurring aggressive land-taking across the West and fortifying a base of support in new regions. Hoisting the squatter standard enabled party leaders to rally behind a humble, heroic symbol that coded neutral on the divisive question of slavery.

Policymakers in previous decades had struggled not just to contain squatters but to define who and what exactly they were. The "intruder" label, conveying illegal occupancy, adhered for decades. So, too, did the designation "white Indian." Physician Benjamin Rush, a leading public figure in the early republic, explained in an 1806 essay that the "first settler is nearly related to an Indian in his manners—In the second [settler], the Indian manners are more diluted: It is in the third species of settlers only, that we behold civilization completed." For Rush, this third category of settler alone merited the appellation "farmer," completing "the progress from the savage to civilized life." English writer Henry Bradshaw Fearon also perceived grades of civilization within America's backcountry populations. In an 1818 book recounting his travels in the United States, he divided country folk into three types: the squatter, the small farmer, and the wealthy farmer. He defined the squatter as a "half-civilized and half-savage" man "who '*sets himself down*,' upon land which is not his own, and for which he pays nothing." By contrast, the small farmer had actually paid for his plot and toiled alongside his wife and children to secure an independent, if "wretched," existence. At the top of the social order stood the wealthy farmer, who possessed hundreds of acres, produced livestock and other goods for distant markets, and enjoyed high standing, often as a legislator or judge.[4]

Another common perception of squatters in the early nineteenth century was that they were not so much subsistence farmers as small-time speculators, occupying and improving land they did not own for the sole purpose of selling it, and then repeating the process over and over. In February 1806, Representative Jeremiah Morrow of Ohio noted that settlers of this description had tripled the value of land in an area of Indiana Territory. "There are some small tracts of land, on which what are called *squatters* are settled, and where already improvements have been made, which would sell for four or six dollars per acre," he told colleagues, in what may have been the first use of the term in Congress. Decades later explorer and politician William Gilpin fixed a precise measurement on the mobility of these professional squatters, calculating that they migrated twenty-four miles annually, built a rough hovel to see them through one season's planting and harvest, and then sold their "improvements" and continued west. Writer John Mason Peck set their movement on a grander scale. Discussing the upper Mississippi Valley in the 1830s, he observed, "Migration has become almost a habit, in the West. Hundreds of men can be found, not fifty years of age, who have settled for the fourth, fifth, or sixth time on a new spot. To sell out, and remove only a few hundred miles, makes up a portion of the variety of backwoods life and manners." Before moving, the roving pioneers would sell their rude cabins and agricultural improvements to the next wave of emigrants who set about building substantial houses, clearing fields, planting orchards, and establishing mills, schools, churches, courthouses, and other trappings of "civilized life."[5]

Some observers, including novelist James Fenimore Cooper, portrayed squatters as outright nomads. Cooper's 1827 novel, *The Prairie*, features a character named Ishmael Bush, "the Squatter," who appears on the Great Plains just after the Louisiana Purchase when Pawnees, Sioux, and other Native peoples held dominion over the vast grasslands. A giant of a man, accompanied by his "Amazon" wife Esther, a brood of children, and some stray livestock, he "pursued his way, with no other guide than the sun, turning his back resolutely on the abodes of civilization, and plunging, at each step, more deeply if not irretrievably, into the haunts of the barbarous and savage occupants of the country." Bush claims the whole of the western wilderness as his home. "The air, the water and the ground, are all free gifts to man, and no one has the power to portion them out in parcels," he pronounces, rejecting both the Euro-American system of fee-simple land tenure and claims by Native Americans to the territory he occupies.[6]

If early characterizations of squatters shared a theme, it was a lifestyle of mobility broken up by spells of settlement. The lifeways of this "squatting, erratic race of settlers" attracted the notice of Joseph M. White, Florida's territorial delegate to Congress, who wrote in an 1828 letter to Senator Thomas Hart Benton of Missouri:

> This kind of population is extremely numerous in the southern States. They have no slaves to aid them in their labor; they have no means of purchasing; and the system of tenantry used in the northern States is scarcely known. This is the class of poor but industrious people who labor the earth with their own hands, and whose wives manufacture their own cotton clothing, and who go to seek better fortunes in Florida and Alabama, and become squatters on the public lands. A cart, a horse, and a few cows are frequently the only property they bring with them; they sit down on the public lands, and make small improvements to furnish them the means of temporary subsistence.[7]

The Jacksonian trope of the squatter as a pathbreaking yeoman was not spun out of whole cloth. There were in fact many thousands of actual flesh-and-blood squatters staking claims to western lands, creating communities, and pressing politicians to take up their cause and help them gain title to property. While nobody maintained an official count of the number of squatters in the United States at any given time, lawmakers and newspapers occasionally hazarded estimates for particular localities. In a January 1831 House speech, for example, Congressman Joseph Duncan of Illinois estimated that there were some 10,000 squatters residing in a northern region of his state. Fellow Democrat Ambrose Sevier, Arkansas's territorial delegate to Congress, noted approvingly that he represented "many counties containing thousands of inhabitants . . . in which not one foot of the public lands has ever been surveyed." Similarly, Senator John Tipton, an Indiana Democrat, spoke of entire counties that had sprung up on public lands beyond the reach of the federal government. In 1838, Senator James Buchanan of Pennsylvania referred to more than 30,000 squatters in "that part of Wisconsin west of the Mississippi called Iowa." Others put the number as high as 50,000. Squatters themselves offered their own clues. For instance, in an 1830 petition to Congress, unauthorized settlers in Louisiana spoke of 500 families having taken up residence "upon the high lands, East of the Red River" of Natchitoches Parish. Similar collections of squatters were commonplace throughout the Mississippi Valley.[8]

Most squatters came from eastern states where land had grown increasingly scarce. They tended to migrate "in columns," observed writer Robert Baird, "moving from the East almost due West, from the respective states from which they originated." New Englanders and New Yorkers typically settled in the northern parts of Ohio, Indiana, and Illinois, and in Michigan and Wisconsin; Pennsylvanians and New Jerseyans often moved to the middle latitudes of those places, while inhabitants of the mid-Atlantic tidewater regions and the South—many of them of Scots-Irish descent—settled in the southern parts of Ohio, Indiana, and Illinois, and in Alabama, Mississippi, Louisiana and elsewhere in the Old Southwest. Still, it was typical for some interregional mixing to occur in frontier locales. There were also significant numbers of squatters who had immigrated from England, Ireland, Germany, and elsewhere in Europe.[9]

What defined squatters was not so much a common place of origin or ethnic heritage but a set of land-taking and home-making practices. For those seeking to move west, reliable intelligence about prospective destinations was essential. The most common source of information was word of mouth as well as letters sent back east to family, friends, and local newspapers. District land officers had detailed knowledge about available tracts and their quality. Emigrant guides like those written by Robert Baird and John Mason Peck provided general descriptions of landscapes, soil quality, and the state of development in particular regions as well as tips for getting settled. Presupposing that emigrants had cash in hand, for example, Peck put the cost of setting up a 320-acre farm at $1,145 dollars, land included. Few actual squatters had such resources at their disposal or sought such large landholdings.[10]

Once the move was afoot, migrants would seek to make their homes on fertile ground with easy access to water and timber. The first task on arriving at a suitable location was building a shelter, usually a one- or two-room log cabin with a clapboard roof, stone chimney, and dirt or shingle floor. Rebecca Burlend, an immigrant to Pike County, Illinois, from Yorkshire, England, described one such cabin in detail:

> The walls of the house consisted of layers of strong blocks of timber, roughly squared and notched into each other at the corners; the joints filled up with clay.... [A]djoining one side were a few boards nailed together in the form of a table, and supported principally by the timber in the wall. This was dignified with the name "sideboard." In the centre of the room, stood another small table, covered with a piece of coarse brown calico; this was the dining table. The chairs, four in number, were the most respectable furniture in the house. . . . Besides these there were two stools and a bench for common use,—a candlestick made from an ear of Indian corn, two or three trenchers and a few tin drinking vessels. One corner of the house was occupied with agricultural implements, consisting of large hoes, axes, &c. . . . Various herbs were suspended from the roof with a view of being medicinally serviceable, also two guns, one of them a rifle.[11]

Squatters combined hunting and small-scale farming. They would clear a few acres and plant a crop of corn among the stumps of freshly felled trees and construct a crib to hold the grain. Often they had a milk cow and some hogs, gradually adding livestock as their fortunes permitted. Family members—female and male, young and old—produced mainly for their own household use, though, once established, they might clear additional acres and plant wheat, oats, cotton, and other crops, selling or bartering them for goods.[12]

In petitions to Congress seeking title to their lands, squatters described their labors in detail to bolster their claims. For instance, Robert Grant, among the first white residents in McDonough County, Illinois, recounted how he took possession of a quarter section—160 acres—in November 1833, and "got logs for a house, made rails and stakes & during the remainder of the year . . . made preparation to settle on . . . improve and cultivate the same." In a note of triumph he reported that he "did persevere & in the month of February 1834 moved his family to & settled on said quarter and during the year 1834 enclosed and cultivated near fifty acres of corn with a good and substantial fence." He later constructed "a good large frame house."[13]

Squatters like Grant had a very specific aim when they recounted their toils to legislators: the passage of preemption laws. Preemption gave squatters a legal toehold in the system by allowing them to occupy and improve land first and later acquire title through private entry rather than at public auction at the minimum government price of $1.25 per acre. During the previous decades, Congress occasionally had granted preemptions on a limited basis to specific settlers, such as builders of gristmills north of the Ohio River, and farmers and others in Indiana, Illinois, and Missouri. But policymakers could not bring themselves to endorse squatting as a general practice. As an 1824 decision by the House Committee on Public Lands affirmed, "It cannot be perceived by what principle persons having no color of title, should, after lands on which they have settled were known to belong to the United States at the time of making such settlement, claim the pre-emption right to such lands."[14]

For Jacksonian Democrats, however, the principle was crystal clear: squatters' indomitable grit and enterprise had led them to stake out homes in the West. It was hardly their fault that they had settled lands ahead of treaties with Indians or in advance of General Land Office operations. Preemption served as a corrective mechanism to get squatters and the apparatus of the state back in sync. Extending a hand to them and trumpeting their virtues was smart politics at a time when the country was growing fast, and states, old and new, were increasingly placing the franchise within the reach of white men across the class spectrum.

Land and Power in Early America

Democrats' embrace of squatters represented a brash variation on longstanding themes. Since colonial times, political leaders in America had engaged in an uneasy dance with backcountry settlers eager for landed independence. On the plus side, the influx of white settlers into western domains established beachheads for future settlement, extending Britain's imperial reach on a continent where rival powers vied for supremacy. Yet these emigrants frequently occupied land titularly held by the Crown or wealthy elites and nearly always belonging to Native peoples with whom they often clashed. Harnessing the benefits of this unwieldy population while keeping them in check required a deft hand.

The year 1763 marked a critical juncture in power dynamics in North America. Britain had just defeated the French in the Seven Years' War, and the late military incursions into the Ohio Country cleared the way for thousands of migrants who made the roads to the west come "alive with Men, Women, Children, and Cattle." Yet hardly had the ink dried on the Peace of Paris when an alliance of Native American tribes under the leadership of Ottawa chief Pontiac captured British forts along the Great Lakes, placing the Crown unexpectedly on the defensive. In an attempt to regulate frontier growth, Britain issued the Royal Proclamation of 1763, forbidding colonists from settling west of the Appalachian Mountains and from purchasing lands reserved for Indians. While practically unenforceable, the proclamation angered a population growing increasingly restive over London's attempts at asserting control. When members of Parliament proposed halting further land grants in the American colonies, writer and politician Edmund Burke, in a 1775 speech to his fellow lawmakers, pointed out the folly of trying to curtail westward settlement there.[15]

> You cannot station garrisons in every part of these deserts. If you drive the people from one place, they will carry on their annual tillage, and remove with their flocks and herds to another . . . without a possibility of restraint; they would . . . soon forget a government by which they were disowned; would become hordes of English Tartars; and pouring down upon your unfortified frontiers a fierce and irresistible cavalry, become masters of your governors and your counsellors, your collectors and comptrollers, and of all the slaves that adhered to them.

The surest way to secure the colonists' loyalty, Burke added, was to continue granting land and imbuing titles with a stamp of officialdom, thereby ensuring "that the ruling power should never be wholly out of sight." Attempting to hedge them in would "be neither prudent nor practicable."[16]

The founders of the US republic faced daunting challenges of their own when it came to administering the nation's western expanses. The country emerged from the Revolution deeply in debt but with numerous states that possessed immense domains west of the Appalachians. One after another, starting in 1780, those states ceded their western lands to the federal government, leading to the creation of the public domain. Congress stipulated that the public lands "shall be disposed of for the common benefit of the United States," providing an important source of revenue as well as physical space for the country to develop. The domain continued to grow as the United States acquired additional territory from Indians and bordering nations and empires, eventually comprising hundreds of millions of acres and stretching to the Pacific Ocean.[17]

Over the decades policymakers created an elaborate system of laws and land office infrastructure to regulate the survey, sale, and settlement of the public lands. There was an abiding tension between gentleman speculators who scrambled to secure title to the lands previously held by British elites and small-time settlers looking to secure a freehold after having fought to overthrow an imperial power. George Washington, preeminent among the wealthy speculators, expressed outright contempt for squatters. On a 1784 visit to inspect his extensive claims in the Ohio Valley, he was aghast at what he perceived to be a lawless mob trading in and squatting on the lands. By the following year, Congress had grown sufficiently alarmed over squatters on Indian lands north of the Ohio River to send troops to evict them. Soldiers set fire to their cabins and destroyed their crops. But once the smoke cleared, the squatters returned to rebuild. As president, Washington came to believe that "anything short of a Chinese wall, or a line of troops" would fail to repel the barrage of illicit settlers on public and tribal lands. His secretary of war, Henry Knox, argued for bringing white intruders to justice, while formalizing treaty-making and trade policies with Indians.[18]

One of the principal dividing lines in American politics from the earliest days of the republic was between those who viewed the public domain as a source of speculative capital and government revenue—an outlook held by Washington and Federalists led by Alexander Hamilton—and those who deemed settlement by small farmers as the primary goal. Thomas Jefferson fell into this latter camp, articulating a powerful vision of the United States as a republican nation led by virtuous yeoman with room to push westward "to the thousandth and thousandth generation." Ideally, from the federal government's perspective, the sequence of events after it acquired new lands was to survey the terrain under the grid system of townships and sections originally prescribed by the Land Ordinance of 1785 and then promptly sell them, thereby turning the public domain into private property held in fee simple by white, male citizens.[19]

Broadly speaking, land policies over the decades moved from a Hamiltonian approach that favored moneyed interests—for example, requiring the purchase of large parcels at prices that mainly individuals with access to credit could afford—to a more Jeffersonian method of making small tracts available for less money to expand the yeomanry. In 1820, for example, following a major economic panic precipitated in part by rampant land speculation, Congress passed a law barring credit sales of public land. The measure also decreased the minimum purchasing size from 160 acres to 80 and reduced the price of public land from $2 an acre to $1.25, where it would remain for decades to come. As a result, a farmer could obtain an 80-acre tract for $100. Of course, many squatters could not afford even this price, and, if they could, they were often ahead of federal surveyors, claiming terrains not yet on the market.[20]

As president, Jefferson advanced his dream of an agrarian empire by orders of magnitude with the Louisiana Purchase of 1803, bringing into formal US possession more than 500 million acres stretching from present-day Louisiana to Montana. Over the next two decades—a period of Jeffersonian dominance—federal officials experimented with policies to attach the polyglot populations of the Mississippi Valley to the United States, assimilate Indian peoples, and repel the influence of foreign actors, principally the British. The Jefferson and Madison administrations added to the system of trading factories with tribes to try to dislodge British traders and developed the General Land Office to increase the efficiency of public land transactions. For the most part, however, the government failed to meet American settlers' demands for the speedy award of secure land titles.[21]

While deeply sympathetic to small freeholders, Jeffersonians prized rule of law and envisioned US westward migration as an orderly process. Like their Federalist rivals, they condemned squatters for flouting the law with their land grabs and provoking conflicts with Indians. Jefferson himself signed the Intrusion Act of 1807, which authorized the president to direct the removal of squatters from public land. Try as they might, though, the nation's leaders could not stem the tide of illicit settlement. The floodgates into the Mississippi Valley burst open following the defeat of Shawnee chief Tecumseh's intertribal confederacy in 1813 by William Henry Harrison's forces and of the Red Stick Creeks the following year by troops under Andrew Jackson's command. President James Madison called for the eviction of the squatters in the Mississippi Valley but could not enforce his order. A federal judge in Mississippi Territory expressed a common view in an 1816 letter to Madison, questioning, "How can a jury be found in Monroe County to convict a man of *intrusion*—where every man is an *intruder*?"[22]

Jackson, supremely popular after vanquishing the Creeks and then the British at the Battle of New Orleans, urged draconian policies toward Indians. He dashed off a letter to President James Monroe on the day of his inauguration in 1817, candidly expressing his philosophy on Indian affairs. "I have long viewed treaties with the Indians an absurdity not to be reconciled to the principles of our Government," he stated. It was high time for the country to end the "farce" and force terms of its choosing on Native peoples, who were "subjects" and not citizens. This approach would open up vast territories to settlement by white Americans, making the nation less vulnerable to invasion by Europeans.[23]

A new order was afoot in the nation's administration of western domains. The influx of white settlers into the Mississippi Valley after the War of 1812 contributed to a shift in policymakers' views of squatters. The creation of a half-dozen new western states—Louisiana, Indiana, Mississippi, Illinois, Alabama, and Missouri—between 1811 and 1821 gave western interests increasing sway in national affairs. Along with the new states—whose constitutions placed voting rights within reach of white men of all classes—arose populist-minded politicians more receptive to the demands of the "common man." For this new breed of statesman, squatters were natural constituents. Celebrating them and catering to their needs was good politics.[24]

Hardy Partisans

The Democratic Party that gathered force around Jackson's successful 1828 presidential campaign had its fingers on the pulse of these changes. While heirs to the Jeffersonian vision of a yeoman empire, Jacksonian Democrats took a different tack to squatters than their predecessors. In their eyes, these unlawful settlers were not a source of mayhem but rather agents of safety and civilization. Far from incompatible with agrarian democracy, they were its very essence. Where in Jefferson's time settlers sought to escape the short reach of the state, squatters under the Jacksonian dispensation had the liberty to extend it. True, squatters technically had broken the law by claiming public lands ahead of sales, Democrats conceded. But as they saw it, the land system was to blame for turning enterprising settlers into criminals simply because government surveyors and land office personnel failed to keep pace with this "hardy race" of pioneers who, they argued, brought enormous benefit to the nation. Accordingly, Democrats set about trying to fix the system, promoting policies that decriminalized squatting and encouraged further migration and land-claiming. As they pursued these measures, party leaders gave squatters a bold rhetorical makeover, attempting to remove the stigma of trespass and equate them with the beloved Jeffersonian yeoman.[25]

In 1830, western lawmakers including Missouri Democrat Thomas Hart Benton pushed for a sweeping preemption law that would grant squatters across the surveyed portions of the public domain the right to procure at $1.25 per acre up to 160 acres that they had illegally settled and cultivated. A long-time Jackson associate, esteemed as "the great and untiring champion of western interests," Benton was the chief architect of Democrats' land reforms, despite his complicated relationship with Jackson. Though a trusted aide to the general during the Creek War, he and his brother had exchanged gunfire with him during a melee at a Nashville hotel in 1813, with Jackson taking bullets to the shoulder and arm. Benton later relocated from Tennessee to St. Louis, where he prospered as a lawyer, editor, and land speculator. His true passion was westward expansion, a cause he championed for thirty years as a US senator.[26]

Benton believed that settlement and cultivation made lands valuable to the United States, not revenues gleaned from their sale. His agenda consisted of three components: preemption, graduation—a policy that would progressively lower the price of public lands the longer they remained unsold—and donation of unsellable lands to settlers and states. Preemption, he argued, represented a win-win proposition for settlers and the government. It enabled the squatter to obtain "a choice home in a new country, due to his enterprise, courage, hardships and privations in subduing the wilderness." Meanwhile, "the government gets a body of cultivators whose labor gives value to the surrounding public lands, and whose courage and patriotism volunteers for the public defence whenever it is necessary." Benton did not mention the other obvious benefit of preemption: its appeal among western voters.[27]

Benton and Jackson became staunch political allies, infuriating the opposition with their approach to western development. Former president John Quincy Adams blasted Benton's land policies as no better than "robbery," designed "to excite and encourage hopes among the Western people that they can extort the lands from the Government for nothing." Samuel Foot, an anti-Jacksonian senator from Connecticut, also vehemently disagreed with Benton's land program. In December 1829 he created a firestorm when he introduced a resolution calling for the termination of the post of surveyor general and for the suspension of public land surveys until the millions of unsold acres already on the market found buyers—proposals Benton lambasted as "hostile to the West." As for preemption, Foot argued that the policy would cede the reins of westward expansion to squatters, forcing the government forever to play catch-up. "The land system is virtually broken down," he declared, "and we are gravely told, 'it is best for us it should be so,' and nothing remains for us but to give the squatters pre-emption rights; and, instead of legislating for them, we are to legislate after them, in full pursuit to the Rocky Mountains, or to the Pacific Ocean." A spate of evils flowed from preemption, Foot believed, not least that squatters showed little restraint when it came to seizing Indian lands. This was an especially fraught issue in the spring of 1830 given that another measure was inching through Congress at the same time and with far more rancor: a bill for Indian removal.[28]

Particularly close to Andrew Jackson's heart, the removal bill authorized the president to transfer US lands west of the Mississippi to southern tribes in exchange for their homelands east of the river, thereby opening up millions of acres to white settlement. "The solemn plighted faith of the Government to the Indians, 'to protect and defend them in their possessions,' forms no barrier," Foot lamented during a May 20, 1830, debate, adding that the treaties "guarantying their possessions forever, [mean] nothing further, and no longer, than [sic] until some good land or mineral is found in their possession, and then they must remove." The Connecticut senator made an impassioned plea to fellow lawmakers to refrain from taking this plunge into national disgrace. But he and his anti-Jacksonian allies could not beat back the prevailing tide. The Indian Removal Act and the Preemption Act both cleared their last legislative hurdles the following week, and Jackson signed them into law on May 28 and May 29, respectively. Indian removal and squatting—two of the growing nation's oldest practices—went from being frontier customs to laws of the land.[29]

A combination of party affiliation and sectionalism drove the votes on preemption and Indian removal. Democrats enjoyed a nearly two-to-one advantage over the opposition in the House and a slight majority in the Senate. With Jackson in the White House, they could set the agenda and pass even controversial measures. The party's congressional delegations were especially dominant in the south Atlantic region, where Democrats controlled all eight of the Senate seats and forty-three of fifty-one of the House seats, and in the Southwest, where nine out of ten senators and twenty-four out of twenty-eight representatives belonged to the party. Northwestern states (with Missouri included) were more evenly divided—only three of the eight senators and eleven of the nineteen congressmen were Democrats—but were on their way to becoming Jacksonian strongholds in Congress. Meanwhile, New England formed the bulwark of the opposition, with eleven of its twelve senators, and twenty-eight of its thirty-nine representatives being anti-Jacksonians.

Preemption passed the Senate on January 13 by a 29–12 vote. Democrats were the measure's strongest backers, providing twenty votes in favor and only one against. However, geography was a salient factor as well. All eight of the Northwest's senators voted for preemption despite the majority being anti-Jacksonians, including Missouri's David Barton, a leading proponent of the policy. Meanwhile, every negative vote was cast by senators from New England and the mid-Atlantic, including the sole dissenting Democrat, New

Jersey's Mahlon Dickerson. Similar dynamics prevailed in the House, where preemption passed on May 29 by a 100–58 vote, with 74 votes in favor coming from Democrats. Broadly speaking, Democrats and westerners propelled preemption to passage.[30]

The polarizing Indian Removal Act sparked intense debate and ultimately greater voting participation than preemption in both chambers. The measure passed the Senate in April by a vote of 28–19, and the House in May by a slim 102–97 margin. In the House, 99 of the 102 votes in favor came from Democrats, while in the Senate not a single Democrat voted against the bill. Taken together the votes on preemption and Indian removal show a strong partisan tilt: of the sixty-five House members who voted for both measures sixty-three were Democrats, hailing from all sections of the country. Cheap, secure land for white settlers proved a powerful rallying point among Jacksonian partisans, giving legs to the coalition of planters and plain republicans.[31]

The Preemption Act of 1830 signaled a new dispensation for those seeking public land, affirming occupation and improvement—prior to acquiring title—as a legal basis of ownership. Groundbreaking as it was, the law was limited in that it was backward-looking, applying only to squatters who already resided on their land and had planted a crop on it in 1829, and who registered their claim within a year of the law's enactment. Still, its passage stirred expectation. New waves of westward-moving emigrants, having found a suitable spot for settlement, pressed lawmakers to accord them the same privilege. The effect of preemption was to foster a settle-first-legalize-later mentality. This aggressive land-taking ethos by squatters, in turn, emboldened Democratic leaders to assert US sovereignty over larger areas of the North American West.[32]

Preemption became the linchpin of the statesmen-squatter alliance, connecting them in a common objective: extending the measure indefinitely with an eye toward securing its permanence. In making the case for the policy, politicians and settlers developed stock phrases and arguments that rebranded squatters as virtuous improvers, congealing into the character of the intrepid white yeoman who displaced "savages" and planted the flag of American civilization in the West while defending the nation's vulnerable borders. Heroes, not violent intruders, they deserved deference rather than scorn.

State legislatures played a key role linking Democrats in Washington to their constituents in the West. In memorials to Congress endorsing preemption and other land reforms, state lawmakers stoked the mythos of the virtuous pioneer yeoman. A December 1831 memorial by the Mississippi legislature, for example, advocated the creation of "a permanent yeomanry" and preventing "wealthy capitalists" from excluding "the poor *pioneers* of the wilderness from the hope of securing a fixed and permanent home." Illinois lawmakers composed a similar memorial to Congress in 1832, touting the importance of cultivating "a population of freeholders." The memorial portrayed squatters as "pioneer[s] of the wilderness" and "worthy heads of families" who had risked everything to forge their humble prairie farmsteads. If Congress failed to intervene with favorable land policies, these squatters risked being driven off by "merciless speculators." The pro-yeoman pitch unified Democrats across sections.[33]

Benefiting from the prevailing currents, squatters flooded Congress with preemption petitions describing their experiences in their own words and contributing to the construction of the pioneering yeoman trope. Whether from Michigan Territory or Mississippi, Illinois or Arkansas, the petitions showed remarkable uniformity in style and substance. Seekers of preemption portrayed themselves as upstanding yeomen undertaking the noble work of nation-building in the face of grave perils. They strongly rejected the notion that they were trespassers who had defied the law by occupying land without title and often manifested a strong sense of entitlement to those terrains. George B. Willis and more than a hundred fellow squatters in Putnam County, Illinois, for example, wrote Congress in 1831, candidly admitting that "they reside on the public lands of the United States," but insisting that "as pioneers of a new country and opening the way for extensive settlements, they do not view themselves as intruders, but as rendering an actual benefit to the government." Moses Finch and other settlers on land acquired by the United States from the Potawatomis in southwestern Michigan freely confessed to having occupied public land without authorization, but argued they were serving the national interest by "forming settlements; opening roads; [and] improving the Country," all of which lessened the "dangerous Indian aggression and the expense of protection to frontier settlements." They self-identified simply as belonging to "a hardy and enterprising class of men wishing to Better their condition." Looking to secure a preemption right of his own, William Matheson of Clarke County, Alabama, emphasized to lawmakers that he had established a sawmill and gristmill and constructed a levee along a stretch of the Alabama River to prevent flooding—infrastructure that benefited the entire region. Matheson also owned numerous slaves but, like his northern counterparts, portrayed himself as a pioneering cultivator whose exertions hastened the march of American progress.[34]

Squatters also defined themselves by who they were not: "speculators." Petition after petition railed against these most contemptible creatures and sought protections against their nefarious designs. O. P. Lacey and fellow settlers in Berrien County, Michigan, contrasted the "boldness of the pioneer—the untiring toils of enterprise" with the "mania of speculation." Arkansas squatter Isaac Darneille styled the speculator "the destroyer of the poor man's just claims, the evil genius, the ruin of the country" who stood in diametric opposition to "the actual settler, the farmer, the real cultivator of the soil." The demonizing of speculators involved a subtle frontier code. Speculation in land had been an American calling since the days of the Puritans and reached new levels in the early nineteenth century, involving rich and poor, urban and rural, and partisans of all political persuasions. In fact, many farmers themselves doubled as speculators, purchasing extra acres in hopes of selling them when land values rose. In the lexicon of the frontier, however, there were different grades of speculators—improvers who pioneered settlements and made the wilderness bloom, and leeches who kept to their cities or plantations and merely watched their profits grow from the sale of remote lands. Settlers were forgiving of the small-scale speculators in their communities but excoriated absentee urban capitalists who tied up choice lands in speculative schemes that impeded development.[35]

Many blamed greedy speculators for forcing them to become squatters in the first place. In their petition to Congress, L. H. T. Maxson and dozens of fellow "Emigrants from the east and south" described their high hopes when they set off for Indiana. Writing in the third person, according to convention, they asked lawmakers to "judge their disappointment and surprise when on ariving [*sic*] with their families they found almost all the good land ... in the hands of speculators and non residents." Worse, the crafty capitalists wanted as much as $20 per acre, far above the government price of $1.25, and much more than Maxson and neighbors could pay. In their testimonial they reported seeing no other remedy but to squat on government land not yet on the market. Undaunted, they set about "making extensive improvements, building mills, erecting school houses, and forming societies," all the while finding themselves "daily threatened by the rich speculator that our lands will be sold from under us, together with our improvements and our families turned out ... pennyless." They concluded with a plea "that Congress ... pass a law giving to the actual settler the preemptive right to the lands on which they live." Squatters in "Cherokee Country" in Alabama made a similar appeal to lawmakers. "We do hope that you will not suffer our improvements to be [thrown] into hands of the speculators who do not buy to cultivate but to deal out to the honest farmers at four times its real value." The drumbeat for preemption as a foil to rank speculation continued.[36]

For some, like Isaac Darneille, speculators did not merely drive honest men to squat on public lands but added insult to injury by mocking them in the process. Having settled in Arkansas Territory in the 1820s "to instruct and civilize" Cherokees and other Native peoples, Darneille struggled to make ends meet. In a wide-ranging petition written in a hand palsied from a fall from his horse, he lamented that, unlike Indians whom the government often provisioned with goods and money when forcing them to migrate from their homelands, "The poor white emigrant who travels at his own expense from the East to the West finds himself with a family of a wife and five or six children to support by his own labor, without money; and besides this, he must have a home. Yes, a temporary home. He sits down on the public lands; (and he is then called a *Squatter in derision*; not by the settlers in this country, but by the unfeeling speculator)." Darneille, of course, failed to distinguish between migrations forced on Native peoples and the voluntary moves that he and other white settlers embarked upon.[37]

Unlike Democratic politicians, who sought to imbue the term "squatter" with positive connotations, squatters themselves often took umbrage at the label, agreeing with a letter writer to an Arkansas newspaper who fumed, "The word 'squatter,' is a most undignified part of speech." Over time, many settlers in the West came to wear the term as a badge of honor. In his 1853 account of life in western states, J. L. McConnel wrote of frequent encounters with squatters "wandering toward the setting sun, in search of pleasant places on the lands of 'Uncle Sam.'" He paused to consider the term, commenting, "'Squatter' is now, in the west, only another name for 'Pioneer,' and that word describes all that is admirable in courage, truth, and manhood!" The journey from epithet to honorific is a testament to decades of rhetorical work by Democrats and white squatters to rebrand them.[38]

In their preemption petitions in the 1830s, squatters positioned themselves as pillars of the patriarchy, often highlighting their status as "heads of families," with wives and children to support—a point that Jacksonian elites also emphasized when defending them. Numerous petitioners professed that it was precisely their determination to fulfill their provider role that spurred them to move west in the first place. William Smith of Noxubee County, Mississippi, spoke in highly personal terms of his circumstances, describing himself as "a poor man with a wife and three children who are dependent on him for support." He faced uncertainty over preemption rights to his land and, he pleaded, without help from Congress, he would "be cast upon the pitiless world with no prospect ahead save penury & want." Unmentioned was that fact that Smith was an attorney and the son-in-law of respected and wealthy Revolutionary War veteran Joel Barnett. Indeed, Smith had been one of nine signatories to a letter from Barnett to Andrew Jackson in 1834, praising the president for his "known and acknowledged friendship to the pioneers of a wilderness country" and asking him to intervene to secure to them title to lands reserved for Choctaw orphans, fearing they would otherwise fall into the hands of non-resident speculators. His fortunes may have turned, but it was unlikely that he was destined for the almshouse. Meanwhile, the ease with which these settlers solicited the aid of the most powerful men in the country spoke volumes. In rare instances, frontier women also petitioned Congress for preemption rights; one was Mary Robison, a widow in St. Joseph County, Michigan, who wrote that in the five years since her husband's death she "has continued to enlarge the improvements" on their farm, bolstering her case to receive title.[39]

Closely linked to their roles as providers and protectors was squatters' notion of themselves as standard bearers of civilization and American advancement. Pressing for preemption rights, squatters in northern Illinois informed Congress of their progress "converting the haunts of the prowling wolf and the roaming savage, to the delightful abodes of civilized man." A preemption petition from settlers along the Illinois and Michigan Territory border noted, "Many of us were the among the first who explored the Country and encouraged by the policy of the Government made it our abode. . . . We have risked our lives and property for the protection and defense of this frontier." The white migrants to "Cherokee Country" in Alabama, based their own preemption request in part on the notion that, by moving into that part of the country, "we contributed largely in . . . causing the Cherokee people to Remove to their homes in the far West." Such views made plain their belief that the government had invited them to take over Native lands.[40]

Indian testimonials and experiences with Jacksonian land policies stood in stark contrast to claims by squatters and their representatives about bringing progress and prosperity to the West. Catharine Cheike, a Cherokee woman, wrote to Congress through an intermediary in 1831, explaining that she was entitled, under treaty, to 640 acres in Alabama. But squatters had occupied her land, forcing "a woman, unacquainted with the language[,] maners [*sic*] and laws of the whites . . . from her home." "Wicked and designing"—not "virtuous" or "enterprising"—were the words Cheike used to describe these men. Between a government bent on Indian removal and settlers occupying their lands, Native peoples felt squeezed on all sides.[41]

Many white squatters couched their expectation of preferential treatment in tones of grievance, suggesting that they were victims of their race.

Isaac Darneille believed it was their very whiteness that placed him and his
Arkansas neighbors in harm's way. "We anticipate the day, which we believe
to be not far distant, when the Creeks and Seminoles from Georgia, Alabama
and Florida, full of hatred and resentment against the white people, will come
to the same country west of Arkansas, and will . . . rise up against the citizens
of Arkansas and Missouri, where the settlements are sparse, the inhabitants
few and the conquest easy," he wrote in a petition to Congress signed by
fellow settlers. Darneille added a recommendation that he deemed not
simply the best policy but the one "required by the laws of nature," namely,
"to remove, without delay, all the obstacles heretofore thrown into the way
of the white settlers and emigrants to this country. Let them have the land."
For good measure he urged squelching any movement to free slaves, crying,
"Emancipate the blacks and the poor white man and his children shall become slaves to the rich."[42]

Savvy in the ways of quid pro quo, Darneille wrote in an 1836 missive to
Arkansas's US senators, Ambrose H. Sevier and William S. Fulton, "It will
give me the greatest pleasure to do anything in my power to serve you or either
of you in anything you may be good enough to hint or suggest to me." It is not
altogether surprising that a hard-luck squatter felt comfortable reaching out
to national statesmen, given how far these Democrats went to prove themselves worthy of their affection. Sevier in particular had earned their trust,
having pronounced in a Senate speech that the "squatters were his particular
friends, and he meant to stick to them." These pledges of admiration and support strengthened the bonds of Squatter Democracy.[43]

Frontier inhabitants listened carefully to cues from Washington and
aligned themselves with allies in Congress, often addressing them in personal
terms. Glen Burnett of Clay County, Missouri, for instance, penned a letter
to Thomas Hart Benton, seeking his help with a local preemption dispute.
"We look to you as our common friend and the supporter of the *poor man*,"
he avowed. Democratic congressman Joseph Duncan of Illinois enjoyed similar standing. Throughout the early 1830s, he introduced scores of preemption
petitions into the House on his constituents' behalf, lauding "the hardy, enterprising, poor man that first ventured into the wilderness." His sympathetic
understanding of their travails naturally inclined squatter constituents to so-
licit his help. One of them was William Stewart, among the original white
settlers in Putnam County. He wrote to Duncan on December 20, 1832,
seeking his intervention in a preemption case. Tellingly, Stewart opened with
a few words of appreciation for Andrew Jackson, a man who inspired special
affection among white settlers.[44]

Jackson's 1832 annual message to Congress elevated his already high standing in the West. In it the president outlined his philosophy for the best use of the public lands. "It can not be doubted that the speedy settlement of these lands constitutes the true interest of the Republic," he declared. By his calculations, the "adventurous and hardy population of the West" had poured some $40 million into federal coffers via land sales. The president insisted that it was "best to abandon the idea of raising a future revenue out of the public lands" and "to afford to every American citizen of enterprise the opportunity of securing an independent freehold." This endorsement of settlement by freeholders over generating revenue as the top priority in the disposal of US public lands won hearty approval from many westerners, including William Stewart. In his letter to Duncan, he wrote, "You will be pleased to hear that Gen. Jackson's late message . . . has made us all 'Jackson men.'" Old Hickory's landslide reelection in 1832, in which he swept the West except for opponent Henry Clay's home state of Kentucky, had affirmed that the electorate was indeed brimming with "Jackson men."[45]

Wooing white squatters became a rainmaker and a sharp point of distinction between Jackson's party and the opposition led by Clay. Pushing for new preemption laws, Democrats continued to breathe life into the squatter yeoman character, using many of the same stock phrases and arguments as squatters themselves, reinforcing the ties between statesmen and settlers, Washington and the West.

Democratic politicians framed dynamics of settlement as a struggle of good versus evil. Their principal aim was to allow the righteous ones—"actual settlers"—to hold onto their lands and defend them against diabolical speculators. Preemption, they argued, was better suited to achieve these goals than the system of public land auctions, which were frequently dominated by speculators. Joseph M. White, Florida's delegate to Congress, took the lead in educating his colleagues about the cruel realities of land auctions, indulging in anti-Semitic literary license with a reference to Shakespeare's Shylock.

> A land sale is advertised; the purchasers attend; the poor settler has scraped together just enough to purchase at one dollar and a quarter per acre. The Shylocks and speculators say to him, give me one, two, or three hundred dollars, or I will buy your improvement, and turn your wife and children into the woods. The money is not to be had, and a note, horse, gun, or cow, is given. . . . The Government is not benefited, and one of its citizens who would, at any moment, hazard his life in its defence, is oppressed and defrauded.[46]

White insisted that this woeful scenario was not fanciful. In fact, he added, "I have even heard of instances in which the last cow has been taken from a poor man." Believing that preemption would stop this "vile and infamous traffic," he called for extending that right to more squatters.

Heavy-handed and dripping with moral drama, Democratic advocacy for squatters did nevertheless embody a theory of political economy. Jacksonians promoted conquest and rapid settlement of the West by small farmers, while also in principle favoring a small government footprint. Who better, in their view, to advance these aims than the "hardy pioneers" who—armed with little more than shotguns, a few household effects, and preemption rights—ventured into frontier regions, created farms and communities, constructed infrastructure, and protected the nation from invasion?[47]

The Democrats' vision of national development contrasted sharply with that of anti-Jacksonians, who organized as the Whig Party in 1834. Whigs disapproved of Democrats' slapdash approach to political economy and advocated orderly growth, with agriculture and manufacturing developing in tandem. Henry Clay's American System of economic development called for tariffs to protect domestic manufacturers and redistribution of public land proceeds to states for internal improvements like roads and canals. Squatters represented a grave liability to this program, because they not only undermined methodical development but also usurped a key source of income by occupying the choicest lands.[48]

For Whigs, auctions administered by the General Land Office represented a sound mode of disposing of public lands since they entailed a modicum of order—generally occurring after a district land office had opened and surveyors had measured the land into saleable units—and because competitive bidding would net the government the most revenue. Preemption, by contrast, promoted a mad dash for prime lands resulting in haphazard growth. "Why not at once throw open all the public lands for a general scramble, and abolish the auction system?" queried Congressman Horace Everett of Vermont sardonically. His colleague Lewis Williams, a North Carolina Whig, observed that the Intrusion Act of 1807 and preemption laws were incompatible, and that the government was sending mixed messages by keeping both statutes on the books. In an 1832 preemption debate, he noted, "The Government [has] a general law forbidding squatters to settle on the public lands. Either that law should be repealed, or this not passed; for this [goes] to invite these citizens to do the very thing which the other law prohibit[s]." On one point Democrats and Whigs agreed: federal policies had an important bearing on the course of national growth. Democrats, however, preached a hands-off approach, while Whigs demanded a more active, controlling influence.[49]

Preemption became a vehicle for the rival parties to elaborate their diverging positions on western development. Because these statutes remained in effect for limited periods, their enactment set in motion a recurring cycle. With one act poised to expire, a fresh spate of frontier petitions praying for preemption would pour into Congress and propel intense debates during which Democrats would champion the squatters' cause, while leading Whigs lashed into them—usually for the law to pass. "It is now too late to question the pre-emption policy," asserted Florida's White in 1832. Whigs ultimately conceded the point, recognizing that they could not stop the prevailing politics of settlement. "Did any gentleman, seriously believe that [preemption] would not be re-enacted, and continue to be re-enacted from year to year, so as, in fact, to be perpetual?" sighed Samuel Vinton of Ohio during an 1834 debate. "The squatters were favorites with some gentlemen in [the] House, and always would be." The consistent passage of preemption laws reflected squatters' increasing clout in Washington. Equally important, the policy gave them a reliable tool for securing their hold on western lands.[50]

Amid record land sales in the 1830s, the Whig argument that preemption deprived the government of income became difficult to sustain. Even with preemption claims steeply rising—from 2,623 acres in 1829 to 637,597 acres in 1834—public land sales reached all-time highs, peaking at more than 20 million acres sold in 1836, compared to 1.2 million in 1829. The roaring land business helped put the government in the black for the first time since the country's founding. In the face of these windfalls, Clay advanced his policy to distribute surplus revenue to the states for internal improvements and other initiatives. Democrats resisted this proposal, arguing that federal involvement in infrastructure projects overstepped the government's proper bounds. When Clay finally managed to get his distribution bill passed in 1832, Jackson vetoed it. If nothing else, the Democracy was consistent in its calls for nation-building on a shoestring and limiting Washington's role, even if in practice party leadership got behind select improvements when these benefited partisans, and they welcomed an active government role in removing Indians from western lands.[51]

Whig charges that squatters sowed chaos and disrupted growth were also debatable. Without question, migrants often outpaced the government as they pushed westward and provoked conflicts with Indians whose lands they occupied. In some respects, though, they were an organizing force. They formed squatter associations, also known as claim clubs, which mimicked the core functions of the General Land Office in places where the federal government had yet to set up shop, run survey lines, or even negotiate with Indians for their land. Such organizations prescribed rules for claiming land and appointed key personnel like surveyors and a "register" to process claims and provisionally award titles. Above all they were defensive organizations, protecting members from claim jumpers. When public land sales finally commenced in their region, members would assemble en masse and muscle out any would-be purchaser reckless enough to try to outbid an "actual settler" from their ranks. For Democrats, squatter associations were instruments of order that made the party's laissez-faire approach to development workable. For Whigs, they merely abetted lawlessness.[52]

Democrats engaged in such elaborate myth-making to convert a long-reviled figure into a cause célèbre that Whigs certainly had grounds for skepticism about their rivals' passion for squatters. Rhetorically, for example, they positioned the squatter as a yeoman with no particular relationship to slavery, either for or against. In reality, squatters were no more indifferent to slavery than their advocates in government. A number of preemption petitioners, including William Matheson of Clarke County, Alabama, were large slaveholders who spoke pro-yeoman, anti-speculator jargon to further their own ends. Meanwhile, squatters George Willis and William Stewart of Putnam County, Illinois, were not only opposed to slavery but leaders of a regional chapter of William Lloyd Garrison's American Anti-Slavery Society. While lurking as a potential source of friction, slavery did not threaten the cohesive power of Squatter Democracy among party leaders in the early years because the squatter yeoman trope served the land-claiming ambitions of northerners and southerners alike.[53]

Social class was another category that lent itself to equivocation. Democratic elites came to apply the term "squatter" so loosely that any white man seeking land, whether a struggling farmer or a prosperous planter, might well anoint himself a squatter, the less details the better for packing a rhetorical punch and promoting cohesion. As a result, "squatter" became a term of acclamation among Democrats, while "speculator" turned into the dirtiest of words. However, the men who sang squatters' praises most passionately were often the wealthiest and most apt to speculate in lands. Robert J. Walker was a case in point. A slaveholding speculator who became the most persistent, inventive, and exuberant champion of squatters, he embodied the paradoxes and peculiar power of Jacksonian Squatter Democracy.

The Ascent of the "Mississippi Squatter"

In the fall of 1833 hundreds of men converged on an alligator-rich stretch of the Yalobusha River in north-central Mississippi, turning a wilderness outpost into a tent city. Chocchuma, as the place was known, was little more than a muddy clearing with a few rough-hewn structures crowded by canebrakes, willows, hickories, and oaks. But from late October through December, it lured pilgrims from as far away as Alabama, Virginia, and Washington, DC, in search of land. With hundreds of thousands of fertile acres up for bid, the government auction at Chocchuma was one of the most eagerly anticipated in a decade that saw public land sales in the United States soar to new heights.[54]

Chocchuma was part of the Choctaw Cession—more than 10 million acres in Mississippi and Alabama, much of it ideal for growing cotton. The Jackson administration secured this bounty in the Treaty of Dancing Rabbit Creek of 1830, brokered by US and Choctaw leaders against the will of most tribal members. In the first big test case of Jackson's Indian removal policy, federal agents began expelling the Choctaws to lands west of the Mississippi. The General Land Office set up operations at Chocchuma to prepare for the auction, giving rise to a temporary town that included a land office, tavern, and little else.[55]

Dancing Rabbit Creek expressly forbade settlers from occupying Choctaw lands until the tribe had removed, a process still ongoing in the fall of 1833. Many squatters, however, had ignored that provision and settled in the region before the sale. Some applied to the government for preemption rights, to no avail, and would have to compete at auction to hold onto their lands and improvements.[56]

With cotton prices at their highest levels in more than a decade, swarms of speculators and prospective settlers converged on Chocchuma for the sale. Political elites from Mississippi and beyond joined the fray, including governor-elect Hiram Runnels, US Senator John Black, soon-to-be Speaker of the US House John Bell of Tennessee, and assorted other congressmen, senators, and judges, both Jacksonian and anti-Jacksonian. Greenwood Leflore, the Choctaw chief and slaveholding planter who had pushed for the Treaty of Dancing Rabbit Creek and received liberal land concessions from the federal government in return, also attended. When bidding commenced on October 21, men massed around the land office where an auctioneer barked out the township and range coordinates of successive tracts and took bids. Many watched in dismay as rival companies of speculators from Alabama, Mississippi, and Tennessee dominated the proceedings, driving prices far above the starting government rate of $1.25 per acre.[57]

On the third morning the sale took a dramatic turn. Robert J. Walker of Natchez, a diminutive man with an air of command, called for the crowd to gather around him in front of Colonel Pratt's tavern. The thirty-two-year-old lawyer headed a powerful group of Mississippi speculators at Chocchuma. He announced to the restless men that the speculating companies from different states that had openly competed in early bidding were joining forces in order to create a single company to protect the interests of squatters. Walker sketched out how the plan would work: the company from that point forward would do all the buying and transfer an eighth of a section—eighty acres—at cost to each squatter who agreed to refrain from bidding himself. By eliminating competition, all parties would get land at or near the baseline government price. The company would then auction off to the highest bidder the thousands of acres it had purchased (and not transferred to squatters) and divide the profits among its shareholders. Squatters, Walker stated pointedly, would not get a better deal. He added that the company's terms reflected Andrew Jackson's fervent desire for the people to get cheap land, knowing as well as anyone the magical effect his name would have on settlers. Many agreed to the company's terms. When sales resumed that afternoon, the fierce competition that had marked the first two days subsided.[58]

Alarming accounts of the apparent collusion that gave speculators almost complete control of the auction at Chocchuma filtered back to Washington, prompting the chairman of the Senate Committee on Public Lands George Poindexter of Mississippi, a one-time Jackson ally turned virulent foe, to launch an investigation, making the land sale at Chocchuma one of the most scrutinized and politicized of the period. Thrust into the national spotlight, Walker, a skilled attorney, wasted no time mounting a spirited defense. He declined the investigating commissioners' request to travel to Jackson, Mississippi, to testify in person. Instead, he penned and circulated a pamphlet justifying his actions at Chocchuma. In the text addressed to his "Fellow-Citizens," Walker did not deny that he and his associates had created a consolidated company of speculators but claimed they did so "not to realize profit to myself," but to secure preemption rights for squatters who had been denied them. "I found the emigrant surrounded by wife and children, who, with him, looked forward to the public sales as the probable period which was to expel them from the little spot which they had selected and improved, and throw them forth again into the wilderness, without a roof to shelter or a home to protect them," he wrote.

Walker insisted that before he agreed to unite with the other speculators, he had extracted a promise that they would transfer ownership rights at the minimum price to squatters—a de facto preemption. "I adopted the last and only alternative . . . that would save the settlers," he explained, adding, "it is and ever will be to me a source of inexpressible gratification that I was thereby enabled to procure a pre-emption for so vast a number of the citizens of Mississippi." Speculators seizing control of land sales for personal profit was nothing new. But his explanation that altruism toward squatters had motivated his actions was a novelty.[59]

Confronting Poindexter's charges of having monopolized the land sale and exploited humble settlers for personal gain, Walker sought to distinguish between different varieties of speculator—those who intended to set down roots in the region and contribute to its development and those who merely swooped in to buy up land and turn a quick profit. In his defense, he emphasized repeatedly that his principal aim in joining forces with other speculators was to thwart the evil designs of predatory capitalists from out of state and rescue vulnerable squatters. Of course, as an attorney from cosmopolitan Natchez hundreds of miles away who had no evident intention of settling in the Chocchuma area himself, he was the very embodiment of an elite, absentee speculator. These facts did not dissuade him from positioning himself rhetorically as a champion of the people.

Justifying his actions at Chocchuma, Walker wrote of the "vast" number of poor squatter families he had saved from eviction. Yet just how many such people had settled at Chocchuma, and what exactly Walker accomplished for them, are questionable. A number of the so-called squatters whom Walker helped acquire land were prosperous men like John L. Irwin, the former speaker pro tem of Mississippi's legislature, and Titus Howard, owner of numerous slaves. Indeed, of the approximately 70,000 acres Walker acquired from the government largely as a bidder for the unified company of speculators, scarcely 3,000 went to individuals who might conceivably fit the hardscrabble yeoman profile he evoked. Based on Walker's version of events, one could believe he had made the long trip to Chocchuma for the sole purpose of saving squatters. Yet it wasn't long before wealthy slaveholders, including some of the most powerful and well-connected Jacksonians such as Polk and Jackson's own adopted son, Andrew Jackson Jr., possessed the lion's share of the best Chocchuma land, and African-descended slaves outnumbered whites in the region.[60]

Suspect and self-serving as they were, Walker's claims could not be dismissed out-of-hand. After all, he had been promoting the cause of squatters for years. If he was celebrating a politically expedient figment of his own fancy as much as real human beings, few would refute that at least a few actual yeoman types acquired freeholds through his interventions. One way to gauge the substance of his claims is to consider how his contemporaries responded to them. Published in August 1834, Walker's pamphlet created a sensation in Mississippi, where it enjoyed wide circulation and dominated talk among the political classes. Days after its publication, William M. Gwin, Mississippi's US marshal and brother of Samuel Gwin, the land office register at Chocchuma who was the main target of the Senate investigation, wrote to Andrew Jackson, reporting that Walker was in a strong position to challenge Poindexter for his Senate seat. For Poindexter to get reelected, Gwin growled, "he will have to walk over the dead bodies of *three* persons before he takes his seat. Mr. Walker my brother & myself." With the well-connected Gwin managing his campaign, Walker went on to wage an aggressive statewide race. To escape the taint of being an out-of-touch Natchez aristocrat, he purchased a plantation in rustic Madisonville, citing that as his residence.[61]

On March 3, 1835, Senator Poindexter issued a scathing report of his investigation's findings. Poindexter had tried unsuccessfully to block Samuel Gwin's appointment in the first place and he did not mince his words about the "profligate scenes" that had taken place at Chocchuma under his watch. The land officer had essentially abandoned his role as a public servant and ceded control of the sale to speculators "united for the purpose of monopolizing all the good lands . . . overawing bidders, and driving all competition out of the market." Poindexter was unpersuaded by Walker's explanation that benevolence motivated him to lead the band of speculators. "The agents of the company undertook to dictate terms to the actual settlers, and claim to themselves great credit for having *permitted* each occupant to purchase . . . a tract not exceeding one quarter section," he wrote. "All who refused to enter into this arrangement, and there were but few, had no other alternative but to bid against the large capitalists . . . but the instant he submitted to the authority of the company his improvements were secured to him at one dollar and twenty-five cents per acre. One of the agents," he added in a nod to Walker, "boasted that he had passed a pre-emption law in effect which had been rejected by Congress." For Poindexter this was all highly illegal, representing no less than the greatest "enormities . . . to have occurred at any time in any land district of the United States."[62]

To be sure, the report reflected the sentiments of a number of witnesses who had testified about the auction. Some grumbled about "wealthy men" taking "almost entire control of the sales." But the account failed to capture perhaps the most salient truth about Chocchuma: the so-called squatters in the region—well-to-do and humble alike—were on the whole pleased with how the sale played out, given that most got the land they wanted at the minimum price. These men feted Walker with a public dinner at the close of the auction and passed a resolution expressing their "warmest gratitude for his generous and manly protection of the interest of the settlers at the Chocchuma land sales." More significantly, in a January 1836 vote, members of the Mississippi legislature propelled Walker into the very US Senate seat held by Poindexter. Representatives from the sixteen new counties carved out of the Choctaw lands, including men who had acquired land directly from Walker on favorable terms, overwhelmingly supported the squatter-friendly speculator, putting him over the top on the fifth ballot.[63]

Walker's election exemplified core features of Squatter Democracy: the dispossession of Indians and speedy survey and sale of their lands, the celebration of a mythic yeoman, poor but virtuous, and the delivery of spoils in the form of land, speculative windfalls, and political office to a wide cross-section of white males—elites and non-elites, slaveholders and non-slaveholders—willing to come along.

Robert J. Walker won faithful constituents at Chocchuma, and he would vigorously champion their interests as he rose to the heights of power, first in the Senate, then as the engineer of President James K. Polk's election, US treasury secretary, and governor of Kansas Territory. In his first month in the Senate, he introduced a comprehensive land bill with provisions for preemption rights and a reduction in prices for "actual settlers." The freshman lawmaker used the occasion to deliver a passionate defense of squatters, taking the opposition—Henry Clay above all—to task for using the word pejoratively. "Sir," he pronounced, "our glorious Anglo-Saxon ancestry, the pilgrims who landed on Plymouth rock, the early settlers at Jamestown, were squatters— they settled this continent with less pretension to title than the settlers upon the public lands." Christopher Columbus and Daniel Boone also were squatters, he added. By referencing the country's hallowed origins—with nods to the North and South—Walker was making the case that America had always been a nation of squatters and was great because of it.[64]

Walker then turned his focus closer to home, observing that many of his "most enlightened" constituents were squatters. He singled out John L. Irwin, speaker of Mississippi's House who had been his associate at Chocchuma. He also mentioned John F. H. Claiborne, a genteel and powerful figure in Mississippi politics. Grouping such men into the category of squatter revealed just how capacious the term had become. Indeed, squatters were not simply America's founders and great pioneers. In Walker's eyes, they were indistinguishable from slaveholding gentry.[65]

Walker ended his speech on a favorite note: squatters as the manly defenders of the United States in a dangerous world. He invoked the calamity of the British invasion of Washington during the War of 1812. In a master stroke of Democratic rhetoric he extolled backwoodsmen and Andrew Jackson in the same sentence, claiming that "if but one thousand of these much-abused squatters, these western riflemen, had been at Bladensburg, beneath their great commander, never would a British army have polluted the soil where stands the Capitol of the Union. No, sir, they would have driven back the invader ere the torch of the incendiary had reached the Capitol, or they would have left their bones bleaching here . . . alike in death or victory, the patriot defenders of their country's soil, and fame, and honor." The gallery erupted in applause. Even Clay complimented his young colleague for his "burst of eloquence." The Kentuckian said he had meant no disrespect to squatters but added that he "hardly thought they would have saved the Capitol unless they had given up their habits of squatting."[66]

The Whig press mocked Walker's "high, flowery, and earnest eulogium upon the squatters," as New York's *Commercial Advertiser* characterized it. According to the fledgling senator, the bemused writer quipped, squatters' triumphal march did not start with the discovery of America but with "Old Adam himself" in the Garden of Eden. And the great squatter procession continued up to the present, with the leaders of the Democratic Party and their constituents taking the lead. "Benton's American people were all squatters," and Democrats "the squatter party" the piece continued, accusing Jacksonians of exploiting the squatter trope to drum up popular support. *Boston Courier* scribe Timoleon (the pseudonym of Isaac Orr) puzzled over the direction of Democratic politics and wondered what the country was coming to. "Duped, misguided, miserable American people," he wrote. "Why do you send your cheats, and brags, and buffoons, and squatters here, to torture us?" He was particularly struck by Walker's pugnacious nature, which he deemed remarkable from a man who barely measured five feet tall. "Frighten him! You might just as well frighten a gnat or moscheto [*sic*], which will come back to stick in its proboscis the five hundredth time after you have driven it away," he groaned. Some in the press dubbed Walker "the Mississippi Squatter." But the laughs died down when, within a year of his arrival in the Senate, he became chairman of the Committee on Public Lands, the very body that had investigated his role at the Chocchuma land sale and deemed his actions criminal.[67]

Walker staked out a position for himself as the squatters' man in the Senate, calling the public lands "a sacred reserve for the cultivator of the soil" and promoting land reforms favorable to settlers' interests. Even as he championed squatters, he lost no chance to rip into speculators, prompting Whig Senator Thomas Ewing to observe caustically "that those who denounce these 'speculators' the most loudly and the most frequently on this floor and elsewhere, are those . . . who are themselves the most deeply engaged in the vocation which they thus condemn."[68]

Walker's appearance on the national stage injected a shriller and more divisive tone into the squatter culture wars and demonstrated the effectiveness of Squatter Democracy as a mode of partisan warfare. If foes found him vaguely ridiculous and annoying, settlers in the West prized the passion of their defenders, especially in the face of continued Whig abuse. A group of unauthorized settlers in northern Illinois wrote to Congress, expressing their "feelings of surprise and regret" at the harsh characterizations of squatters "echoed from the walls of the capitol." They saw it as their role to set the record straight and talk about their contributions to the country.

> If you ask . . . "who are the settlers on the unsurveyed public lands"? . . . [W]e are your brethren . . . engaged in the quiet pursuits of agriculture and its kindred employments; and in a country which three years ago was little better than a desolate waste are now to be seen comfortable dwellings surrounded by valuable improvements. Water power is being improved, and saw & grist mills are built or rising in every direction. Towns and villages are already springing up. The tract has been divided into counties by our state legislature; and we have magistrates who administer equitable laws.[69]

Other petitioners were less measured in their responses to perceived attacks on their character. Squatters in Racine County, Wisconsin Territory, assured lawmakers they were not "fugitives from justice, wishing to be free from the operation of laws," nor were they "midnight house-breakers." Instead, they came from "the most respectable families and the most desirable situations in the Eastern or Middle States, of their own choice, bringing with them much property, because they could find here a better soil, a more genial climate, and a wider field for the exercise of enterprise and talent." In seeking preemption privileges they did not believe they were demanding "the reward of crime, or large premiums for the violation of the laws, but manfully and honorably seeking their just rights." Claims of respectability featured prominently in pro-squatter discourse.[70]

Despite rising frontier pique, Henry Clay and others in his party did not refrain from maligning squatters. In December 1837, Walker reported a new preemption bill, sparking the most strident debates yet. Clay took the bait, making inflammatory comments that would haunt him for years to come.

Squatters were "a lawless rabble," he reportedly charged. "What right had they to the public domain more than any other description of plunderers to the goods they may seize upon?" Senator John Tipton of Indiana registered shock. "Does [Mr. Clay] not know that . . . the emigrants from the old to the new States are in the constant habit of entering upon the best public land they could find, building cabins to shield their families from the pelting of the storm, and cultivating the soil, regardless whether the land had been surveyed or not, with the expectation and intention of paying the Government for the lands whenever they should be brought into market[?]" Tipton pointed out that four entire counties in Indiana were populated by squatters and that "I am personally acquainted with many of them: they are educated, moral, and highly respectable. Many of them would lose nothing by a comparison with members on this floor; and if the honorable Senator holds a different opinion, it is because he has been misinformed." James Buchanan, Democratic senator from Pennsylvania, applauded the thousands of squatters in Iowa who "had cleared away the forests, had erected farm houses and barns, planted orchards, cultivated the land" and created thriving towns. "Could you now expel such an entire community from their homes," he asked, expecting any decent American would emphatically answer "no."[71]

Foreshadowing conflicts to come, one Democrat pushed back against his party's pro-squatter ways. Ever the wildcard, John C. Calhoun had been Jackson's vice president but fell out with the administration and was an increasingly caustic exponent of slavery. Never one to toe the Jacksonian line, he charged that Iowa—then a part of Wisconsin Territory—had been "seized on by a lawless body of armed men, who had parceled out the whole region, and had entered into written stipulations to stand by and protect each other, and who were actually exercising the rights of ownership and sovereignty over it—permitting none to settle without their leave, and exacting more for the license to settle, than the Government does for the land itself." In taking aim at squatters and their claim clubs, Calhoun rejected the Democrats' assertion that squatters brought civilization, virtue, and order to the frontier West. He effectively spouted Whig doctrine. His thinking may have been influenced by the South Carolina nullification crisis, during which upcountry freeholders had rejected the secessionist impulses of coastal slaveholding elites, a dynamic that did not go unnoticed by Andrew Jackson, who hailed "the united voice of the yeomenry." Calhoun perhaps recognized that his party's solidarity with squatters masked fundamental incompatibilities between plain republican farmers and slavemaster planters. If the contest came down to which section would benefit most from following squatters west, Calhoun seemed to intuit the North would win that race.[72]

Though Calhoun's tirade held worrisome implications for party unity, Democrats kept their focus on Clay. Roused to combat by the Kentuckian's anti-squatter bombshells, Walker dared Clay to "lead the forces which are to drive from their homes and consume the dwellings of these hardy pioneers." Clay coolly countered, "Do we live in a country of laws, or not?" A squatter might as well stake a claim to the White House, he suggested. "Suppose," Clay continued, "a pre-emptioner was to go there and say, Mr. President, this house is too large for you; I am an honest, industrious cultivator, one of the bone-and-sinew men, and claim a pre-emption to part of this house. Would he not have as much right to squat down there, as to squat down on the public lands?" Walker ridiculed Clay for his obsession with the White House, the ultimate object of his ambition. He then jabbed at the sorest spot of all, the so-called corrupt bargain between Clay and John Quincy Adams that had allegedly plucked the election of 1824 from Andrew Jackson and handed it to Adams, who made Clay his secretary of state. "Sir," Walker said, "I never knew of but one *squatter in the White House*, who could be truly called an intruder there, and that was one who was placed there in 1825, with the aid of the Senator from Kentucky, against the will of the people."[73]

The preemption bill passed 30–18 in the Senate and 107–53 in the House. As in 1830, Democrats controlled both chambers and the votes on preemption reflected notable partisan dimensions. In the Senate, twenty-nine Democrats and only one Whig approved the measure, while twelve Whigs and six Democrats voted against it, including Calhoun. As with the 1830 act, support among northwestern senators was strong—with nine out of ten approving it. Unlike in 1830, when the opposition held the majority of those seats, Democrats in 1838 controlled all but one. Support for preemption had tapered off in the south Atlantic, even among Democrats, a trend especially pronounced in the House where thirteen Democratic congressmen supported the bill while twelve joined with all eleven Whigs representing the region to oppose it. Still, with the exception of Calhoun, Democrats from all sections had come to the passionate defense of squatters and secured preemption's passage by comfortable margins. Martin Van Buren signed the act into law on June 22.[74]

By decade's end, Squatter Democracy had carried the day on rhetorical and policy fronts. A figure once universally vilified had become, over the course of the 1830s, the darling of the Democratic Party and preemption the law of the land. The marriage of interests between Washington-based elites and flesh-and-blood squatters across the expanding West gained traction because it delivered on its fundamental promise: land in exchange for political support. A continent beckoned and Democrats had found a powerful means to conquer it—or so it seemed.

2

Bad Birds

A CRACKLING FIRE sent plumes of fragrant smoke through the Council House at Chicago on September 14, 1833, as a trio of US officials convened with head men from the "United Nation" of Potawatomi, Chippewa, and Ottawa tribes for talks aimed at convincing them to cede their homelands and move west of the Mississippi. They passed around a peace pipe before lead commissioner George Porter, governor of Michigan Territory, blessed "the Great Spirit" and opened the deliberations. "We are happy to observe, my children, that you have not listened to the bad birds which have been flying around you, but have come up to the council of your own free will," he pronounced. "We approach you all my children, as friends. We take you fast by the hand, and offer you our best advice."[1]

Over the course of the next two weeks Porter doled out a great deal of advice, making plain that the ultimate authority was Andrew Jackson. "Your Great Father the President of the United States has a perfect knowledge of the condition and interests of his red children. . . . He loves them, and does all he can for their happiness and good," he began. He went on to catalogue the Indians' woes. "You complain that the white man has pressed too closely upon you—that he has environed you on all sides and deprived you of the pleasure of the chase," he said. Fortunately, the president had a vision to help: "Your Great Father . . . believes, that if you will all consent to go across the Mississippi then you will live much better, and that he will be a shield to you against any farther molestation from the white man and protect your Lands from his encroachments." So it went, day after day. Porter's tone shifted from professions of sympathy to subtle wheedling to not-so-subtle threats. "Your Great Father is the greatest war chief that any of you have ever seen," he declared at one point, hinting at the carnage awaiting any "bad birds" who

Dangerous Ground. John Suval, Oxford University Press. © Oxford University Press 2022.
DOI: 10.1093/oso/9780197531426.003.0003

resisted fatherly advice. "Yet he loves his red children." If this was love it was the toughest kind.[2]

In treaty councils up and down the Mississippi Valley and beyond, US officials sounded the same notes, paying homage to the Great Spirit, pointing to swelling white populations in Indian domains, pressing for cessions of their homelands, promising a prosperous existence west of the Mississippi, and delivering stern warnings not to heed the bad birds. They portrayed themselves as powerless to control the tide of white emigration even as Democrats encouraged squatters to claim western domains. Benjamin F. Currey, the federal agent for Cherokee emigration notorious for his zeal in enrolling Indians to remove, stated the obvious to Andrew Jackson when he noted approvingly, "Rapid settlements by the whites in the vicinity of the Indians have a most powerful influence in determining them to go west."[3]

The president himself put the best possible spin on Indian removal, arguing that migration was not merely a "benevolent" policy essential to Indian survival but an opportunity for their betterment. To illustrate he pointed to white settlers in the West. "Our children by thousands yearly leave the land of their birth to seek new homes in distant regions. Does humanity weep at these painful separations from everything, animate and inanimate, with which the young heart has become entwined? Far from it," he proclaimed in his 1830 annual address, touting his Indian policy. "It is rather a source of joy that our country affords scope where our young population may range unconstrained in body or in mind, developing the power and faculties of man in their highest perfection." Jackson did not distinguish between the voluntary movement of white squatters who went with the blessings and weight of the government behind them and the compelled marches of Indians whom the United States and its land-hungry white citizens had forced out.[4]

Democrats depicted Indians as nomadic and lacking the capacity to properly value and utilize land, therefore disqualifying them from ownership. Native peoples like the Cherokees who had adopted Euro-American systems of land ownership and cultivation, erected sophisticated structures of constitutional government and expertly wielded the available mechanisms of suasion—from petitions, to editorials, to high-level litigation—also faced unrelenting pressure to give up their territory. The Cherokees, in their fight to remain, tested the limits of US jurisprudence, yielding landmark Supreme Court rulings in *Cherokee Nation v. Georgia* (1831), in which Chief Justice John Marshall designated Indian tribes "domestic dependent nations," and in *Worcester v. Georgia* (1832), which recognized their sovereignty outright and struck down Georgia's attempt to subordinate the tribe to state laws. But neither Jackson nor Georgia officials showed any inclination to relent in their campaign to force out the Cherokees.[5]

There was a cruel irony in dispossessing legally astute, self-governing agriculturalists because of their allegedly "wandering" ways, thereby forcing them to roam. No one felt this bitter reality more acutely than John Ross, principal chief of the Eastern Cherokees. He and a small delegation from his nation were in Washington in 1835, making a last-ditch attempt to stave off removal. In a January 23 letter they appealed directly to Jackson, reminding him "that hundreds of their people, many of whom are women and children, may now be homeless wanderers, suffering with cold & hunger, for no crime, but, because they did not love their Country less." The president did not respond, prompting Ross to write to Secretary of War Lewis Cass proposing to cede extensive tribal territory in Georgia in exchange for reserving tracts bordering their domains in Tennessee and Alabama. Cass reported back two days later that Jackson had considered the proposition and remained convinced "that any arrangement short of a general removal of your people would neither relieve the difficulties of the present nor prevent those of the future."[6]

Jackson had long held that formal treaty negotiations with Indians were "an absurdity" but was perfectly willing to go through the motions as long as they sped to a predetermined outcome: Indian land cessions and removal. It was Native people who could thus be forgiven for thinking that treaty negotiations were a farce. Indians from Florida to Michigan, New York to Louisiana, faced intense pressure from the United States and its footloose white populace to leave their ancestral lands. Sometimes they heard directly from President Jackson himself, as the Seminoles did in a February 16, 1835, letter:

My Children: I have never deceived, nor will I ever deceive, any of the red people. I tell you that you must go, and that you will go. Even if you had a right to stay, how could you live where you now are? You have sold all your country. You have not a piece as large as a blanket to sit down upon. What is to support yourselves, your women and children? The tract you have ceded will soon be surveyed and sold, and immediately afterwards will be occupied by a white population. You will soon be in a state of starvation. You will commit depredations upon the property of our citizens. You will be resisted, punished, perhaps killed. . . . If you listen to the voice of friendship and truth, you will go quietly and voluntarily. But should you listen to the bad birds that are always flying about you, and refuse to remove, I have then directed the commanding officer to remove you by force. This will be done. I pray the Great Spirit, therefore, to incline you to do what is right.[7]

The Indians stood their ground and the Second Seminole War broke out before the year's end. When military force failed to vanquish the Seminoles, Congress passed the Armed Occupation Act of 1842, granting 160 acres to men over eighteen "able to bear arms" who settled in or near the conflict zone. Thomas Hart Benton, the prime mover of the legislation, described the logic of settler-led conquest. "The heart of the Indian sickens when he hears the crowing of the cock, the barking of the dog, the sound of the axe, and the crack of the rifle," he declared. "These are the true evidences of the dominion of the white man; these are the proofs that the owner has come and means to stay, and then the Indians feel it to be time for them to go." In encouraging white families to settle on the Seminoles' homelands Jacksonians furnished proof of their belief that the only good squatter was a white squatter.[8]

Federal policies combined with state laws and on-the-ground practices by squatters to create domains of whiteness in the American West. White Americans wanted land and, to a remarkable degree, their elected officials openly did their bidding. In a memorial to Congress Mississippi's legislature pushed for policies to expedite "the exchange of [the state's] present unfortunate and degraded population of red men for a numerous, hardy and industrious one of free white men." Their counterparts in Indiana passed a joint resolution in 1832 soliciting Congress to approve a donation of land "to all white, actual settlers, who are not the owners of any land." The journals of the Senate and House from the 1830s abound with bills providing for the relief of destitute white settlers and for the extension of preemption laws even to those claiming Indian reserves.[9]

In pleading for preferential treatment, squatters cast themselves as victims deserving of government largesse. Squatters on public lands in Putnam County, Illinois, for example, wrote that they had fallen victim to "Indian hostilities" during the Black Hawk War of 1832 and urged lawmakers to grant them preemptions to secure their tenure. Solon Robinson, the Connecticut-born agricultural innovator who settled in Lake County, Indiana, composed a petition with his neighbors in 1835, chronicling how they had settled and improved land "under the full faith that the right of purchase would be secured to them by a pre-emption law of Congress," only to learn that a Potawatomi chief claimed the same tract under an 1832 treaty. "During the past summer we have been threatened that our dear bought homes, for which we have toiled and some of us suffered great hardships and privations, should be wrested from us for a reservation to one of the original owners of the soil," they lamented, praying for legislation to secure to them at the minimum government price the lands they claimed. Zadoc Martin, operator of a ferry along the Platte River in Missouri, noted in his own plea for preemption that he and his family felt constantly "exposed to Indian depredation." In an era of wholesale Indian removal, as Native peoples fought to remain on their ancestral lands, it is striking to find white squatters depicting themselves as the ones vulnerable to dispossession.[10]

Squatter associations or claim clubs worked to secure western terrains for white Americans. Most federal land statutes including preemption did not include language on race. Nevertheless, claim clubs set ground rules to keep non-whites out. Solon Robinson's Squatters' Union of Lake County, Indiana, exemplifies this dynamic. The organization formed on July 4, 1836, in the northwestern corner of the state on lands that until recently had belonged to Potawatomis. Its constitution resolved "that every White person . . . making or causing to be made, an improvement on a claim, *with the evident design of becoming a settler thereon*, shall be entitled to be protected in holding a claim on one quarter section." They established the offices of register, to process land claims, and arbitrator, to adjudicate disputes. Though existing preemption statutes did not apply to them, the Lake County squatters did not despair. With their pledges of mutual support and with pro-squatter sentiments prevailing in Washington, Robinson and his neighbors felt emboldened to establish settlements "under the full assurance that we shall now obtain our rights, and that it is now perfectly as safe to go on improving the public land as though we already had our titles from government." Their faith reflects the extent to which white Americans viewed the public lands as their patrimony and how they could weaponize preemption to seed the ground for a society rooted in white supremacy.[11]

Some Whigs pushed back against the pretensions of claim clubs. Senator Thomas Ewing of Ohio accused the Lake County Squatters' Union of undermining the authority of the United States by attempting to establish its own sovereign government—an "*imperium in imperio*"—and flouting federal laws. The allegation underscored what Whigs perceived as a gross double standard. On the one hand, Democrats had rejected the sovereignty of Native peoples. Yet they encouraged white squatters to establish what amounted to their own principalities on US public lands.[12]

Laws and settlement practices aimed to convert western lands into domains of whiteness, welcoming Euro-American land-seekers while placing every manner of impediment in the way of non-whites wishing to retain or claim territory. People of color had to run a gauntlet of racist structures just to scout a place for settlement, arrive safely, and commence the hard work of securing a subsistence, all the while facing threats of violence and severe limitations to civic participation and possibilities of advancement.

The story of Free Frank McWorter illustrates how heavily the deck of frontier land-claiming, farm-making, and settlement-building—arduous endeavors for anyone—was stacked against African Americans. McWorter was born into slavery in South Carolina in 1777 and was sent as a teenager to develop his master's farm in Kentucky's Pennyroyal region. Enslaved people played a central role in breaking ground and developing infrastructure in thinly populated frontier regions of the Southwest, and McWorter became a jack-of-all-trades, farming corn, tobacco, and wheat, caring for livestock, constructing cabins, and performing many other tasks for his owner and other white settlers to whom his owner hired him out. In 1799 he married Lucy, an enslaved woman owned by a relative of McWorter's master in a distant settlement.[13]

McWorter convinced his owner to allow him to hire out some of his own time to earn wages. So long as he satisfied his owner's work demands, he had considerable autonomy to pursue side endeavors. McWorter took to mining potassium nitrate in the caves of the region, establishing his own saltpeter manufactory. By 1817 he had saved enough money to purchase Lucy's freedom for $800. Two years later he purchased his own freedom for the same amount and assumed the byname "Free Frank." Over the next decade he continued in the saltpeter trade while also engaging in small-scale land speculation. In 1829 he traded his saltpeter operation for his son Frank's freedom. He also acquired 160 acres in southwestern Illinois's sparsely populated "Military Tract," where land tenure took the form of warrants redeemable by soldiers but typically fell into speculators' hands. Thus, McWorter was able to procure title outright to land in a remote region, providing a layer of protection against potential clashes with white squatters and their claim clubs.[14]

Securing title prior to settlement was essential. The public domain was not a place where land-seeking African Americans could safely venture in search of the ideal spot to farm, nor could they go to a district land office and consult a plat map without fear of a hostile reception. Unlike white settlers, McWorter and other African Americans had no association of fellow squatters to afford mutual protection or a government eager to reward their pioneering efforts with preemption rights.

Racism was ubiquitous, even in a free state. Illinois comprised territory from the Northwest Ordinance and approved a constitution in 1818 that affirmed the ordinance's ban on slavery over the objections of an influential proslavery minority. At the same time, the constitution perpetuated unfree labor by allowing contracts of indenture and prevented African Americans from voting. In 1829 the legislature passed a law requiring proof of freedom and a $1,000 bond for any black person wishing to settle in Illinois. Few settlers of any race could afford such an expense. Even those African Americans who possessed the capital would enter a society determined to keep them out. Simply moving across borders exposed free African Americans to the perils of slave catchers eager to send black people into bondage.[15]

Despite the steep obstacles, Free Frank McWorter, his wife Lucy, their manumitted son Frank, and three of their freeborn children, Squire, Commodore, and Lucy Ann, departed for Illinois in the fall of 1830. He was nearing his mid-fifties and Lucy sixty. Before leaving they had to convince the owners of their other enslaved children, Solomon, Juda, and Sally, not to sell them, pledging they would return and purchase their freedom as soon as they could raise the money.[16]

The McWorters established a farm in Pike County. Though older than many settlers, Free Frank and Lucy possessed the range of skills needed to flourish on the frontier. In addition to agriculture, Frank had the experience and acumen to make a go of the land business, which enabled him both to purchase his remaining enslaved children and establish the town of New Philadelphia, a unique instance of an African American man founding a town prior to the Civil War. By 1840 New Philadelphia's population exceeded 160 people, black and white.[17]

While the McWorters and many others triumphed against the odds, every step of their journey required extraordinary efforts in a system rigged in favor of white squatters. Across the West, people of color pushed against the white supremacist currents of Jacksonian land politics. Leopold Pokagon, leader of a band of the Potawatomis in Michigan's St. Joseph River Valley that bore his name, found his own path of creative resistance. In 1830, already in his mid-fifties, Pokagon got baptized as a Catholic, forming an alliance with influential French diocesan officials in the region who soon after established a mission near their village. Other members of the Pokagon band took baptism as well, even as the population of white settlers around them exploded.[18]

Leopold Pokagon was present at the Council House in Chicago in September 1833 for the treaty negotiations with the United States. He saw fit to enlighten the commissioners on nuances of Potawatomi culture. "Some of us are called 'wood Indians' altho we are Potawattamies, and others are called 'Prairie Indians,'" he explained. His group and other bands in Indiana and

FIGURE 2.1 Leopold Pokagon in an undated portrait by the artist Van Sanden. Courtesy of The History Museum, South Bend, IN.

Michigan fell into the former category. Like their counterparts on the Illinois prairies, they had already ceded most of their lands in previous treaties and faced pressure to relinquish the rest. "You have, my fathers, asked us to sell our *Land* to our Great Father. We do not know *what* land you want. We have *small* tracts of Land." Irritated, Porter pressed for more cessions: "These are the Lands which your Great Father instructed us to buy of you. You have, my children, told your Great Father that you were willing to sell these lands. . . . We repeat to you, that your Great Father cannot be trifled with." Porter insisted that ceding the lands was for their own good, given intensifying conflicts with white settlers who accused Pokagon's villagers of killing their hogs. The situation could easily escalate, he warned. "When your Great Father sends his warriors amongst you, there will be no time to make a treaty."[19]

Memories remained fresh of the 1832 Black Hawk War when the US army and Illinois militias mobilized against Sacs and other tribes for resisting removal. Earlier in the talks Porter had invoked the conflict to issue threats, emphasizing that Indians who continued to resist encroachments on their territory would face similar force. "You all know, my children, that during the last year some of your red brethren between here and the Mississippi river listened to bad birds, closed their ears to good council and acted most wickedly," he said. "In their case, your Great Father did what on such occasions he always does. He first gave these wicked men good advice; but they refused to listen to it. He then sent one of his War chiefs among them. . . . When the war was over with these wicked red men, your Great Father treated with them at the Cannon's mouth, and upon such terms only as his humanity dictated." The cajoling was both perverse and unnecessary given that many Potawatomis, including Pokagon's band, had assisted the US government in the conflict with Black Hawk.[20]

Whether sweet-talking or menacing with threats of war, Porter's message was unmistakable: cede your homelands and migrate west. Do not be bad birds. This was the Jacksonian script, and he adhered to it. Two weeks of such talks produced the Treaty of Chicago of September 26, 1833, under which the Chippewas, Ottawas, and Potawatomis relinquished their domains in Illinois and Wisconsin for 5 million acres west of the Mississippi. In supplementary provisions signed the following day, Pokagon and other Potawatomi chiefs ceded their Michigan lands.[21]

The agreement set three years as the deadline for departing. But Leopold Pokagon found a way to avoid leaving the land of his fathers. Because he and members of his band were Catholics, he convinced the commissioners to allow them to relocate to L'Arbe Croche, a settlement founded by French Jesuits on Ottawa lands in northern Michigan. That arrangement proved temporary, however, as the Ottawas came under significant pressure to relinquish their domain and move west. Meanwhile, Missourians protested against the settlement of Indians in their state as called for in the Treaty of Chicago, leaving hundreds of Potawatomis—many already in the process of migrating—in limbo. Amid the wrenching uncertainty, Pokagon wrote to Andrew Jackson on January 26, 1835, complaining of the strong-arming he had faced in Chicago in 1833. He had gone there to collect annuities, he explained, but payments were withheld for weeks as US officials demanded a treaty to cede their lands.[22]

During the whole of that time the Commissioner and several other persons engaged for the pourpase, came every day, one after an other to us, insisting that we would make a treaty: we answerd every one that we would not. they insisted principaly upon me Pokegan day an

night in sutch an insuportable maner that I hardly could get an hour
to rest: they promised me all that I could wish: I always refused, and
all my people did so during the said three weeks, although they were all
excessively tired by their importunities. Seeing they could not previal
upon us by that way, they began to thraten us and the governor Poorter
told us that you father was a very big man with large wings covering
the whole earth and doeing with the earth and the people what you
pleased, and if we would not willingly give our consent to the treaty
that you would come with your big cannon and great knives and
chasse us all awy. . . . [N]ow great father is this a fair maner of threating
with your children and can you ever aprove by your sanction sutch a
treicherous means?

Pokagon said moving west would expose his band to unique perils given
that they had marched against Black Hawk at the behest of the United
States. He concluded by asking the president to "reject that decetful treaty of
Chicago . . . [and] order to move the settlers from our reserve. . . . We will live
in good peace with the whites cultivate our lands and we shall pray the master
of live that he will reward you for your justice."[23]

Whether the government responded is unclear but Leopold Pokagon
found yet another way to stay in the land of his birth. He combined money
granted under the Treaty of Chicago with contributions from his community
to buy hundreds of acres around Silver Creek in southwestern Michigan and
re-establish a settlement that survives to this day.[24]

Indian removal and systemic barriers to settlement by non-whites—save
for slaves in certain regions—aimed to convert the domains of the United
States into a white man's country. Those policies and structures faced pushback at every turn, from the militant resistance of the Seminoles and Sacs, to
the political savvy of the Cherokees, to the extraordinary resilience and cre-
ativity of people like Free Frank and Lucy McWorter and Leopold Pokagon
and his band. Their persistence delivered an unmistakable rebuke that no
amount of repression could overturn the reality and enduring power of a mul-
tiracial West.

3

Crockett, Hard Cider, and the Whigs' Rustic Turn

"MISTER SPEAKER . . . [that there] honourable gentleman as spoke last, called my constituents squatters! Well, so they be's squatters, and so be I a squatter; I glories in the name." With these words, a fictionalized Davy Crockett, congressman from Tennessee, launches into his "celebrated squatter speech." The hero of *Crockett's Yaller Flower Almanac, for '36*—created by New York engraver and publisher Robert Elton—this particular iteration of Crockett goes on to teach his "lily-fingered" colleagues a thing or two about squatters and what they're made of. "The squatter, sir, goes out in the back woods, sir, *whor* the foot of man never was, and what if they sees a panther *thor*, and a wolf *thor*, sir, they builds 'em a hovel here, and a log house *thor*, and a court house *thor*, sir, and, sir, in less time than you can say Jack Robinson, they've a *hull* state squatted. Ax an Ingin varment, and he'll tell ye's the pale faces are all squatters." Crockett snarls a warning to his effete associates that if they're of a mind "to poke fun at squatters, I'll let 'em know as how they barks up the wrong sapling. Yes, Mister Speaker, I is a squatter, and have squatter constituents, and hopes as how the day will come when the American people shall squat the face of this tarnal 'arth, from the *Hatlantic* ocean to the *Specific*!!!"[1]

Ornery, profane, and racist, this Crockett character defiantly positions his fellow squatters as America's unsung pioneers and conquerors of the non-white peoples of the West. Every inch the embodiment of Squatter Democracy, he seethes at his fancy colleagues' slights and dares them to utter just one more cruel word. His hyper-bellicosity, denial of Indians' humanity, and mangling of the English language contain more than a whiff of Whiggish caricature of

Dangerous Ground. John Suval, Oxford University Press. © Oxford University Press 2022.
DOI: 10.1093/oso/9780197531426.003.0004

uncouth backcountry Democrats. Was this make-believe speech a send-up or a homage to pro-squatter politicians? Likely it was both. While many of the almanac makers were Whigs, commercial interests typically trumped ideological conviction in their productions. Understanding the public's appetite for tall tales from the frontier, these publishers happily delivered. Elton, in particular, appeared to have a business-before-politics philosophy, printing cartoons and almanacs that lampooned partisans of all stripes.[2]

If Elton's affiliations and motivations remain obscure, the same cannot be said for Davy Crockett. His persona in popular culture may have made him the brawling, cussing avatar of Democratic pro-squatterism, but David Crockett, the actual man from Tennessee, was a level-headed, if colorful, Whig, scrupulous enough to resist the currents of his place and time and vote against the Indian Removal Act. His party affiliation was counterintuitive given the habitual squatter-bashing by Whig leaders. Yet, rather than run from Crockett, they embraced him as somebody who could appeal to country folks. In fact, party operatives eagerly assisted in the creation of the mythic Davy Crockett, the salty-tongued, squatter-loving antihero. Their strategic deployment of this larger-than-life character underscores the Whigs' recognition of the power of pro-squatter politics, and the party stood ready to appropriate its trappings. Nowhere was this clearer than in their "log cabin and hard cider" campaign for the White House in 1840.[3]

The Whigs' rustic turn demonstrates the extent to which pro-squatter politicking had come to exert a defining influence on American political culture. Faced with the choice of jumping on the squatter bandwagon or getting run over, Whigs climbed on board. Democrats, however, were ill-inclined to cede the reins of their favorite workhorse. In 1844, they would make squatter-driven conquest of Texas and Oregon the centerpiece of their presidential campaign, positioning undaunted white settlers at the leading edge of geopolitical jockeying for sovereignty over those western domains.

As the era of Manifest Destiny dawned, the humble squatter yeoman figure began to morph, in popular depictions, into something more akin to the brash Davy Crockett character bent on claiming every inch of the continent for Uncle Sam. The marauding hell-raiser heralded the rise of the genre of southwestern humor and seared into many minds a vivid image of what a squatter was. This character had proslavery leanings, a noteworthy development because it marked the beginnings of a pronounced disjuncture between the symbolic squatter and actual settlers in the West, the majority of whom rejected the institution. The bid by competing interests to claim the squatter to advance their agendas reflects the symbol's potency and malleability—a combination of characteristics that made it an increasingly unpredictable factor in American politics.[4]

Davy Crockett

The emergence of Davy Crockett as the archetypal American squatter in the late 1830s and early 1840s attests to the blurring partisan lines of squatter politics. Despite the challenge of disentangling David Crockett the man from Davy Crockett the myth, some facts are beyond dispute and help explain the rise of this cultural icon. Crockett was born in 1786 in an area of western North Carolina that would soon become part of the new state of Tennessee. Nineteen years Andrew Jackson's junior, he enlisted in the militia under Old Hickory's command during the Creek War. Amid the slog and deprivations of the campaign, a number of the troops nearly mutinied against their hard-driving general. Jackson was not known for sparing insubordinates the rod, but Crockett walked away unscathed. In 1821 he won a seat in the Tennessee legislature representing a poor district in the southwestern part of the state.[5]

Throughout his political career Crockett posed a thorny challenge to Jackson and his lieutenants, including fellow Tennessean James K. Polk. These founding Democrats built their brand on appeals to ordinary folk. But from the vantage point of Crockett and his western Tennessee constituents, Jackson looked less like a man of the people and more like a Nashville aristocrat who lorded over a sprawling plantation and speculated prodigally in lands. He occupied a rarified world very distant from their own. Crockett joined the minority of Tennessee legislators who voted for Jackson's opponent in the election for US senator in 1823—a heresy that Jackson and the powerful machine that galvanized around him did not forget. But Crockett's supporters appreciated his independent streak and sent him to Congress in 1827.[6]

A single overriding obsession marked Crockett's otherwise undistinguished career as a lawmaker: getting a land bill passed to secure the claims of the poor farmers in his district. Land tenure in their neck of the woods was complicated. For decades much of the territory was tied up in warrants promised to Revolutionary War soldiers. Land speculators acquired most of the warrants and fought to keep squatters out. The settlers' toehold grew even more tenuous in 1829 when Tennessee's US congressional delegation, led by Polk, pressed for a law that would turn over hundreds of thousands of acres to the state for the support of higher education. Crockett considered it pure treachery that Tennessee's elite would take land from his struggling district and sell it off to fund schools for the rich. "The children of my people never saw the inside of a college in their lives, and never are likely to do so," he thundered. Insisting he had to answer to a "higher authority"—his constituents—Crockett framed the fight in David-versus-Goliath terms. "I find myself under the necessity of defending one poor district against all the rest of the State of Tennessee."[7]

Crockett showed a deft populist touch when he described the men who had elected him to Congress. "None of them are rich," he explained, "but they are an honest, industrious, hardy, persevering, kind-hearted people. I know them—I know their situation. . . . [I]f their little all is to be wrested from them, for the purposes of State speculation; if a swindling machine is to be set up to strip them of what little the surveyors, and the colleges, and the warrant holders, have left them, it shall never be said that I sat by in silence, and refused, however humbly, to advocate their cause." He pleaded on behalf of these "hardy sons of the soil . . . men who had broken the cane, and opened in the wilderness a home for their wives and children." Crockett preached a language that Democrats were fast making their own. The plainspoken legislator was ahead of his time in another respect as well. He proposed granting these poor settlers up to 160 acres of free land, foreshadowing homestead policies that decades later became the consuming focus of fellow Tennessean Andrew Johnson and other land reformers. Somewhere in this cascade of oratory, one suspects, were the origins of the "celebrated squatter speech" showcased in *Crockett's Yaller Flower Almanac, for '36.*[8]

Anti-Jacksonians—who later formalized as the Whig Party—embraced the congressman from west Tennessee. For all their denunciations of squatters, they were delighted to have in their corner a backwoods figure who could go toe-to-toe with the vulgar Jacksonians. Party operatives milked the Crockett mystique, strategically deploying him as a foil to the Democrats and Jackson, the greatest living legend of all. In the 1830s, a series of Crockett biographies came out, mainly written by Whig hacks in the service of campaigns. The Crockett character from these volumes relished any chance to tweak Jackson and allies in the world-turned-upside-down way that only he could pull off. (Martin Van Buren, Jackson's vice president and heir apparent, was a favorite target.) Of course, the "real" Crockett also possessed a provocative sense of humor that he put to good use in debates. Recollecting that Jackson had declared an interest in "giving homes to poor settlers," the congressman deadpanned, "the President was almost turning [into] a Crockett man." He wanted there to be no doubt who was the squatters' best friend in Congress.[9]

Colorful as he was, Crockett lacked the stature to seriously challenge Andrew Jackson as a political force. It was especially hard to make the case that Jacksonian Democrats were the anti-squatter party, given their extravagant praise of the "hardy pioneers" and sustained push for preemption laws amid Whig condemnations and stonewalling. Throughout the 1830s Democrats owned squatter politics. The best Whigs could do was trot out a comical, hatchet-tongued frontiersman from time to time to try to beat them at their own game. Thus, as Squatter Democracy gathered strength, Crockett became a valuable asset to Whigs.[10]

A spate of Crockett biographies and almanacs began pouring forth in the 1830s, borne by a revolution in printing that made such publications available for pennies. Where the biographies trafficked in folksy anecdotes, often of a political cast, the almanacs converted Crockett into an antic superhero. One vignette boasted that he "makes nothing of sleeping under a blanket of snow, and no more minds being frozen than a rotten apple. He lives, moves, rides, walks, runs, swims, fights, hunts, courts, marries, and has children, on a great scale!" Besides that, he "can grin the bark off a tree—look a panther to death—take a steam boat on his back—[and] stand three streaks of lightning without dodging. . . . To sum up all in one word—*he's a horse.*" His neighbors, too, in this rip-roaring telling, were "half horse, half alligator"—a description that humorists would regularly apply to squatters. The real-life Crockett only added to the legend when he ventured to Texas in late 1835 to support the

FIGURE 3.1 "Davy Crockett" and his wife, neighbor, and dog battle a bear in *Davy Crockett's Almanack, 1837*. University of Tennessee Libraries, Knoxville, Betsey B. Creekmore Special Collections and University Archives.

revolution launched by white American settlers and Tejano allies. When he died at the siege of the Alamo on March 6, 1836, he already occupied a middle ground in the culture between reality and myth. Crockett's demise augmented his folk-hero status and stature as the archetypal American squatter.[11]

Hard Cider

If the manipulation of the Crockett character marked a flirtation by Whigs with pro-squatter politics, the election of 1840 represented a full embrace. Initially the race appeared set to proceed along a familiar track. Democrats relished the prospect of taking on the compromised Henry Clay and held fast to the Squatter Democracy playbook. The *Piney Woods Planter* of Mississippi was just one Democratic paper to dredge up Clay's "lawless rabble" slander from the 1838 preemption debates. Whigs continued to provide fresh fodder, including a Vermont newspaper that griped that Democrats had "bartered the public lands for squatter votes, and permitted a host of lazy, idle vagrants to master Uncle Sam, pilfer his purse—his wig, cane and hat, and then run away."[12]

Yet Democrats faced challenges of their own, including a struggling economy and general disdain for incumbent president Martin Van Buren. Back in the 1820s, the Little Magician had envisioned an alliance between southern planters and "plain Republicans" that became a template for the Democratic Party. Although he was Jackson's chosen successor and had the backing of prominent western Democrats including Thomas Hart Benton, the New Yorker did not inspire the zealous support of backcountry folks like his predecessor or even his own vice president Richard M. Johnson of Kentucky, hailed by many as the soldier who killed Shawnee warrior Tecumseh. Van Buren had hardly proven himself to be the most faithful squatter advocate. In his first annual message to Congress, in 1837, he had criticized preemption, declaring that the policy "tends to impair public respect for the laws of the country." Sounding positively Whiggish, he pointed out the incompatibility of preemption and anti-intrusion statutes: "Either the laws to prevent intrusion upon the public lands should be executed, or . . . they should be modified or repealed." The suggestion that squatters had committed acts of intrusion by settling on public land betrayed an eastern sensibility out of touch with Democrats' squatter-friendly creed. Van Buren proposed what he believed was a reasonable compromise: grant one more preemption law for those who had settled on public land under the expectation that the policy would abide, and take steps to "prevent intrusions hereafter." A Democratic president grudgingly endorsing preemption with an eye towards scrapping the policy left a bad taste in many westerners' mouths, even if he also touted Benton's "graduation" policy to lower the price of land.[13]

Throughout the 1830s, Democrats had thoroughly dominated in western states but Whigs made inroads, particularly on the issue of federal funding for internal improvements, which the Party of Jackson selectively opposed on ideological grounds. With elections on the horizon, a palpable malaise pervaded Democratic ranks. The economy had boomed during Jackson's two terms but bottomed out by decade's end. Speculation had run wild during the "flush times" of the mid-1830s. Jackson had tried to contain it with the Specie Circular, a directive composed by Benton that required payment in gold or silver for public land. When the economy tanked in the Panic of 1837, Martin "Van Ruin" bore the brunt. A settler in Kalamazoo, Michigan, identifying himself simply as an "old squatter in these diggings," captured the general spirit of gloom in a newspaper letter addressed to his "brother farmers." Whigs were "making a great cry," he noted, but everyone had gotten caught up in the land speculation bubble. "Didn't you and I, and all of us think property was worth five times what it really was? and shouldn't we make some allowances for the acts of men under such feelings?" he queried. Anyway, the time for whining had long passed. What the country needed was action, the squatter insisted. "Be sure you're right, then go ahead," he declared, uttering a catchphrase well-known in "diggings" across the land. This was Davy Crockett's motto. It was an uncertain time when Democratic squatters turned to the Whig Crockett to revive flagging spirits.[14]

Despite the economic hardships and Van Buren's dubious affinity for settlers, the Little Magician may well have captured the "squatter vote" had he faced Henry Clay. But at their convention in Harrisburg in December 1839, Whigs got behind William Henry Harrison, who won lasting fame as commander of American forces in the Battle of Tippecanoe and other campaigns against Tecumseh's confederacy and had held numerous high-profile offices in the ensuing years. In doing so, Whigs sloughed off their patrician style and adopted a more populist tone. A tone-deaf Democratic journalist mocked Harrison as a cider-swilling, cabin-dwelling simpleton and, in the process, handed Whigs their theme for the campaign: hard cider and log cabins.[15]

Whigs hailed Harrison as a down-to-earth frontiersman who was in every way the "people's candidate." Van Buren, by contrast, was an effete easterner and crafty arriviste. A young Horace Greeley launched *The Log Cabin* newspaper out of New York City. Western Whigs cheered the loudest of all for the homespun turn the party had taken. In Mississippi they touted Harrison's

FIGURE 3.2 Whig presidential candidate William Henry Harrison greets soldiers in this
woodcut from the 1840 campaign. Library of Congress, Prints and Photographs Division,
LC-2008661359, https://www.loc.gov/item/2008661359/.

bona fides on land matters. "[O]ur State has become populous and thriving
and the poor squatter has been enabled to secure to himself his little home,"
wrote the *Southern Argus*. "And he who now asks their suffrages, is one who
for a long term of years when employed in the public service of his country
was the inmate of a *log cabin* and has thoroughly felt its privations." Now it
was time for "the yeomanry of the country" to "unite their exertions to elect
him who can fully appreciate their situation and wants." Solon Robinson,
founder the Squatters' Union of Lake County, Indiana, led local log cabin
rallies and took to referring to himself, tongue-in-cheek, as the "King of all
the squatters." They celebrated "Old Tippecanoe" at barbecues and torch-
light parades, singing with glee: "All hail to the glorious West / Log cabins
and yeoman to you; / The land of the brave and the blest, / And home of old
Tippecanoe." To the tune of "Auld Lang Syne," supporters crooned: "Should
good old cider be despised, / And ne'er regarded more? / Should plain log
cabins be despised / Our fathers built of yore?"[16]

Throughout the campaign, Whigs stayed on message, delighting in
Democrats' mounting frustration that they had no more unkind words for
squatters. Congressman George Profitt of Indiana imagined his opponents'
rising pique: "We cannot get these rascally Whigs to say one word against
the 'squatters.' We cannot, with all our ingenuity, provoke them to utter one
syllable against the 'Log Cabin' men." The *Connecticut Courant*, meanwhile,
published news of a mass defection of Democrats who attended a large "Log
Cabin" meeting in Easton, Pennsylvania, in June 1840. "ONE HUNDRED
AND TWELVE persons, nearly all of whom had previously been active
partizans of Van Buren, and the remainder neutral, publicly announced that

they would 'vote in favor of Wm. H. HARRISON and JOHN TYLER,'" the paper reported. The signs augured well for Whigs.[17]

In an election that saw record turnout, Whigs captured not just the White House by a commanding margin, but Congress too. Harrison carried nineteen states to Van Buren's seven, including several in the West like Michigan, Mississippi, and Louisiana that Van Buren had won four years earlier. Having studied their rivals, Whigs draped themselves in the symbolism of the backwoods farmer. In a post-mortem of the election, Jacob Thompson, a Mississippi Democrat, affirmed the importance of Whig overtures to squatters.[18]

> Look through the excitement and debauch which existed on the surface of the canvass of 1840, and analyze the secret springs which control the actions of men, and you will find that no one fact or circumstance had so powerful a control over the minds of the great masses in the Mississippi valley in winning their affections to General Harrison as that he had been a pioneer himself, a settler, in the western sense of that term, had lived in his log-cabin, and had favored all laws which had tended to the protection and security of the squatter. Here was the consideration which threw confusion into the ranks of the Democratic party. This was the lever by which the Whig party raised themselves from a hopeless minority into a most unexpected and triumphant majority. The supposed sympathy of General Harrison, and the imputed aversion of Mr. Van Buren for the poor man, for the humble citizen, is the true secret of the great and tremendous political revolution of 1840.[19]

Van Buren was a poor fit to lead Squatter Democracy. His neo-Jeffersonian vision of a cross-sectional party of northern republicans and southern planters was faltering in the face of a rising West. Van Buren would remain out of step with the expansionists in his party in coming years as he balked at annexing Texas.

The Whigs' pivot toward pro-squatterism did not last long, nor were Democrats prepared to cede such productive ground. Harrison died one month into his presidency, leaving the White House to John Tyler—"His Accidency"—a wealthy Virginian who quickly fell out with party leadership. Henry Clay reclaimed his position as Whig chief and familiar features of the Second Party System began to reassert themselves. Democrats including Robert J. Walker and Missouri's two US Senators, Thomas Hart Benton and Lewis Linn, led the charge for a "permanent" preemption law. When Whigs appeared to waver, Linn reminded them that the deceased Harrison had won the White House "as a pre-emption man." "Votes were claimed for him expressly on that ground," Linn maintained. "He was spoken of by his friends as 'a log cabin man,' and we were told that he would extend his favor to the inhabitants of log cabins all over the United States."[20]

The preemption debates of 1841 followed much the same script of years past. When Clay expressed his wonted qualms, Linn underscored the injustice and sheer futility of trying to remove thousands of squatters from the public lands. As American citizens, he said, "we ought to feel proud while witnessing the march of the Anglo-Saxon race in its onward progress for the benefit of the human species." Linn certainly saw reason to rejoice: "Let the free race of American pioneers go onward West, carrying their love of liberty and all their free and beneficent institutions with them." Rather than contempt there should be a monument established, "if not to these bold and enterprising men, at least to the noble-souled women who had followed their husbands into the wilderness, and shared their toils and dangers." He ended with a rousing pitch for a permanent preemption law. If anybody believed that Democrats had abandoned their pro-squatter ways, Linn's rhetoric—echoed by his colleagues—put that notion to rest.[21]

Debates may have reverted to form but, unlike before, they did not stay gridlocked for long. Henry Clay remained as intent as ever on passing legislation to distribute public land proceeds to states. To secure its passage, he agreed to combine the measure with the "permanent prospective preemption" bill long sought by Democrats. The Preemption Act of 1841 thus was a hybrid creation. Part preemption, part distribution, it contained perennial priorities of both Democrats and Whigs, who held the majority in both chambers. The measure passed the House in July by a vote of 116 to 108 and the Senate 28–23 in August, its hybrid nature scrambling partisan lines. Indeed, the provisions to distribute public land proceeds to states and fund internal improvements proved distasteful enough for leading pro-squatter Democrats including Benton and Walker to vote against the bill. At the same time, its passage made preemption permanent, a goal they had sought for years. Moving forward, squatters could claim up to 160 acres of surveyed public land, regardless of when they took up residence. Tyler signed the act into law on September 4, making preemption the status quo on the public lands of the United States.[22]

Passage of the Preemption Act of 1841 by a Whig-controlled Congress marked a watershed victory for pro-squatter partisans and signaled an important shift in public land politics. Preemption ceased functioning as a wedge issue, central to one party's agenda and anathema to the other's. A standing law, it no longer snarled Congress in angry debates, dragging squatters through the mud of partisan strife. In subsequent years, attention increasingly turned to homestead measures that provided for free land, further jumbling party alignments in the process.

In the nearer term, Democrats emerged from the wilderness of 1840 with a vengeance. Setting their sights on recapturing the White House and Congress, they rallied behind a militant program of squatter-driven expansion, provoking tensions with Mexico and Great Britain. The presence of Henry Clay atop the Whig ticket in 1844 provided fertile ground for Squatter Democracy to surge anew.

4

"Great American Measures" and the Election of 1844

Who Is Seatsfield?

The question spread through literary circles with burning urgency in early 1844 when it became known that the renowned German critic Theodore Mundt, in his compendious *History of Modern Literature*, had anointed the unknown author the "greatest American writer of fiction." "This great national painter of the characteristics of his native land, has unfolded the poetry of American life and its various relations" more brilliantly than even Washington Irving or James Fenimore Cooper, Mundt proclaimed. Such glowing praise from a top European critic mortified the staff of the *Boston Semi-Weekly Advertiser*, which published Mundt's assessment in March. How was it possible that they had never even heard of this "hero of our literature"? Chastened, they set about trying to learn everything they could about the elusive Seatsfield, scouring the best bookstores and libraries and consulting the literati. In desperation, they appealed directly to their readers to help solve the mystery "and absolve our country from the shame of ignoring an author, who has been crowned with the laurels of transatlantic criticism."[1]

Two weeks later Newark's *Centinal of Freedom* announced some leads into the mystery of the "great Unknown." Seatsfield, their sources told them, was a native-born American with a German wife who resided in Switzerland. Despite his US nationality, he wrote in German. And his books, which demonstrated "an extensive knowledge of American manners, character, relations and scenery," remained untranslated into English. "In Germany," the piece continued, "they are very popular, being read with avidity by all classes . . . and have contributed not a little to the reputation of American

Dangerous Ground. John Suval, Oxford University Press. © Oxford University Press 2022.
DOI: 10.1093/oso/9780197531426.003.0005

literature in that critical land!" The plot thickened when the *National Intelligencer* of Washington, DC, ran a letter from a reader who claimed to have actually met the enigmatic Seatsfield. "Though presented to us as an American," the source recounted, "we at that time could not suppress some suspicion that he had been born and educated in Germany.... By some he was reputed to be an ex-Jesuit, while others thought him a political refugee from Austria." By that time interest in this prodigy had reached a fever pitch.

> If a comet unknown and unannounced by astronomers should dance athwart our system, or a meteor explode in our atmosphere, scattering its fragments into our dwellings, the sensation of wonder and sur- prise could not be stronger than this literary amphibial has produced. Who is Seatsfield? A man that gives the slang of our backwoodsmen[,] descriptions of our "Sleigh-Rides," "Huskings" and "Elections," in a German diction as pure as Goethe.... Where is Seatsfield? here, there, everywhere; a mysterious and ubiquitous being wearing an invisible cloak, who can circumgirate the earth in a second.[2]

If Seatsfield sounded superhuman, even otherworldly, proof of his earthly ex- istence was not long in coming. On May 1, the *New York Herald* announced that a "new era in American literature" was dawning with translations of Seatsfield's works on the way. "The whole herd of authors or writers on American scenery and character, will sink into insignificance when compared with the brilliant, powerful, and graphic sketches of Seatsfield," the *Herald* predicted.[3]

Sure enough, the publishing house of J. Winchester in New York City printed installments of a work that shortly after would be collected as a single volume titled *Life in the New World; or, Sketches of American Society.* The sprawling work demonstrated that Seatsfield—actually Charles Sea*l*sfield, *nom de plume* of the very real Austrian-born writer Karl Anton Postl—did possess, if not earth-shattering talent, then at least a familiarity with all walks of American life, from urban high society to the rustic abodes of the back- country. One subject especially riveted the author's imagination: squatters.[4]

Hot off the presses on May 23, 1844, Sealsfield's "The Squatter Chief; or, The First American in Texas" could not have been more timely. The tale captured dynamics of American squatter imperialism even as real-life squatter incursions into Texas and Oregon roiled international diplomacy and dominated the unfolding US presidential contest. It also showed the extent to which squatters had emerged as culture heroes among Democrats and their admirers.[5]

"The Squatter Chief" opens in an earlier flashpoint of imperial rivalry: Louisiana, circa 1800. At that time, sovereignty over the region was in flux, oscillating between Spain and France. The action begins with a group of high-born French officers, led by a Count Vignerolles, trekking through the swampy terrain. They encounter a buckskin-clad character who leads them to a thriving settlement of sturdy cabins surrounded by rolling fields of tobacco, corn, and cotton, cultivated by enslaved people. They quickly discover that it is neither Europeans nor Creoles nor Indians who hold sway in this part of the world, but American squatters.

Before they know it, Vignerolles and companions find themselves in a rough assembly room, where Nathan Strong, "the mighty squatter chief," presides over a gathering of more than 100 of his rugged brethren. Though put off by the "grotesque" appearance of the group—dressed to a man in "hunting-frocks and leather-jackets"—the Frenchmen detect something in them "so dignified, so republican" that they cannot help but give their full attention to the proceedings. Strong starts the meeting by reminding the assembly how in only a few years their colony, through diligent toil, has succeeded in converting a hostile wilderness into a beacon of civilization.

> I mention these things, fellow-citizens, not from any vain ambition, nor from a notion of having done any great and daring deeds. No! that's not my way. It's only squatter-doings that we've done. We know it; thousands have done the same thing before, and thousands will do it after us.[6]

Despite these professions of humility, the Frenchmen perceive that Strong and compatriots see their simple "squatter-doings" as part of something altogether epic: the clash between empires for sovereignty over the vast Louisiana country. In the squatters' minds, the beachhead they have established has made US acquisition of the territory inevitable. "Our doings will certainly join Louisiana to the Union—a destiny for which Heaven has intended it," Strong declares during a separate exchange. Vignerolles and his fellow officers consider such talk a "plain declaration of war." In spite of themselves, though, they cannot help but grudgingly admire Strong's resolve. "There he stood," Vignerolles recounts, "the farmer in his leather-jacket—the republican, backwoodsman and woodcutter, who, with inconceivable *sangfroid*, raises his shield against the Spanish government, conquers its troops, stands in a hostile position to the governor and the government, settles, with hundreds of his countrymen, in this strange and hostile land, and does it so quietly, so comfortably . . . as if he had thrashed one of his backwoods neighbors and carried his rights of settlement, title deeds and claims, within his fist or waist-coat pocket. We stared after him, for such a character we had never yet met." Americans in the Jacksonian era, by contrast, were growing increasingly accustomed to squatter protagonists conquering new domains.[7]

When Sealsfield published the original German version of "The Squatter Chief" in 1837, Texas had just won independence from Mexico, following a bloody insurgency led by Anglo-American colonists. In fact, the tale furnishes an imaginary backstory to the real Texas Revolution. Having shown how Nathan Strong and his squatter community had conquered Louisiana for the United States, the author had his flinty hero move on to become "the first American in Texas," where he replicates his successful colonization experiment. By novel's end in the 1820s, Strong is firmly established in Texas as "chief of nearly a thousand squatters." For verisimilitude the narrator adds, "To the east of his plantation, a certain Colonel Austin has founded a second colony." By concluding the novel with his disciplined squatter conquerors rooted in Stephen F. Austin's Texas, Sealsfield signaled his approval of the revolution and takeover of the region by slaveholding American settlers.[8]

In point of fact, American immigrants had begun flooding into Texas in the 1820s in the wake of Mexico's independence from Spain. Many, like Austin, availed themselves of the *empresario* system devised by Mexican Federalists to encourage Anglo settlement as a means of stimulating trade and agriculture and defending against attacks by Comanches and Apaches. Many others entered illegally, chasing windfalls in land and cotton. This influx of squatters, mainly from the US South, propelled Texas's non-Indian population from approximately 2,500 in 1821 to more than 40,000 in 1836. By that time, Anglos and their slaves outnumbered Mexicans by roughly ten to one.[9]

Unlike their Federalist counterparts, Mexico's Centralists saw nothing but ill resulting from what international observers termed the "immense hordes of squatters" overrunning Texas, many openly contemptuous of Mexican institutions, laws, and customs. An alarmed Manuel de Mier y Terán, the commanding general of Mexico's northeastern states, believed the same dynamics that had made Americans "masters of extensive colonies" once belonging to Europeans, and possessors of "spacious territories from which have disappeared the former owners, the Indian tribes," were repeating themselves in Texas. US territorial conquests followed a pattern, he wrote in an

1829 letter to Mexico's minister of war. The first step was asserting sovereignty "based on historical incidents which no one admits." Then the US government would cite "a national demand" for the desired territory, encouraging "adventurers" to settle there. Once on the ground, these squatters would agitate against the host government, leveling charges of inefficiency and sowing dissent. As insurrection spread, the United States would make demands for a diplomatic solution involving a transfer of territory under terms "as onerous for one side as advantageous for the other." Such tactics had divested Spain, France, and Britain of enormous amounts of New World territory. "If Mexico should consent to this base act," Terán warned, "it would degenerate from the most elevated class of American powers to that of a contemptible mediocrity, reduced to the necessity of buying a precarious existence at the cost of many humiliations." To prevent this calamity, the general called for the swift suppression of any uprising that might flare up in Texas and for establishing a colony of 1,000 Mexican families to secure the nation's precarious hold on its borderlands.[10]

Perceiving an untenable and potentially explosive situation, Mexico passed a law in 1830 forbidding further immigration by Anglo-Americans or introduction of slaves into Texas. But the law did little to stop the onslaught of Anglos, enslavers among them. Indeed, the statute's most notable outcome was sparking outrage that eventually burst into open rebellion. Davy Crockett and his brothers-in-arms perished at the hand of General Antonio López de Santa Anna's forces at the Alamo in March 1836. But, soon after, their fellow revolutionaries—Anglo and Tejano—won the war.[11]

After Texas independence, freshly minted senator Robert J. Walker endorsed resolutions calling for US recognition of the new republic—a move that exacerbated tensions with Mexico, which rejected Texas's independence. In a May 1836 speech, Walker paid tribute to the Anglo-American revolutionaries, insisting that even in the darkest hours of the Alamo siege "his confidence in the rifle of the West was firm and unshaken." Walker expounded on what he deemed the racial incompatibility between the United States and Mexico, arguing that "the valley of the Mississippi never could have permitted Santa Anna to settle Texas with the mixed colored races of Mexico . . . Africans, Indians, Mettizoes, Mulattoes, and Zamboes, speaking twenty different languages, and constituting the most poisonous compound that could be amalgamated." The senator from Mississippi wanted more than acknowledgment of the "Lone Star Republic's" sovereign status. Over the next eight years, he trumpeted the cause of US annexation of Texas with a passion bordering on obsession.[12]

Whigs, especially in the North, deemed annexation an endorsement of ungodly plunder. In an 1837 letter to Henry Clay, Unitarian minister and prolific author William Ellery Channing portrayed the Texas Revolution as a wicked land grab by slaveholders and their squatter minions. "Our people throw themselves beyond the bounds of civilization, and expose themselves to relapses into a semi-barbarous state, under the impulse of wild imagination, and for the name of great possessions," he bemoaned. "Slavery and fraud lay at its very foundation. It is notorious, that land speculators, slave-holders, and selfish adventurers were among the foremost to proclaim and engage in the crusade for 'Texan liberties.'" Believing annexation would only ratify the evil, Channing urged the Whig leader to use all his influence to defeat the measure. "With Texas, we shall have no peace."[13]

The question of annexation waxed and waned for the next several years and became the central issue in the election of 1844. Walker took the lead in defining the national debate. For him, like other Democratic propagandists, it was not a question of annexation but rather "reannexation." As he portrayed it, Texas historically had belonged to France and came into US possession under the Louisiana Purchase. The United States had ceded Texas to Spain in 1819, but Mexico subsequently won independence from Spain, and Texas, in turn, had successfully revolted from Mexico. His famous "Texas letter"—written in response to Democrats in Kentucky who solicited his and other prominent partisans' views on the subject—portrayed the "reannexation" of Texas as vital to national interests. Where Whigs like Channing had depicted the Texas Revolution as out-and-out depredation, Walker styled it the just overthrow of a "treacherous and sanguinary military dictator" by "the American race." With Texas authorities expressing overwhelming support for annexation by the United States, he claimed, it was high time to grant their wish, or risk heaping scorn on "the great fundamental principle of popular sovereignty."[14]

The senator from Mississippi noted that Texas would bring immense material advantages to the United States, emphasizing its "magnificent public domain" of 136 million acres, extensive coastline, and vast mineral resources. Great Britain, too, hungrily eyed this valuable territory. For Walker the issue came down to a fundamental clash of civilizations that would define the course of American and world history. "It is a question," he contended, "between the advance of monarchy and republicanism throughout the fairest and most fertile portion of the American continent, and is one of the mighty movements in deciding the great question . . . which of the two forms of government shall preponderate throughout the world." Walker positioned American squatters as foot soldiers in this world-historical battle. Far from being the freebooters whom Clay, Channing, and other Whigs had denounced, they were protectors of American interests. Invoking the Battle of New Orleans and flattering his Blue Grass interlocutors, Walker declared, "If war should ever again revisit our country, Kentucky knows that the steady aim of the western riflemen, and the brave hearts and stout hands, within the limits of Texas, are, in the hour of danger, among the surest defenders of the country, and especially of the valley of the West." Warming to the subject he wanted to know, "Who will desire to check the young eagle of America, now refixing her gaze upon our former limits? . . . Who will wish again to curtail the limits of this great republican empire, and again to dismember the glorious valley of the West?"[15]

A leading proponent of Democratic pro-squatterism and a consummate unionist, Walker understood the importance of winning the hearts and minds of southerners and northerners alike. Therefore, while a slaveholder himself and a supporter of the institution, the Pennsylvania-born senator had to defuse the explosive charge that annexing Texas would spread slavery. Here he introduced an innovation—the "safety valve" theory— aimed at putting antislavery advocates at ease. For generations, the question of what would happen with freed slaves had bedeviled debates over emancipation. Texas provided the solution, Walker argued. Far from extending slavery, annexation would actually contribute to its eventual extinction because Texas would serve as a "safety-valve" through which emancipated slaves would funnel into the warm climes of Latin America, where diverse populations would welcome African-descended people. Slavery "will slowly and gradually recede, and finally disappear into the boundless regions of Mexico, and Central and Southern America," he predicted. On the other hand, without Texas, the people of the North could look forward to a day when they would face a deluge of emancipated blacks, many of them likely to be insane, deaf, and dumb according to the notoriously skewed figures from the 1840 census, which portrayed free African Americans as far more susceptible to derangement and disease than slaves, and which Walker appended to his Texas letter.[16]

In another move to balance sectional interests, Walker linked Texas annexation to the desire among many northerners and northwesterners for exclusive US possession of Oregon, jointly held with Great Britain under an 1818 treaty. The Willamette Valley teemed with American emigrants whose surging numbers emboldened Democratic leaders to assert sovereignty over the region. Coupling the annexation of Texas, slated to be slave territory, with sole possession of Oregon, likely to be free, proved a potent formula for expansionist Democrats.

With his bellicose calls for territorial growth spearheaded by democracy-loving patriots from the North and South, Walker hammered home key points of the Democrats' pro-squatter expansionist ideology. Initially published in February 1844 by the *Globe*, the influential former mouthpiece of the Jackson and Van Buren administrations, the letter became an instant sensation. His hardline stance lit a fuse on an issue that Martin Van Buren and Henry Clay, the presumed frontrunners heading into the presidential race, had hoped to avoid. In April 1844 both men published statements against immediate annexation. Clay's position fell well within the Whig mainstream, and he easily won his party's nomination on May 1. Van Buren faced steeper hurdles. His views placed him at odds with Democrats from the South and Southwest, who came to the Baltimore convention on May 27 ready for battle. At the outset of the gathering, Walker proposed a resolution requiring that the nominee capture two-thirds of the delegates' votes, rather than a simple majority. Van Buren led in early balloting but could not break the higher threshold. After several more ballots, delegates settled on James K. Polk, the former speaker of the US House and Tennessee governor who strongly supported annexation and westward expansion in general.[17]

The annexationists from the West and South had denied Van Buren his dream of recapturing the White House, alienating many northern Democrats in the process. However, they took pains to keep the rift from becoming an unbridgeable chasm, tapping Pennsylvanian George M. Dallas, uncle of Walker's wife Mary, for the vice presidency (after Van Buren ally Silas Wright of New York declined). Walker, meanwhile, prepared a platform that carefully balanced northern and southern interests, including calls for "the re-occupation of Oregon and the re-annexation of Texas." This was the very blueprint of parallel expansion, promising something for North and South. The platform was also intended to provoke Britain and Mexico, which still considered Texas its own.[18]

Whigs mocked such belligerence and advanced a sober platform of national improvement that emphasized government efficiency and a "well regulated and wise economy." Confident that Clay, a distinguished statesman, dwarfed the Democrats' "dark horse," party operatives attempted to set the terms of the 1844 election by repeating a simple, sneering question: "Who is James K. Polk?" Their own partisan papers gleefully supplied answers. A "slaveholder—a duellist [*sic*]—and the *whipped* Locofoco Candidate for Governor in . . . the last election," quipped one Pennsylvania publication, using a favorite Whig pejorative for radical Democrats. The *New-Hampshire Sentinel* deemed Polk unworthy of remark except to say that he was a rabid expansionist "ready to plant the stars and stripes upon the Pacific." A boon to Whigs, Polk's nomination was another mark of shame on his party. "The whole Democratic party at the North, have surrendered, as usual, to the fell spirit of Southern Slavery," the *Sentinel* maintained. The Whig press projected that this obscure, slavemaster imperialist would get whipped.[19]

Democrats took up the Whigs' mantra and turned it on its head, highlighting Polk's close association with Andrew Jackson and his own family's rugged western roots. Who is James K. Polk? None other than "Young Hickory," a protégé of the Old Hero himself. The *Pittsfield Sun* of Massachusetts called him a Democrat *"of the straightest sect,"* and son of "hardy pioneers of the South West." James K. Polk, the writer crowed, *"will be the next President of the United States."*[20]

With Clay topping the Whig ticket, the voices of Squatter Democracy rose from the wilderness to form a steady chorus. Amos Kendall, Jackson's postmaster general and pioneer of political spin, circulated a tract titled "Henry Clay Against the Frontier Settlers," which cited chapter and verse Clay's many heresies, including his opposition to preemption and graduation bills, and his perennial calls for a distribution policy that would place public land revenue "into the hands of a little aristocracy in each State." The pamphlet broadcast Clay's familiar litany of squatter putdowns—"intruders," "thieves," "lawless rabble," "plunderers," "pirates"—and ended with a passionate appeal: "PEOPLE OF THE NEW STATES! . . . Will you acknowledge Mr. Clay's slanders to be JUST, by *taking the slanderer for your President?* NEVER! NEVER!! NEVER!!! *Yes, NEVER will echo around our vast frontier, until the sound shall reach the ocean, and be thrown back in one continuous NEVER, NEVER, NEVER!!"* Democrats were back in their wheelhouse, lauding squatters and whipping up resentments over old slights.[21]

Other partisans played the squatter card, fanning grievances with nearly identical arguments. In a letter to Democrats in Vicksburg, Mississippi, former congressman William M. Gwin, Walker's longtime confidante, contrasted Clay's record on the public lands with both Walker's and Polk's. Like Kendall, he repeated Clay's anti-squatter rhetoric, emphasizing just how close to home those insults hit. "Now, fully one third of the voters of Mississippi and of the new States, or the ancestors of these voters, were settlers upon the public lands," he wrote. "These are the men, the brave and hardy pioneers of the West, whom Mr. Clay thus brands with infamy." Gwin hardly needed to tell savvy squatters which politicians had their backs.[22]

A resurgent Squatter Democracy rattled Whigs, who anxiously watched the ground they had gained in 1840 slip away. Clay and his allies attempted to reverse the squatter-bashing of the past. Before Clay had even secured the nomination, the *Boon's Lick Times* of Fayette, Missouri, ran an article under the headline "Political Dishonesty," that took a Democratic newspaper to task for reprising the highly charged preemption debates of 1838. That paper's account contained "sentiments [Clay] never uttered," the writer insisted. The *Boon's Lick Times* included a letter from Clay himself to a friend calling depictions of his speech from January 29, 1838 "a gross caricature of what I said." Clay conceded that he opposed preemption, "but I never used the epithets, which were put in my mouth, against the pre emptioners themselves, many of whom I know to be respectable, and my friends." Such attempts to amend the record underscore Whig concerns that they risked losing a constituency with whom they had made inroads.[23]

In truth, Clay and party were entirely overpowered on the squatter front. That much was clear on a Saturday in mid-October 1844, as hundreds of Democrats, women and men, young and old, gathered on the banks of the Mississippi in Louisiana's Carroll Parish for a campaign rally. A rostrum, festooned with flowers, stood in the shadows of towering oaks. Beside it, a portrait of George Washington commanded viewers' eyes, along with the emblazoned names of Polk and Dallas. American flags fluttered. A portrait of Jackson hung nearby, completing the Democratic shrine. On hand was an ancient cannon, brought over from Natchez and bearing the name "Mississippi." "Expection [*sic*] stood tiptoe," one attendee reported, "and as the morning sun began to make the pale twilight blush to crimson, the strange roar of that old heavy iron cannon . . . began to make the forests reverberate, and send back, in redoubling thunder, the majestic intonations of freedom." The crowd was so enchanted by the "old iron-hearted democratic cannon," they rechristened it: "THE SQUATTER."[24]

Speaker after fiery speaker added to the thunder, while revelers hoisted banners condemning the "old arch enemy of the settlers, the despotic Henry Clay." Mississippi congressman William H. Hammett pulled out a newspaper clipping of an old debate and barked out Clay's squatter denunciations, eliciting howls. Through it all, as day turned to night, there was that percussive roar: the "voice of the 'Squatter,' bellowing over the domains of the squatter nation." The scene combined the civic spirit of Sealsfield's squatters with the uproarious antics of the almanac Crockett. But in this instance, a real-life squatter chief stood poised to take command. He may have tussled fifteen years earlier with the sainted Crockett over land for poor Tennesseans, but his brash calls for Texas and Oregon and embrace of squatters helped James K. Polk reclaim Louisiana, Mississippi, Michigan, and Indiana for Democrats, and win the West and the White House.[25]

Streaks of Squatter Life

Amid the sound and fury of a reinvigorated Squatter Democracy a curious development became manifest: popular depictions and appropriations of the squatter increasingly imbued the character with proslavery sympathies. Certainly this was the case at the rollicking event in Carroll Parish, where, in addition to the thunderous rebukes to the anti-squatter strawman Henry Clay, orators clamored for the annexation of Texas, a vast region that most expected would become not one but several new slave states. The association of squatters and slavery was already evident in Sealsfield's "The Squatter Chief," where enslaved black people toil in the fields of Nathan Strong's community. The narrator, Count Vignerolles, initially finds this aspect of squatter life deplorable. But as he assimilates into their society, he sheds his aversion to slavery and eventually becomes a slaveholder himself. "It is not impossible to hold slaves, and yet remain human," he concludes, giving voice to Sealsfield's southern sympathies.[26]

It was, however, a dodgy proposition to try making the squatter a symbol of the Slave Power. The dominant trope of Squatter Democracy was the pioneering yeoman, and this figure, even in the South, was not a slaveholder—certainly not a large one. Sophisticated champions of slavery expansion, like the novelist William Gilmore Simms, understood this reality. A denizen of Charleston, South Carolina, Simms portrayed squatters and planters as fundamentally different creatures. Certainly both had a place in an expanding South, just not at the same time. As Simms saw it, squatters could be forerunners of slave society, but not members of it. A character in the novel *Border Beagles* explains, "The business of the squatter always carries him over the line of the old settlements." These "rash, violent" pioneers were "peculiarly fitted for the conquest of savages and savage lands." But, conquest accomplished, they sold their improvements to planters and moved on.[27]

Perhaps because of this inherent incompatibility, proslavery appropriations of the squatter symbol, as well as popular renditions associating squatters and slavery, often veered toward the antic and cartoonish. Not surprisingly, Davy Crockett, a small-time slave owner in real life, was never far away from the mayhem. *The Squatter's Almanac, 1845* featured the folk hero more alive than ever, tearing across the West astride a bear, ready to assert America's title to the far corners of the continent. This ultra-jingoistic Crockett embodies the Democrats' expansionist platform of 1844. "You see, feller citizens," he growls, "I'm . . . of the rale American grit, an . . . go in for Texas and the Oregon . . . for they both belong to Uncle Sam's plantation, jist as naturally as a cabbage leaf belongs to a cabbage stalk." While advocating parallel expansion—Texas for the South, and Oregon for the North—this character tilts proslavery. In one vignette, he takes it upon himself to find out who's behind the "nigger kidnappin along the Mississippi." He quickly discovers the missing enslaved people have been swallowed by a half-mile-long crocodile and duly slices open the beast to free them: "129 kidnapped niggers . . . all alive and grinnin." The vile idiom here was not so much planter propaganda as what passed for southwestern humor, in which slavery was part and parcel of the territory but not a central concern.[28]

Southwestern humor ushered in the age of the picaresque squatter, a member of an "original race" in the West distinguished by violent swagger and spicy speech. Absent were Leggett's virtuous victims of fortune, Sealsfield's disciplined empire builders, or even Cooper's self-sufficient, if decidedly menacing, nomads. As John S. Robb wrote in the introduction to his popular *Streaks of Squatter Life, and Far-West Scenes* (published under the pseudonym Solitaire), "the western *squatter* is a free and jovial character, inclined to mirth rather than evil. . . . An encounter with the hostile red skins, or the wild animals of the forest is to him pleasurable excitement, and his fireside or campfire is rich with story of perilous adventure, and which seems only worthy of his remembrance, when fearfully hazardous in incident." A Pennsylvania-born Whig based in St. Louis, Robb mastered the short, comic sketches that became a staple of newspapers in the 1840s. The vignettes in *Streaks of Squatter Life* follow the protagonists as they wrestle with "bars," traverse the mighty Mississippi in explosion-prone steamboats, and extract themselves from quicksand by clutching the tail of a mammoth "catty" (catfish). Nearly always stupefied from the effects of "corn juice," they brawl for the affection of a girl, or, more often than not, just for the hell of it. Enslaved people enter the picture from time to time, not as main characters, but as part of the scenery, occasionally compelled to follow the commands of a besotted white squatter.[29]

The whiteness of Robb's squatters and their partisan allegiance are badges of belonging, making them proud sovereigns of their own domains inclined to take down a peg or two anyone who would dare to defy or look down on them. They were thoroughgoing Democrats, tribal in their politics, quick to mock "slicked up finefied sort[s]" with "aristocracy notions," and sing the praises of their patron saint Andrew Jackson:

Thar aint throughout this western nation,
Another like old Hickory
He was born jest fur his siteation—
A bold leader of the free.[30]

One story, "The Standing Candidate," features a campaign event centering around the bedraggled figure of Sugar, so named because of the extra-sweet whiskey with which he plies voters. The narrator recounts: "*Sugar* had long been the *standing candidate* of Nianga county, for the legislature, and founded his claim to the office upon the fact of his being the first 'squatter' in that county—his having killed the first *bar* there, ever killed by a white man, and, to place his right beyond cavil, he had '*stilled* the first keg of whiskey!" Despite his bona fides, Sugar was in the habit of renouncing his candidacy in favor of others. On this occasion one of the stump orators gets on a roll, paying tribute to their forefathers, "how they had been trained to war by conflict with the ruthless savage, their homes oft desolated, and their children murdered,—yet still, ever foremost in the fight, and last to retreat, winning the heritage of these broad valleys for their children, against the opposing arm of the red man, though aided by the civilized power of mighty Britain, and her serried cohorts of trained soldiery!" The speech sends tears rolling down Sugar's cheeks and convinces him to back this squatter who had "painted with truth and feeling the claims of the western *pioneers!*"[31]

Another story in the collection—"The Pre-emption Right"—departs from the rambunctious tone and revives the classic Whig critique of Democratic land policies and squatter depredations. The action takes place in "Upper Missouri country," where a hard-drinking, card-playing Kentuckian named Dick Kelsy has built a cabin under the shade of a riverside cottonwood. "Tall, raw-boned, good-natured and fearless, he betrayed no ambition to excel, except in his rifle," the narrator explains. One day a stranger appears whose general sullenness and abusive treatment of his wife make bad impressions. Kelsy tells the man he'd best be on his way. However, the stranger has a trick up his sleeve. Pretending that his wife is sick, he convinces the squatter to let him build a shack on his property so she can rest. He then tiptoes off to the local land office and files a preemption claim, based on this "improvement" he has made. When Kelsy learns of the ruse, he dispatches the intruder execution style. Beholding the mound of dirt marking the dead stranger's grave, Kelsy's slave Sam has the last exultant word: "Dat's Massa Dick's signature to dis land claim—dat is!" The presence of Sam, while incidental to the storyline, once

FIGURE 4.1 Sugar, "the standing candidate," stirs his sweet whiskey on the stump in an engraving by Henry W. Herrick from John S. Robb's *Streaks of Squatter Life, and Far-West Scenes* (1858). Retrieved May 20, 2021, from https://www.gutenberg.org/files/46329/46329-h/46329-h.htm.

again reflects the growing association between squatters and slavery in 1840s popular culture.[32]

"The Pre-emption Right" reasserts Whig criticisms of lawless squatters operating outside the codes of civilization. Despite the Whigs' anomalous flirtation with pro-squatter politics in the 1840 election, this backwoods figure remained first and foremost a symbol of Jacksonian Democrats, who returned the squatter to his pride of place in their militantly expansionist platform of 1844. By mid-decade even Davy Crockett had been repurposed from a flesh-and-blood Whig from Tennessee into the antic embodiment of Squatter Democracy and avatar of a new doctrine: Manifest Destiny. Proponents of slavery expansion rallied behind the squatter figure with particular verve, and popular portrayals increasingly rendered squatters as wholly compatible with slaveholding society. Yet while squatters cheerfully abided slavery in the pages of penny almanacs, actual settlers in the West tended to distance themselves from the institution. This disconnect would tear at the fabric of Squatter Democracy and factor in the rise of Free Soil.

5

Manufacturing Destiny

"I WILL START with my family to the Oregon [Territory] this spring," wrote Jesse Applegate of St. Clair County, Missouri, to his brother Lisbon in April 1843. "This resolution has been conceived and matured in a very short time, but it is probably destiny." The thirty-one-year-old Applegate was not a grandiose man, but he did possess the self-assurance that accompanies exceptional intelligence and all-around competence—qualities that had turned a man born into humble circumstances into a respected teacher, land surveyor, and confidante of some of Missouri's leading citizens. He and his wife Cynthia maintained a farm in the Osage River floodplain, raising livestock and a growing family. Yet lingering privations caused by the Panic of 1837 pressed heavily on a region cut off from major transportation routes. "This state of things," Applegate would recall, "created much discontent and restlessness among a people who had for many generations been nomadic, and had been taught by the example of their ancestors to seek a home in a 'new country' as a sure way of bettering their condition." A self-styled squatter, Applegate remained open to the possibility that fate had grand things in store. So when destiny called, he and Cynthia packed up their farm, trekked up to Independence with children and cattle in tow, and joined an emigrant train to Oregon.[1]

Applegate was not the only American talking "destiny" in the 1840s. The term had become a buzzword as national leaders and citizens across the land grew cognizant of an untapped potential. With Democrats holding the reins in Washington, and squatters claiming western domains, the United States muscled out rival empires, neighboring nations, and Native peoples to assert sovereignty from sea to sea. To some, the sweep westward had an air of inevitability, almost as if it were the work of a divine hand. Such was the line taken in the summer of 1845 by John L. O'Sullivan's *Democratic Review*, a literary

Dangerous Ground. John Suval, Oxford University Press. © Oxford University Press 2022.
DOI: 10.1093/oso/9780197531426.003.0006

and political magazine aligned with powerful Jacksonians. Pondering the trajectory of national growth, the magazine spoke in terms of physics—possibly metaphysics—noting "the inevitable fulfilment of the general law which is rolling our population westward." The subject at hand was Texas. After months of bitter debate that had divided the country largely along proslavery and antislavery lines, Congress approved US annexation of the breakaway republic earlier that year. The *Review* deemed any further opposition entirely unwarranted.[2]

Fixing its sights on points farther west, the *Review* claimed it was America's "manifest destiny to overspread the continent allotted by Providence for the free development of our yearly multiplying millions." Having introduced a potent phrase into the lexicon, the writer predicted that California was ripe to "fall away" from "imbecile and distracted" Mexico by the same natural law. The agents of conquest would not be conventional soldiers but rather an "irresistible army" of Anglo-Saxon emigrants "armed with the plough and the rifle, and marking its trail with schools and colleges, courts and representative halls, mills and meeting-houses." These were men and women who braved all manner of hardships and dangers to conquer their homes, giving them "a better and a truer right" to the land "than the artificial title of sovereignty in Mexico a thousand miles distant."[3]

Manifest Destiny echoed core tenets of Democratic pro-squatterism, portraying white settlers as catalysts of miraculous transformations who, by their mere yeomanly presence, converted benighted backwaters into blessed American lands. Consistent with the preemption principle, Manifest Destiny made settlement and improvement the bases for legitimate title and the true source of sovereignty. The author also avowed neutrality on slavery. Indeed, the preachers of Manifest Destiny envisioned North and South alike reaping windfalls from continued conquest. The Democrats' 1844 platform pairing Texas annexation and sole US possession of Oregon remained the operative playbook. The South got Texas even before Polk took office. Oregon appeared close at hand.

Had the *Review*'s quasi-mystical vision come to pass—had a phalanx of pioneer yeomen gone forth and peacefully conquered California by dint of their "squatter-doings," as Sealsfield's Nathan Strong might say—there would have been little grounds for division among Democrats. Yet it took a real army and an actual war to wrest the vast, bountiful region from Mexico. To many northerners it appeared as if the Slave Power was giving the marching orders. The multiple, concurrent fronts of conquest scrambled the sectional calculus and threw Democratic expansionists into confusion. Combined, the claiming of Oregon and the US-Mexican War marked a major turning point in the career of antebellum squatters. In 1845, these "hardy pioneers" were land-taking agents of Manifest Destiny and by and large remained a unifying influence in the Party of Jackson. Three years later they were arbiters of slavery's survival or extinction and a divisive, destabilizing force within Democratic ranks.

Going to Oregon Anyhow

If innate migratory propensities set his steps in motion, Applegate's appointment with destiny had proximate political and geopolitical causes as well. The treaty under which the United States and Great Britain jointly occupied the Oregon Country faced new tests as more and more Americans settled in the Willamette Valley and demanded protection, including guaranteed rights to the lands they occupied. In response, national leaders adopted a more truculent tone toward Britain and encouraged further emigration, increasing the prospects of confrontation.

For Democrats, Oregon represented the next and final phase of squatter-driven conquest of the North American West. Congressman Tilghman Howard of Indiana expressed this view in an 1840 speech, arguing that only "by filling up the great valley of the Oregon with settlers—squatters if you please, of Anglo-Saxon blood" would "the tide of Western emigration cease to overspread the public domain." The phrasing is telling. Oregon—which stretched north to present-day Alaska and east to Wyoming—was not a US possession in 1840. It certainly did not fall within the nation's system of public lands. But Democrats like Howard spoke of its place in the US public domain as a fait accompli, making it ripe for white American squatters to claim.[4]

Determining who did hold sovereignty over Oregon was complicated. The United States and Great Britain each claimed to have a superior right to the Oregon Country based in part on the doctrine of discovery—the United States resting its claim on the "discovery" of the Columbia River by sea captain Robert Gray in 1792, the British citing Captain James Cook's passage along the Oregon coast in 1778 and George Vancouver's own coastal explorations mere weeks before Gray's arrival. The rival nations reached a tentative accommodation with the Treaty of 1818, which declared that the territory and waterways south of the Forty-Ninth parallel, between the Rocky Mountains and coast, were "free and open" to the citizens of both countries for a period of ten years. This so-called Joint Occupation Treaty, however, said nothing about which nation exercised outright sovereignty. In effect, the treaty, which was renewed in 1827, invited settlement but not ownership, creating uncertain conditions for any would-be land claimant. On one point, there was no dispute: the doctrine of discovery left little room for recognizing possession of land by Clackamas, Chinooks, Cayuses, Kalapuyas, and other Native peoples.[5]

In the two decades following the treaty, the British presence—mainly Hudson's Bay Company (HBC) traders and trappers—dwarfed America's scant footprint. Granted a monopoly on British trading rights by Parliament, the HBC was the dominant colonial institution in the region, enjoying broad kinship-based commercial ties with tribes across the West. Replete with warehouses, cultivated fields, and a stately gathering hall, the company's head-quarters at Fort Vancouver, on the north shore of the Columbia River about 100 miles inland, became the hub of an extensive western trade. Inhabitants included British, French Canadian, Irish, Hawaiian, Iroquois, and other per-sonnel, many joined by their Métis and Native American wives.[6]

The balance of power began to tilt slightly in 1834 when the Reverend Jason Lee, a Methodist, arrived in the Willamette Valley with a party of American missionaries and traders who felt called to bring Christianity to the Indians and to reap earthly rewards as well. The mission remained small, but Lee saw promise in their new home. "There is the germ of a great State," he wrote to Massachusetts congressman Caleb Cushing in 1839. Two years later, the British population of 1,200 still tripled the number of Americans in Oregon. But those figures would soon shift dramatically as news of Oregon's natural bounty captured the imaginations of expansionist politicians and eager emigrants.[7]

Land was the main lure for settlers and a primary selling point for promoters of emigration who emphasized the region's astonishing fertility, mild climate, and "innumerable pleasing landscapes," as explorer George Vancouver had written decades earlier. Claiming that bounty was no simple proposition, however, in a part of the world where the Americans and British neither fully asserted nor disclaimed sovereignty and where diverse Indian peoples remained in possession of their homelands.[8]

The nebulous status of sovereignty posed a dilemma for emigrants. The Joint Occupation Treaty—to say nothing of boosters inside Congress and out—seemed to encourage settlement. But what guarantees would squatters have to the homes and farms they created, given that the United States lacked the authority to issue land patents in Oregon? Steeped in uncertainty, they pressed Congress to recognize their claims by extending American laws over the region. "We need a guarantee from the Government that the possession of the land we take up and the improvements we make upon it will be assured to us," Lee wrote in his 1839 letter to Congressman Cushing. Noting that the "settlements will greatly increase the value of the Government domain in that country, should the Indian title ever be extinguished," the missionary concluded, "we can not but expect... that those who have been pioneers in this arduous work will be liberally dealt with in this matter." In seeking guarantees to land based on "possession" and "improvements," Lee invoked the cardinal principles of preemption, which rested on the doctrine that "proving up" a claim by residence, construction, and cultivation of crops conferred rights of ownership. Lee's statement that settlements would raise the value of the "Government domain" was similarly savvy. A long-standing argument of preemption backers was that squatters, by establishing farms and communities in the wilderness, enhanced the worth of the surrounding public lands, creating a win-win scenario for the government and its pioneering citizens.[9]

If Lee's missive conveyed an expectation that Oregon would sooner or later become part of the US public domain, others spoke as if it already was American land. Such was the case with the Reverend David Leslie and colleagues who sent a wide-ranging petition to Congress in 1840. Referring to themselves in the third person, according to custom, the petitioners wrote, "they have settled themselves in said Territory, under the belief that it was a portion of the public domain of . . . [the United] States." They discovered it was not. Compounding their distress were rumors that Britain had granted prime territory between the Columbia River and Puget Sound to the Hudson's Bay Company and that "said company is actually exercising unequivocal acts of ownership over said lands thus granted, and opening extensive farms upon the same." The United States could ill afford to cede such an "invaluable possession," they insisted, urging Congress "to establish . . . a Territorial Government in the Oregon Territory." Doing so would at last convert Oregon into a US domain, affirming their "right of acquiring, possessing, and using property."[10]

The preemption mindset of Americans in Oregon fostered an aggressive land-taking ethos, converting American squatters into imperialist agents— the legs of Manifest Destiny. Intimately versed in the workings of the General Land Office, many of these newcomers arrived in the Willamette Valley acculturated in the laws and customs of the US public land system, including the squatter-friendly policy of preemption. In the absence of US laws governing the region, they set about, in "provisional" fashion, replicating key aspects of that system to assert and secure their property rights. The precedents established in the 1830s—and enshrined in the Preemption Act of 1841—incentivized land-taking under the expectation that the government sooner or later would recognize their claims. Ultimately, though, they needed actual US jurisdiction over the territory to guarantee legal title and pushed hard for Congress to act.[11]

The long-running battle between Lee's Methodists and Dr. John McLoughlin, HBC's chief factor, over mill sites in Willamette Falls (later named Oregon City), pivoted on the principle of preemption. Favorably located along trade routes, Willamette Falls boasted what some considered the "finest water power in the known world"—perfect for turning the water-wheel of a sawmill or gristmill. McLoughlin possessed the foresight to envision a town flourishing there. A physician as well as a trader, the Canadian-born McLoughlin was an outsized presence in Oregon, not simply because of his long white locks and six-foot-four frame but because he was the commanding force behind the HBC's far-flung operations in the North American West. Lured by the falls, he would later recount, "I . . . selected for a claim, Oregon City, in 1829, made improvements on it and had a large quantity of timber squared." By emphasizing his "improvements," McLoughlin sought to legit-imize his claims, which included a sizable island in the middle of the river.[12]

The same natural features that had caught McLoughlin's eye also attracted the Methodists. Seeking to break their dependence on the HBC, particularly for bare essentials such as flour, they devised an ambitious plan of mill and mis-sion construction. Willamette Falls looked like the ideal place. Besides its ob-vious natural advantages, the area appeared up for grabs. McLoughlin did not live there; he continued to reside twenty-five miles north at Fort Vancouver. This left room for Lee and his brethren to establish a superior claim to pre-emption, which privileged actual residence. One of the Methodists erected a dwelling, and by 1841 the mission's steward George Abernethy had opened a mill and store on the island. Passage of the Preemption Act of 1841 only emboldened the Methodists in their land-taking pursuits.[13]

For his part, McLoughlin was stunned to discover the Americans had "jumped part of my claim." More than a land grab, it was a slap in the face of a man who for years had made it his business to provide shelter and sus-tenance to beleaguered American newcomers, including many in Lee's party in 1834. Now, they "assumed the right to judge of my rights" and rejected the validity of his claim. Going on the offensive, McLoughlin platted his claim into town lots—hiring a cash-strapped Jesse Applegate to perform the survey work—and demanded payment from settlers in exchange for deeds to the land. Lee considered the demand preposterous and told the doctor to his face "that I thought it assuming rather high grounds for a private individual to give deeds to land in this neutral Territory to which the Indian title had not been extinguished." For Lee, Euro-American occupation of Indian lands was acceptable, but McLoughlin's issuing deeds to them crossed a line.[14]

By 1843, widespread discontent among Americans in Oregon City led them to petition Congress yet again, this time seeking protection from what they described as systematic oppression by McLoughlin and the HBC. Having selected lands, they were busy improving their claims, they wrote, when "Dr. McLoughlin, who still resides at Fort Vancouver, comes on the ground, and says the land is his, and any person building without his permission is held as a trespasser." McLoughlin's directives struck them as part of the HBC's campaign to snuff out "the improvement and enterprise of American citizens." Containing the signatures of sixty-five men, topped by that of Robert Shortess—a cerebral, ultra-nationalistic American who had arrived in 1840—the petition reflected a nuanced understanding of frontier codes. The arch villain was the speculator, the rich absentee owner who engrossed valuable tracts of land with one purpose: to sell them off and make a killing. The petitioners cast McLoughlin—a scheming Brit in their eyes, and a Catholic at that—in this role. The moral antithesis of the speculator was the hardworking actual settler who labored to forge a home for his family in the western wilds. This, of course, was the role the petitioners assigned to themselves. Unfortunately for them, there was no advantage to being a squatter on lands that fell outside the US public domain, the one realm where preemption reigned. The petitioners sought to change that inconvenient fact. "Laws are made to protect the weak against the mighty," they wrote, urging Congress to afford them "the protection of the United States Government."[15]

Accounts of an absentee British speculator depriving American pioneers of what was rightfully theirs, and on the grounds that they were the "trespassers," struck the rawest of nerves among Democrats back in Washington. They had been pushing for years to bring Oregon into the US fold to prevent just this sort of thing. Missouri's two US senators, Thomas Hart Benton and Lewis Linn, both outspoken squatter advocates, had taken particularly active roles in advancing American interests. Beginning in 1838, and continuing until his death in October 1843, Linn introduced a series of bills and resolutions for the organization of a territorial government in Oregon, complete with military installations and generous land policies. Linn submitted one such resolution in December 1839, calling US title to Oregon "indisputable" and directing the president to give notice to Britain of the nation's intent to terminate the Joint Occupation Treaty. He also recommended extending US laws over Oregon and raising a regiment of riflemen "for the purpose of overawing and keeping in check various Indian tribes, or any foreign forces." Finally, Linn called for granting 640 acres of free land to every white man eighteen or older who had cultivated those lands for five straight years. This last proposal planted a seed that would germinate and ripen in the years to come.[16]

The quantity of 640 acres—an entire "section" in public lands parlance—represented a fourfold increase from the maximum allowed under preemption laws. Unlike those laws, which required payment of $1.25 per acre, the grants Linn proposed would be free to white squatters. Backers of the measure emphasized the need to encourage Anglo-American families to undertake the burdensome trek and establish fixed settlements in the contested region. Samuel R. Thurston, Oregon's first territorial delegate to Congress, would underscore the high costs of the overland journey. "To get ready, to go, and to settle again, will take him a year," he explained, referring to the typical male emigrant. "He must . . . buy oxen and wagons, and horses and cows, and an outfit and provisions to last six or seven months." One scholar puts the migration expenses for a party of four at just under $600; others contend the cost of equipment alone stood between $800 and $1,200, or between approximately $25,000 and $40,000 today. Benton summarized the matter well when he noted, "Nobody would go there without the inducement of land."[17]

Grants of 640 acres were prominently featured in Linn's 1843 Oregon bill, which again sought to place the region under US control and protection. The senator from Missouri explained that the bill's goal was "to encourage emigration, by an assurance to those emigrating that they should have the benefit of the jurisdiction of our laws, and the security of their settlements. Without these encouragements," he added, "there would be no emigration of our citizens, and England would be left to occupy the whole country, through the agency of her Hudson's Bay Company." Benton adopted a characteristically bellicose tone in supporting the measure. "I go now for vindicating our rights on the Columbia," he roared, "and, as the first step towards it, passing this bill, and making these grants of land, which will soon place the thirty or forty thousand rifles beyond the Rocky Mountains, which will be our effective negotiators." Linn's measure squeaked through the Senate in February 1843 on a 24–22 vote, with seventeen Democrats voting in favor and only three against, including John C. Calhoun, who argued that the government need not directly intervene but should rather pursue a policy of "masterly inactivity" and let the proliferation of Americans determine the balance of power in Oregon. Subsequent debates would show Calhoun's deepest fear was adding non-slave territory to the nation.[18]

The bill gave encouragement to thousands of would-be emigrants who took their cues from Congress. One of them was Jesse Applegate, who dashed off his letter to brother Lisbon noting that "destiny" had a hand in his decision to strike out for the Pacific. Holding out hope of eventual House passage of Linn's bill, he counseled, "If you are going to Oregon by all means go this spring for if Linn's Bill pass next year every man and every man's neighbor will move in that direction." Although the proposed act, with its generous land provisions, languished in the House, waves of American migrants believed Oregon was theirs for the taking. "I am going to Oregon anyhow," declared one unfazed emigrant. The "Great Migration" of 1843 was on.[19]

Linn's bill may have launched a thousand wagons, but its demise in the House made it cold comfort for Americans already in Oregon who remained in a legal no man's land. The ongoing dispute between the Methodists and McLoughlin only underscored the uncertainty surrounding land claims—and practically all questions of law and governance in Oregon. Frustration spurred action. During the spring of 1843, settlers convened at Champoeg and Oregon City and laid the groundwork for a provisional government. As a first step they appointed a committee to draft a constitution. Within weeks, the committee completed its work, crafting a charter that drew on the Northwest Ordinance of 1787, including an especially consequential passage from that landmark act: "There shall be neither slavery nor involuntary servitude in said territory." In July, the white, male electorate approved the constitution or "organic acts," giving Oregonians a Provisional Government and law code that would remain in effect, as the preamble stated, "until such time as the United States of America extend their jurisdiction over us." What began as a turf war between McLoughlin and the missionaries resulted in a robust experiment in self-government. Before decade's end, that experiment would stoke national discord, as proslavery politicians moved to block Oregon's admission into the United States because of the slavery ban.[20]

The organic acts included the "Law of Land Claims," whose various provisions replicated core functions and practices of both the General Land Office and squatter associations. Settlers had to mark their boundaries and register their claims. Consistent with preemption principles, the law mandated actual occupation and "permanent improvements" as conditions for ownership. Those who abided by these rules would acquire title as well as protection against trespassers. While deeply informed by the ethos and institutions, both formal and extralegal, of the US public land system, the Provisional Government's land law also bore the marks of its difficult and idiosyncratic birth. The statute made special allowances for claims of "any Mission of a religious character"—a clause that benefited the Methodists. At the same time, it took aim at McLoughlin by barring individual claims "upon City or Town sites" when such claims worked "to the detriment of the community." One feature in particular marked the land law as a child of Oregon and its chief patron Senator Lewis Linn: allowing settlers to claim up to 640 acres of free land. All told, the law revealed their determination to secure in a contested corner of the continent the privileged position white squatters enjoyed on the US public lands.[21]

Destiny in Conflict

As Oregon's white men took strides toward self-determination and guarantees of property rights, leaders in Washington began agitating the "Oregon question" with newfound fervor. In his inaugural address in March 1845, President Polk re-asserted that the nation's title to Oregon was "clear and unquestionable" and celebrated the Americans who were "preparing to perfect that title by occupying [Oregon] with their wives and children." It was a paean to an army of preemptioners on the move and a testament to squatters and statesmen marching in lockstep.[22]

Facts on the ground inspired such boldness. The year 1845 alone saw 3,000 new US settlers arrive in Oregon, doubling the territory's white population. By 1846, the number of Americans had surged to nearly 8,000. Those realities were not lost on the British, who felt their grip on Oregon slipping. Assessing the bleak outlook, a London editorialist summarized the problem succinctly: "The Hudson's Bay Company is a strong company, so strong that it consists of the stronger sex only. The American squatter takes his wife with him. The child follows." Numerically overwhelmed by marauding squatters and their fecund wives, Britain would soon find itself forced to withdraw from the region unless it undertook a program of colonization, the editorialist bleakly concluded.[23]

Colonizing nations rested their claims to indigenous territories on a variety of foundations, including discovery, exploration, and actual settlement. American and British officials marshaled every scrap of evidence they could, dating back centuries, to litigate these arguments and make the case for their country's superior claim to Oregon. But for John L. O'Sullivan's *New York Morning News*, US rights to the region transcended all such considerations. The "true title," according to a December 1845 article, "is by the right of our manifest destiny to overspread and to possess the whole of the continent which Providence has given for the development of the great experiment of liberty and federative self-government entrusted to us." This was the second recorded use of the term, coming on the heels of the *Democratic*

Review's innovation the previous summer. The writer likened America's right to Oregon to that of a tree to the very earth and air it requires for its growth. For Britain, Oregon would never amount to anything but "a mere hunting ground for furs and peltries." Under the United States, by contrast, "it must fast fill with a population destined to establish . . . a noble young empire of the Pacific." The Democratic intelligentsia continued to preach the gospel of squatter yeoman conquest.[24]

With Manifest Destiny fast becoming Democratic orthodoxy, militants in the party renewed their calls for the "whole of Oregon," north to the 54°40' line of latitude. "Fifty-four Forty or Fight!" became their rallying cry. The loudest voices came from northern and western Democrats who demanded that Polk make good on campaign pledges, especially after they had supported their southern colleagues' quest to annex Texas, which resulted in a sweeping expansion of slavery in the United States.

But events intervened to change the outlook on Oregon. Acquisition of California had one been of Polk's top priorities since entering the White House, though he kept this goal close to his vest. In the spring of 1846, his administration provoked a conflict with Mexico to seize it and other western lands. The commencement of hostilities gave impetus to resolve the Oregon dispute quickly and peacefully, as the United States could hardly risk fighting two wars simultaneously. The resulting compromise with Great Britain, signed on June 15, 1846, split the Oregon Country at the Forty-Ninth parallel. Many northern Democrats felt betrayed, especially after they had backed Texas annexation. As one Democratic newspaper in Ohio put it, "Our rights to Oregon have been shamefully compromised. . . . NO MORE SLAVE TERRITORY!" Such critiques overlooked the continual efforts by Polk and advisors including Treasury Secretary Robert J. Walker and Secretary of State James Buchanan to balance sectional interests, but they did reflect growing frustration.[25]

Americans in Oregon, meanwhile, welcomed the treaty as the dawn of a new era when they could finally count on the resources and protections of their country and, at long last, receive US patents for their land claims. Additional steps were needed, however, to secure these privileges, the most important being the organization of a territorial government, which required an act of Congress. Only then would the formal apparatus of the United States arrive in earnest: Indian agents, military units, land offices and surveyors, and other key personnel and infrastructure that would make the conquest of the region complete. To their immense frustration, Oregonians would wallow in a state of limbo as the war with Mexico dragged on, absorbing most of the nation's attention.

Observers saw the Mexican conflict as yet another chapter of American squatter imperialism. The opening shots occurred in early 1846 when forces under General Zachary Taylor had crossed the Nueces River—considered the international border by Mexico—and positioned themselves just north of the Rio Grande. Having provoked the enemy into a deadly skirmish, Taylor then led his army into northern Mexico—movements the *London Spectator* viewed as "but an episode in the great plot."

> General Taylor's force is but the precursor of the real army of invasion—the squatter and back-woodsman, men in whom it is a hereditary and invincible instinct always to depart from before the approach of civilization, to avoid every spot where law has become established, and never to feel themselves thoroughly at home except on debatable ground. By men like these coming in by twos and threes, then by scores and hundreds, and finally in multitudes, like carrion birds to the quarry, the Northern provinces of the Republic will be overrun; and thence the process will be continued until the whole territory is filled and mustered by these unprincipled and desperately energetic immigrants.[26]

The notion of an American squatter army on the march found its most vivid expression in the character of Major Jack Downing, the invention of Whig newspaperman Seba Smith of Maine. A simple farmer who worshipped Andrew Jackson, Major Jack had a penchant for turning up at all the flashpoints of the day and sending dispatches describing his firsthand view. Readers could not have been surprised then when his missives began appearing from the Mexican front. In one, addressed to Polk, he reported that soldiers were busy claiming Mexican land.

> We keep pushing the business here; we've got pretty well through the vital parts of the country, and the army has now commenced spreading out and turning squatters. But we haven't near enough to spread all over the country yet without leaving them too scattering. I hope you will hurry on the thirty thousand more men that you promised, as fast as possible; that would make us near a hundred thousand strong; enough to spread out squatters into all parts of the country, and the annexin business would be pretty well over.[27]

Mexico was just the beginning. Major Jack foresaw the squatter army cutting a path of conquest throughout the Americas. The general dynamic he described was similar to the *Democratic Review*'s vision of Manifest Destiny. But Major Jack's take was meant as blistering satire.

Whig critiques of American squatters run amok struck a familiar chord of the Second Party System. However, a new—and, for Democrats, ominous—development was how militant expansionism was compounding rifts within their own party. Despite efforts to appease North and South by pursuing a course of parallel growth, Democrats were fracturing as they executed their program. Texas had created divisions within the party, first when Walker and comrades jilted Van Buren for the pro-annexation slaveholder Polk. While the general election had temporarily restored unity as Democrats focused on defeating Clay, the spurned Van Buren faction nursed the grudge. Further stinging from the Oregon Compromise, a number of northern Democrats, like their Whig counterparts, came to see the war with Mexico as part of a slaveholder power grab.

Determined to draw a line in the sand, Congressman David Wilmot of Pennsylvania, in August 1846, attached a seventy-one-word amendment to an appropriations bill, barring slavery from any territory gained from Mexico. Like Oregon's provisional constitution, the Wilmot Proviso derived its anti-slavery wording from the Northwest Ordinance. Wilmot was no abolitionist, instead professing himself to be the defender of poor whites who might better their condition by claiming and developing western lands. "I have no . . . morbid sympathy for the slave," he insisted. "I plead the cause and the rights of white freemen. I would preserve to free white labor a fair country, a rich inheritance, where the sons of toil, of my own race and own color, can live without the disgrace which association with negro slavery brings upon free labor. I stand for the inviolability of free territory." Wilmot and allies were all for expansion, but not if it served as a Trojan horse for slavery. As they saw it, the West was the rightful domain of hardworking white Americans, not slaveholders and their human chattel. Wilmot himself dubbed the measure the "white man's proviso." Their racism was pronounced but differed from the racism of orthodox Jacksonians in a key respect—it deemed slavery an unequivocal evil for white men, if not for the enslaved themselves. The Wilmot Proviso passed the House but not the Senate. Nevertheless, it cast a shadow over nearly all congressional action related to US westward growth for the next fifteen years.[28]

The most prescient of the Jacksonian unionists recognized the danger immediately. Thomas Hart Benton believed the proviso had no possible upside even for antislavery advocates, given that Mexican laws had banished slavery from New Mexico and California and would remain operative until repealed. "The proviso," he opined, "was nugatory, and could answer no purpose but that of bringing on a slavery agitation in the United States. . . . Every where, in the slave States, the Wilmot Proviso became a Gorgon's head . . . and the synonyme [*sic*] of civil war and the dissolution of the Union." Benton faulted not only "nullifiers" like Calhoun for the uproar but "abolitionists" as well, deeming those groups "two halves of a pair of shears, neither of which could cut until joined together." Wilmot's proviso sharpened the edges, leaving Squatter Democrats scrambling to disarm both sides.[29]

Wilmot, while formally remaining a Democrat, galvanized the incipient Free Soil Party, whose name adroitly encapsulated its core agenda: western lands, free from slavery and free of cost, for poor whites. Territorial expansion and white squatters' rights had been core elements of the Democratic platform since the party's inception, but they found the formula had been hijacked.

The advent of Free Soil came at a time of transition in land reform. With the triumph of preemption, capped by the passage of the 1841 law, reformers turned their focus to passing a homestead act. Not surprisingly, it was a Democrat—Congressman Robert Smith of Illinois, an ally of Stephen A. Douglas, a rising star in the party—who took the lead in advancing such a measure. In January 1844, Smith offered a resolution calling on the Committee on Public Lands to examine the expediency of granting free land to the "head of a family . . . not now the owner of land, and who, through misfortune or otherwise, is unable to purchase." But homestead advocacy flowed from multiple sources. If Smith and Douglas advanced pro-squatter western Democratic prerogatives, another set of reformers had different interests in mind: those of exploited factory workers in the East. George Henry Evans, an immigrant from England and fixture in New York's labor activist circles, founded the National Reform Association (NRA) in 1844 to improve the lives of the growing class of urban workers confronting the grinding realities of industrial capitalism. Evans and associates focused single-mindedly on making free public land available to such workers so they could escape the bonds of "wage slavery" and lead self-sufficient, productive lives. The NRA left an enduring mark with a catchphrase hatched in the winter of 1845–46: "Vote Yourself a Farm."[30]

Democrats, initially, were more inclined than Whigs to tout similar aims. But NRA's homestead crusade received its most high-profile endorsement from Horace Greeley, the Whig editor of the *New-York Tribune*. "The principle of a Free Soil for a Free People must be vindicated and established," the *Tribune* declared in July 1846. Because Whigs, Free Soilers, and other activists embraced homestead, often as a way of stopping slavery in its tracks, the policy generated strong pushback from southerners, making it a non-starter for the unionists heading the Democratic Party, including Polk and Robert J. Walker, who as treasury secretary oversaw the General Land Office and regularly weighed in on policy. These reflexive centrists understood that maintaining power required unity across sections—a balancing act that, in turn, demanded a posture of neutrality on the question of slavery's spread amid the aggressive territorial growth of the period. The Free Soil Party, which emerged in the fall of 1846 and came to include a number of antislavery Democrats, had no such constraints and made homestead a centerpiece of its platform.[31]

The Wilmot Proviso and the advent of Free Soilism posed mortal threats to Democratic pro-squatterism. Since its founding, the party had strived with marked success to hold together a cross-sectional coalition, in part by promoting an expansionist platform that brought spoils for all. Partisans from the North and South could rally behind the squatter yeoman because the symbol relegated slavery to the background and furnished a heroic image that corresponded to the way many Americans saw themselves. The Wilmot Proviso forced the issue to the fore, making it impossible to gloss over the contentious question of slavery's place in the West. Politicians promoting expansion would have to choose sides. For Free Soilers, this did not pose a problem. Their raison d'être was to make western lands available to poor, non-slaveholding whites. When they championed yeomen, they actually meant independent smallholders, not enslavers. For Democrats, by contrast, dissembling on slavery had become the default position. As a party whose strength rested on its broad national appeal, it had to appease northerners and southerners alike. If their leaders began showing preferences, the coalition would crumble.

Backed into a corner, party chiefs called for settlers, not Congress, to decide the slavery question for themselves. Lewis Cass, a US senator from Michigan and formerly Andrew Jackson's war secretary, gave expression to this doctrine of "popular sovereignty" in a widely published letter from December 1847. Cass had initially—privately—supported the Wilmot Proviso but backpedaled when he realized how fast it would torpedo his presidential dreams. Like any national Democrat with ambitions to lead the party, he had to thread the needle between those who believed Congress possessed the authority and responsibility to set slavery policy in US territories and leading southerners who insisted that any prohibition on slavery there violated their constitutional rights. Cass arrived at what he thought was a middle path. "Leave to the people, who will be affected by this question, to adjust it upon their own responsibility, and in their own manner," he insisted, "and we shall render another tribute to the original principles of our government, and furnish another guaranty for its permanence and prosperity." By taking the onus off politicians and placing it on pioneering migrants in the West, popular sovereignty offered Democratic bosses space to keep equivocating on slavery.[32]

Popular sovereignty harmonized with Democrats' pro-squatter approach to political economy, which in principle favored limiting the government's role and giving white Americans across the class spectrum free rein to claim and develop the West. The policy was also known as "non-intervention" because it dictated a hands-off stance by Congress. It seemed simple, straightforward, and in sync with American ideals of popular government. The doctrine also appeared neutral, because it was so vague.

As presented by Cass and later proponents, popular sovereignty left unanswered a crucial question: At what point were settlers to decide the slavery question? On first arrival in a territory? Or at the very end stages of territorial existence when voters approved a constitution and sought admission into the Union as a state? Opponents of slavery favored the former interpretation because small family farmers tended to be more mobile than slaveholders and would likely arrive en masse and ban slavery before it could gain a foothold. Slavery supporters, while generally critical of the popular sovereignty doctrine, backed the latter interpretation because it at least offered a chance for planters to establish slavery during the territorial phase and advocate its continuation after statehood. The premise here was that it would be harder to ban something that already existed than to nip it in the bud. Because popular sovereignty was ambiguous on details, both sides could find scope to support it in theory. But eventually abstract questions of process would demand answers as actual settlers in real places determined their social institutions. What at first seemed like a panacea turned into a hornet's nest the moment anyone poked it.[33]

Trouble with Oregon

Years before Cass offered his popular sovereignty formulation, Oregonians had in fact adjusted the slavery question "upon their own responsibility, and in their own manner." They did so in 1843 when they approved their constitution prohibiting slavery. They also approved a subsequent statute outlawing free blacks from settling in the territory, punishable by public lashings. Combined, these measures staked out a white supremacist free-soil position, although a proslavery minority as well as a small number of African Americans—free and enslaved—continued to reside in Oregon. Once Oregonians sought US territorial status, they found themselves in the crosshairs of national slavery strife, a reflection of the heightened stakes and sensitivities in the Wilmot Proviso era.[34]

Settlers in Oregon and their elected officials yearned for integration into the United States. Provisional governor George Abernethy expressed the impatience of many in his annual message in December 1847. "Our situation is not a pleasant one, on account of the uncertainty of it," he said. "We may be, in less than six months, under the laws and government of the United States; and we may, on the other hand, exist in our present state several years." Individual Oregonians took up the pen to demand confirmation of their land claims. In a petition to Congress, Daniel McKissick related how he had carefully tracked the debates over Oregon for years and had based his decision to emigrate on cues from Washington. Having become "satisfied in reference to the validity of the American claim to all that part of the Oregon Territory which we have ultimately obtained," he headed west with his family in 1843, traveling from Missouri with Jesse Applegate's party and putting down roots in a remote area about a hundred miles south of Oregon City. With his eyesight failing, the last thing he needed was questions about the legality of his claim. Reminding lawmakers of his service to the nation—both as a veteran of the War of 1812 and as an Oregon pioneer—McKissick asked that the land "be confirmed to him or his heirs." The message was clear: he had helped the United States secure title to Oregon, and he wanted the nation to return the favor.[35]

In the fall of 1847—mere weeks before several Cayuses and Umatillas attacked the Whitman Mission, resulting in greater US military involvement in the region—Abernethy dispatched J. Quinn Thornton, the Provisional Government's supreme judge, to Washington to urge Congress and the president to take action. While in the capital, Thornton presented a detailed petition, portraying US acquisition of Oregon as the handiwork of intrepid American yeomen. "Whatever may have been the strength of the American title resting upon discovery, exploration, cession, and contiguity," he wrote, "an actual possession of the country by an agricultural people was wanting to render that title clear and indisputable." For their troubles, these settlers wanted official territorial status—an important milestone on the road to statehood. They also wanted recognition of their land titles.

The inhabitants now in the country believe that they have some claim to a confirmation of the title to the homes which they have made, based upon the promises implied in your repeated legislation, in the fact that they have overcome many of the difficulties of the journey to Oregon; and by their settlements have introduced agriculture and civilization upon our shores on the Pacific, and by doing so gave to the nation an actual occupancy, which was the only circumstance wanting to make the title to the country clear and unquestionable.[36]

Thornton emphasized that without pioneering American yeomen staking claims to the far-off land, the United States would not have redeemed its "clear and unquestionable" title. When it came to claiming Oregon, the language of land tenure was the lingua franca of citizen and state.

Proslavery fire-eaters sought to quell any talk of adding free domains to the nation. On June 1, 1848, Congressman Robert Barnwell Rhett used the occasion of a naval appropriations bill to introduce three resolutions from southern states rejecting restrictions on rights to bring "property" into territories "acquired by conquest or treaty." The Wilmot Proviso was unconstitutional in his view. But the South Carolina Democrat reserved his most scathing critiques for popular sovereignty. A territory, Rhett argued, was "a temporary dependency," the chief purposes of which were to "sell the public lands" and "create new States." It was patently absurd and downright dangerous to allow squatters in US territories—mere political embryos—to set policies that would have a permanent effect. "I maintain that the Territories are subordinate, are subject to the great sovereignties in this Union—the States, the people of the States, where alone, under our system of free government, sovereignty resides," he stressed. This states' rights position, which echoed that of fellow South Carolinian John C. Calhoun, remained the principal thrust of slavery defenders in debates over western lands. Ironically it demanded the use of federal power to protect slaveholder rights against local antislavery majorities in the territories.[37]

Pointing to post-war California and to Oregon, Rhett conjured a picture of chaos and imminent tyranny: "On the first organization of a Territory, a handful of men, consisting of Mexicans from whom we have won it, or of foreign adventurers, fugitives from justice, speculators, and squatters, meet together, and, under the sanction of laws we make for them, gravely determine whether the citizens of the United States . . . shall be allowed to enter the territory." The South and its cherished institution could never make any headway among this motley mass. "If this doctrine of territorial sovereignty is acted on, not another southern State may be added to the Union," Rhett proclaimed. "The Wilmot Proviso in Congress is harmless compared with this doctrine." The scramble to claim land by emigrants with opposing views on slavery had the potential to create "ill-blood amongst the settlers of our Territory where hitherto peace has prevailed," he warned. And that blood would be on the politicians who supported popular sovereignty—"a political device, to harass or circumvent the South." For Rhett, the capacity to carry human property into western territories was a fundamental right that southern Democrats would fight for at "the price of our party cohesion"—indeed, even at the cost of the union.[38]

Rhett's Democratic colleague Richard Brodhead of Pennsylvania responded with a speech that captured the unsteady ground on which old political alliances stood. The husband of Jefferson Davis's niece, Brodhead sympathized with southern concerns about their rights and the future of slavery. A committed unionist, he took aim at what he saw as extremism on all sides, Free Soilers and slavery crusaders alike. Those pushing an agenda of antislavery in the territories "were obliged to resort for support to the extreme of fanaticism, and they had certain catchwords which marked them as a party, and were used for party ends alone. Among these was that of 'free soil.' What did this mean?" Brodhead asked. "Had it any intelligible meaning?" The congressman ridiculed what he perceived as northerners' fondness for wacky fads and hypocrisy in bemoaning slavery when they had racist statutes themselves. "There exist[s] a sickly sentimentality in some of the northern States, that [is] finding its outlet sometimes in Fourierism, sometimes in Millerism, and sometimes in anti-slavery," he declared. Added up, it amounted to impertinent meddling in other people's affairs.[39]

Brodhead also chided Rhett and other southerners whose views struck him as both extreme and inconsistent. When abolitionist petitions had poured into Congress in previous years, southern lawmakers prevented their being read on the grounds that the federal government had no business involving itself with slavery. Now the South demanded federal protection for slavery, even as Wilmot and associates asserted Congress's authority to ban it. For his part, Brodhead professed approval of the doctrine of popular sovereignty, calling for "an entire neutrality in the Government on the whole subject" and "letting the Territories work the machine for themselves." Rigid neutrality of slavery remained a hallmark of Democratic centrism.[40]

Tellingly, Brodhead's most pointed critiques focused not on Rhett's views on slavery but on his disrespect toward squatters. Though Rhett's reference to squatters had been in passing, Brodhead chided his colleague for speaking ill of a cherished icon. "The gentleman from South Carolina had objected to permitting a 'handful of squatters' in the Territories to settle this question of slavery there for all time to come," Brodhead observed. He found this wholly unacceptable: "We [are] a nation of squatters; and it [is] squatters who, by their industry and hardy enterprise, had made the country what it [is]." Brodhead said he would "trust a company of squatters to make a constitution under which to live" certainly more than he would "a pack of dreaming Fourierites shut up in cities, who knew nothing of life in a new country." Squatters were not the problem, he argued, but the solution, and it was entirely appropriate to grant them the authority to resolve what politicians in Washington clearly could not.[41]

Despite southern opposition, the effort to organize Oregon Territory moved forward thanks to powerful supporters, including Stephen A. Douglas, chairman of the Senate Committee on Territories. Early in 1848, he introduced a territorial bill for Oregon that upheld the slavery ban. Calhoun and his allies used all their strength to kill it. At stake, warned the Great Nullifier, was nothing short of "the continuance of the Union."[42]

In February of the previous year, Calhoun had introduced a series of resolutions to protect slaveholders, declaring that territories were the "common property" of the states and that any law that would "deprive the citizens of any of the States of this Union from emigrating with their property into any of the territories of the United States," was unconstitutional. During the Oregon debates, he repeated his core contention that southerners had a constitutional right to bring their "property" into US territories. He maintained that allowing territorial inhabitants to subvert that right would overturn the constitutional order, making territories masters of the United States, by which he meant "the States of the Union in their federal character"—a key distinction for a diehard states' rights advocate. Popular sovereignty was reckless and frankly ridiculous, he railed, given that the "first half-dozen of squatters would become the sovereigns, with full dominion." In years to come Douglas would remember this as the moment when the term "squatter sovereignty" emerged to bedevil Democrats, though Calhoun did not use that exact phrase. The mercurial South Carolinian had a history of attacking squatters. Increasingly, other southern Democrats were voicing similar views—a worrisome development for a party that had long rallied behind this shapeshifting figure. Even more ominous, Thomas Hart Benton deemed "the dogma of squatter sovereignty"—that is, the principle that settlers had the ultimate right to decide the slavery question for themselves—to be in error, but on opposite grounds from those of Calhoun. Where the South

Carolinian argued that no ban on slavery whether by Congress or squatters was constitutional, Benton believed that Congress alone had the authority to enact such a policy in a territory.[43]

Oregonians retained the firm support of Douglas, Benton, and other backers of the territorial bill. In an effort to secure its passage Douglas offered an amendment to extend the Missouri Compromise's 36°30' line to the Pacific, assuring that lands north of the line would be free while those south would be open to slavery. This garnered the support of a broad swath of Democrats, from Benton and Douglas to Calhoun and Jefferson Davis of Mississippi. President Polk also backed the concept. The amendment passed the Senate 33–21 on August 10 but the House nixed it the following day 121–82 on the strength of northern votes. The Senate acceded to the House's removal of the compromise amendment, approving the Oregon territorial bill by a slimmer margin of 29–25. Predictably, Benton and Douglas voted in favor, Davis and Calhoun against. Despite the warnings of imminent disunion, Polk signed the bill into law on August 14.[44]

The president's approval came despite his objections to the Oregon bill's slavery ban. Nevertheless, as a staunch unionist he saw fit to make good on a pledge that dated back to the heady days of the 1844 campaign. Back then it would have been hard to imagine that making Oregon a US territory could divide Democrats so bitterly, especially given the expectation all along that it would be free, just as Texas would be slave. While men like Cass, Benton, Walker, Douglas, and Polk continued to abide by the notion that the continent held spoils for pro- and antislavery partisans alike, a cadre of hardline southerners would no longer brook any limitations on slavery. The Democracy was fracturing on the very pro-squatter expansionist grounds that had been its traditional source of unity and strength.[45]

This reality hit home with stunning force when news filtered in from Buffalo, at the very moment the Oregon debates reached their crescendo, that the Free Soil Party had named their presidential candidate: Martin Van Buren, the architect of the Jacksonian Democratic Party and its alliance of planters and plain republicans. As Jackson's trusted vice president and hand-picked successor, he had struggled to keep this coalition on course as the country surged westward. Burned one too many times by proslavery partisans, he jumped ship in dramatic fashion. "Mr. Van Buren is the most fallen man I have ever known," Polk snarled in his diary, upon learning that the Little Magician had accepted the Free Soil nomination.[46]

Heading into the 1848 race, Democrats had little of the swagger they had shown four years earlier when they appeared ready to conquer the world.

Since then, they had presided over the conquest of a considerable portion of the continent, nearly doubling the nation's territory. Yet theirs was a party in disarray. Polk was not running for reelection, having pledged that he would serve only one term. So they settled on Jacksonian stalwart Lewis Cass. An unapologetic expansionist and champion of Indian removal, the Michigander was happy to countenance slavery in the name of party unity. His popular sovereignty formulation, despite what fire-eaters alleged, was not an antislavery doctrine but rather a slippery expression of neutrality, designed to help Democrats wiggle through the impasse over the polarizing issue.

The squatter remained a potent symbol for many Democrats to rally around. Newspaperman Loring Pickering of the *St. Louis Union* launched a new publication, *The Squatter*, to promote the party in the upcoming election, earning cheers from a fellow partisan to "*squatt* right down amongst the whigs and claim pre-emption on the true dremocratic [*sic*] grounds." A raucous gathering in Natchez demonstrated that Squatter Democracy still had life farther south as well. The customary cannon fire resounded from the city's steep bluffs as stump speakers praised the man atop the Democratic ticket. John F. H. Claiborne, the genteel politician whom Robert J. Walker had singled out for praise in his 1836 squatter speech, stretched the truth when he dubbed Cass "the father of the present pre-emption system, which gives the settler and squatter a home and wealth in the wilderness or on the prairie." But the underlying point was sound: Cass was a strong backer of preemption. He was also one of the party's most aggressive imperialists, having gone all in for Texas, Oregon, Mexico, and Cuba.[47]

Whigs, meanwhile, returned to their 1840 form, forsaking Clay for another military commander from the West. The nomination of Mexican War hero Zachary Taylor smacked of hypocrisy given the party's broad opposition to the conflict. Furthermore, Taylor was a Louisiana slaveholder—though not an especially doctrinaire one. Tactically, the nomination of "Old Rough and Ready" was shrewd, as the general was almost certain to attract significant support from southern Democrats. Certainly this appeared to be the case in Charleston, South Carolina, where local Democrats declared their support for Taylor, dismissing Cass's popular sovereignty as "a doctrine too monstrous to be tolerated." In a resolution, they affirmed:

> The opinions of Gen. Cass . . . that the inhabitants of a territory, before they are invested with the attributes of self-government and sovereignty—tenants of the public lands at the sufferance of the States—mere squatters—have the right to appropriate the

territory that may be acquired by the treasure or gallantry of all the States, and to exclude from its limits the property of fourteen of the States—has been repudiated by the Press and the people of the whole South.[48]

Rather than unify Democrats across regions as before, the squatter sharpened divisions at the very moment the party needed to stand as one. The *Richmond Whig* noted with glee that "the nomination of Gen. Cass falls like a 'shower-bath' on the people of Virginia. . . . They do not believe him sincere; and with Mr. Rhett, they think that his Squatter Doctrine is worse than the Wilmot Proviso."[49]

The confused state of Squatter Democracy came through clearly in a humor piece written for the *St. Louis Weekly Reveille* by none other than John S. Robb, author of *Streaks of Squatter Life*. In it, an artist named Sam Stockwell floated down the Mississippi making drawings. One rainy afternoon he happened upon a squatter standing outside the riverside cabin he shared with his wife Betsy and children. The conversation quickly turned to the coming election.

"Are you a Taylor man?" inquired Sam.

"No, by thunder," said he.

"Do you go in for Cass, then?" inquired Sam.

"Well, I calculate not, stranger," shouted he.

"What! Do you *support* Van Buren?" continued the artist.

"No," shouted the screamer: "I *support* Betsy and the children, and it's d--n tight screwin' to get along with them, with corn at only twenty-five cents a bushel."

"Good bye: stick to Betsy and the children," said Sam: "they are the best candidates out"; and raising anchor, he floated off. As he sped onward, the squatter's voice reached him once more, and its burthen was: "Hurrah for Gineral Jackson, the old Mississippi, and *me and Betsy*."[50]

Amusing as it was intended to be, this burlesque of Jacksonian Squatter Democracy had a sobering message for partisans: as the 1848 vote drew near, the squatter figure had come untethered from its traditional partisan moorings. Amid the uncertainty, the squatter in the story wanted nothing more than to return to the glorious days of Jackson, when settlers knew who their friends in Washington were.

As it turned out, Cass won every state West of the Mississippi, save for Taylor's Louisiana, while capturing the entire Old Northwest, Maine, and his own birth state of New Hampshire. In the South he took Virginia, South Carolina, Alabama, and Mississippi, showing that the Democrats remained a force in their traditional grounds. But it was not enough. He and his main opponent each won fifteen states, but Taylor's electoral college victory was decisive: 163–127. In addition to Louisiana, he won Florida, Georgia, and North Carolina, as well as Tennessee and Kentucky. He was especially dominant in the Northeast and mid-Atlantic, including the all-important state of Pennsylvania, an erstwhile Jacksonian stronghold. In New York, favorite son Martin Van Buren received 120,000 votes to Cass's 114,000; combined, those tallies exceeded the 219,000 votes that Taylor received in the Empire State.[51]

While Free Soilers could not seriously contend for the White House, given their almost complete absence of support in the South and their scant party apparatus, they did play the role of spoiler, topping Cass's vote tally in Massachusetts and Vermont, as well as in New York. On the flip side, the party took enough votes in Ohio from Taylor to return it to the Democratic column. Free Soil candidates also won House and Senate seats.[52]

Free Soilism was a direct threat to Squatter Democracy because it offered a competing brand of pro-yeoman expansionism that was unambiguous in its goals: a West populated by white smallholders and unsullied by slavery. This was precisely the form of society toward which Democratic pro-squatterism conduced, given its fundamental promise of granting yeomen access to land. Where Free Soilers could forthrightly profess their aims, Democrats had to hedge in order to maintain their appeal across sections. The perceptive Horace Greeley comprehended Democrats' dilemma. A champion of homesteads for farmers, the editor retained a reflexive Whiggish disdain for squatters, viewing them as the boisterous rubes depicted by John S. Robb. Nonetheless, he saw them as crucially important to ending slavery, in spite of themselves. "The squatter may be as empty-headed or wrong-headed as he can—may spend his evenings in bar-rooms execrating Abolitionists—but if he gives his days to useful toil he is preaching an anti-Slavery harangue," a *Tribune* editorial read. Independent squatter yeomen and slavery were like oil and water, the piece suggested. They could not co-exist. It was a devastating point, fraught with implications for Squatter Democracy, which was staggering because its master symbol appeared incapable of advancing slaveholder and small family farmer ambitions at the same time.[53]

Oregon was a case in point. Its settlement revealed that the independent family farmer likely would prevail on the ground when American emigrants flooded into a distant domain. In a period when slavery-friendly squatters thrilled and amused the reading public, actual squatters took possession of western lands and forged societies that by and large rejected slavery, even as they excluded free black people. This reality was not lost on southern firebrands who fought to block the organization of Oregon Territory under the free-soil terms favored by the majority of its inhabitants.

Oregonians rejoiced when the territorial bill passed, envisioning a new era of peace and prosperity. The act did have a significant downside from their perspective, though—it voided the land laws of the Provisional Government, creating anxiety about whether the United States would honor their squatter rights.[54]

Oregon Donation Land Act

Samuel R. Thurston, Oregon's first delegate to Congress, arrived in Washington late in November 1849 for what would be one of the most consequential—and contentious—sessions in history. Issues of greatest magnitude snarled both chambers. Would California be admitted as a free state and territorial governments organized for New Mexico and Utah? Would they be slave or free, and who would decide? Would popular sovereignty carry the day in those western domains? What about slavery in the nation's capital? Would it be banned once and for all? Perhaps most controversial, would the fortified Fugitive Slave law demanded by the South meet with approval? These questions formed the components of the compromise measures of 1850, which held the key to the rupture or survival of the Union.

Thurston quickly perceived that the poles in national politics were no longer Democrat and Whig, but North and South, the latter, in his mind, by far the more shrill and unreasonable. His introduction to this new dispensation proved jarring. A diary entry from December 13, 1849, records his impressions soon after arrival.

> The House . . . commenced its session and the whole day was spent in a most disgraceful altercation. The Southern democrats made some 15 or 20 speeches, all declaring that if the Wilmot Proviso should be applied in the dispositions of the new territories, or if Congress should abolish Slavery in the District of Columbia, in either case, they and the South would dissolve the Union. The North replied that they should do what they could to prevent the farther extension of slavery, but if the South outvoted them, they would not dissolve the Union for that.

Having witnessed the angry exchanges, Thurston concluded, "The South would not vote for Jesus Christ in person unless they were satisfied that he was with them on the slavery question."[55]

Thurston had strong opinions about these matters. Born in Maine and trained as a lawyer, he was a thoroughgoing Democratic centrist of the northern ilk. He deplored slavery but loathed abolitionists. Nevertheless the thirty-three-year-old delegate resolved not to get swept up in the drama and vitriol. He came to Washington with a broad agenda for helping Oregon Territory get up and running, with one goal towering above the rest: passing a land bill that recognized Oregonians' claims and held out inducements to future emigrants. To those ends, Thurston fixed on a strategy he would scrupulously follow: "I . . . shut up the book of *partisan* politics . . . and opened one in which the Whig and the Democrat, and the Free-soiler, the Northern man and the Southern man, might read in harmony together."[56]

From everything he had seen so far, Thurston knew he faced stiff odds. Of particular concern, land reforms had hit snags in Congress. Homestead backers had made repeated attempts to push through legislation and had failed, mainly because of resistance from southerners who feared it was a Free Soil contrivance that would abet small farmers and halt the spread of slavery. The very month Thurston arrived in Congress, Stephen Douglas introduced a homestead bill granting 160 acres of the public lands "to the actual settler who shall reside thereon and cultivate a portion thereof, for a period of four years." However, it was a dead letter in the eyes of many southern lawmakers who viewed homesteading as a rearguard attack on slavery.[57]

There was, however, one proslavery advocate who broke the mold, and his case reveals an abiding, uniquely southern strain of pro-squatter advocacy. Congressman Albert G. Brown, a former governor, represented a "piney woods" district of southeastern Mississippi that included prosperous planters and struggling farmers. In an 1850 homestead debate, Brown singled out squatters as patriots who would not hesitate to lay down their lives in defense of the country, thus meriting gratitude in the form of land. This was the old Squatter Democracy line. But for Brown the identification with squatters went deeper, as he made clear in an 1852 speech in support of a homestead law.

> I know something, Mr. Chairman, of squatter life. . . . I will tell you why my heart is with these people. When I was a boy—a very little boy—an honest, but poor man, settled (squatted is a better word) in the country where I yet reside. Removing from South Carolina, he pitched his tent amid the unbroken forests in the dead of winter. . . . He was in a strange

land, without money and without friends. But with an iron will, such as none but squatters have, he attacked the forest. It receded before him, and in three short months the sun, which had been shut out for many centuries, was permitted to shine on a spot of earth in which the squatter had planted corn. Day by day he might have been seen following his plow, while his two sons plied the hoe. Toil brought him bread—and he raised up his sons to know, as Heaven's wise decree, that "by the sweat of their brows they should gain their bread." . . . Despise not these squatters. Among them is many a rough diamond. They, and their sons, may rise to the first honors in the Republic.

Brown's very personal portrait depicted a hardworking yeoman who sacrificed so that his sons might thrive and the nation advance. At the same time, he had this to say about the South's defining institution: "I regard slavery as a great moral, social, political, and religious blessing—a blessing to the slave and a blessing to the master." Brown was the rare southern Democrat who could still keep the issues of land-claiming and slavery separate. To his mind, giving settlers free land was pro-squatter but not antislavery. His personal history allowed him to hold these seemingly contradictory positions when others could not. Of course, when he spoke of squatters he was romanticizing an early phase in his father's career. Yes, the man had occupied a patch of public land and toiled to make it productive. But subsistence farming was never the goal. The elder Brown prospered as a cotton planter, becoming one of Copiah County's largest slave owners and serving as justice of the peace. If his father's story taught Brown anything, it was that squatters posed no threat to slavery. Quite the contrary, they could extend its reach, since today's squatter might well become tomorrow's enslaver.[58]

Brown's love songs to squatters carried a tune from an earlier time that few southerners were still willing to sing. While homestead legislation had a broad array of supporters in 1850, from western Democrats like Douglas, to Free Soilers, to antislavery Whigs like Greeley and Senator William Seward of New York—and even the odd slaveholder like Brown—it could not overcome stiff southern resistance.

The issue weighed heavily on Thurston. After all, Oregonians were seeking a full section of free land—four times more than homestead advocates sought—and in a territory that had banned slavery. Still, he pressed on, advancing a bill that provided for a donation of 640 acres to married white men—and "American half-breed Indians"—who were US citizens (or intended to become ones) and had lived on their plot and cultivated crops for four straight years. In the case of married men, half the land—320 acres—would be in the wife's name. ("This surely was a woman's Rights Bill," Thurston's wife Elizabeth noted approvingly.) Single men would receive 320 acres. As incentive to future inhabitants, the proposed act also offered grants of 320 acres to married couples and 160 acres to single white males who arrived in Oregon within three years of its passage. Thurston succeeded in getting the land bill reported in the House on April 22, and spent the next months "assiduously electioneering" for the legislation in speeches, letters, and private meetings with lawmakers.[59]

The proposed law was an overt policy of social engineering along racial lines, taking a resource wrested from Indians and making it the private property of white people. Some lawmakers blasted the provision to donate land to whites only. Free Soil congressman Josiah Giddings of Ohio, underscored the wrongheadedness of such a policy, noting that it would invite "low, vulgar, vicious" white toughs from New York City "to select farms in Oregon; while Frederick Douglas [*sic*], a man of high moral worth, of great intellectual power, of unrivalled eloquence . . . is to be excluded, rudely driven from that region." Giddings asked rhetorically: "Will history record this as an exhibition of the narrow, the groveling prejudices which govern the American Congress? Is this to be a specimen of our Legislation at this middle of the nineteenth century?"[60]

Thurston frequently "startled" his interlocutors with the magnitude of the land grants as well, but patiently "appealed to their *sympathy* on the ground that our married men came to Oregon with the expectation of a full section; that they had taken it, and that they had large families growing up, which would make it necessary in a very short time, for the father to subdivide this section into farms of small dimensions for his boys." Nor were men the only Oregonians looking to Congress: "I assured them that our *mothers* were watching with intense anxiety their action."[61]

Thurston's non-partisan gambit played well at home, even as Oregon itself entered a new era of partisan politics. Although they bore the fissures of the national party, Democrats would dominate there for several years. Polk had installed Joseph Lane, a proslavery Indianan, as governor, while voters had chosen the antislavery Thurston to represent them in Congress. There was no love lost between the territory's two most powerful Democrats. But when it came to the land bill, they and other Oregonians rallied behind a jingoistic stance of American versus British interests, rather than Democrat versus Whig or proslavery versus antislavery. "I know that you will never by any act of yours, take from good *American Citizens* their property and give it to any . . . foreigner," Lane wrote to Thurston in January 1850. The governor let drop that there were rumors to the effect that Thurston was planning "to put the Island and mills, purchased of Abernethy, in the hands of the old Dr."—a reference to McLoughlin and his long-simmering conflict with the Methodists in Oregon City.[62]

Regarding Thurston's sympathies, there was no question they lay with the old "Mission party" and not the "wiley [*sic*] old Jesuit," as one associate dubbed McLoughlin. It made no difference that McLoughlin had quit the HBC, settled in Oregon City, and announced his intention to become an American citizen. Thurston appeared to go out of his way to ensure that under no circumstance could the old doctor obtain a land grant. "He has devoted long years of his life in the service of British Kings and Queens, in seeking to wrest the whole Territory from our Government," Thurston explained to his constituents. "His heart does not palpitate with true American blood." For his part, McLoughlin struggled to comprehend Thurston's enmity. He knew there were charges that he had sided with the Cayuses during outbreaks of violence and had blood on his hands, but he had trusted that decades of opening his arms to Americans in need would dispel such slander. "If the immigrants had all been my brothers and sisters, I could not have done more for them," he sighed. It appeared he would be the one white man in Oregon denied property, despite the fact that he was among the first to make a claim.[63]

Apart from McLoughlin and his friends and business partners, Oregonians by and large approved of Thurston's course. "Your Land Bill gives entire satisfaction to all parties," gushed Wesley Shannon, a Democratic partisan, when the measure passed the House in August 1850. "You are far more popular here than ever *Genl.* Jackson was in Tennessee and are considered much the *greater man.*" William Bryant, chief justice of the territory's Supreme Court, deemed him deserving of the "lasting gratitude of your Constituents and all friends of Oregon." He urged swift action in the Senate.[64]

It was around this time that Jesse Applegate wrote his own letter to Thurston. Tracking the evolving land bill, Applegate chafed at a provision requiring grantees to occupy their land for four years before they could receive title. "If this 4 years *confinement* is intended to check the restless spirit and desire of change of the nomadic race to which I belong I consider it not only impolitic but oppressive," he wrote. The United States "owe their existence" to that "restless spirit," which first appeared "on the rock of Plymouth and added every acre to this wide spread republic," Applegate maintained.

Since the Revolution the nomads and squatters have subdued the valley of the Mississippi; they have added Texas and Calafornia [*sic*] to the Union, and *we* have given them Oregon and they propose to pay us for this magnificent gift by doling out a few acres of our own land *coupled with a condition* . . . at variance with our habits and subversive of our right and liberties.[65]

As he penned these words, Applegate may have reflected on his epic 1843 trek west at the head of a "cow column"; or his death-defying efforts in 1846 to open a new southern trail into Oregon; or the years of backbreaking work and public service to establish a home and functioning society. His thoughts may also have turned to his father, a Revolutionary War veteran who traversed the Cumberland Gap to settle in Kentucky, where Applegate was born. Given all that squatters had sacrificed and all they had accomplished, he considered it a grave injustice for anyone to denigrate "this most deserving class of citizens." He still fumed over Henry Clay's insults and long-standing opposition to preemption laws. "Mr. Clay," he wrote, "owes his high place to a state wrested from the bloody hand of the savage by Danl. Boone and his associate squatters."[66]

With his critiques of Clay and his reverence for Thomas Hart Benton, whom he dubbed "the 'Cyrus' raised up by the Deity to lead the star of American empire to the shores of the Pacific," Applegate bore the hallmarks of a true Democrat. Indeed, his paean to squatters as America's great nation-builders echoed the Squatter Democracy creed. In fact, he was a staunch Whig and fervently antislavery. Family members detected the influence of Edward Bates, a leading Missouri Whig who had befriended Applegate during the young man's days as a land surveyor in St. Louis and would go on to serve in Lincoln's cabinet. In his letter to Thurston, Applegate underscored the role that he and his fellow squatters had played in making Oregon a US domain, a feat, he argued, that entitled them to ample grants of land with no strings attached. It was a sign of the times and the shifting ground of squatter politics that a Whig would make such a case to a Democrat. What he and Thurston both shared was a vision of the West as a slavery-free zone for white farming families.[67]

In the weeks following House passage of the Donation Land bill, Thurston struggled to get the Senate to act on the measure. Whenever it encountered an obstacle, he detected the hand of his nemesis. "I have no doubt myself that the agents of Dr. McLoughlin are operating against it," he confided to his diary on August 13. The doctor was but one of his worries. When Stephen

Douglas moved to take up the legislation in the Senate in early September, a spirited debate ensued. Jefferson Davis of Mississippi, in a pointed exchange with fellow Democrat Benton, demanded to know: "Who is it that owns the land, the squatters or the United States?" Davis was dead set against ceding the public lands to antislavery squatters. Working in Thurston's favor was Oregon's transnational context. The squatter figure had loomed large in the brinkmanship between the United States and Great Britain for supremacy over the Oregon Country. With the region firmly in US hands, many in Congress could see justice in rewarding those who helped vanquish a despised foreign foe. As the debates carried on, Thurston held his breath while the bill made a thousand "hairbreadth escapes." To his infinite relief, the Donation Land Act cleared its final hurdles and passed the Senate on September 19.[68]

The northern press trumpeted the vindication of "Squatter's Rights in Oregon." In shepherding the measure through, Thurston became the critical link connecting some 7,400 individual claimants to more than 2.6 million acres of Indian homelands in Oregon. In that regard, he carried his party's white squatter advocacy to its natural endpoint. Even his rival Joseph Lane conceded he had "acted very handsomely" on behalf of Oregonians. Thurston did not have long to savor the triumph. On the steamer home in early 1851, he contracted dysentery and died off the coast of Mexico, just shy of his thirty-fifth birthday.[69]

In certain respects, the claiming of Oregon represented the high-water mark of Squatter Democracy. Democrats in the White House and Congress and their allies in the press brashly asserted the nation's "clear and unquestionable" title to the bountiful land still occupied by Native peoples and also claimed by Great Britain, and they encouraged emigrants to redeem that title by settling there. Americans flooded into the contested domain, bringing with them the land-taking practices of the US public lands system and enacting them on the ground. Their overwhelming numbers and assertions of ownership helped tip the balance of power in America's favor. In return for their troubles, these squatters demanded title to the lands they claimed, resulting in the Donation Land Act of 1850, a novelty in the history of US land laws for its unusually large grants of free land and overt white supremacy. It would take years of hand-wringing and arm-twisting for this policy to bear fruit, but white squatters eventually got the land. For helping to secure their titles, Democrats, in turn, strengthened their standing with the people.

While scene to the full fruition of Democratic pro-squatterism, Oregon was also where this brand of politics began to seriously fracture. Since the party's advent, the squatter had been a unifying symbol—the heroic white face of conquest—behind which northerners and southerners could rally to advance a resource-hungry agenda without showing their hand on slavery. After Wilmot drew his antislavery line amid the war with Mexico and Cass responded with the doctrine of popular sovereignty, the sleeping dogs of sectional discord awoke snarling. It was into this fray that Oregonians stepped when they sought territorial status. Although they had banned slavery with little fanfare years earlier, they became, in the view of southern firebrands, prime evidence of squatter sovereignty run amok when they pushed for formal integration into the United States. With popular sovereignty emerging as Democratic orthodoxy, the squatter was no longer simply a land-claiming pioneer planting the American flag on Pacific shores, but an existential threat to southerners' most prized form of property: enslaved humans. Given Oregonians' surpassing interest in land, it is no small irony that their bid to secure their property rights contributed to a profound shift in national squatter politics.

6

Sacramento's Squatter Riot and the Aftershocks of Manifest Destiny

ON DECEMBER 7, 1849, Charles Robinson was hard at work constructing a cabin on Sacramento's sloped riverfront when three men, bearing firearms and a writ from the city council, came and tore it down. They applied themselves to the task of destruction with efficiency and verve, smashing the wooden boards to splinters, removing the shelter's frame, and making off with hundreds of dollars' worth of planks and other materials. Notably, this wrecking crew did not consist of hired muscle but rather three of the most powerful men in the fast-growing town: the marshal and two prosperous businessmen, including the fearsome Samuel Brannan, the Mormon adventurer and entrepreneur famed for being the first Gold Rush millionaire.[1]

Earlier that morning, Brannan and his associates, joined by a lawyer for John Sutter—the empire builder from Switzerland who became a Mexican citizen and claimed ownership of much of the Sacramento Valley—had marched into the city attorney's office complaining that Robinson's construction "is doing us great damage, inasmuch as it obstructs our way, injures the sale or lease of our property and in a great measure shuts us out from public view." They urged officials to do whatever it took to "restore to us our ancient rights." The city wasted no time obliging, commanding the marshal "to abate the nuisance," which meant removing Robinson and the house he was constructing.[2]

A graduate of Amherst College and practicing physician, Robinson was not someone to trifle with, as Sacramento's leaders would discover. The thirty-one-year-old Massachusetts native had come to California earlier that year via the arduous overland route as much for adventure as out of gold lust. Resolute

Dangerous Ground. John Suval, Oxford University Press. © Oxford University Press 2022.
DOI: 10.1093/oso/9780197531426.003.0007

and tall, with sharp blue eyes, he possessed the kind of charisma that "would inspire men to do and to dare in the cause of human liberty," a friend recalled. To his tormentors, though, there was nothing inspiring about him at all. He was, as the official complaint put it, a "nuisance," an intruder, a squatter—the scourge among the business elite of this booming town.[3]

The confrontation on the banks of the Sacramento River came less than two years after the United States had violently seized California from Mexico, and months after news broke that the streambeds of the Sierra Nevada glittered with gold. Hundreds of thousands of fortune seekers raced into California, with mining pans and picks among their essential gear. As the weather turned cold and wet, many scuttled into Sacramento from the surrounding hills, putting up tents and shanties wherever they could find a suitable patch of ground in the flood-prone town and setting the stage for showdowns with those who considered the terrain their own property. The ensuing turf wars sparked the Squatter Riot of 1850, which erupted at the very moment lawmakers in Washington stood poised to vote on California statehood amid rising rancor over the meaning and thrust of "squatter sovereignty."

Three days prior to the attack on Robinson's cabin, President Zachary Taylor, in his first annual message to Congress, described epic events taking place in the golden land. Though it had become part of the United States only the previous year, California had witnessed meteoric growth as emigrants rushed in. Taylor reported in his message that leading citizens there had recently met in convention "and it is believed they will shortly apply for the admission of California into the Union as a sovereign State"—thereby leapfrogging the usual territorial phase for new US domains. Should they move forward, the Whig president added, "I recommend their application to the favorable consideration of Congress."[4]

Taylor did not mention that the convention that had taken place the previous September and October in Monterey had approved a constitution—one that barred slavery. Instead, as if to preemptively defuse the inevitable blowback, Taylor obliquely emphasized that Americans had a right to choose their own institutions, "in such form as to them shall seem most likely to effect their safety and happiness." He cautioned lawmakers that "we should abstain from the introduction of those exciting topics of a sectional character which have hitherto produced painful apprehensions in the public mind." The president was preaching popular sovereignty. He was also engaging in wishful thinking. When southerners, Democrat and Whig, got wind of the terms of Californians' statehood bid—and Taylor's endorsement of them—they could hardly believe their ears. A slaveholder president from Louisiana, who had led a conquering force in Mexico, now approved California racing into the Union as a free state?[5]

If Oregon had been a bitter pill to swallow, California was pure poison. After all, from the beginning, most presumed that Oregon would be free. That was the understanding in 1844 when Democrats paired the region with Texas as twin pillars of their agenda. Also, it stood north of the Missouri Compromise's 36°30' line of latitude, which, although specifically applying to the lands of the Louisiana Purchase, functioned symbolically in many people's minds as a dividing line between slavery and freedom across the West, even if the House had rejected its extension in debates over the Oregon territorial bill. California was different. Much of it lay south of 36°30', fueling hopes that it might well become a slave domain. Furthermore, a disproportionate number of the volunteer soldiers who had fought in the war that had snatched the region for the United States in the first place hailed from slaveholding states. Finally, and perhaps most significantly, whereas Oregon was merely a territory, Californians sought to skip the territorial phase altogether and apply directly for statehood. If successful, they would tip the balance of fifteen free and fifteen slave states.

In seeking to squelch California statehood, slavery advocates picked up where the Oregon debates had ended. "This new doctrine, asserting the right of the squatters on the public domain to assume sovereignty over it, in its territorial state, was concocted only for a Presidential campaign," scoffed Georgia congressman Robert Toombs, referring to Cass's unsuccessful White House run. "It failed of its purpose, and now is brought into general contempt." It was during the fierce debates over California that the term "squatter sovereignty"—hinted at during the uproar over Oregon—became an epithet among fire-eaters from the South. Henceforth, in the buildup to the Civil War, as ideologues clashed over squatters, they did not debate land rights so much as the power to determine slavery's fate. Abolitionists also perceived that Taylor had stolen Cass's thunder. "We certainly think the 'great Michigander' is entitled to damages for this unceremonious poaching of Old Zach upon territory where the former had acquired, through great political tribulation, the solemn rights of a 'squatter,' " quipped the *Anti-Slavery Bugle* of Ohio.[6]

While politicians in Washington clashed over California's course and positioned symbolic squatters as invaders of slaveholders' rights, actual, self-styled squatters in the golden land, borne by the winds of Manifest Destiny, focused on acquiring land. It was as if statesmen and squatters occupied parallel universes. Once popular sovereignty emerged as a predominant mode of resolving the slavery debate in the American West, a degree of illegibility arose between those who continued to understand squatters principally as land claimants and those who conceived of them as sovereign actors empowered to determine whether slavery would or would not take root in particular locales. It required time for minds to adjust to this shift. For the time being, the two sides shouted past each other.

To a considerable degree, Charles Robinson and the Sacramento squatters he would lead resembled their forebears in other frontier settings. They asserted that the lands they desired fell within the US public domain and staked claims to choice plots. To bolster their claims, they positioned themselves as virtuous yeomen oppressed by land barons and speculators, all the while applying time-honored land-claiming structures and strategies such as squatter associations and preemption rights to secure their foothold. Furthermore, they said little about slavery, not so much for ideological reasons but because claiming land truly was their aim. In all of these senses, they were heirs of Democratic pro-squatter politics.

In other ways, Sacramento's squatters were a novelty. They became the first major movement to appropriate the squatter label to advance their agenda. Hailing from a variety of sections and representing a range of partisan affiliations and positions on slavery, they inclined toward a free-soil brand of squatterism that prioritized free land for white yeomen. Indeed, a number of their leaders were progressive northerners with close ties to George Henry Evans's National Reform Association. On the whole they were not overtly antislavery. But like emigrants to Oregon, they would prove that mass migration and land-taking by squatters from the eastern United States ultimately favored a land free of slavery.

Land of Gold

California was a cornucopia and cultural crossroads. Miwoks, Nisenans, and other Native peoples had dwelled in the foothills and grasslands for centuries. Old Spanish missions, *pueblos*, and *presidios* dotted the coast, while *ranchos* devoted to raising cattle, horses, sheep, and goats sprawled over the rolling hills and valleys. After winning independence from Spain in 1821, Mexico had continued the practice of awarding land grants—a number of them topping 50,000 acres—to prominent Californios. Some established prospering farms. Most reserved them for grazing livestock.[7]

The mystical rhetoric about Manifest Destiny had positioned California as the promised land of an "irresistible army" of Anglo-Saxon farmers who, by virtue of being white American cultivators, would naturally come to possess the region and spread enterprise and republican institutions. In the minds of the *Democratic Review* scribes, these squatters possessed "the natural right of self-government belonging to any community strong enough to maintain it." But war, not squatters, delivered California into the American fold.[8]

As negotiators from the United States and Mexico converged on the Mexican village of Guadalupe Hidalgo in early 1848 to make peace, California's immediate destiny became manifest in the streams of the Sierras. A worker constructing a mill for John Sutter on the banks of the American River spotted "some kind of mettle . . . that looks like goald [*sic*]." The frenzied rush in the wake of the discovery catapulted California's non-Native Anglo-American population from less than 15,000 in 1848 to over 200,000 in 1852. While most came in quest of precious metal, they could hardly fail to notice the astonishingly fertile valleys and plains that surrounded them.[9]

The Treaty of Guadalupe Hidalgo, signed on February 2, 1848, promised to honor the property rights of Mexican landowners, but its pledges did not translate into practice. To newly arrived Americans, the sparsely populated terrain seemed almost completely up for grabs. Jacksonian land politics had conditioned such perspectives. Under preemption, occupation and improvement were the benchmarks of legitimate ownership. Beholding vast stretches of seemingly uncultivated territory, Americans scoffed at what they perceived as Californios' unproductive use of land. "Were it not for the Indians who work about the farms for little or nothing, (and generally get cheated out of that,) there would be no land cultivated in California," one American writer acidly observed. "[T]he people are so indolent and careless."[10]

The swarms of settlers and miners, backed by pro-squatter politicians, created an onslaught unlike anything California's Indian and Mexican populations had faced before. With the United States in formal possession of California, Thomas Hart Benton addressed American squatters in a letter circulated in the press in the fall of 1848. He rued that Congress had yet to pass a land law similar to the one proposed for Oregon and advised each settler "to make [h]is own location, taking care to avoid interferences with one another, or with old claims considered good"—in essence: organize squatter associations to regulate land-claiming until US surveyors and lands officers were on the ground. The lawyer who had once generated considerable business sorting out the old Spanish and French claims in Missouri offered California's squatters some free advice: "Avoid if possible, law suits about land above everything else. They are a moth which eats up the crop, and often the land itself." It was the kind of counsel a consummate squatter-friendly politician would offer. A new order was afoot, challenging even those best positioned to with-stand the influx of American settlers and their powerful sponsors.[11]

John Sutter was many things but indolent was not one of them. Fleeing an unhappy marriage and mountains of debt in Europe, he arrived in the United States in 1834 seeking to revive his fortunes. Sensing that California offered opportunities to match his ambitions, the immigrant rustled up an explora-tion party and, in the summer of 1839, headed up the Sacramento River to scout out a location for an estate. As he wended his way along the waterway, Sutter made a point of blasting his large cannons to impress the Miwoks, who dominated the region to such an extent that neither Spain nor Mexico had been able to take control. With Indian labor, Sutter built a redoubtable fort on the banks of the American River in Sacramento that became a haven for Europeans and Americans moving through the area. Brimming with energy, he established a blacksmith shop, stables, stockyards, a textile manufactory, vineyards, and other enterprises at the fort.[12]

Having naturalized as a Mexican citizen, Sutter applied in 1841 for a land grant of eleven leagues (roughly 50,000 acres). In his application he emphasized the enlightening effects his presence was having on the region's Native inhabitants, noting that his settlement, named New Helvetia in honor of his Swiss heritage, served as "a strong barrier to the incursions of the barbarous tribes" and as "a school of civilization." Californios in the vi-cinity, like Mariano Guadalupe Vallejo, did not know quite what to make of Sutter, reportedly given to staggering around with a bottle of wine in hand. But Governor Juan Alvarado responded positively to his application, praising Sutter for "his steady perseverance and truly patriotic zeal in favor of our institutions, reducing to civilization a portion of the savage Indians." The phrasing about "reducing to civilization" rings with cruel irony given ac-counts that Sutter fed his Indian peons in a pig's trough.[13]

Sovereignty remained in flux in California, and Sutter scrambled to nego-tiate the changes. When a ragtag group of Americans, allied with US army ex-plorer John C. Frémont, husband of Benton's daughter Jesse, revolted against Mexican rule in 1846 and announced the advent of the Bear Flag Republic, Sutter allowed them to use his fort to detain Vallejo and other Californios. Bear Flag was short-lived but betokened changes to come. Sutter, however, was less worried about the prospect of a new nation claiming sovereignty over California than about his own debts. As the US-Mexican War came to a close, he focused on constructing a sawmill in the Sierra Nevada, hiring a crew of Mormon army veterans. It was one of those workers, James Marshall, who first discovered gold. Fortune hunters raced into the region—some using the trail through the Sierra Nevada forged by famed African American mountain man James Beckwourth.[14]

Amid the onslaught, Sutter moved to Hock Farm, his estate to the north, and the family sold off Sutter's Fort and other Sacramento properties to American speculators, who found they could command top dollar for them. Those who witnessed the courtly, tippling Sutter doing business with the crafty Americans saw trouble brewing. "Sutter is a goodmeaning pleasant man, but the most sappy headed fool you can conceive of—& excited with wine usually & half his time half drunk," remarked merchant and horticulturist William R. Prince, a transplant from New York. "[T]he Yankees have used him & flattered him, & made him believe that he owns the greater part of [California]."[15] If Sutter and the speculators appeared poised for a collision, they were united by a common threat: squatters, scores of them, taking possession of prime lots in Sacramento.

By the spring of 1849, the surge of unauthorized settlers had grown sufficiently alarming for Sutter to take out a standing ad in local newspapers. "*Notice to squatters,*" it announced, "All persons are hereby cautioned not to settle without my permission, on any land of mine in this territory." His hard line pleased Sacramento's business elite, who held top positions in the nascent city government, along with titles to many of his lots. Usurpation of Sutter's property threatened their own investments. As winter approached, evicting squatters and razing their dwellings became a regular event in Sacramento. Prince, the merchant, would later fume that the system favored speculators. "[T]he local courts here are dead against the Squatters & they can get no justice from them & they decide to eject them in all cases & then the Sheriff is ordered to tear down their buildings & clear them off." What the authorities did not count on was the strength of the resistance.[16]

Gold Rush California existed in a tenuous state. Nominally the United States was in control, but it lacked the institutional footprint to impose rule of law. For enterprising individuals this presented both opportunity and danger. Charles Robinson perceived the fluid state of affairs upon arriving in the summer of 1849 as a member of a New England company of prospectors that had formed near Boston and made the overland trek across the continent. Reflecting back on what inspired him to set aside his growing medical practice in Fitchburg, Massachusetts, he quipped that even "staid" Yankees were not immune from the "gold fever." Robinson found his way to the Bear River in the Sierra Nevada foothills and began panning for precious nuggets. A quick study, he took stock of his situation and noted, "In the absence of the civil code, every man was a law unto himself and constituted in his own person judge, jury, and executioner."[17]

On a personal note, Robinson discovered that he had little appetite for gold prospecting. During a visit to purchase supplies in Sacramento, some thirty miles south of his camp, the venturesome doctor had a change of plans. Impressed by the town's proximity to the mines, its easy access to the coast via navigable waterways, and the high prices its merchants commanded, he decided to open an "eating-house" with some of his Massachusetts associates. With meals selling for up to $1.50 apiece—more than $50 today—they would be sitting on their own gold mine. This became particularly evident when heavy rains commenced, flushing hundreds of hungry miners out of the hills and into town for the winter during a season of historic flooding, later followed by a cholera outbreak.[18]

In addition to serving meals, Robinson occasionally dispensed medicines to ailing townsfolk. One day walking along the levee with two friends, he recognized a man whom he had just treated. Illness, it seemed, was just the beginning of this man's woes. He had constructed a crude dwelling out of logs and sheets of canvas, and retired there to convalesce. But the marshal and his henchmen—"well charged with whiskey," in Robinson's telling— had other ideas. They dragged the sick fellow from his shelter and destroyed

FIGURE 6.1 A bustling Sacramento in December 1849, growing crowded with buildings and tents. Drawing by George V. Cooper; lithograph printed by William Endicott and Company. Library of Congress, Prints and Photographs Division, LC-93511486, https://www.loc.gov/item/93511486/.

it. Horrified, Robinson and companions called a public meeting to spread the word about this "damned outrage," drafting a handbill and plastering it "on wagons, mules, and things movable and immovable." They were probably as surprised as anybody when an estimated crowd of 3,000 turned up at the levee at the appointed time, some out of keen interest, others perhaps because an impromptu gathering offered a diversion from their daily grind. Robinson, a novice stump orator, got up and announced the formation of a squatter association, generating thunderous applause with his pledges to protect settlers.[19]

On the heels of the gathering, he received his visit from the marshal's wrecking crew at the cabin he was building on the waterfront. Turning the tables on his tormentors, he accused them of trespassing and sued for $3,000 in damages. The court dismissed his suit but Robinson and allies pressed on with their fight. In a written motion seeking a new trial, his attorneys argued that the city council had no legal authority to force their client's removal— let alone destroy his property—because it was "a mere voluntary association having no greater or other power than an individual would." In effect, local authorities had no special claim to power, they asserted, leaving squatters on equal legal footing with them to claim and enjoy property. They failed to persuade the court, which only strengthened their resolve. The squatters vowed *"for every hut they pull down we will destroy a palace."*[20]

Robinson and friends took steps to formalize their squatter association, printing up a broadside detailing its rationale for forming and terms of membership.

> The Sacramento City Settlers' Association, believing the ground, generally, in and around Sacramento City, to be Public Land; and desiring to promote the prosperity and harmony of persons settling thereon, has Resolved, That . . . Every Member of the Association will use his best exertions for the support of his fellow-associates, against any and every innovation of their JUST RIGHTS.

The organization's officers included a president—Robinson—a vice president, treasurer, a three-person board of arbiters to adjudicate claims, a secretary, and a surveyor/register. Membership dues and monthly fees would pay for the cost of surveying unoccupied lands into lots of one, four, and 160 acres, depending on whether they were in the city or outskirts, and the association would grant provisional titles—only one per settler—until US courts determined the rightful owners.[21]

With its pledges of mutual protection and provisions for surveying lands and awarding titles, the group was a classic claim club. Crucial to its legitimacy was the argument that they were operating on US public land where preemption reigned. Robinson and his associates rejected the validity of Sutter's title and, by extension, the property rights asserted by the speculators who had purchased lands from him. Sacramento, they argued, fell outside the boundaries of the 1841 land grant, which was invalid anyway in their eyes because it had been awarded by the Mexican governor of California and not by the central government in Mexico City. Merchant William Prince, a squatter sympathizer though not one of their number, summarized their position: "The Squatters say . . . most justly that if he (Sutter) claims the Hock farm, he can't claim here (Sacramento), & that at all events he can only have 11 leagues be it where it may."[22]

Like American emigrants in Oregon, the squatters in California arrived thoroughly acculturated in the norms and practices of the US public land system, including preemption. It was not possible for them to behold the fertile valleys—shamefully "unimproved" in their view—and accept their status as off-limits simply because a distant monarch in Madrid or some corrupt Mexican official had long ago capriciously scribbled his name on an ill-defined grant, thus ceding princely tracts to a coterie of favored families. Sutter's claims were sketchy at best. By virtue of US conquest of California, they argued, the ground they claimed formed part of the nation's public domain, affording them the right to occupy, improve, and own.[23]

Sacramento's squatters proved adept at leveraging the mechanisms of American civic power within their grasp. Shortly after the formation of their group in December 1849, they turned to a trusty tool: the petition. The heading of their document to Congress spoke volumes: "Petition for the free occupancy of the Public Lands of the United States in California by actual Settlers." Characterizing the lands they occupied as "Public Lands of the United States" was an essential, much-used framing device that placed squatters in their rightful domain. The petition explained how they had made the arduous journey "with the expectation and full belief that our Government had purchased from Mexico the Territory of California." But upon arrival, "we found ourselves trespassers on the soil, subject to the will of pretended owners; denied the right to plant a tent, to build, occupy, or cultivate, except by submitting to enormous prices for rents or purchases." They urged Congress "to apportion the public domain to actual settlers" and "preclude the gambling speculations now so rife amongst us." The references to US public lands and their implicit entitlement to them as Americans in a conquered region, the celebration of "actual settlers," and demonization of speculators all revealed fluency with the essence of Democratic pro-squatterism.[24]

The petition, however, bore signs that a novel squatter movement was afoot—one that did not march in lockstep with Democrats. The call for "free occupancy of the Public Lands," in particular, smacked of free-soil home-steading notions. Robinson and his allies had a range of political affinities, reflecting both their individual backgrounds and the fluctuating condi-tion of national party politics. Within their growing movement there were both "anti-slavery squatters" and "pro-slavery squatters," the latter much in the minority. The leaders mainly fell in the former camp. Robinson was a Whig who opposed slavery. His close associate, Irish-born journalist James McClatchy, was a labor activist with free-soil affinities who had been active in New York in the homestead-focused National Reform Association (NRA) and had ties to Horace Greeley. NRA founder George Henry Evans drew a direct line between his organization and the Sacramento squatter movement, seeing in Robinson and allies nothing less than the advance of "Free Soil in California."[25]

For Sacramento's civic leaders, the squatter movement was first and fore-most a problem of economics and public security, not one of partisan poli-tics, particularly given the inchoate state of party structures in California at that stage. The so-called Sutterite faction, comprising the city council and businessmen like Brannan who had purchased Sutter's lands, anointed them-selves the "Law and Order Party" and moved to terminate the squatter nui-sance. William Prince detected impure motives. "It is these speculators, many of whom will be ruined if they can't sell the lots, that are so deadly against Squatters," he observed. Early in 1850, Council President Albert M. Winn, a native Virginian, delivered an address deploring the "great evil" posed by squatters and proposing measures to remove these "intruders." "It is plain to every intelligent man disposed to be just to his neighbor, that those who pay high rents or high prices for property for the purpose of carrying on a legitimate business cannot compete with those who occupy public grounds without expense," he declared. Winn offered a resolution authorizing law en-forcement to clear "all obstructions" from the public landings and streets. The squatters dug in their heels.[26]

The Settlers' Association opened an office in the heart of town as its ranks swelled to include scores of members mutually pledged to protect each other's property from authorities whom they deemed unlawful. They won sympathy even from locals determined to stay neutral. "My feelings & *prin-ciples* but not my interests, are strongly on the side of the Squatters," wrote

Samuel W. Brown, chairman of a mining and trading company, to his wife in Connecticut. Meanwhile the appearance of new tents and shanties in town, and western-style log cabins farther north at the junction of the Feather and Sacramento rivers bore testimony to an exploding squatter population.[27]

The Sacramento squatter movement began attracting notice far beyond California. The *Daily Picayune* of New Orleans published a detailed account of the intensifying conflict, professing uncertainty about "whether the landholders will give way or the squatters." The *Texian Advocate* detected a palpable sense of unease among the large property owners "lest their claims . . . not be recognized by Uncle Samuel." As tensions escalated, the writer noted, "The squatter movement in Sacramento City, frightens them not a little."[28]

Sacramento's squatters skillfully appropriated the tropes of Democratic squatter politics, using the same pro-yeoman, anti-speculator rhetoric to assert rights to lands once belonging to Mexicans and Native Americans and employing similar organizational structures and land-taking strategies. But their mixed backgrounds, diverse political affinities, and connections to northeastern land-reform movements set them apart from earlier generations of squatters who, by and large, found succor in the Democratic Party. They did not say much about slavery, mainly because land was their all-consuming focus, but the movement gathering force in Sacramento would embody southerners' worst fears about what to expect if squatters were left in charge of western lands.

Compromising Measures

When the thirty-first Congress commenced on December 3, 1849, the Mexican Cession—some 325 million acres stretching from New Mexico to California—cast an ominous shadow as lawmakers confronted whether the territories and states carved out of those lands would be slave or free. These and related questions sparked months of angry debate, drawing in some of the lions of a passing age, including "the Great Compromiser" Henry Clay and a dying John C. Calhoun.

Calhoun considered California "the test question" for whether the Union would survive or splinter. The sixty-seven-year-old South Carolinian entered the Senate chamber on March 4, 1850, propped up by an assistant. Too infirm to speak, he had a colleague deliver his oration, which diagnosed the nation's maladies. Calhoun depicted the history of the republic as a slow, deliberate strangulation of the slaveholding South. The Northwest Ordinance of 1787, the Missouri Compromise of 1820, the establishment of Oregon Territory in 1848, and the current effort to make California a free state all enhanced northern strength, while bringing his own beloved region to its knees.

Calhoun identified the culprit of the current crisis: popular sovereignty, wielded by footloose settlers. "Are you prepared to surrender the sovereignty of the United States over whatever territory may be hereafter acquired to the first adventurers who may rush into it?" he asked. California's bid to become a free state was "revolutionary and rebellious in its character, anarchical in its tendency, and calculated to lead to the most dangerous consequences." Only by rejecting it could lawmakers restore harmony and maintain sectional balance in the Union. Having said his piece, the Great Nullifier retired to his sickbed and died before the month was out.[29]

Stephen A. Douglas defended Californians' course. The indefatigable young chairman of the Senate Committee on Territories believed the West was rightly the domain of valiant white pioneers who, left to their own devices, would establish thriving frontier communities and thereby enhance the nation's wealth and power. He trusted that the continent held spoils for Democrats of all stripes, and if everybody got a piece, the people and party would prosper, even as they agreed to disagree about slavery.

Throughout his career, Douglas had proved himself adept at balancing sectional interests. In Illinois, he had to walk a line between the antislavery majority and the sizable number of proslavery inhabitants with southern roots. The state had rejected slavery but instituted policies that perpetuated coerced labor and excluded free blacks. Douglas no doubt took instruction from his adopted state's history, concluding that local populations could settle the issue without resort to mass violence. A Vermont native, he saw the value of a society of free farmers—a core constituency. Yet his wife came from a wealthy North Carolina planter family and inherited a cotton plantation in Mississippi, which Douglas helped oversee. Above all, a Jacksonian unionist and insatiable expansionist, he had little patience for those he considered the extremists in the North or South. He understood that for himself and his party to flourish required the maintenance of the cross-sectional coalition that was the Democracy's hallmark and traditional source of strength. Keeping that alliance intact, in turn, required extensive new lands and party leaders committed to strict neutrality on slavery.[30]

Douglas came to view Cass's popular sovereignty formulation as the surest solution to the chronic fighting and gridlock over slavery in the West. Allowing local majorities to decide their institutions kept faith with principles of republican self-government, he maintained, and represented the best hope for peace among Democrats, while allowing for continued territorial expansion. Responding to Calhoun's denunciations of California's squatters, the Little Giant shot back in a speech on March 14, "What rights ... have they usurped?" He provided the answer himself: "Not the rights of property, for they expressly recognize the right and title of the United States to the public domain." He considered it axiomatic that "all mankind have an inherent and inalienable right to a government." Californians had made their choice and done so in a lawful and orderly fashion. They wanted statehood without slavery. "The question is already settled, so far as slavery is concerned. The country is now free by law and in fact—it is free according to those laws of nature and of God ... and must forever remain free." It was a stark bit of truth-telling. However, Douglas was not denouncing slavery; he was endorsing popular sovereignty. He was also stating the obvious. With its high sierras and variable climate, California, to his mind, was no slave country. Besides, its own constitutional convention had rejected slavery.[31]

What Douglas and supporters of majoritarian democracy saw as popular sovereignty, slavery boosters slammed as "squatter sovereignty." In their bid to block entry of California as a free state, slavery apologists echoed arguments by Calhoun and Robert Barnwell Rhett during the Oregon debates that emphasized the dangers of allowing roving emigrants to establish the social institutions that would prevail in new western states. The California state-hood bill "gives a full and solemn recognition, by the Congress of the United States, to the doctrine of *Squatter Sovereignty*," charged the Democratic *Georgia Telegraph*. The coinage—one of the first examples on record—discarded twenty years of rhetorical work by Democrats to rebrand the squatter from outlaw to pioneer and also painted this controversial figure in the same damning light Whigs once had. To accord wayward migrants the sovereign status to determine slavery's fate was, in the writer's estimation, the fatal flaw of popular sovereignty. Yet this was precisely what was happening. "The citizens of half the States of this confederacy [are] to be excluded with their property from a territory ten times as large as Georgia, by a band of adventurers, in defiance of all previous precedents, and the express provisions of the Constitution," the *Telegraph* lamented.[32]

The squatter sovereignty decried by enslavers was not the sovereignty that self-described squatters in California were enacting on the ground. In Sacramento, Charles Robinson and allied squatters did not see themselves as "a band of adventurers" out to stop slavery's spread. The sovereignty they asserted was as American citizens staking claims to what they considered US public land. Tensions continued to escalate through the spring and summer of 1850 as more and more miners gave up the quest for gold and moved into town, claiming lots of their own. Adding to the stress, the speculative bubble that grew during the Gold Rush showed signs of bursting. With property values on the wane, owners fought for every inch of land they had purchased from Sutter and other land barons in the region. Taking aim at "the squatter innovation" that was causing so much unrest, the *Placer Times* declared it was high time to confront "a cancer which threatens the very vitality of our body, social and politic."[33]

The conflict came to a head on August 10, 1850, when county judge Edward J. Willis ruled against a squatter named John Madden who had built a cabin on a lot claimed by one of Sacramento's councilmen. Not only did Willis order him to vacate his home and fine him $300 but he denied Madden the right to appeal. "Outrage!!" blared the broadside that squatters posted the next day throughout Sacramento. "Shall Judge Willis be [a] Dictator? . . . Squatters and all other Republicans are invited to come to the Levee, this evening, at 8 o'clock, to hear the details." Hundreds convened for what a local paper described as a "rich and racy" gathering on a principal thoroughfare. Representatives for both sides gave spirited speeches and engaged in heated banter with the crowd. When called to address the masses, the popular Robinson stepped forward and growled that he "was ready to have his corpse left on his own bit of land, [before] he would yield his rights." The small-town Massachusetts doctor appeared ready to redeem his claim to western soil at the cost of his life.[34]

The next day Robinson published a manifesto vowing defiance should the sheriff or anybody else attempt further harassment of squatters, even if authorized by a court. Squatters, the manifesto assured, would not disturb anyone who remained neutral. But, he warned, those who moved against them would "share the fate of war." The physician-turned-revolutionary was a picture of calm and unflinching grit. Inside, though, he harbored doubts. Retiring to his tent that night, Robinson wrote a letter to his fiancée back east. "On whom can I depend?" he asked. "How many . . . squatters will come out if there is a prospect of a fight? . . . How many speculators will fight? . . . Will the world, the universe and God say [our cause] is just?" He was keenly aware he was testing the moral boundaries of land rights.[35]

With a confrontation looming, authorities hauled off James McClatchy and another prominent squatter on August 13, detaining them in the prison brig on the Sacramento River. Robinson remained at large. That night he met with allies and devised a plan to reclaim Madden's property. On Wednesday, August 14, he and James Maloney, the Settlers Association treasurer and a

Mexican War veteran, rode out to the designated meeting spot—a large oak at the edge of town—"but found not a solitary squatter." They went from tent to tent, shanty to shanty, and raised a force of a dozen or so men. Maintaining a defiant posture, they commenced marching under a scorching sun, led by the erratic, saber-wielding Maloney atop a "cream-colored horse." Onlookers—some friendly, some not—followed in the squatters' dust. "Armed men on foot & on horseback [were] passing up the Levee confusedly & hastily & shouting as they went," an eyewitness reported.[36]

According to Robinson, the sword-bearing Maloney made a fateful decision when he marched the small "squatter army" onto bustling J Street, home to numerous shops, saloons, and gambling-houses. This drew into the fray some of Sacramento's "most desperate characters." Perhaps having second thoughts, Maloney began rounding the corner of J and 4th streets, where his forces collided with mayor Hardin Bigelow, sheriff Joseph McKinney, and their posse. Gunshots rang out. The mayor toppled from his horse, badly wounded. A bullet struck the city assessor, whose wife had given birth just that morning, killing him almost immediately. Maloney had his horse shot out from under him and died in a hail of bullets. A second squatter lay lifeless in a pool of blood.[37]

Amid the chaos somebody shot Robinson point blank in the side, the lead bullet passing through his body just below the heart. The injured squatter managed to drag himself into a hotel, where a physician was summoned. The sheriff rushed in, directing his men to bear the hemorrhaging Robinson by cot to the prison ship. Meanwhile, the city council declared a state of martial law to "insure the defense of the city against further depredations of the Squatters." US troops marched in to quell the mayhem. The townspeople braced themselves for a violent night. "Many rumors are current with regard to the intentions of the Squatters, & there is much noise & disorder in the streets & occasional report of firearms," Samuel W. Brown wrote to his wife.[38]

The next day Sheriff McKinney and his men raided a boarding house on the American River owned by a man suspected of harboring fugitive squatters. The resulting shootout left several more dead, including McKinney himself and a "Negro squatter." Troops remained garrisoned in and around Sacramento for days. When the dust finally settled, shaken residents took stock of the calamity. "Dearest Charlotte," wrote merchant William R. Prince to his wife back in New York, "You will without doubt hear astounding news concerning this town." Sacramento, he assured, was still standing, though the people remained on edge. Prince offered an account of the "most unnecessary squabble" that had taken place a mere block from his store. "The Squatters," he concluded, "had no course left but to defend themselves." If the scrupulous merchant was any indication, public sympathy lay with Robinson and his fellow insurgents—indicating that their appeals as actual settlers taking on lordly speculators had resonated.[39]

The "Squatter war" in California sent shivers down the spines of slavery advocates back east, especially as Douglas moved closer to securing Senate passage of the California statehood bill. In a last-ditch attempt to prevent California's entry as a free state, Democratic senator Hopkins L. Turney of Tennessee introduced an amendment on August 6 that would extend the Missouri Compromise 36°30' to the Pacific, leaving southern California open to slavery. Douglas and Benton had been willing to support such a policy to get the Oregon territorial bill through in 1848 but stood with the majority who defeated the amendment 32 to 24. On August 13, the Senate passed the California statehood bill with a 34 to 18 vote that exposed a profound rift within the Democratic Party. Every northern Democrat approved the measure and all but two Democrats from slave states opposed it, revealing that support for squatter-driven expansionism had assumed a decidedly sectional cast. The *Daily Morning News* of Savannah, Georgia, rued that the bill "gives the vast area of territory lying between New Mexico and the Pacific ocean . . . to the free soil adventurers, and squatters now depredating upon the public domain in those regions." The link between Free Soilism and squatters spoke volumes. Seen from the South, the squatters of California appeared hostile to their interests. It mattered little that men like Robinson had put their lives on the line to obtain land, not to end slavery. The fact was their crusade took place in a part of the world that had barred slavery. If this was the world "squatter sovereignty" was making, the South would have none of it. California statehood passed the House in September, 150 to 56.[40]

In California, squatter politics took a more formal turn. Aboard the prison brig Robinson made a surprisingly swift recovery. His popularity had surged as a result of his daring leadership of the squatter movement. While still a captive and awaiting trial for murder, he was elected to the state assembly. Released on bail and awaiting the start of the legislative session, Robinson and James McClatchy launched a newspaper to continue their crusade. The short-lived *Settlers and Miners Tribune* devoted most of its coverage to litigating the particulars of the squatter cause. They elaborated a credo of "squatterism," positing it as an antidote to "Sutterism." "When . . . Sutterism or any other 'ism' is ruining the country, squatterism should step forth to save it," they wrote in the inaugural issue in late October. Sutterism meant monopoly, speculative greed, and feudal decadence, while squatterism meant setting down roots, improving one's property and community, and advancing republican institutions. It also meant non-partisanship. "Squatterism, like Republicanism, in a land like ours, should be far above all parties," the editors affirmed, wrenching yeomen free from any partisan yoke.[41]

Rallying behind the "Squatter" flag, Robinson, McClatchy, and comrades directed their energy to electoral politics, articulating a platform and fielding candidates for local and state races. The "Squatter party" held a mass meeting in Sacramento's public square in November 1850, where they passed a series of resolutions, including one that highlighted their independence from the major parties. Celebrating "the vigorous infancy of the Squatter movement," they proclaimed, "we cannot give our support to any man for any office, who is afraid or backward in avowing here, there, and everywhere, that he is a Squatter in principle. . . . [W]e recognize in every American citizen the inalienable right to a portion of the public domain, free as God gave it." Free land for actual settlers was their agenda. The aim was to take squatterism—their particular homestead-infused blend—from the fringes and place it in the political mainstream.[42]

On the campaign trail Robinson and the Squatters remained committed to the principle of non-partisanship, staking out neutral ground vis-à-vis Democrats and Whigs. "By occupying this position," Robinson explained in a letter to his fiancée, Sara Tappan Doolittle Lawrence, "both parties seek our votes & put up candidates in our favor. They have adopted our platform & I presume will carry it out. In fact neither party dares oppose us, & I expect little, or no opposition in the Legislature." The Squatters' neutrality strengthened their position, Robinson observed. "Every one has given up all open opposition to us, and we 'damned Squatters' are as much respected as any one."[43]

Robinson and party boldly appropriated the squatter label. The potency of the name owed much to the cultural legwork of Democratic pro-squatterism whose proponents, over the previous twenty years, had toiled to remove the stigma of trespass from these scrappy settlers and position them as the heart and soul of the expanding nation. The California insurgents had repurposed the pro-yeoman thrust of Squatter Democracy for their own independent ends. While not explicitly antislavery, their brand of squatterism had a distinct whiff of Free Soilism to it, a feature that would become especially evident a few years later when Charles Robinson took up residence in Kansas and led the free-state movement there.

In the nearer term, scribes in San Francisco faulted the administration of Democratic governor John McDougal for expediently jumping on the

FIGURE 6.2 Charles Robinson depicted in a cabinet card photograph from 1861, the year he took office as the first governor of Kansas. Courtesy of Kansas State Historical Society.

Squatters' bandwagon as they acquired new power and privileging them "in contra-distinction to all other classes of California population not enrolled under the banners of Squatter Democracy." This was perhaps the first time the term Squatter Democracy was used in print and underscored what the author believed was an attempt by California Democrats to co-opt the Squatter movement. Indeed, as California's squatters grew increasingly influential, vestiges of the old Democratic statesmen-squatter alliance reasserted themselves. It was hardly a surprise when the Squatters, turning to Congress to confirm their land titles, found a particularly strong ally in William M. Gwin, one of California's original US senators. Gwin had been Andrew Jackson's top lieutenant in Mississippi in the 1830s. He coordinated the campaign that launched Robert J. Walker into the Senate in 1836 and later touted the squatter-friendly views of Walker, Polk, and other top Democrats. Though proslavery, he was savvy enough to know what played well with constituents in his new West Coast home. At the top of the list was access to cheap land, including the terrains tied up in land grants awarded long ago by vanquished foes.[44]

In his Senate seat, Gwin pushed hard for squatters' claims, securing passage of the Land Act of 1851 that created a board of commissioners to assess the validity of Spanish and Mexican land titles. Championing white settlers, Gwin resorted to the old tropes of Squatter Democracy. In an August 1852 speech promoting legislation to protect settlers from "remorseless" speculators, he blasted Whigs for blocking his efforts and launched into a panegyric on the virtuous squatter yeoman.

> Who is there with mercenary rancor enough to pursue such settlers, and denounce and stigmatize them in opprobrium as "squatters?"— a class of men whose triumphs are everywhere written upon the face of this continent—the men, bold and adventurous, who fled from the tyranny of the Old World, and at Jamestown, Virginia, the Plymouth rock of Massachusetts, and St. Mary's, in Maryland, laid the foundations of the settlements which have spread over the broad bosom of this mighty Republic from the Atlantic to the Pacific . . . before whom forests have disappeared, under whose hands cities have arisen, with whom the arts and sciences are in their highest development, by whom tyranny in every form, political, social, and religious, has been overthrown, the dignity, glory, and independence of man has been asserted and maintained, and the American Republic advanced to the front rank of the nations of the earth! This is the class of men whose interest I am proud to advocate; to whose cause every faculty I possess shall be devoted.[45]

Gwin cast America's rise as a story of squatters' progress. His historical references paid tribute to Yankee New England, the Old South, and also Catholic Maryland—a shrewd selection designed to appeal to core Democratic constituencies. He gave speculators the obligatory drubbing. If there was anything surprising about the speech, it was how anachronistic it was. This was especially evident in his choice of framing device—delivering the oration as a rebuke to a reputedly anti-squatter Whig, the ultimate strawman of Squatter Democracy. Gwin's address could have emanated word for word from the lips of any number of Democrats in their jousting with Henry Clay in the 1830s or in their full-throated defenses of Oregon settlers in the 1840s. Here was an attempt to stoke the old sense of grievance and resentment, while strengthening bonds of trust between statesmen and squatters by securing the latters' claims to conquered land.

Yet not even high-flown oratory could turn back the clock or obscure just how much the underlying politics had changed. The squatter whom Gwin extolled was a relic of the past. In the wake of clashes over Oregon and California, this figure circulated less predictably and legibly than ever in national politics, spooking proslavery partisans in particular. Indeed, few southern Democrats joined Gwin in celebrating squatters in the golden land.

It would have been a much simpler world if Democrats were still mainly fighting Whigs. But the fiercest battles over squatters had turned internecine. This was evident during an 1851 Senate exchange when Jefferson Davis dismissed Californians as "trespassers upon the public domain." Lewis Cass took it personally. "I crossed the Ohio river and went to the Northwestern Territory when there was not an acre for sale," he shot back, recalling his migration from Ohio to Michigan Territory where he served as governor from 1813 to 1831. "And now, when that practice has continued for fifty years . . . are we going to make California an exception, and institute suits against every man, woman, and child there because they are trespassers?" Davis retorted dryly, "If I chose, I could go into an argument upon squatter sovereignty; but I think we have had all the argument heretofore upon that subject that is called for." The two Democrats talked past each other. Cass spoke of land-claiming settlers. Davis, still smarting from California entering the Union as a free state, kept coming back to squatters as violators of slaveholders' rights.[46]

Davis, who made an unsuccessful run for Mississippi governor in 1851, faced the awkward question of why he had supported Cass, the father of "squatter sovereignty," in the presidential election of 1848, spurning his own father-in-law Zachary Taylor. Times had changed was all he could answer. California, he explained, "gave the highest practical importance to the doctrine of 'squatter sovereignty.' Its character was changed from speculative to real." The future president of the Confederacy saw clearly that, as in Oregon, the squatters of California had advanced free-soil interests, whether that was their avowed goal or not. Having been burned twice, slavery defenders attempted to co-opt the squatter to prevent the loss of any more ground.[47]

7

A Squatter's-Eye View
of Bleeding Kansas

THE NOTE TO Charles Robinson did not mince words, though it did mangle
his name. Written on a scrap of paper and addressed to "Dr. Robertson," it
read: "Yourself & friends are hereby notified that you will have one half hour
to move the tent which you have on my undisputed claim. . . . If the tent is
not moved within the half hour we shall take the trouble to move the same."
It was signed "John Baldwin and Friends." And so the Sacramento squatter
leader found himself on the cusp of another turf war. This time he was not
spearheading a crusade for a piece of the golden land but contending for an
even bigger prize: Kansas. It was October 1854, four months after the passage of the Kansas-Nebraska Act that organized those territories for settlement. The controversial law repealed the Missouri Compromise of 1820,
which, by clearly demarcating where slavery could exist and where it could
not, had been the linchpin of a shaky peace between North and South for
more than thirty years. Kansas and Nebraska both stood north of the 36°30'
line of latitude, previously barred from slavery. According to the terms of the
new statute, they would be settled under the principle of popular sovereignty,
meaning settlers themselves would decide whether those territories would be
slave or free.[1]

As he had in California, Robinson felt secure in the rights that he and his
associates asserted to terrain outside the town of Lawrence, the fast-growing
hub of their settlement. They had arrived a few weeks earlier and purchased
the parcel in dispute from one of the original white inhabitants. It came as a
rude surprise, then, when Baldwin turned up insisting the tract was his and
occupied it with a group of heavily armed friends from nearby Missouri.
Robinson and his allies moved in swiftly to re-assert their claim, resulting in

Dangerous Ground. John Suval, Oxford University Press. © Oxford University Press 2022.
DOI: 10.1093/oso/9780197531426.003.0008

a standoff that saw the two parties "scowling defiantly" at each other across a grassy distance of some fifty feet. When a lawyer delivered Baldwin's scrap-paper missive, giving "Dr. Robertson" half an hour to move his tent or else, Robinson remained unfazed. A battle-scarred veteran of California's squatter strife, he understood that land-claiming in a new territory was often a game of bluster and brinksmanship. He wasted no time replying to Baldwin: "If you molest our property, you do it at your peril."[2]

Kansas has been accurately portrayed as the bloody battleground between proslavery and free-state factions acting as proxies for South and North in the national showdown over slavery. Overlooked is the fact that much of the violence began as fights over land and that rival squatter factions frequently directed the skirmishes. Indeed, "Bleeding Kansas" cannot be understood without attending to the central role of squatters and their quest to claim and hold onto land. Democrats in Congress and the White House had thrown open the doors to settlement before clearing Indian titles or commencing surveys. Squatters filled the resulting vacuum. Doing what they had always done, they organized clubs to secure their members' claims, lending a degree of order to the otherwise chaotic process of settling a new country. In and of themselves these dynamics were not unusual in the frontier West. But in Kansas, national slavery agitation created a pressure-cooker environment that made the politics on the ground uniquely volatile. It was not long before squatter associations became instruments for waging battles over slavery, contributing to the upheavals that shook the territory and the nation.[3]

For the previous quarter century, Squatter Democracy had harnessed the symbolic appeal and on-the-ground presence of white settlers to advance an agenda of conquest and partisan gain. Oregon and California, each in its own way, had marked high points of the statesmen-squatter alliance rooted in the quid pro quo of land for political support. They also became fracture points between northern and southern Democrats because popular sovereignty was emerging as the dominant mode of resolving the slavery question, and flesh-and-blood squatters played a central role in providing answers. Crucially, in both cases popular sovereignty became a point of contention after settlers had made their decision on slavery. There was no ground war between competing sides—indeed, the issue was resolved before it had become a source of pro-longed strife. In Oregon, the Provisional Government—with voter ap-proval—had banned slavery in 1843 before Oregon was even a US territory. In California, the statehood convention in the fall of 1849 had done something similar. Both bodies had exercised popular sovereignty, to be sure, but organi-cally and of their own accord, and not as a result of a policy prescription from

Washington. In both cases, squatter-led settlement had naturally produced free-soil societies, sparking southern ire after the fact.

Kansas was different. Settlement there took place expressly under the principle of popular sovereignty, as dictated by the Kansas-Nebraska Act. All parties—squatters and statesmen, proslavery and antislavery—understood the ground rules from the start: actual settlers by dint of claiming land and exercising the franchise attendant to residency would determine whether slavery or freedom would triumph. Having learned from hard experience that squatter sovereignty was all too "real," to paraphrase Jefferson Davis, proslavery partisans could no longer simply denounce squatters and the doctrine that empowered them to decide whether slavery would die or survive. It was too late for that. So they made a bold play to claim the squatter for their side.

On the plains of Kansas competing forms of squatterism came into open conflict: one, a novel brand tailored for the occasion by proslavery squatters who aligned themselves with fire-eating southern Democrats—an increasingly potent faction within the party—and the other, a strain embodied by free-state squatters, many of whom shared affinities with Free Soilers and affiliated with the burgeoning Republican Party. Both varieties were spawns of Jacksonian pro-squatterism. The alliance between Democratic politicians and western settlers over the past quarter century had turned the squatter into a powerful talisman eminently worth claiming. In Kansas, however, old-guard Jacksonians—who to a surprising degree continued to occupy the highest rungs of power—struggled to contain the forces they had helped unleash. Amid the escalating violence in Kansas, men like Stephen A. Douglas, Lewis Cass, Robert J. Walker, Franklin Pierce, and James Buchanan tried sticking, with varying degrees of commitment and success, to an avowed neutrality on slavery, even as they espoused land-taking by white Americans in the West. That position had long been party orthodoxy and a key component of the squatter politics that had carried the American flag to Pacific shores and kept the Democracy in power for so long. Opening up new territories had brought personal enrichment as well, in lands, mines, and railroads. The leading Jacksonians knew better than anyone how much there was to gain when partisans agreed not to make bones about slavery.

Having run out of room to dodge, the Jacksonian apostles of popular sovereignty ceded authority to squatters to resolve the inflammatory issue, setting the stage for rival bands to wage a ground war that would determine slavery's place in America. They miscalculated that Kansas's abundant resources would concentrate settlers' minds and turn down the heat on slavery agitation. Squatters with passionate ideological commitments—and not statesmen retrenched in kneejerk neutrality—defined the direction of events. In doing so, they put the Jacksonian elder statesmen through a severe trial, forcing them at long last to show where they stood and, in some instances, to actually take a stand.

The squatters in Sacramento may have been independent, but they still behaved like traditional squatters in the sense that their primary goal was claiming land. In Kansas, thanks to popular sovereignty, squatters were set up to fight a war over slavery, via the medium that was their natural habitat: land. Because the issues of land and slavery were so intertwined, it is no simple matter to tease out where land hunger ended and fights over slavery began. Charles Robinson, for example, was not in Kansas merely to acquire prime real estate. He was the on-the-ground agent of the antislavery New England Emigrant Aid Company and as such worked to facilitate settlement from the Northeast as a means of making Kansas free. Claiming land and fighting slavery—or claiming land to fight slavery—was his mandate and remained so throughout a crusade that made him both the leader of the free-state movement and a major landowner in Kansas. John Baldwin also presented a complicated profile. Originally from Illinois, he had lived in Missouri, a slave state, before settling in Kansas with several of his brothers and becoming a ferryman on the Kaw River. He harbored proslavery views and hostility toward "Yankees," making him "an object of tender affection" among fire-eaters.[4]

Robinson, it bears noting, did not consider Baldwin's occupancy of his land an act of Slave Power aggression. It was, in his view, first and foremost a land grab. A number of claimants in the Lawrence area "cared nothing for the slavery question," he observed, hastening to add that some "took advantage . . . of the pro-slavery sentiment" in their bid to profit on lands. William Cutler, author of a comprehensive early history of Kansas, was less equivocal in his assessment of the dispute between Robinson and Baldwin, noting, "The strife grew bitter, and although purely one of conflicting property rights . . . was represented, or misrepresented, to be a quarrel between the Pro-slavery men and Abolitionists." Cutler went too far in painting slavery out of the picture, but his viewpoint pushes back against a tendency to forget the importance of land to settlers in Kansas Territory. It would be more accurate to say that disputes over land were often just that. But in the powder keg that became Bleeding Kansas, claiming land was never a straightforward proposition. Land-taking would determine the course of the fight and, with it, the future of slavery in the United States. Jumping a claim belonging to somebody on the other side of the ideological divide had the power to light a fuse—and often did.[5]

That fuse, it so happened, stretched from the nation's capital, set in place by Democrats who mistook it for a lifeline.

A Perfect Humbug

One of the most thoroughgoing political animals the United States has ever produced, Stephen A. Douglas lived and breathed the elements of partisan existence, crafting policies to advance the fortunes of his cherished Democratic Party, along with his own dreams of power and wealth. Chairman of the Senate Committee on Territories, he was in the perfect spot for a man of his vaulting ambition, helping to steer national growth at a time when the United States took colossal strides across the continent. Looking westward, Douglas delighted in new territories and states he had helped establish: Wisconsin, Iowa, Oregon, California, Utah, and New Mexico, among them. Yet marring the vista was an ungainly gap in the region known as Nebraska—a large chunk of the Louisiana Purchase stretching from present-day Kansas through North Dakota—awaiting a territorial structure. This unorganized, undeveloped domain hindered the work of connecting the far West with the rest of country via railroads and telegraph lines. Douglas's own net worth—particularly his real estate holdings in Chicago—stood to benefit from a railroad to the Pacific.[6]

Organizing a territorial government for Nebraska—something Douglas had been trying to accomplish for years—promised personal and political rewards. As recently as 1853 his bill to create Nebraska Territory had died, mainly because southerners saw it as a threat. Not only would the proposed territory almost certainly become a region of non-slave states, but it also would pave the way for a transcontinental railroad route that would veer away from the South. His goal unrealized, Douglas looked for ways to make a Nebraska bill more attractive to his southern colleagues. In consultation with proslavery fire-eaters such as David R. Atchison of Missouri, he worked on a re-tooled bill and introduced it into the Senate in January 1854. The bill came to be known as the "Kansas-Nebraska Act" because it proposed creating not one but two territories. By every expectation, Nebraska, which extended from the present-day state of that name through the Dakotas, would become free. But Kansas, abutting the slave state of Missouri, might well become slave territory if the people who migrated there had any say. There was, of course, a major impediment: the Missouri Compromise, which barred slavery north of the 36°30' line of latitude. Douglas's bill dispensed with this difficulty by nixing the Compromise—a move he, Atchison, and others strong-armed President Franklin Pierce into endorsing during an unannounced Sunday visit to the White House. The bill they crafted left it to settlers to decide the slavery question for themselves—"as their constitution may prescribe at the time of their admission" into the Union as a state. This formulation reflected a vision of popular sovereignty that proslavery expansionists could get behind since the decision would come at the end of the territorial phase, by which time slaveholders would have had ample opportunity to establish themselves.[7]

If Douglas had shown himself willing to defy proslavery partisans over Oregon and California, he synchronized with them on Kansas. In important ways, the Kansas-Nebraska Act fit in the traditional Squatter Democracy mold by contemplating a course of settler-driven growth with potential spoils for northerners and southerners alike. During heated debates, Douglas offered conventional expansionist arguments to justify his legislation, communicating a sense of inevitability in the growth of the United States. "You cannot fetter the limbs of the young giant," he warned. "He will burst all your chains. He will expand, and grow, and increase, and extend civilization, christianity, and liberal principles." This was the language of Manifest Destiny re-worked around the image of a freedom-loving colossus rumbling across North America. In addition to nationalistic appeals, Douglas framed the debate over the Kansas-Nebraska bill as a referendum on popular sovereignty and majoritarian democracy, underscoring "the great, sacred, fundamental right" of the people to determine their own institutions. "Nothing can be plainer than the honesty of the simple position, that every community has a right to legislate for itself," he declared. Despite Douglas's attempts to win over colleagues on nationalistic grounds, the bill landed in Congress like a bomb.[8]

Shell-shocked lawmakers struggled to make sense of a measure that, in the words of one Democrat, "spit upon . . . the sacred acts and pledges of our fathers." After all, the Missouri Compromise had helped to keep the peace for more than three decades. Ohio congressman Salmon P. Chase and allies published a widely circulated tract—"Appeal of the Independent Democrats"—that envisioned a potent new alliance between antislavery Democrats, northern Whigs, and Free Soilers who would "erect anew the standard of freedom" and rescue the country from slavery's grip. "We will not despair," they pronounced, "for the cause of human freedom is the cause of God." But Douglas himself did not despair nor flinch, responding to critics: "I accept your challenge; raise your black flag; call up your forces; preach your war on the Constitution, as you have threatened it here. We will be ready to meet all your allied forces." The war of words presaged bloody battles to come.[9]

Blowback from the law compounded sectional rifts within both Democratic and Whig ranks. Slavery advocates generally embraced the bill despite unease that popular sovereignty left open the possibility that squatters could abolish slavery if they so chose. Democratic leaders, meanwhile, made support of the bill a litmus test of loyalty, alienating many in the North. To be a Democrat, lamented Maine congressman Samuel Mayall, meant a man "must go into all manner of popular vice and political delusion; he must go for breaking down the compromises of the Constitution; he must go for propagating the institution of slavery over our fair Republic, . . . [and] for 'non-intervention and squatter sovereignty'; because we are told on this floor that it is in keeping with Democratic principles." Mayall affirmed his love for genuine yeomen but could not tolerate what he viewed as faux squatter sovereignty, which he deemed a front for slavemasters. "I never will prove recreant to the brawny arm and hard fisted yeomanry," he vowed, in language reminiscent of David Wilmot's. "Never, by any act or vote of mine, shall free labor be reduced to the level of slave labor. I want this Territory for free labor and free men." The bill was sold on false pretenses, Mayall alleged. "A perfect humbug is squatter sovereignty; there is no such thing in the bill. Popular subjection and control are its leading characteristics." Far from leaving settlers free to decide for themselves, it would saddle them with a territorial government directed by doughfaces in Washington.[10]

Words like these from a fellow Democrat no doubt displeased Douglas and other backers of the bill. But Mayall was an obscure first-term congressman from Maine. When similar arguments came from Thomas Hart Benton, it was time to worry. In 1854, Benton was a member of the House of Representatives. He had lost his Senate seat in 1851 after serving in that body for five terms, largely because he had become a forceful voice in asserting Congress's responsibility to halt the spread of slavery in western territories. He had maintained strong support among non-slaveholding farmers but encountered fierce opposition from proslavery Missourians. His prominent role in 1850 Compromise debates, including his arguments on behalf of California statehood, ultimately cost him the seat he had held for thirty years. Undaunted, he was able to resume his principled stand from the House. Benton was all for opening Kansas to settlement, just not under the terms of the Kansas-Nebraska bill, which voided the Missouri Compromise. "I have stood upon the Missouri Compromise for above thirty years; and mean to stand upon it to the end of my life," he vowed.[11]

Benton viewed Douglas's bill as a betrayal of policies dating back to the founding of the republic to contain slavery, including the Northwest Ordinance of 1787. "Oh, squatter sovereignty! [W]here were you then?" he mocked. "The illustrious principle of non-intervention had not then been invented. The ignoramuses of that day had never heard of it." The Constitution and precedent all made plain that Congress had the power to legislate on slavery in the territories, he argued. Benton underscored the shallowness of the sovereignty afforded by the Kansas-Nebraska bill by pointing out that on all questions other than slavery it left Congress to its customary role of territorial administration. Even the purported sovereignty to decide on slavery was dubious given the outright denial by fire-eaters that the institution could be banned by anyone. Benton was all for squatters, but not this "burlesque upon sovereignty." Making a unionist appeal, he declared that the issues at stake transcended geographical sections, calling himself "a southern man" who voted "nationally on national questions." All told, the Kansas-Nebraska bill represented "a bungling attempt to smuggle slavery into the Territory, and all the country out to the Canada line and up the Rocky Mountains." He was not willing to cave to Slave Power pressure even if it cost him politically.[12]

Benton's pushback was a defining moment for Squatter Democracy. He had been the intellectual architect of pro-squatter expansion since his arrival in the Senate in 1821, lending this blend of politics genuine heft. Typically racist, he was an enslaver and staunch proponent of Indian removal. What separated him from his Squatter Democrat peers, however, was a bracing degree of frankness. As he grew in years and experience he had little use for the dissembling style of his close colleagues who tied themselves in knots trying to appease North and South. He was not willing to twist the Constitution to say what it did not, or breezily discard hard-won compromises, or abdicate the responsibilities incumbent on Congress as a co-equal branch of the government. He was not afraid to tell hard truths. His outspokenness against the Kansas-Nebraska bill further damaged his political fortunes, turning him into a one-term congressman.

If Benton's attacks on the Kansas-Nebraska bill raised doubts about whether Squatter Democracy still abided, Lewis Cass put them to rest. A progenitor of popular sovereignty and another Jacksonian heavyweight, he took it upon himself to revive the old pro-squatter creed. Defending "squatter sovereignty" from Benton's fusillades, the Michigan senator proclaimed,

It is up-hill work, Mr. President, in this country, for any man, however splendid his talents or commanding his position, to contend
against this doctrine. It landed with our fathers upon the beach of
Jamestown and the Rock of Plymouth, and has been treasured in their
hearts through all their trials and difficulties, to this, the great day of
its glorious consummation. It has accompanied the pioneers through
the passes of the Rocky Mountains, and has planted itself, with the
beloved flag of our country, upon the very shores that look out upon
China and Japan. "Oh, squatter sovereignty! [W]here were you then?"
emphatically asks its great opponent, alluding to territorial history.
I was then—may then be answered to this invocation—I was then in
the Declaration of Independence, and I am now, as ever, in the hearts
of the American people, and am firmly established in the tables of
their law.

Cass set squatter sovereignty as the essence of American liberty and celebrated the "pioneers" who carried it forward. The speech harkened back to
the days when the mere invocation of squatters electrified partisans. However,
in resurrecting these bromides in the service of the Kansas-Nebraska Act,
Cass treaded dangerously close to what critics like Benton deemed doughface
territory. It was a clear sign that Squatter Democracy had lost its cohesive
force when Jacksonian giants from the West like Benton and Cass clashed
over squatter-driven expansion.[13]

Democrats could take some solace in the fact that the Whigs were fracturing even worse than they along a north-south axis as a result of the Kansas-
Nebraska bill. The majority of southern Whigs backed the measure, many
migrating into a Democratic Party increasingly under the sway of proslavery
men. Northern Whigs, like numerous northern Democrats, blasted it. Out of
the crucible of partisan strife emerged, as Chase foresaw, an Anti-Nebraska
organization that would morph into the next great force in American politics: the Republican Party.[14]

Douglas doggedly stuck to what he considered the middle path of popular sovereignty—the only viable route to save his splintering party and advance his own interests. He weathered the maelstrom whipped up by his bill
and even grew accustomed to seeing his likeness burned in effigy. In the short
term, he found vindication when the Kansas-Nebraska bill handily cleared the
Senate 37–14 in March and the House 113–100 in May. Both chambers had
Democratic majorities and the results had pronounced sectional dimensions.
Senators from slave states supported the bill 23–2, while non-slave-state

senators split 14–12. The House roll call revealed similar dynamics, with an overwhelming majority of southerners voting for it and northern Democrats splitting almost down the middle, revealing a major breach in the party's northern wing. President Franklin Pierce's signature on May 30 merely drove the stake into a badly divided a party.[15]

The Kansas-Nebraska Act represented a moment of truth for popular sovereignty, taking it from the abstract realm of political theory and testing it on America's plains. In the aftermath of the settlement of Oregon and California, proslavery and antislavery factions alike comprehended the reality of squatter settlement of the slavery question and began preparing accordingly. Even before final passage, the focus had started to shift from the Capitol to the grasslands of Kansas, which many foresaw as the site of a coming ground war. Addressing himself to the "gentlemen of the slave States," Whig Senator William H. Seward of New York declared, "Since there is no escaping your challenge, I accept it in behalf of the cause of freedom. We will engage in competition for the virgin soil of Kansas, and God give the victory to the side which is stronger in numbers as it is in right." Proslavery politicians and editors answered in kind with urgent appeals to would-be emigrants to Kansas. "Citizens of the West, of the South, and Illinois! stake out your claims," enjoined a Missouri newspaper, "and woe be to the abolitionist . . . who shall intrude upon it, or come within reach of your long and true rifles, or within *point-blank shot of your revolvers.*" British journalist Thomas H. Gladstone framed the stakes succinctly. "Kansas," he wrote, "is made the battle-ground of a great principle. 'Squatter sovereignty' . . . must there work itself out."[16]

Squatters Love a Vacuum

When the Kansas-Nebraska Act passed in May 1854, there were fewer than 1,000 white people residing in Kansas. The territory was home to numerous Indian tribes; some were of long standing, such as the Kansas, Kickapoos, and Osages, while others, like the Potawatomis, Sacs, and Foxes had arrived under the squeeze of Jacksonian removal policies. The act opened the sluices of white settlement, with further inducement coming in the form of a pre-emption provision passed in July 1854. "Kansas fever" swept the nation as Americans caught wind of the region's extraordinarily rich prairie lands. By summer, the number of white settlers had become a "chaotic flood," estimated between 5,000 and 10,000.[17]

Even as the population surged, the federal government lagged behind. Public land surveys did not commence until late 1855, no land offices opened until 1856, and the federal government had yet to clear the title to Native American lands. Misinformation and confusion complicated the settlement of Kansas and contributed to the chaos there. Where were the boundaries of the Indian reservations? Could white emigrants settle on those lands? Even the status of preemption remained uncertain. "I see it rumored in the papers that we will have no preemption right of claims," one settler wrote to John Calhoun, surveyor general of Kansas and Nebraska. "If this turn out to be so it may have quite a serious damper upon the Emigration to these [Territories]. . . . [W]e are at a loss to know the truth of the matter. Can you give us any information on this point?"[18]

Amid the uncertainty and lagging federal presence, settlers filled the void with time-honored frontier institutions. The Squatter Association of the Whitehead District was one of the first such organizations in the territory. On June 24, 1854, less than a month after the Kansas-Nebraska Act passed, the group held "a large and enthusiastic" inaugural meeting in the newly founded town of Whitehead on a bend of the Missouri River in Doniphan County. These squatters chose their site wisely. When US surveyors ran their lines sometime later they found well-timbered bottomland veined with rivers and creeks and deemed much of it "first rate" for agriculture. The area encompassed Kickapoo, Iowa, Sac, and Fox Indian reservations, the boundaries of which were a source of confusion and contention.[19]

Most of the Whitehead association's forty-four original members were Missourians who, according to the founding charter, had become "citizens of Kansas Territory, intending to fix our homes upon its fertile soil." In an effort to "secure safety, certainty and fairness in the location and preservation of claims," the Whitehead squatters passed more than a dozen resolutions at their inaugural meeting, mainly dealing with protocols of settlement. Members could claim a maximum of 160 acres and had to clearly demarcate their boundaries and commence construction of a cabin or pitch a tent within thirty days. "Any person building his cabin or tent within less than half a mile of another, shall be deemed an intruder," subject to forcible expulsion, one resolution warned. A squatter association was, above all, an agency of mutual defense. Accordingly, members created a Vigilance Committee to enforce rules and adjudicate disputes. This committee functioned both as a court and the strong arm of the law. When, for example, a man named George Jameson took possession of land claimed by William K. Richardson, an officer of the association, and refused to cede the spot, the committee summoned the requisite muscle to evict him. In general, though, members submitted to the committee's rulings like "philosophers."[20]

In the absence of federal surveys, describing claims as accurately as possible was critical since settlers would ultimately have to prove occupancy and improvement to secure a preemption right from the US government. With no district land office operating in Kansas until much later, squatters in Whitehead and elsewhere mimicked functions of the General Land Office, including creating the post of register to keep track of "the name and description of all Squatters and their claims." While such mechanisms brought a modicum of order, they were merely stopgaps and no substitute for the stamp of officialdom that could come only from the United States and its land officers. Accordingly, in December 1854, James R. Whitehead, founder and namesake of the association, wrote to Surveyor General Calhoun, noting the anxiety of settlers for the official surveys to commence so they could have their boundaries confirmed before spring planting time. "There would be much good resulting from an early knowledge of our true lines, men would go to work with more energy and without a fear of having one half of their improvements wrested from them by an insidious neighbor," Whitehead suggested. "Many claim difficultys [*sic*] now of a serious nature would be settled, and many more that would occur will be prevented." However, surveys would not formally commence for months—an abiding source of frustration for restive settlers across Kansas.²¹

The rules and structures of the Whitehead Squatters Association by and large mirrored those of similar organizations in other places and times across the American frontier. But resolutions adopted at their first meeting and enshrined in their founding charter suggested their group was a new breed of claim club, specifically adapted to Kansas and the role in which squatters there had been cast. In the first resolution, they proclaimed themselves "in favor of bona fide Squatter Sovereignty," acknowledging "the right of any citizen of the United States to make a claim in Kansas Territory, with the ultimate view of occupying it." However, the Whitehead group made clear it did not mean just anyone. The tenth resolution drove home their affinities: "We will afford protection to no abolitionist as settler of Kansas Territory." The eleventh and final resolution, meanwhile, made plain where the organization stood on the burning question of the day: "We recognize the institution of Slavery as already existing in this Territory, and recommend to Slaveholders to introduce their property as early as practicable." These provisions underscore their recognition that securing a foothold for the South's peculiar institution required a critical mass of slaveholding settlers. The Whitehead association's slavery-related clauses were an innovation in squatter practice, revealing that in Kansas, settling the land and determining slavery's fate were two sides of the same coin.²²

Whitehead squatters were not alone in their proslavery sympathies. Their counterparts in Salt Creek Valley, near Leavenworth, banded together even earlier, forming an association with anti-abolitionist provisions. Other proslavery squatter associations moved farther west, including one in Tecumseh, setting the stage for conflicts with free-soil squatters.[23]

Antislavery forces, meanwhile, were making preparations of their own. Months before any squatter associations had formed in the proslavery districts of Kansas, the founders of what would become the territory's most effective antislavery organization sprang into action some 1,500 miles away in New England. When it became clear that the odious Kansas-Nebraska bill would pass and that settlers would determine slavery's outcome, opponents of the measure steeled themselves for battle. Eli Thayer, a Worcester schoolmaster, conceived of a plan to facilitate settlement by northern families in a bid to keep Kansas free. He barnstormed the region to drum up support for what would become the New England Emigrant Aid Company, winning backing from Boston philanthropist Amos Lawrence and from Charles Francis Adams, the 1848 Free Soil vice-presidential candidate and son of John Quincy Adams.

In classic New England fashion, the Emigrant Aid Company wedded humanitarian impulses with prospective financial rewards. While supported by philanthropists intent on ending the scourge of slavery, it was also a corporation whose investors sought monetary returns. The model called for purchasing land, assisting emigrants' moves to the territory, and selling them the property the company had acquired. If successful, it would foster a population of settlers whose modes of agriculture, ideological predispositions, and numerical supremacy would make Kansas a free state, while also reaping dividends for investors.[24]

Even the most carefully constructed plan would go nowhere without the right man to implement it on the ground. To that end, a fortuitous event occurred. Charles Robinson, having taken a bullet as the leader of Sacramento's Squatter Riot, founded the *Settlers and Miners Tribune*, and briefly served in the California legislature, returned east in 1851 after authorities dropped the murder charges against him. Back home in Massachusetts, he married his beloved Sara Tappan Doolittle Lawrence. Perhaps he briefly envisioned an existence as a small-town doctor. But the Kansas-Nebraska Act pricked his conscience.

Robinson had heard murmurings about this fellow Thayer, who was traversing the Northeast to win backing for his campaign for a free Kansas. He felt sufficient interest to investigate the man for himself. As he described in his memoir: "At length, to satisfy himself fully, to see of what material this man (Thayer) was made, whether he was a mere agitator, or a man who had convictions for which he would risk his life if necessary, the squatter attended one of his Boston meetings." Sitting in the back of the meeting hall as Thayer laid out his vision for Kansas, "the squatter"—a label Robinson proudly bestowed upon himself—was moved. "No man could listen to him without partaking of his spirit, neither could any person, after listening, entertain any doubts of the feasibility of his plan, or of his ability to put it in successful operation," he observed. The admiration evidently was mutual. Not long after this initial encounter, the trustees of the Emigrant Aid Company summoned Robinson to Boston to discuss the enterprise.[25]

With his firsthand knowledge of the West and its cutthroat modes of land-claiming, Robinson had useful information to impart. He also had some familiarity with Kansas, having passed through the region on his overland journey to California in 1849. A diary entry from May 11 of that year shows it made a vivid impression. "The feelings that come over a person, as he first views this immense ocean of land, are indescribable. As far as the eye can reach, he sees nothing but a beautiful green carpet, save here and there perhaps a cluster of trees; he hears nothing but the feathered songsters of the air, and *feels* nothing but a solemn awe in view of this infinite display of creative power." Thayer, of course, was not looking for a mystical poet but a flinty squatter. The battle-hardened Robinson was the right man to help the Emigrant Aid Company find its footing in Kansas.[26]

If his Sacramento experiences had taught him anything it was the old maxim that "possession is nine-tenths of the law." Accordingly, Robinson's most pressing concern was establishing a suitable beachhead for the New Englanders. He favored a memorable landmark on the old California Road that he recalled from his cross-country travels five years earlier—the high ridge or "backbone" dividing the valleys of the Kansas and Wakarusa rivers. That ridge, later named Mount Oread in honor of Thayer's academy for young women, loomed over an expanse of rich prairie, studded here and there with oak, walnut, hickory, hackberry, and elm. Besides the good soil and timber, the site had the advantage of being "situated on the south side of the Kansas River . . . navigable for steamboats." The Emigrant Aid Company bought out the lone settler living on their prospective town site, paying him $500 and converting his cabin into a store. The first party of New Englanders arrived in the summer of 1854 and named their new home for their patron Amos Lawrence. A second group followed a month later, traveling from the Missouri border in ox-drawn wagons packed with trunks, Dutch ovens, kettles, pans, coffee pots, sacks of flour and sugar, dried apples, hams, and other essentials, including trusty firearms, for they "had read in the papers of the threats to shoot all the Yankees that attempted to go . . . into the new Territory." With the fresh arrivals, Lawrence was on its way to becoming the heart of the free-state movement.[27]

By the end of September Robinson and fellow squatters had founded the Lawrence Town Association, which set the rules for claiming and purchasing land and adjudicating conflicting claims. One of its first orders of business was selecting a surveyor, who, within days, had platted the townsite and also run survey lines through the tall grass to mark off farm claims. With the surveys came land sales. The association held auctions in September, selling more than fifty parcels, some to Robinson in a personal capacity and as agent for the company. He ended up building his residence on top of Mount Oread, becoming king of the hill that had attracted his notice when he traveled to California in 1849.[28]

Lawrence developed rapidly with the establishment of a boarding house, a sawmill, and a variety of shops. By the start of 1855 the area's white population topped 7,000—making it the most populous in the territory. The majority of residents came from New England and the "Yankee" regions of the Midwest, but not all. Unlike the Whitehead Squatters Association, which excluded "abolitionists," the Lawrence Town Association did not pass resolutions barring proslavery settlers. Robinson was unambiguous on that point: "A pro-slavery man was entitled to all the rights, privileges, and immunities of the most favored Free-State man." Of course, it was widely assumed that the influx of New Englanders would settle the slavery question favorably—the underlying premise of the Emigrant Aid Company. But some of the first settlers were in fact proslavery and demanded a voice in local affairs. Missouri-born Achilles Wade, for example, was not shy about tweaking the "Estron (Eastern) folks" for their bossy ways. Wade seemed especially annoyed at restrictions on timber use. "By taking timber from all the western People thay call it onest (honest)," he wrote to Robinson, adding, "I sepose it onest as much a[s] Steling nigroes." The gibe had a clear implication: "Estron folks" were complicit in aiding fugitive slaves—and hoarding wood.[29]

The mixing of antagonistic populations engendered some creative accommodations in early territorial days devoid of formal governmental institutions. "Squatter courts"—established to rule on land disputes and other questions of law—were prime examples. The best known of these convened from time to time in the Lawrence area at a dry goods store west of town on the California Road. Its officers were a mix of free-state and proslavery men. The chief justice was John A. Wakefield, a "plain-spoken and thorough Free-soiler." William H. R. Lykins, a proslavery man, served as marshal. Juries comprised a mix of the two sides. "There were, perhaps, a dozen claim contests tried before such juries, a few by mutual agreement tried without juries," recalled Wakefield, adding that the court's decisions were "strictly enforced and quietly submitted to." Ultimately, though, the squatter courts had a limited reach. "As a rule," according to Robinson, "squatters settled their disputes in person, appealing to no higher authority than physical force or bluster."[30]

The face-off between Robinson and John Baldwin on the hillside outside Lawrence illustrates the point. Drawing on his Sacramento experiences, Robinson formed a military company of roughly fifty men and commenced a series of marching exercises, back and forth, as a show of martial discipline (though one of the marchers recalled a certain "greenness" to the proceedings). A recruit asked if, in the event the Missourians advanced, they should deliberately fire over their heads and Robinson reportedly replied that he "would be ashamed to fire at a man and not hit him." A deadly fracas appeared imminent. But then an unexpected thing happened. One of the men on Robinson's side sauntered over to the Missourians' camp, where he received the kind of welcome generally accorded to a friend. Evidently this man had infiltrated the New Englanders' ranks as a mole of sorts. He spoke a few words to Baldwin and gang, who, in a surprise move, picked up and left, but not without a final threat to raise a force of 30,000 men to vanquish the "Yankees." Similar scenes would play out across Kansas in the months ahead and not end so peacefully.[31]

Strategic land-claiming was an important feature in the struggle between free-state and proslavery men. Preemption, in particular, proved a handy, if often abused, tool. Studding the plains were rudimentary log structures marking preemption claims, yet a person could travel for miles and encounter only scant evidence of actual habitation. *New-York Tribune* editor Horace Greeley found this to be the case as late as 1859. One day he and a companion stood on a bluff near Atchison gazing at the beautiful prairie that stretched for miles. In that expanse, Greeley spotted a mere half dozen ramshackle dwellings and even those had little in the way of fences or crops. Yet, his friend informed him, all the land as far as the eye could see was preempted. "Preempted!" Greeley shouted. "The squatters who took possession of these lands must every one have committed gross perjury in obtaining preemption." One particularly impudent individual marked his or her claim with a birdhouse.[32]

Given their proximity, Missourians had a significant head start and asserted rights to a good deal of ground in Kansas, though many never actually settled there, infuriating emigrants from the North. Robinson charged proslavery partisans with fraudulently claiming territory for the sole purpose of ejecting "all Free-State men on a pretense of prior claims to the land." He drew parallels to his experiences in California, in which individuals possessing Spanish and Mexican land grants held title to vast domains: "It was the Sacramento game over again, with squatter's title instead of Sutter's deeds." Needless to say, he considered this an outrageous misuse of "squatter's title." "The truth seems to be that the slave interest demanded Kansas, and it was to be secured at all hazards, legally or illegally," he concluded. Proslavery men lobbed similar charges at the "Yankees," their generic name for settlers from the North.[33]

Land claims sparked conflicts between these northerners and the proslavery Missourians—branded "Border Ruffians"—deepening battle lines. Tensions flared in the winter of 1854 between the Topeka Town Company, whose members overwhelmingly supported a free state, and the nearby, proslavery Tecumseh Squatter Association. Cyrus K. Holliday found himself in the middle of the skirmishes. A twenty-eight-year-old Pennsylvania native, he had already had a brush with financial success as a railroad entrepreneur and would eventually become a railroad magnate in Kansas. What drew him there initially was land. Holliday arrived in Lawrence in October 1854, became associated with the Emigrant Aid Company, and proceeded west to scout out a suitable site for his own company town, accompanied by Robinson who was ever on the lookout for fresh terrains. Holliday co-founded the Topeka Town Company on December 5, 1854. A December 10 letter home to his wife Mary conveys the hardships of frontier life as well as a palpable sense of hope. "It is a long time since I have seen anything in the shape of a bed," he wrote. "I have a Buffalo Robe and two blankets in which I roll myself and lay down to rest upon the bare ground with boots, hat, overcoat and all on. Our food is mush, molasses and bacon, mixed plentifully with dirt three times each day. Thus we live in Kansas." Despite the gritty diet, his optimism shone through. "A more lovely country I certainly never saw." Two weeks later he wrote Mary again, reporting progress: "At Topeka I have a city interest and have taken a farm claim, both of which I hope to hold. But if I succeed in holding the claim it will be necessary for me to live upon it—hence I think I will put a house upon it, and we will live there when you come on to the Territory." Holliday made clear his intention to honor the golden rule of preemption: actually settling on the land he claimed.[34]

Holding claims in Kansas was easier said than done. On Saturday, January 6, 1855, Holliday recorded in his diary, "Today for the first time had to assume the sovereign powers of the squatter; and in common with a number of our men removed from one of our City claims a squatter who the day before had jumped the claim." The "sovereign powers of the squatter" for Holliday amounted to the right to possess land and defend it with force, if necessary, from all comers. Two days later he penned a diary entry describing how he and fellow Topeka men were set upon "by a committee of the Tecumseh Squatters association requesting us to leave one of our City claims. We reasoned the case with them and finally escaped lynching." On January 15 he wrote, "Today the first strong outbreak of squatter sovereignty occurred . . . in this section." Holliday withheld the details, noting only, "I hope I shall never be called upon to witness such a sight again." His diary entry for February 7 reads, "Last Wednesday some 16 or 18 of us went to Tecumseh in order to again administer *justice according to the law of the land.*" In Kansas, the law of the land came down to whatever it took for squatters to hold onto their claims.[35]

The clashes between rival factions were propaganda battles as well as turf wars, centering on what it meant to be a legitimate squatter. To "Yankees" like Holliday and Robinson, Missourians violated basic squatter codes. They had no interest in permanently settling in Kansas, these critics alleged, but merely made a show of "proving up" claims—typically by stacking a few logs to give the impression that a cabin was under construction. The charade had dual aims: financial and political. First, like speculators everywhere, they wanted to amass valuable property to eventually sell. But they also sought to claim residency in order to secure voting rights and influence the course of events in Kansas. As Thomas H. Gladstone, a correspondent for the *London Times*, observed, "Many affirmed their right to a vote in the territory, although they only threw down an axe upon the ground."[36]

The New Englanders had a knack for caricaturing the Border Ruffians as ignorant, whiskey-crazed louts. This was precisely how writer Mary A. Humphrey portrayed such men decades later in her novel, *The Squatter Sovereign.* In it a southerner, whose great passions in life are booze and chewing tobacco—"licker" and "baccy"—jumps the claim of an Ohioan who is away. A member of the absent man's squatter association confronts the intruder, prompting the latter to shoot back, "Stranger, thar's some folks as kin take oaths as well as others, an' thar's a thousan' or more of us boys swore by the Eternal, to drive every last dog-goned Aberlition sneak outen this hyer Territory, an' we mean to do it too." Such threats buzzed back and forth like hornets. But, as Charles Robinson himself explained, "The Free-State men were in no mood to be driven off."[37]

Missourians were equally inclined to caricature the New Englanders and question the legitimacy of their presence in Kansas. The Lawrence men were "tyrants," "mercenaries," and ruthless "speculators" all too ready to trample on anyone who stood in the way of their unholy pursuit of gain. Worse, they were "abolitionists" intent on subverting the rights of slaveholders. It mattered little that few of the emigrants from the North identified as abolitionists—a term that, for many, connoted extremism. Most were farmers, mechanics, and the like seeking fresh opportunities. They opposed slavery in Kansas and believed that the growing presence of people like themselves would ultimately yield a free state. To slavery advocates, however, they were "invaders." At a proslavery squatter gathering on January 11, 1855, a speaker blasted the "stock-jobbers and money-getters" of the Lawrence Town Association, portraying them as "men of exchanges . . . covered from head to foot with the leprosy of materialism, until it shall submerge all opposition, by secret and unjust invasions." They passed a resolution specifically aimed at Charles Robinson, should he be rash enough to rally his "shot-gun battalion" and deprive slaveholders of their rights. "We, the Sovereign Squatters of Kansas Territory," they vowed, "will take his Honor and battalion, and deal with them according to law, rules, and regulations . . . that we may adopt." Proslavery and the free-state factions alike painted their foes as lawless imposters, unworthy of the squatter name.[38]

Squatter Versus Squatter

The squatter propaganda wars intensified in early 1855 when a weekly broadsheet, the *Squatter Sovereign*, rolled off the presses in the bustling riverfront town of Atchison, on the Missouri border. The proslavery Atchison Town Company had seeded the publication with a $400 donation. Its publisher and editor, a young doctor from Virginia named John H. Stringfellow, was passionately proslavery. In fact, he took pride in being among the handful of slaveholders who brought their human property into the contested territory.[39]

The *Squatter Sovereign* claimed the squatter for the slaveholding South. Stringfellow and his co-editor Robert S. Kelley styled themselves and their readers as the genuine squatters of Kansas and advanced a particular interpretation of sovereignty favorable to slaveholder interests. The paper's masthead announced: "*The Squatter claims the same Sovereignty in the Territories that he possessed in the States.*" This succinct formulation communicated a states' rights understanding of sovereignty whereby "the people" as citizens of the equal, independent states of the Union constituted the supreme authority of government. Accordingly, any policy that abridged "property" or other rights of a citizen of any state moving into a US territory was unconstitutional.

The editors articulated their guiding philosophies and political affinities in the inaugural edition on February 3, 1855:

> The political complexion of our paper will be Democratic, but as our name imports, will more especially be devoted to the advocacy of such measures, as will in our opinion conduce to the best interests of the "Squatter." Fully recognizing the truth of the great principle adopted in the Kansas-Nebraska Bill, popularly denominated "Squatter Sovereignty"—the right of the people to legislate for themselves, in all matters of a local character, in which their interests alone are involved, we shall repel all attempts on the part of others to interfere in the domestic affairs of our Territory—whether those attempts be made in Congress, or elsewhere. On the great question to be decided, on the formation of our State Constitution, we declare in advance, that we are in favor of the institution of negro slavery, and our effort will be to introduce its recognition in that instrument.[40]

Democratic, pro-squatter, and proslavery—this was a novel amalgamation of interests and bold reframing of squatter politics by enslavers. The squatter as imagined by the *Sovereign* was a slavemaster himself or at least entirely amenable to slavemaster concerns. Others had found compatibility between squatting and slaveholding—the speeches of iconoclastic southern Democrats like Albert G. Brown, for example, and literary depictions by Charles Sealsfield and John S. Robb. The leading pro-squatter Democrats had themselves always reserved a place for slaveholders. Yet politicians like Walker, Douglas, Cass, and Polk generally strived to balance sectional interests and toe a neutral line. The *Squatter Sovereign* tossed all such caution out the window. Turning the usual southern critique of squatters as usurpers of slaveholders' rights on its head, they co-opted squatters as foot soldiers for slavery's expansion. True squatters, they argued, were white, male defenders of slavery—in other words, people just like them. Having remade the squatter in their own image, Stringfellow and colleagues felt comfortable backing the doctrine of squatter sovereignty. Indeed, by naming their sheet the *Squatter Sovereign* they presumed to embody the archetypal squatter and wield to the hilt the sovereign authority vested in him. Left in their hands the decision about slavery would produce only one outcome: a slave state. This was a squatter incarnation that even John C. Calhoun would have adored.[41]

The *Squatter Sovereign* became the leading fire-eating organ in Kansas, sounding the same notes over and over: slavery was biblically sanctioned and benevolent; abolitionists were evil; the New England Emigrant Aid Company was a collection of venal Yankee cowards. Other proslavery editors began to take notice of the verbal cannonades thundering out of Atchison, commenting with appreciation that the *Squatter Sovereign* "advocates with power and ability the pro-slavery and true squatter rights, in Kansas." Here again was a novel formulation—"the pro-slavery and true squatter rights"— unthinkable in the early days of Jacksonian Squatter Democracy. Among those rights, the paper made clear, was a swift return of runaway slaves.[42]

Because legal voting required residency, land-claiming and political power went hand in hand. Stringfellow understood clearly that if slavery was to triumph it would happen because proslavery men gained possession of the earth. Accordingly, the *Squatter Sovereign* devoted much of its energy to mobilizing voters with the overriding goal of making Kansas a slave state, commanding readers to turn out "in support of 'Squatter Sovereignty,' and Southern Rights." "We very much mistake the character of the Squatter, if they will permit any *selfish* motives to govern their votes," the editors cajoled.[43]

As he rallied proslavery squatters, Stringfellow conceived another strategy to amass power: harass federal officials sent from Washington and cow them into submission. Andrew Reeder, the Pennsylvanian tapped by Franklin Pierce to be territorial governor, had an especially large target on his back. The firebrand editor and associates spewed endless venom at him for an alleged antislavery bias, dubbing Reeder the "President of the 'Underground Railroad' in Kansas Territory." The enmity of southern men was not lost on the governor, who reported to Stephen A. Douglas that his antagonists "pursue a policy of unrelenting unscrupulous denunciation and bitter abuse against every man who is not an open proslavery partisan. . . . They recognize no medium between a pro Slavery man and a 'nigger thief.' "[44]

The March 1855 elections for territorial legislature would be a crucial first test of the strength of both sides and set the tenor of territorial governance. Goaded by Stringfellow, David Atchison, and other influential fire-eaters, thousands of Border Ruffians—many allegedly toting pistols and bowie knives—flooded in from Missouri for the March 30 vote. In total, more than 6,000 ballots were cast, despite there being only 2,905 registered voters in Kansas. Stringfellow's "squatter sovereigns" had rallied to the cause beyond his wildest dreams. Almost every district was won by a proslavery candidate, including the editor himself, who would soon ascend to the post of speaker of the territorial House.[45]

The fraudulent election hit free staters like a punch in the gut. Dismayed and determined to strike back, Charles Robinson wrote to Massachusetts-based Unitarian minister Edward Everett Hale, a prominent backer of the Emigrant Aid Company, decrying the turn of events. "Can such outrageous conduct from Missourians be longer tolerated?" Appealing to the minister's militant side, he let drop that "our people are forming military companies & are determined to protect their rights even should it set the Union in a blaze. We want 200 of Sharp's rifles & two cannon for Lawrence people." Even with a new cache of arms, things continued to go downhill for the free-state side. The attacks on Governor Reeder rattled Franklin Pierce, who replaced him, in August 1855, with the openly proslavery Wilson Shannon, a former congressman and Ohio governor. Robinson and associates had had enough. Denouncing the "bogus governor" and the "bogus legislature," they recognized it was time to organize in earnest.[46]

Having dismissed the elections and constituted authorities as shams, anti-slavery partisans prepared the ground for their own stand-alone government, electing delegates to a forthcoming convention "to form a constitution, adopt a bill of rights for the people of Kansas, and take all needful measures ... preparatory to the admission of Kansas into the Union as a State." During the fall 1855 convention in Topeka, delegates led by James Lane, a Mexican War veteran and former US congressman from Indiana, drafted a constitution prohibiting slavery. Like Oregonians a decade earlier, they would later approve a ban on black settlement in the territory, thus adopting a white-supremacist, free-soil posture. Robinson opposed this policy but was in the minority. Still, he and his free-state compatriots could boast that they were on track to vindicate squatter sovereignty for white male Kansans.[47]

Robinson had come a long way from his California days. In Sacramento he had headed a squatter movement crusading against powerful land barons and speculators. Squatterism meant breaking up large land syndicates and enabling landless emigrants to acquire a freehold. Back then, he had an affinity for free soilism, but the terms of the fight dictated only cursory engagement with that position. Land really was the thing. Events in Kansas forced him to take a more expansive view of the role of a squatter chief. While land-claiming was foundational to his movement, it was just the first step toward building a government that embodied the core values of its constituents, including their desire to live in a society free from slavery.

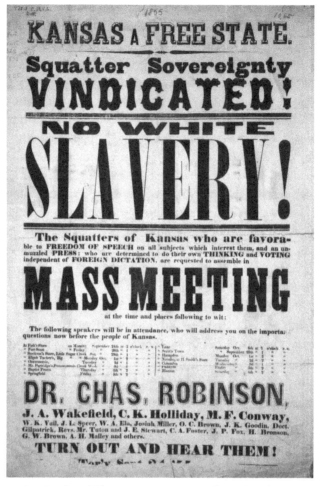

FIGURE 7.1 An 1855 broadside announces a series of meetings in support of a free Kansas. Courtesy of Kansas State Historical Society.

Democrats in Washington and their surrogates on the ground moved to derail the free-state movement and fortify their own party in Kansas. John Calhoun, handpicked by Stephen A. Douglas to be surveyor general of Kansas and Nebraska, convened a gathering in the proslavery town of Leavenworth in November 1855. Arguably the most influential man in the territory, Calhoun oversaw a small army of surveyors and other personnel tasked with the all-important, complicated job of running their lines across millions of acres—measuring and parceling them out for sale—and bringing order to the crush of settlement in an increasingly volatile part of the world. That role alone made him a key actor, but his close ties to Stephen Douglas turned him into a truly towering figure. Douglas trusted his old Illinois associate to be his eyes, ears, and voice, steering events in the direction he commanded, including making Kansas a Democratic stronghold.[48]

Calhoun warned the 300 men—a majority of them proslavery—convened at Leavenworth not to alienate moderate Democrats who supported a free state, lest they risk the worst outcome of all: handing the territory over to the "abolitionists." "I took the ground that it was decidedly more important to make Kansas a democratic state than a free or slave state," Calhoun reported to Douglas. He was pleased to say that the crowd concurred and resolved to unite under the banner of a Law and Order Party, an organization that John H. Stringfellow had helped organize, so named to underscore the purported lawlessness of antislavery men. "From this day you may count Kansas right," Calhoun assured his patron, predicting that the free-state rebellion would be "crushed . . . with an overwhelming force." The surveyor general expressed confidence that sensible farming folks—a party mainstay since the days of Jackson—would work their magic in Kansas, focusing on their families and fields rather than slavery and quietly winning the territory for Democrats. "There is not on earth a more democratic people than the Kansas settlers," he insisted.[49]

As it turned out, anything but "law and order" prevailed. On November 21, a proslavery man shot and killed Charles Dow, a young free-state supporter who was on his way home from a blacksmith shop outside of Lawrence. The assailant, Franklin Coleman, swore it was a land dispute that had sparked the violence, but Robinson and others were convinced it was a premeditated murder meant to intimidate free staters. Not surprisingly, the *Squatter Sovereign* offered an account sympathetic to Coleman, saying that the trouble began when "three Abolitionists, with Sharps rifles" turned up at his claim and ordered him to go. "He was allowed ten minutes to leave or he would be shot." According to the *Sovereign,* Coleman sped off as commanded, but soon returned "well armed" and shot Dow in self-defense. The paper applauded him for taking a stand, alleging that "Pro-Slavery citizens in the vicinity of Lawrence have been brow-beaten and insulted, their stock killed, houses burned, and lives threatened." So began the Wakarusa War—pitting free-state squatters against proslavery ones.[50]

Governor Shannon summoned militias to intimidate and suppress the free staters. Proslavery men responded to the call. Atchison, home of the *Squatter Sovereign*, and Tecumseh put together companies of soldiers. Leading the Atchison forces was none other than John H. Stringfellow. By early December, the *Sovereign* reported, "an army of about twelve hundred

men were ready and anxious to administer such rebuke to the offending party
as our executive might think proper." Free staters in and around Lawrence prepared for an invasion, erecting "fortifications & breastworks" for defense and
assembling their own military unit of several hundred men. Robinson served
as commander. Fronting their respective armies, Robinson and Stringfellow
appeared headed for an all-out "KANSAS WAR!" as the *Sovereign* put it
none too subtly.[51]

Having received alarming reports about hundreds of Missourians bearing
down on Lawrence, Robinson urged Governor Shannon to head off the
advancing militias. He also wired President Pierce, seeking federal intervention. In the meantime, he sent out calls closer to home, dispatching messengers
"to all parts of the Territory to call upon the squatter to come to our aid." On
December 6, Cyrus Holliday paused amid the heart-thumping mobilization
to pen a letter to his wife Mary from "Head Quarters" in Lawrence. "There
is now no kind of question but that there will be the biggest kind of a fight,"
he wrote. Thinking of their baby daughter, he asked his wife to "kiss Lillie for
me. I may never see you or her again; but if not remember I fall honorably as
I trust I have lived." The present state of affairs went far beyond the "outbreak
of squatter sovereignty" that Holliday had described in his diary accounts of
the turf battles between settlers in Topeka and Tecumseh earlier in the year.
This conflict was beginning to look like civil war.[52]

With low-grade skirmishes resulting in further casualties, Governor
Shannon agreed to sit at the negotiating table with Robinson and Lane at the
Free State Hotel. On December 8, they signed a draft of the Wakarusa Treaty,
and the conflict de-escalated.[53]

The sudden flare-up and cessation of violence gave urgent impulse to
the free staters to enact their vision of squatter sovereignty in Kansas. On
December 15, 1855, voters overwhelmingly approved the Topeka Constitution
drafted prior to the Wakarusa War. The newly formed Free State Party met
soon after to appoint officers, choosing Robinson for governor. More than an
idea, the Free State had the trappings of an actual government. It was, in effect, the preeminent white man's claim club. A mass of self-identified squatters
had voted to pass a constitution and establish a regime that answered to their
needs and reflected their values. Truly this was squatter sovereignty if ever
there was such a thing.[54]

To its officers and backers, the free-state movement was a pure expression
of popular will. To practically everyone else it was a dangerous delusion. The
Squatter Sovereign mocked the alternative universe playing out in Topeka and
Lawrence. "According to the dictum of Robinson, Lane & Co., we are now

citizens of the State of Kansas," the paper jeered, underscoring that many steps still lay ahead in the process of Kansas statehood and that national leaders in the White House and Congress viewed the Free State as insurrectionary. The *Sovereign's* rhetoric would grow even more inflammatory. "We are determined to repel this Northern invasion," declared one editorial, "though our rivers should be colored with the blood of the victims, and the carcasses of dead abolitionists should be so numerous in the Territory as to breed disease and sickness, we will not be deterred in our purpose."[55]

The advent of the Free State government coincided with another important development in Kansas politics: the organization of the Republican Party, which first formed in Wisconsin and Michigan in the wake of the Kansas-Nebraska Act to stop the spread of slavery. On January 12, 1856, promoters of the party met in Lawrence and approved a platform that recognized Congress's right to legislate on slavery in the territories and spurned "Squatter Sovereignty" as "the cardinal doctrine of the 'National Democracy!'" To Kansas Republicans the "National Democracy"—the party of Douglas, Cass, and Pierce—had entirely capitulated to the Slave Power and there was no difference between squatter sovereignty as practiced by firebrands like Stringfellow and the proslavery policies of the Pierce administration, which propped them up.[56]

The antislavery press took favorable notice of these auspicious developments. Reporting on the Republican meeting, the *Kansas Herald of Freedom* noted the attendance of the Free State governor, commenting that "Dr. Robinson made a masterly speech." It also found noteworthy the fact that it was James Lane who reported the new party's platform favoring federal intervention, given that, as a Democratic Indiana congressman, he had voted for the Kansas-Nebraska Act that denied Congress a role in setting slavery policy. Kansas, the *Herald* opined, seemed to be having a healthy effect on Lane, "who came here with the squatterophobia, of which he had been long and dangerously sick." Now he appeared "politically convalescent." The article concluded with an appeal to their core constituency: "Unfurl the new banner, squatters of Kansas, and inscribe thereon—NO MORE SLAVE STATES."[57]

Republican squatter advocacy was a product of its historical moment, having grown up in direct opposition to the Kansas-Nebraska Act and in tandem with the free-state movement in Kansas. Its key thrust was as much about keeping slavery out of Kansas and other western domains as it was about abetting land-claiming by yeomen. These were two wheels of the same cart, just as making Kansas a slave domain was intrinsic to the brand of squatterism adopted by Stringfellow and his allies.

Robinson and fellow Republicans remained convinced that Kansas's proslavery forces enjoyed unqualified support from Democrats in Washington, and the Pierce administration did little to dispel that perception. In a message on January 24, 1856, the president took aim at the "revolutionary" free-state movement, whose leaders "without law, have undertaken to summon a convention for the purpose of transforming the Territory into a State, and have framed a constitution, adopted it, and under it elected a governor and other officers and a Representative to Congress." Pierce warned that the movement veered close to a "treasonable insurrection" which he, as president, would be forced to suppress militarily. He noted that Kansas held immense promise for "the pursuit of happiness on the part of the settlers themselves" and expressed his determination to let them chart their own course by ensuring that the "great prerogative of popular sovereignty" be "sacredly respected." Kansas could be a veritable promised land if only the true squatter sovereigns—landtaking Democrats—were allowed to reign. An avid expansionist dubbed "Young Hickory of the Granite Hills" to underscore his Jacksonian bona fides (and New Hampshire roots), Pierce considered the preservation of the Union a high charge. But his strong southern sympathies blinded him to the fraud and iniquities that had spurred antislavery Kansans to action.[58]

The free staters continued to bedevil Pierce, who tended to grow surly when faced with his own haplessness. On February 11, he issued an even sterner admonition:

> I, Franklin Pierce, President of the United States, do issue this my proclamation to command all persons engaged in unlawful combinations against the constituted authority of the Territory of Kansas or of the United States to disperse and retire peaceably to their respective abodes, and to warn all such persons that any attempted insurrection in said Territory or aggressive intrusion into the same will be resisted not only by the employment of the local militia, but also by that of any available forces of the United States.[59]

Fulminating against "the fury of faction" and "fanaticism," the president allied himself with the forces of "law and order"—code in Kansas for slavery-friendly Democrats as evidenced by Calhoun's meeting in Leavenworth the previous November. As far as the free staters were concerned, his references to "unlawful combinations," "aggressive intrusion," and "fanaticism" would more aptly pertain to the Border Ruffians.

Like Pierce, Stephen A. Douglas saw the free-state movement as public enemy number one. In common with other party leaders, he refused to acknowledge the immorality of slavery and considered anyone who strongly opposed the institution a self-righteous troublemaker. Although he had confronted proslavery zealots in the past when they sought to subvert the will of local majorities, the Little Giant inveighed against Robinson and associates for raining on the popular sovereignty parade. Styling free-state partisans the puppets of northeastern abolitionists, he groused, "the whole responsibility of all the disturbances in Kansas rests upon the Massachusetts Emigrant Aid Company and its affiliated societies." While believing himself strictly neutral, Douglas was willing to avert his gaze from the anti-democratic thuggery of slavery supporters in Kansas.[60]

In defiance of national Democrats and proslavery Kansans, the free staters forged ahead in their parallel world. "Governor" Robinson delivered an inaugural address to the new legislature that convened on March 4, 1856. Showing his free-soil proclivities, he gave a ringing endorsement to a homestead law—a policy that the national Republican Party would also embrace (along with Douglas, though with increasing caution). For Robinson the energy and enterprise of the yeomen society he envisioned—which would thrive all the more with access to free land—stood in stark contrast to one marred by the "debasing character" of slavery. In a true squatter republic, responsive to the majority's will, there was no place for the South's abhorrent institution.[61]

Robinson assailed the perversion of squatter sovereignty by the dubiously elected territorial legislature, the administration of proslavery governor Shannon, and all the other "instrument(s) of oppression and tyranny" that tried to force free staters to genuflect before "the dark image of Slavery." To his mind these constituted the real sham alternate universe. The legislature was especially nefarious, chosen "by armed invaders from an adjoining state for the purpose of enacting laws in opposition to the Known wishes of the People." Drawing from resolutions approved at Topeka the previous year, Robinson charged that squatter sovereignty, as distorted by the Pierce administration, congressional leaders like Douglas, and local proslavery forces, was "a miserable delusion." If "Squatter Sovereignty means simply that Congress has no right to interfere with the affairs of a Territory but that the Executive and the People of another state have, then most certainly that doctrine will be very unpopular in Kansas," he proclaimed.[62]

Showing no signs of backing down, the Free State governor was emerging as a cause célèbre in the Republican Party. Benton's son-in-law John C. Frémont, on track to become the party's first presidential nominee, wrote Robinson from New York in March 1856, recollecting their time in California. "You have carried to another field the same principle with courage and ability to maintain it, and I make you my sincere congratulations, on your success—incomplete so far but destined in the end to triumph absolutely." He recalled that Robinson had supported him in his bid to represent California in the Senate, standing up to the proslavery "nullifiers" who worked to defeat him. "I have every disposition to stand by you in the same way in your battle with them in Kansas," he pledged.[63]

Republican senator Henry Wilson of Massachusetts compared Robinson to Miles Standish, the long-ago military leader in Plymouth Colony—a comparison that proved altogether too much for Stringfellow and the *Squatter Sovereign*, which endeavored to correct the record with a biographical sketch of Robinson during his California days.

> Mr. Charles Robinson—the Miles Standish of Kansas—was once a citizen of the State of California; and what was he there? He was the head and front, the leader of a band of desperadoes, as infamous as ever disgraced any age or country. He it was that organized a band in the city of Sacramento for the purpose of warring against the rights of property there. He it was who led that band in that ever memorable, ever to be execrated conflict, in which the peaceful Mayor of the city of Sacramento, and the sheriff, of that county, in attempting to execute the law, were shot down. He was arrested and put into prison, and while there elected to the legislature by these ruffians, these squatters, these men essaying to usurp the rights of property. He went to the legislature as the champion of that spurious . . . squatter sovereignty in California. . . . He left California, and the next time that Miles Standish, *alias* Mr. Governor Charles Robinson, makes his appearance on the stage, he is at his old game, leading desperadoes to the violation of the law and resistance to the legal authorities of the country.[64]

There's an irony to Stringfellow's using the pages of the *Squatter Sovereign* to condemn Robinson as a champion of squatter sovereignty, but for the editor it was a "spurious" form of that doctrine that attempted to "usurp the rights of property"—a point of unremitting sensitivity for slaveholders. The editor showed his hand that he himself was no squatter in the traditional land-taking sense.

The proslavery men and their backers in Washington attempted to root out the free-state movement through judicial maneuvers and outright force. In May a grand jury in Lecompton handed down indictments for treason against Robinson, Lane, and others. Robinson was detained on a steamboat in Missouri and brought to Fort Leavenworth "from whence he should only be taken to be hung," the *Squatter Sovereign* crowed. On May 21 proslavery militias launched an attack on Lawrence. Appeals by residents to Governor Shannon went unheeded. The Free State Hotel sustained massive damage from cannon fire. The marauders made their way to Robinson's house on Mount Oread. Sara Robinson was away but Charles's brother and two others were there and "had only time to take the horses and escape" before the house was torched. Some of Robinson's neighbors rushed onto the scene to extinguish the fire, but the attackers set the house ablaze again after dark. "Your clothes & everything else pertaining to you & myself were destroyed . . . except a few papers & letters & the carriage & harness," Charles Robinson reported to his wife. For his part, militia commander Stringfellow reportedly entered an abandoned shop and "carried off under each arm a box of cigars, having helped himself to them behind the counter, saying, as he did so, 'Well, boys, I guess this is as good plunder as I want.'"[65]

By this time Kansas had become a full-blown national crisis. The day before Lawrence fell, Senator Charles Sumner of Massachusetts delivered a blistering address on the "crime against Kansas," specifically mocking fellow lawmaker

FIGURE 7.2 Free-state partisans stand their ground in Kansas Territory, 1856. Courtesy of Kansas State Historical Society.

Andrew Butler for his devotion to slavery. "The Senator from South Carolina has read many books of chivalry, and believes himself a chivalrous knight, with sentiments of honor and courage," Sumner declared. "Of course he has chosen a mistress to whom he has made his vows, and who, though ugly to others, is always lovely to him; though polluted in the sight of the world, is chaste in his sight—I mean the harlot Slavery." Sumner's censure earned him a near-fatal caning on May 22 from South Carolina congressman Preston Brooks, a relative of Butler.[66]

Two days later, an Ohio native accompanied by several of his sons and other volunteers hacked to death with swords proslavery settlers at Pottawatomie Creek. The massacre by John Brown and his party made "Bleeding Kansas" a byword. From his captivity at Fort Leavenworth, Robinson expressed his gratitude to Brown. "I cheerfully accord to you my heartfelt thanks for your prompt, efficient and timely action against the invaders of our rights and the murderers of our citizens," he wrote. "History will give your name a proud place on her pages, and posterity will pay homage to your heroism in the cause of God and Humanity." Bracing himself for his own treason trial, the Free State governor wrote to his old Sacramento squatter associate James McClatchy, musing, "There is but a step from the sublime to the ridiculous, & but one from the Governor's office to the gallows, so it seems."[67]

Squatter politics left bloody footprints all over Kansas, conditioning how the territory was settled and governed. Attempting to claim the squatter mantle for their respective sides, Charles Robinson, John H. Stringfellow, and their constituents built on the rhetorical work of Democratic pro-squatterism but stood in very different relationships to that force. Chastened by the outcomes in Oregon and California, the proslavery men made an aggressive bid to personify the squatter as they swarmed in to claim land, vote, and define the territory's course, imbuing the symbol with qualities and meanings entirely favorable to slavery's fortunes. The free staters styled themselves as the legitimate squatters and executed an effective ground game of their own, claiming significant amounts of territory as the basis for a free-soil society. They rejected the form of sovereignty practiced by the Slave Power in Kansas and their Democratic abettors in Washington and instead created a government and society that reflected their antislavery, though racist, Republican values. Their splinter Free State government offered a vivid example of actual squatters asserting sovereignty.

Stephen A. Douglas and supporters had banked on the Kansas-Nebraska Act keeping the gravy train of Squatter Democracy rolling—enriching partisans and boosting their party's fortunes as white Americans, whether for or against slavery, took possession of the heartland. For years Democrats had mythologized squatters as the growing nation's backbone and empowered them to claim western terrains, all the while courting them as constituents.

The squatter figure was a workhorse that carried the Democratic Party to dominance and gave Manifest Destiny legs. Ultimately, though, it could not support all the contradictory elements loaded on it. The symbol turned deadly once Douglas and his allies armed opposing squatter factions with the authority to determine slavery's future, and then, rather than act as honest brokers and let the popular will prevail, appeared to stand with a proslavery side willing to cheat and pillage its way to victory.

In a last-ditch attempt to staunch the bleeding, party leaders turned to one of the original architects of Squatter Democracy to go and talk some sense into the squatters waging guerilla war on the plains of Kansas.

8

Squatterdom

ROBERT J. WALKER did not want to go to Kansas. The former treasury secretary made this abundantly clear throughout the fall and winter of 1856 as he rebuffed request after request from president-elect James Buchanan, his former colleague in James K. Polk's cabinet, to assume the post of Kansas governor and quell the agitation over slavery once and for all. He was thriving in 1856. He had a "large fine house" on I Street in Washington, DC, and pursued far-flung business opportunities, investing in sundry railroads and mines, and avidly speculating in lands in Louisiana, Wisconsin, and his old Mississippi stomping grounds. He had turned down Franklin Pierce's offer of the ambassadorship to China but remained a respected elder statesman in the Democratic Party.[1]

Though Walker and Buchanan had sparred in cabinet meetings, the two had remained allies in the years since, and Walker backed "Old Buck" in his presidential run, flattering him before the 1856 Democratic convention in Cincinnati that "you . . . really are the choice of the people." The presidential race posed a tricky challenge for Democrats. Pierce was deeply unpopular, mainly because of his ham-fisted handling of Kansas, yet the party had never dropped an incumbent president. Consensus over the need to dump Pierce had the effect of restoring some unity among Democrats, including turncoat Martin Van Buren, who rallied behind Buchanan. Walker assured the candidate, "As an American democrat, I feel intensely the importance of the present critical posture of affairs, & will do my duty in the coming canvass." He also saw fit to emphasize that, as for himself, "there is not steam power enough in the world, ever to drag me into another political office."[2]

The real drama of the 1856 Democratic convention had less to do with Pierce, whose star had faded, and more with the contest between Buchanan and Douglas. The courtly, cautious Buchanan had an impressive pedigree as a

Dangerous Ground. John Suval, Oxford University Press. © Oxford University Press 2022.
DOI: 10.1093/oso/9780197531426.003.0009

diplomat, senator, and secretary of state. When the controversy over slavery in the territories heated up post-Wilmot Proviso, he backed extending the Missouri Compromise's 36°30' line of latitude to the Pacific. More recently he had come around to popular sovereignty and, at Cincinnati, stole Douglas's thunder by expressing strong support for the doctrine as the way forward in Kansas. The party duly enshrined the principle in its platform, affirming "non-interference by Congress with slavery," as embodied in the Kansas-Nebraska Act, as being "the only sound and safe solution of the 'slavery question.'" Upon reading the platform, Douglas wired from Chicago that he would cede the nomination. "If agreeable to my friends I would much prefer exerting all my energies to elect a tried statesman on that platform to being the nominee myself," he averred, no doubt gritting his teeth.[3]

Walker kept his promise and campaigned energetically for Buchanan, preaching the gospel of popular sovereignty and national unity. He circulated one of his signature pamphlets—this one anointed the "Pittsburgh letter"— in which he argued that Republicans and their candidate John C. Frémont posed an existential threat to the Union because they were a sectional party, something the Founders had warned against. Besides that, they were far too eager to wield federal authority against slaveholding interests. Their platform asserted that it was Congress's "right and imperative duty" to ban slavery, an institution Republicans dismissed as a "relic of barbarism." Walker deployed racist tropes when he charged that the "Black Republicans" had "surrendered the American flag, and taken in exchange the African banner." He ended with a rallying cry: "Friends of the Union, come and unite with us. . . . Come in the name of our common country, now in the agony of an approaching convulsion!" His message was clear: nationalist Democrats, disposed to cede authority over slavery to the patriotic white squatters of the West, would save the country. Given the shocking state of affairs in Kansas, this was a dubious proposition, but it was perhaps the only path forward as a cross-sectional coalition.[4]

Buchanan swept the South and captured enough northern and midwestern states—Pennsylvania, New Jersey, Indiana, and Illinois—to win the White House. For those taking the long view, however, the signs were inauspicious. Where Pierce had won fourteen of sixteen free states in 1852, Buchanan won only these four plus California. The Republicans had established a firm grip on the nation's northernmost reaches from New England to the Great Lakes.[5]

Dissecting the canvass, the *St. Albans Messenger* of Vermont attributed the results to Democratic alarmism and gave the source of this dangerous mischief a name: "squatter Democracy." "The squatter Democracy . . . require the people to continue them in power by electing BUCHANAN President and threaten disunion and civil war if they fail to comply," the writer charged. Beholden to slavemasters, the party used "terror" every bit as effectively as Robespierre and the Jacobins during the French Revolution. "For more than twenty-five years this crack of the slave driver's whip has rung through the halls of Congress and controlled the measures of the government," the article continued. "That crack has now been heard at the polls, and the people have cowed and trembled at the sight of the lash—have yielded to the threats and surrendered the power to a set of men who boldly declared they would rule the country or ruin it." This use of the term "squatter Democracy" denoted the capture of the party by slaveholders and their allies. The reduction of the Democracy to a single descriptor—"squatter"—unmasked the machinations that had helped hold the party together for decades. Democrats could extol yeomen all they liked, but, the writer alleged, the party and its popular sovereignty doctrine proved to be little more than a front for the Slave Power to conquer the country. Events in Kansas and beyond would reveal whether the *Messenger* was correct.[6]

Even as denunciations rained down from Republican quarters, leading Democrats perceived favorable winds. After all, they had retained the presidency, won majorities in Congress, and some of the party's most practiced hands were at the helm. In his inaugural address, Buchanan reaffirmed his commitment to the doctrine of popular sovereignty, calling it "a principle as ancient as free government itself." At the same time, he acknowledged that there was a disagreement about the stage at which territorial inhabitants should render their decision on slavery. Blithely shrugging aside the complications this and related questions had caused his party and country for years, Buchanan said, "This is, happily, a matter of but little practical importance" because it was "a judicial question, which legitimately belongs to the Supreme Court of the United States." Indeed, pending before the high court was a case that the president believed would "speedily and finally" put the matter to rest. He, for one, would "cheerfully submit" to their decision "in common with all good citizens." What Buchanan did not say was that he already knew what the result of the *Dred Scott* case would be.[7]

Scott was a slave purchased by an army surgeon in St. Louis and brought to Illinois and then Wisconsin Territory. He sued for his freedom on the grounds that slavery, while legal in Missouri, was outlawed in those other places. As if like clockwork, two days after Buchanan's inaugural, the court handed down its decision. Written by Chief Justice Roger Taney, the ruling stated that African Americans—slave or free—could not be citizens of the United States and therefore had no standing to bring suit. Furthermore, the federal government lacked the power to restrict slavery in territories—the Northwest Ordinance and other acts notwithstanding. According to the ruling, Scott remained a slave, despite his sojourn in free places. Many had hoped the court would put the question of slavery extension to rest. But *Dred Scott v. Sandford* succeeded only in ratifying the southern view that slaveholders had a perfect right to bring enslaved humans into US territories. For many northerners the ruling furnished full and final proof that slaveholding interests had conquered the Democratic Party and every branch of the government, and there was nothing left to do but fight, regardless of the new president's claptrap about "cheerfully" submitting to the ruling.[8]

The *Dred Scott* decision dealt a blow to proponents of a free Kansas and to the aspirations of African Americans across the land. Benton, in a final published piece before his death, viewed the ruling both as judicial over-reach that defied the Framers' intention for Congress to regulate slavery in the territories and as another disastrously wrong turn by Democrats who had moved "from the abrogation of the Missouri Compromise (which saved the Union) to squatter sovereignty, (which killed the compromise) and thence to the decision of the Supreme Court (which kills both)." Unionist Democrats including Buchanan did, however, stick to their guns on "non-intervention," maintaining that the inhabitants of a territory ultimately had the right to decide the slavery question for themselves when applying for statehood. Whether or not a slavery ban would stick in light of *Dred Scott* was an open question, but the administration moved forward with its avowed commitment to popular sovereignty. The trick was finding the right man to oversee the processes that would enable and inspire voters to express their will.[9]

Buchanan had his heart set on one man for the post of Kansas governor: Walker. When the one-time treasury secretary resisted his overtures, the president persisted, pleading that the fate of the nation hung in the balance and enlisting powerful friends like Douglas to help. The wheedling finally worked. On March 26, 1857, Walker wrote the president, "In view of the opinion now presented by you, that the safety of the union may depend upon the selection of the individual to whom shall be assigned the task of settling the difficulties which again surround the Kansas question, I have concluded that a solemn sense of duty to my country requires me to accept this position." Walker took pains to put in writing the terms of his mandate. As he understood it, his job was to ensure that unalloyed popular sovereignty carried the day on the slavery question.

I understand that you and all your cabinet cordially concur in the opinion expressed by me, that the actual bona fide residents of the territory of Kansas, by a fair and regular vote, unaffected by fraud or violence, must be permitted, in adopting their state constitution, to decide for themselves what shall be their social institutions. This is the great fundamental principle of the act of Congress organizing that territory, affirmed by the supreme court of the United States, and is in accordance with the views uniformly expressed by me throughout my public career. I contemplate a peaceful settlement of this question by an appeal to the intelligence and patriotism of the whole people of Kansas, who should all participate, freely and fully, in this decision, and by a majority of whose votes the determination must be made, as the only proper and constitutional mode of adjustment.

Walker was committed to letting the people determine the status of slavery. If they were denied that right, he warned, "I see nothing in the future for Kansas but civil war, extending its baleful influence throughout the country, and subjecting the union itself to imminent hazard." He took care to document that his views had the president's endorsement, knowing from experience that Buchanan had a tendency to change his mind capriciously. He was also keenly aware that the cabinet contained some touchy characters, including Secretary of War John B. Floyd, a Virginia slaveholder, and Treasury Secretary Howell Cobb of Georgia, a passionate slavery defender. Walker could take some comfort that Lewis Cass, the father of popular sovereignty, was secretary of state, and that his friend and ally Stephen Douglas remained the preeminent force in the Senate on matters related to the territories.[10]

For Walker, his core mission in Kansas boiled down to a simple precept: ensuring a fair vote by eligible Kansans on their constitution, including its provisions on slavery. If Walker entertained doubts about his chances for success he did not let them show. "The duty is severe and hazardous, but I must not shirk from it on that account," he wrote to his sister in April 1857. Besides, he added almost cavalierly, "The slavery question in Kansas, is not so *unsolvable* as you suppose. It is reduced to the simple issue, of slave or free state, and must be decided by a *full* and *fair* vote of a *majority* of the people of Kansas. The same question has thus been decided peacefully in every other state, and why not in Kansas?"[11]

Though a slave owner at different points of his life, Walker was not a virulently proslavery man, even if he had expediently manipulated the issue to drum up support among his constituents in Mississippi. He was no longer beholden to voters, although he may well have harbored presidential ambitions. Raised in Pennsylvania before moving south in his twenties, he had lived in Washington for much of the past two decades and spent a good deal of time in New York as well. He belonged to that species of Jacksonian unionist unwilling to consider the moral dimensions of slavery and blasting "extremists" on either side of the issue. Heading into his new role, he was quite sure how things would play out. Climate, he believed, dictated that slavery would never take hold in Kansas. To his mind, the only undecided question was whether he could help make it a free Democratic state.[12]

Given Walker's prominence, ties to both South and North, unique ability to sway public opinion, and deft touch with squatters dating back to his Mississippi days, it struck many as an inspired choice when the president tapped him to be the governor of Kansas Territory. The *New York Herald* endorsed the incoming governor's calls to place the slavery decision in the hands of "the *bona fide* inhabitants," predicting that such a course "will bury the Atchisons, Stringfellows, Robinsons, and Greeleys beneath the load of their own infamy" and "strengthen the national feeling throughout the country." Dubbing Walker "the foster-father of Texas," *Harper's Weekly* expressed a fervent hope that "he be equally fortunate with Kansas."[13]

With the nation anxiously watching, Walker—the politician who owed his rise to the "hardy pioneers" of the West and who never ceased invoking their sacred name—took his place among the squatters of Kansas in a bid to heal a fracturing country. He arrived in May, after a stop in Chicago to consult with Douglas, whose views on popular sovereignty harmonized with his own. From the moment he stepped onto Kansas soil, his every move became grist for rumor and recrimination. If he interacted with free-state men, the South cried foul. If seen in proslavery quarters, the free staters registered displeasure. Robinson, who had been released from jail but still faced charges of treason, observed with consternation that one of the new governor's first stops was in the proslavery bastion of Leavenworth, where, according to one account, "instead of a speech, he had $250 worth of liquors distributed among the people in the street."[14] Was Walker trying to sway hearts and to what end?

With his usual self-confidence, Walker boldly went where he felt his presence might make a difference in convincing Kansas settlers to resolve their differences peacefully at the polls. He did not shy away from even the most contentious places, including hubs of the Free State. Within days of his arrival he found himself sharing an event stage with Charles Robinson, the Free State governor, at a Unitarian church in Lawrence. Like other federal officials, Walker considered Robinson's governorship illegitimate. But he recognized the man's influence over a sizable portion of Kansans and had the good instinct not to publicly offend, particularly as Robinson "spoke kindly and hopefully of Governor Walker's administration." Another man, identifying himself as "one of the squatters of Kansas," pledged that free staters stood ready "to aid Governor Walker in administering justice in Kansas." Walker kept his own remarks short, indicating that he would expound upon his views and plans in his forthcoming inaugural. He did, however, give his word "that every citizen of Kansas should be protected in the enjoyment of his rights."[15]

On May 27 at Lecompton, site of the territorial legislature and a crucible of proslavery fervor, Walker delivered his inaugural address. In solemn tones

FIGURE 8.1 Robert J. Walker in the early 1860s, photographed by Matthew Brady. National Archives and Records Administration, NARA-528738.

he explained that his chief obligation as governor was "the settlement of that momentous question which has introduced discord and civil war throughout your borders, and threatens to involve you and our country in the same common ruin." His job was not to see slavery triumph or fail but to ensure fair elections. The rest, he said, fell to Kansans "who, by a majority of their own votes, must decide this (slavery) question for themselves in forming their state constitution."[16]

Referencing his long career as an advocate of squatter interests, Walker launched into a subject dear to his heart and to those of his listeners: land. He trumpeted not only preemption, his long-standing special cause, but also "a homestead of a quarter-section of land in favor of every actual settler." This was a rare instance of Walker's endorsing a homestead measure. The policy remained controversial in Democratic circles because many still associated the granting of free land with Free Soilers and their Republican heirs. Given homestead's broad appeal in Kansas, though, it was astute of Walker to support it. He dangled land as a carrot for peace: "In establishing here the great principles of state and popular sovereignty, and thus perpetuating the union, Congress doubtless will regard with indulgent favor the new state of Kansas, and will welcome her into the union with joyful congratulations and a most liberal policy as to the public domain."

The reference to "state and popular sovereignty" was a skillful nod to both South and North, signaling to southerners that he respected states' rights—the basis of slaveholders' claim to perpetuate their institution in US territories—while communicating clearly to northerners that the popular will would prevail in Kansas. The fact that he struck this sectional balance and articulated core principles in the context of favorable land policies showed he remained committed as ever to the Squatter Democracy creed.[17]

Walker turned his attention to slavery, the most vexing problem of all. Here he showed himself to be a thoroughgoing popular sovereignty man. Congress, he argued, did not have the authority "to interfere with the people of a territory on this subject in forming a state constitution." It was up to the people themselves. Striking a hopeful note, the governor suggested that Kansans, by applying popular sovereignty, could bring peace to the entire country. "If this principle can be carried into successful operation in Kansas—that her people shall determine what shall be her social institutions—the slavery question must be withdrawn from the halls of Congress and from our presidential conflicts, and the safety of the union be placed beyond all peril."[18]

The new governor then dispensed a pill that slavery backers would find very hard to swallow. He spoke of "a law more powerful than the legislation of man, more potent than passion or prejudice" that would determine where slavery took hold. "It is the isothermal line, it is the law of the thermometer, of latitude or altitude, regulating climate, labor, and productions, and, as a consequence, profit and loss." Walker explained that slavery simply was not possible in Kansas because the climate would render it unprofitable, "being unsuited to the constitution of that sable race transplanted here from the equatorial heats of Africa." He thought he was stating the obvious, a point so self-evident that nobody could object, and supported by the fact that there were only, by his count, about 200 slaves in the entire territory. Basic laws of nature, not moral outrage, he insisted, would settle the slavery question. Walker did not realize that these and similar words uttered elsewhere would doom his errand in Kansas.[19]

Having delivered a message sure to discourage and dismay slavery partisans, Walker could not resist getting in a few jabs at the free-state movement and the burgeoning Republican Party. By electing to bar black people from Kansas, the free staters had "in the most positive manner, affirmed the constitutionality of that portion of the recent decision of the supreme court of the United States declaring that Africans are not citizens of the United States," Walker avowed, referring to *Dred Scott v. Sandford*. With their white supremacist policies, the free-state men had opened themselves up to this sort of critique.[20]

The governor ended with a dramatic summation of what was at stake in the days ahead, leaning heavily on the tropes of traditional Democratic pro-squatterism. "Upon the plains of Kansas may now be fought the last great and decisive battle, involving the fate of the union, of state sovereignty, of self-government, and the liberties of the world," he intoned. A peaceful resolution would launch Kansas on "an immediate career of power, progress and prosperity, unsurpassed in the history of the world." Walker listed the myriad blessings to come: "the rapid extinguishment of Indian title, and the occupancy of those lands by settlers and cultivators; the diffusion of universal education; pre-emptions for the actual settlers." These were the perennial promises of Squatter Democracy. With Native peoples pushed aside and white Kansans in possession of the land, Walker foresaw railroads, churches, and colleges "carrying westward the progress of law, religion, liberty, and civilization." He envisioned "villages, prosperous and progressing; . . . farms teeming with abundant products, . . . and peace, happiness and prosperity smiling throughout our borders." If the people there continued to stoke strife over slavery, though, "all history will record the fact that Kansas was the grave of the American union." Fortunately, Walker said, the decision was in the hands of "the hardy pioneers and settlers of the west," a reality that boded well for everyone.

> It was men like these whose rifles drove back the invader from the plains of Orleans, and planted the stars and stripes upon the victorious fields of Mexico. These are the men whom gold cannot corrupt, nor foes intimidate. From their towns and villages, from their farms and cottages, spread over the beautiful prairies of Kansas, they will come forward now in defense of the constitution and the union. . . . Before the peaceful power of their suffrage this dangerous sectional agitation will disappear, and peace and prosperity once more reign throughout our borders. In the hearts of this noble band of patriotic settlers the love of their country and of the union is inextinguishable.[21]

As if by muscle memory, Walker positioned the "hardy pioneers" not merely as steadfast defenders of the country from foreign invaders, but as its likely saviors from the menacing divisions within. Notably, he eschewed use of the term "squatter," perhaps recognizing how inflammatory it had become.

Walker's inaugural received mixed reviews, suggesting that the jury was out on the new governor and his chances of pacifying Kansas. The centrist *New York Sun* seemed buoyed by the address, particularly Walker's conviction about sovereignty "belonging to the people." The paper also found it encouraging that Robinson and the free staters had accorded him due deference, writing, "Governor Robinson not only did not dispute the new Governor's title to govern in Kansas, but received him with expressions of the most cordial respect. The people cheered their new Governor, and everything indicated the beginning of a new era of good feeling." But not everyone liked the substance of the speech. The Democratic *Richmond South* alleged that Walker "openly allies himself with the anti-slavery faction, and employs all the influence of his position to deliver Kansas into the power of the Free-State party." Most observers believed Kansas was poised to become free, given that free-state men outnumbered proslavery settlers by roughly two to one. Robinson, for one, felt heartened by the political winds. "That we shall have a free state is well settled," he wrote to James McClatchy in Sacramento. The question was whether that free state would be Democratic or Republican. Robinson expressed optimism about his side's chances. "We intend to set our State government in motion next Winter after seizing upon the [territorial] Legislature & repealing all of the laws, & thus compel Congress to admit us into the Union under the 'Treasonable' Topeka Constitution." The free staters showed no signs of wavering in their determination to see their brand of squatter sovereignty triumph. They were ready to work with Walker so long as he did not try to force slavery on them.[22]

The old-guard Democrats who occupied the nation's top posts— Jacksonian heavyweights like Buchanan, Cass, Walker, and Douglas—had staked their political futures on popular sovereignty in Kansas. Walker's mission hinged on whether he could ensure "full and fair" elections that expressed the popular will, meaning the majority of eligible voters. There were two distinct aspects to that proposition: safeguarding voting so it went off without irregularities and convincing Kansans to turn out. Walker hoped that by guaranteeing the integrity of the vote he would induce people to exercise their franchise. This was no small order considering the fraud that had characterized Kansas balloting and the skepticism Democrats had engendered by countenancing it.

The governor raced around the territory urging Kansans to participate. Despite his efforts, turnout proved disappointingly low in elections for delegates to the constitutional convention slated to begin in Lecompton in September. Out of 9,251 registered voters, only 2,100 cast ballots, the majority of them proslavery. "The black republicans would not vote & the free state democrats were kept from voting by the fear that the constitution would not be submitted [to voters for ratification] . . . & that by voting they committed themselves to the proceedings of the convention," Walker explained to Buchanan. Attempting to save face, he added, "But for my inaugural circulated by thousands & various speeches all urging the people to vote, there would not have been 1,000 votes polled in the Territory & the convention would have been a disastrous failure." Putting the best gloss on things, Walker assured the president there was still reason to hope for a peaceful resolution: "Notwithstanding the small vote, if the convention make a good conservative constitution & submits it to the people, they will vote next fall & we will succeed with a great deal of hard work."[23]

Walker made a careful survey of the political landscape in Kansas and laid it out for Buchanan. He identified 9,000 Democrats who supported a free state, the majority of whom stood solidly behind his policies; 6,500 proslavery Democrats, whose leaders viewed him with marked ambivalence; 8,000 Republicans who, in his assessment, "are against me generally"; and a few hundred proslavery Know-Nothings, also in opposition. The numbers were on his side, he suggested. The key to success would be holding onto Democratic support, in particular preventing the free-state Democrats from defecting to the Republican camp, while banking on the likelihood that proslavery partisans would prefer a Democratic regime to a Republican. Walker's calculus showed that he saw scope for an abiding coalition of plain republicans and planters within a non-slave realm.

In parsing these groups Walker let drop a rather stunning piece of information: "A very large majority of the *squatters*, who came to the Territ[ory] from slave states are said to be for a free State partly from conviction that their *claims* would bring a larger price, & partly because many of them came here expressly to settle in a free state." This was a rare moment of candor for an apostle of Squatter Democracy long accustomed to obfuscating over slavery. Of course, Walker was delivering a fact that nearly everyone, other than Democratic leaders fearful of offending southern firebrands, readily acknowledged: squatter yeomen in the main were not slaveholders. This was obvious in the North. In the South it has always been less clear because some middling farmers owned slaves or aspired to. But western lands offered fresh choices. Given their druthers, Walker reported, southern squatters opted to break free of a society dominated by slavemasters and their degrading institution.[24]

Walker did not find southern squatters' aversion to slavery at all surprising or discouraging. He was convinced that Kansas's climate was ill-suited to slave-based agriculture and considered it perfectly natural that actual farmers had the good sense not to waste their hopes or money on unworkable schemes. As it stood, the total slave population in Kansas barely numbered 200. "The permanent existence of slavery here is . . . preposterous," he wrote to Buchanan, "& I never heard but one proslavery man in Kansas who did not concede the fact—& all admit that a very large majority of the settlers are for a free State." Politically there was much to gain by recognizing this reality because the squatters from the South likely identified with free-state Democrats and opposed Republican rule. The overall picture that Walker painted was of a territory that for reasons of climate and settler preference would be free. Let popular sovereignty work its effects and Kansas would be free and Democratic, he maintained. The administration could diffuse southern rage by creating "a slave state out of the southwestern Indian Territory" and by acquiring Cuba, he counseled. This suggestion harkened back to their days in Polk's cabinet when they directed a program of vast territorial conquests favorable to South and North. Whether Buchanan would heed his advice was uncertain.[25]

The president wrote to Walker on July 12, concurring with his general course. "On the question of submitting the constitution to the *bona fide* resident settlers of Kansas, I am willing to stand or fall," he declared. "In sustaining such a principle we cannot fall. It is the principle of the Kansas-Nebraska bill; the principle of popular sovereignty, and the principle at the foundation of all popular government. . . . Should the convention of Kansas adopt this principle all will be settled harmoniously, and, with the blessing of Providence, you will return triumphantly from your arduous, important and responsible mission." Buchanan's expressions of approval proved fleeting and did little to smooth Walker's path.[26]

The governor's standing in the South continued to plummet as he stuck by his belief that slavery could not take root in Kansas. Democrats in Georgia and Mississippi issued resolutions condemning his course. Walker tried shaking off the criticism: "I am not disturbed by the assaults made upon me in some of the southern states, because I feel a profound conviction of the propriety of my course," he wrote to Secretary of State Cass. To Buchanan, he insisted, "I care not about the abuse heaped on me if the country is saved." Despite these words, the slights must have stung.[27]

Walker faced detractors on all sides. A scribe for the *New-York Tribune* caught up with him at a public land sale at Paola, some fifty miles south of Leavenworth, where the governor addressed a crush of speculators, squatters, "Border Ruffians" and "Abolitionists" who had gathered to "bid upon the blood-stained soil." The writer took the measure of Walker, whose political career had taken off as a result of the controversial land sale at Chocchuma in 1833, and drew a sharp, unflattering portrait:

> He is a diplomat, a man of that cunning school who refine deception into a virtue and call it "statesmanship." . . . He will call every man a "fanatic" who will not sell his principles for a dollar, and will think him one, for the class of politicians to which he belongs can only esti-mate party principles at their market value. He will truckle and trade, and try to distract. But a noble and manly stand for justice and right, against fraud and oppression—will he do it? We will see.[28]

Amid the rising criticism, residents of Lawrence handed Walker an oppor-tunity to revive his reputation in the South. Democrats considered the town a hotbed of "Black Republican" abolitionist scheming. Walker's own worst suspicions were confirmed when somebody slipped him a handbill in July showing that the townspeople were preparing to elect a mayor and other public officers and pass ordinances in defiance of territorial laws. Worse still, the Lawrence insurrectionists were distributing their handbills across Kansas, urging citizens in other locales to follow suit. These "most alarming proceedings" risked an overthrow of the territorial government and "a re-newal of civil war," Walker charged.[29]

Though ill, the governor raced to Lawrence and issued an ultimatum to the people. "I appeal once more to your love of country; to your regard for its peace, prosperity, and reputation; to your affection for your wives and chil-dren; and to all those patriotic motives which ought to influence American citizens, to abandon this contemplated revolution," he commanded. As if speaking to recalcitrant children, the ailing governor observed that all his pre-vious admonitions had "failed as yet to produce any effect upon you," leaving him no choice but to call in General William S. Harney and his dragoons from Leavenworth. When the troops arrived they did not encounter scenes of revolutionary abandon but rather a small town going about its business. They set up camp outside Lawrence; Walker remained with them. The *Leavenworth Times* provided a mock timeline of the governor's intervention, spoofing his overreaction and capturing the agony of a vain and ambitious man forced to confront his own ridiculousness and untenable position.

MONDAY EVENING.—Walker dispatched 792 dragoons this morning to arrest an audacious youngster who was selling peanuts in violation of the organic act and our beloved constitution. Boy to be tried by court-martial for high treason. Governor somewhat boozy.

TUESDAY EVENING.—Walker said he'd be gol-darned if he ever sweat so in his life. Says he has to put on a clean shirt every day—willing to make such sacrifices for the peace of the country and the union. Little boy discharged. Walker imbibes too much.

WEDNESDAY EVENING.—Troops damn Walker, and Walker damns the troops. Both want to know what the devil to do. Weather awful. Governor thinks he wouldn't like the army. Dog heard howling and company sent to arrest him. Dog escaped. The governor three sheets in the wind.

THURSDAY EVENING.—His excellency has the bowel complaint. Takes paregoric. Troops growl and Walker swears like a trooper. The citizens don't seem to mind the presence of the army. The governor says he feels blamed mean and danged small. Gets tight and oblivious.

FRIDAY EVENING.—Walker's got the headache. Says he's been sold—thinks he won't be the next president. Damns republics, and Kansas troops laugh and snicker—whisky shops do a staving business. The gov-ernor says he's going home—don't think his mother knows he's out. All quiet in the city. Walker inebriated. . . . This last dispatch was received just before going to press, and convinces us that the governor has had a most glorious and successful campaign. The rearresting of that peanut boy was a master stroke, and every act of the governor during the momentous crisis was worthy of the hero and the man.

The article ends with a final dig, noting that Walker had one last piece of unfinished business to attend to: preventing a squatter association from performing its work. "We stop the press to announce we understand three settlers in the Neosho country have referred the matter of a disputed claim to a committee of squatters, in violation of the constitution of the United States," the *Times* reported. "Such a highhanded and infamous usurpation of power would sever the union into splinters if allowed to go unpunished and unrebuked, and we hope Governor Walker will march an army down there without delay, accompanying it himself, to prevent bloodshed, and serve the miserable fanatics and lawbreakers as he has served those at Lawrence." The irony was rich. A simple squatter association, doing what such groups had always done and what Democrats had long encouraged them to do—peacefully adjudicating a frontier land claim—committed a high crime capable of destroying the country. As the instigator and enforcer of this overwrought state, Walker, in the *Times*'s send-up, comes across as a besotted buffoon who does not understand even the most basic realities of western life, to say nothing of the dynamics of the conflict in Kansas—a stinging rebuke to a man who considered himself something of a "squatter whisperer."[30]

Observers across the ideological spectrum derided Walker for making a mountain out of a molehill in Lawrence. Samuel Pomeroy, an associate of the Emigrant Aid Company, wrote to his business partner Thaddeus Hyatt that Walker was "playing the fool" at Lawrence. Having bought out the *Squatter Sovereign* from Stringfellow earlier that spring and put the "Free State" banner on its masthead—a symbolic victory in the trenches of squatterdom—Pomeroy intended to have the last laugh. Most ominous for Walker, the southerners in Buchanan's inner circle cycled from skeptical to outright snide. Secretary of War John B. Floyd was decidedly unimpressed by "His Excellency's" anticlimactic crackdown on Lawrence and heaped scorn on the governor's request for additional troops. "I doubt, now, whether the investment in Gov. Walker is going to turn out very profitable," Floyd wrote the president, adding that he and fellow cabinet members found the governor's performance puzzling. "We all feel it to be a sort of game of *Solitaire*, the play of Hamlet with the part of Hamlet left out." In his eyes, Walker cut more of a farcical figure than a tragic one. Floyd dispatched a message to the besieged governor, denying his request for more troops and noting he already had some thirteen companies at his disposal, all "thoroughly equipped and efficient."[31]

It's not hard to imagine Walker's dismay as he read Floyd's response. Here he was, an elder statesman, likely still entertaining presidential ambitions. That honor had gone to a longtime rival for whom Walker always held a mix of respect and contempt. Buchanan sat in the Oval Office taking instructions from slavemasters while Walker slummed it among squatters in Kansas, despised and ridiculed on all sides, and forsaken by the administration that had promised to back him at all cost. After a life of improbable triumphs, seemingly mastering big, complicated forces, he found himself increasingly powerless.

Walker's history of poor health was compounded by creeping malaise. When a band of Cheyennes appeared in the territory, he dashed off a letter to Buchanan that captured his agitated state of mind. Writing in haste, Walker told the president he would travel through the night to get to Fort Riley to meet the danger head on. "I go not in search of military laurels, but in the discharge of my duty," he solemnly wrote. "[I]f any accident befall me, it will leave my Kansas policy as a legacy to my country, & silence the voice of faction, which so falsely charges me with wishing to disturb the equilibrium of our Government, in the treasonable hope of sectional aspirations." In this hour of peril Walker's thoughts turned to those he loved most. "My wife & family must not hear of this movement of mine," he pleaded, wishing to spare them the worry. "You may show this to the Cabinet. God bless you all." With that, the governor rode off into the night.[32]

Isolated and unwell, Walker did retain one key ally. Stephen A. Douglas anxiously tracked developments in Kansas and scribbled a letter to his friend, attempting to cheer him up. "I have just read your Proclamation to the people of Lawrence. You have placed the Rebels clearly in the wrong, and the whole country will sustain you in maintaining the supremacy of the laws," he wrote. Walker's plan to submit for voter approval the constitution drawn up at the forthcoming Lecompton convention also had broad support, Douglas said, "with the exception of a small party at the South"—and their discontent stemmed less from Walker than from disgruntlement over Buchanan's disbursement of patronage. "They were in fact dissatisfied with the national administration, and seized upon the Kansas question as a pretext, and made you the scape goat. But the present state of the question will compel them to rally under your banner and vindicate your course from the beginning," he assured Walker. For a politician capable of trenchant political analysis,

Douglas's assessment was surprisingly off the mark, even if fleetingly com-
forting. Southern fire-eaters were in fact furious with Walker and anyone who
forced them to accept that local majorities could reject slavery if they chose.[33]

In August, Amos Lawrence sent a letter to Charles Robinson from Boston
registering delight at the turn of events: "You seem to have got Walker at last
just where he should be. From all we can learn there has been great discre-
tion used by the Free State men." Days later there was even more reason to
cheer: Robinson was acquitted of treason—the second time the squatter
leader dodged prosecution.[34]

The constitutional convention, with its proslavery majority, kicked off in
Lecompton in September. There had been some hope that John Calhoun,
the surveyor general and Douglas ally, would exert a moderating influence. Elected to represent Douglas County—home to both Lawrence and
Lecompton, the free-state and fire-eater strongholds—he served as president
of the convention. Douglas and Walker expected he would give full backing
to their plan to submit the constitution, once completed, to every "*bona
fide* actual citizen" in Kansas. But fresh political controversies changed the
complexion of events. October elections for the territorial legislature, congressional delegate, and other offices saw rampant voter fraud in proslavery
districts. In the precinct of Oxford the poll-book in which voters' names were
recorded turned out to match the Cincinnati city directory. Walker tossed
out those returns, announcing that, if they stood, "civil war would immediately be recommenced in this territory, extending, we fear, to adjacent states
and subjecting the government of the union to imminent peril." He also
invalidated returns in McGee, explaining that more than 1,200 votes had been
cast despite there being fewer than 100 eligible voters in a county "constituted
from the lands of the Cherokee Indians, which are not yet open to preemption or settlement." As a result of Walker's interventions, free staters won a
majority in the territorial legislature—a fitting result given their numbers
nearly doubled those of proslavery partisans.[35]

Watching these events unfold, the proslavery delegates at Lecompton
comprehended with troubling clarity what happened when the free-state
majority flexed its political muscles without any skullduggery to keep them
in check. A constitution affirming enslavers' "inviolable" right to human
property clearly would never pass if voters had a fair say. Faced with this co-
nundrum, they opted to forego a popular referendum, choosing instead to
send their charter straight to Congress for approval of Kansas as a slave state.
Convention president John Calhoun recognized the outrage this would
spark and sought to dissuade his colleagues. On November 7, they settled on

a compromise—submit to voters the following month a limited question: a "constitution with slavery" or a "constitution with no slavery." Either way, slaveholders could not lose because the choice did nothing to affect the status of slaves currently in the territory.[36]

For Walker these proceedings marked a betrayal of his central mission to ensure a fair vote by Kansans on the whole constitution and an assault on popular sovereignty and norms of democracy. He fumed about "the infamous manner in which Calhoun behaved." But he was a man bereft of a solid base of support and powerless to undo the convention's actions. "The result of all this popular alienation from the Governor, places him now in a very unpleasant position," noted the *Lawrence Republican*. "[W]e fear he never can rise politically here, and that another Governor who came to Kansas a great man will leave, as all before him have left—broken down—used up—politically annihilated."[37]

In the grip of illness and holed up near Leavenworth, Walker snatched up his pen on November 10 and attempted to unravel the nightmare that had ensnared him. Months of pleading, cajoling, and snuffing out fire after fire had brought neither the territory nor the anxiously watching nation any closer to peace. As Walker saw it, the only tangible result he had achieved was making himself universally despised. He was alone, misunderstood, and somehow expected to play the part of greatness. He retooled the words of vengeance spoken by the ghost of Hamlet's father and applied them to his own circumstances: "But howsoever thou pursuest this deed taint not thy heart nor let thy soul conceive against thy Country aught." The governor understood his task was to save America; he just didn't know how.[38]

As he had done to powerful effect throughout his political career in moments of personal or national crisis, Walker put pen to paper and addressed himself to the public. He asserted that "from 1820 down to the present time, a period of 37 years, I have uniformly endeavored to secure the equilibrium of the government." He marched through the highlights: advocating Andrew Jackson's presidency as a young man in Pennsylvania, moving to Mississippi and serving the state in the Senate, leading the charge for Texas annexation and sole occupation of Oregon, crafting the expansionist platform of 1844, getting Polk elected, and serving as his treasury secretary. In that last role, Walker proved a nimble economic theorist and hawkish imperialist, championing the causes of tariff reform and conquest of Mexico. Few could argue with Walker's bona fides as an influential Jacksonian statesman, effective expansionist, and committed unionist, whose interventions had benefited North and South.[39]

Walker reminded prospective readers that he had not wanted to come to Kansas but allowed himself to be talked into it for the country's survival. He arrived guided by "fixed principles" not sectional interests. In his feverish state of mind, he repeated again and again that it was paramount that the "actual, *bona fide*, resident settlers"—not Congress or anyone else—decide whether Kansas would become a slave or free state. Walker then added a caveat: "I am and ever have been a total disbeliever in . . . squatter sovereignty." For a man who had hitched his personal and political fortunes to white squatters in the American West, this disavowal was striking. He had cheered longest and loudest for white pioneers, bidding them to claim the continent, form their societies, and fortify the Democracy. Forced into a corner, he saw the need to set some limits.[40]

In citing "squatter sovereignty," Walker was referring not to people but a process. This remained, after all, the post–Wilmot Proviso world, and Democrats had vested their beloved icon with sovereign authority to resolve the slavery question. The party had then proceeded to tie itself in knots over when exactly squatters could render this momentous decision. What Walker meant by squatter sovereignty was any formal decision on slavery made by territorial inhabitants prior to writing a constitution for admission as a state. He considered this a premature exercise of authority and claimed to be against it.

The governor's reading of popular sovereignty matched the preferred southern interpretation, which placed the vote on slavery at the final phase of territorial existence when inhabitants approved a state constitution. Yet if his tenure in Kansas had taught him anything it was that proslavery partisans would never accept popular sovereignty even at this late stage if the results did not go their way. They had resorted to sophistry, cheating, and outright violence in their quest to make Kansas a slave state. Having contorted himself for decades to accommodate the interests of Democrats across sections, Walker would bend no further. The majority of Kansans wanted a free state, yet slavery proponents had manipulated the process and stood on the cusp of subverting the popular will. As governor he would not allow it.

Had it been possible, Walker likely would have continued to practice the same self-serving, dissembling squatter politics that had rewarded him and his party so handsomely for decades. Rallying partisans from the South and North behind the idealized figure of the squatter yeoman had contributed to Democratic dominance and the conquest of large portions of the continent. When confronted with the dangerous contradictions of their expansionist program, Democrats delayed the day of reckoning by empowering squatters to work their yeoman magic and put the slavery matter to rest. Walker, charged with cleaning up the mess he had helped create, experienced directly the slings and arrows of politics constructed of fictions. Despite promises to further the interests of North and South, Squatter Democracy—premised on securing land for yeomen—favored free farmers, not slaveholders. With free-state and proslavery squatters warring to achieve their incompatible visions, there was nothing left to do but ensure that the will of the majority carried the day. Walker had run out of room to dodge.

The governor filled more than eighty pages with his autobiographical musings and rambling reflections on constitutional theory. For once, though, he did not produce a blockbuster tract that galvanized public opinion. In fact, this manuscript would not see the light of day. Once back on his feet, Walker returned to Washington and resigned his post.

Standing shoulder to shoulder with his embattled friend, Stephen A. Douglas decried the Lecompton travesty. In early December he stormed into the White House and urged the president not to endorse the infamous constitution. The discussion grew heated and Buchanan tried pulling rank on his colleague. "Mr. Douglas," he warned, "I desire you to remember that no democrat ever yet differed from an administration of his own choice without being crushed." He advised him not to follow the example of a pair of upstarts who had attempted to defy party leadership during Andrew Jackson's tenure. For Douglas the invocation of Old Hickory, the man who had stared down the Nullifiers, likely grated in this forlorn hour when Buchanan was capitulating to Slave Power treachery. Rising up, he shot back, "Mr. President, I wish you to remember that General Jackson is dead, sir!"—an eloquent requiem for a bygone era.[41]

Douglas's critics were unimpressed by his eleventh-hour attempt to seize the moral high ground. For all the talk of respecting the majority's will his "*Squatter* doctrine, so much harped upon, has been fully developed, and it has *run into the ground*," observed the *Clermont Courier* of Ohio, surveying Kansas Territory's history. Democratic misrule helped install "a *Squatter* Territorial Legislature, filled up with Missouri citizens; it made *Squatter laws*, and these were enforced by a *Squatter* Administration, with a *Squatter army* to back it." A "Squatter Convention" then crafted a "Squatter Constitution" under consideration by a "Squatter Congress." Everything the Democrats touched turned to "Squatter" and always to slavemasters' advantage. For years Republicans had cried foul, the *Courier* wrote, "and Squatter Democracy answered, by bawling out, *Freedom-Shriekers!*" Douglas joined in their cries, but as far as the *Courier* was concerned it was too late. He and Buchanan had helped make Squatter Democracy a front for enslavers, even if the two men were presently at odds.[42]

The vote on the Lecompton Constitution took place later that month. With barely any free staters participating, the "constitution with slavery" passed. Buchanan backed the results and recommended that Congress approve Kansas's admission into the Union as a slave state, against the will of Walker, Douglas, and most Kansans. Lewis Cass, dutiful lieutenant that he was, publicly supported Buchanan's position, betraying his own popular sovereignty doctrine.[43]

Amid the infighting and the deepening malaise, one Democrat surprisingly found clarity. From Atchison, Kansas, on January 5, 1858, John H. Stringfellow addressed a letter to James Buchanan in which he delivered strong doses of reality. "Kansas will not be permanently a slave state," he announced, and "for the very best of reasons." The erstwhile editor of the *Squatter Sovereign* walked the president through the math: "Of the present actual resident voting population, there are not one hundred who own slaves in the Territory and out of about 15000 voters, not over 3000 who desire slavery to exist here as an institution, and of these few, the number is daily diminishing." Stringfellow gamed out what would happen if the Lecompton Constitution were forced on an unwilling majority: the free staters would resist anew; armed Missourians would return to defend slavery interests, which in turn would draw residents of Iowa and Illinois to the free-state side; and Kansas would become a "real Battle ground . . . our property destroyed, and our families made paupers." And why? "[B]ecause forsooth the people of Kansas will not consent to have a Constitution fastened on them which they do not like."[44]

Stringfellow confessed that he had experienced a change of heart. He believed that true squatter sovereignty—that is, the will of the majority of actual settlers—ought to prevail. Subverting that straightforward proposition simply was not worth the pain.

> I have lived too long in the practical west, to be willing to sacrifice everything, to reduce my family to pauperism for the sake of even that dearest of all Southern abstractions. I have sacreficed [*sic*] as much of time and money, risked life as often, and if the newspaper press of the north be believed, have lost as much of "Sacred Honor" to establish negro slavery in Kansas by emigration and settlement as any Southern abstractionist or fire eater of them all, but when I found Southern men would not bring themselves and their negro property here, but

took from here the little that had ventured in, and that the north were emigrating rapidly with their all, I was not willing to play the Dog in the Manger . . . by neither occupying the country myself, or permitting others to do so by imposing a Constitution on them against their will.[45]

The fire-eating squatter chief had discovered democratic scruples and made his peace with thorny truths, even as Kansas voters overwhelmingly rejected the Lecompton Constitution in a new referendum. Other southern firebrands, however, were less inclined to give up the fight. Having made a play to co-opt the shapeshifting squatter for their cause and lost, proslavery Democrats returned to bashing this figure as an illegitimate usurper of their rights. They also redoubled their attacks on "squatter sovereignty" and its champions.

Democrats were breaking apart on the very pro-squatter expansionist grounds that had once unified them because their avowed fidelity to majoritarian democracy had run afoul of colleagues intent on perpetuating slavery at any cost. For decades the progenitors of Squatter Democracy had kept the peace by avoiding hard truths about the popular will, their own constitutional duties, and the evils of slavery. The main exception, Thomas Hart Benton, had paid a political price for trying to uphold Congress's authority to regulate US territories. In Kansas, Robert J. Walker came face to face with warring squatter factions and found himself compelled to dispense with the usual bromides and take a stand for democracy. It would fall to Stephen Douglas to demonstrate whether a cross-sectional Democratic Party still had viability once the squatter had become a lightning rod. One thing had become perfectly clear amid the wreckage of Kansas: association with this polarizing symbol had lost any upside for a Jacksonian unionist searching for a path to the White House.

9

The Ordeal of the Squatter King

ON JULY 12, 1860, as the bruising presidential campaign entered its final phase, M. H. Birdsong of Sussex County, Virginia, wrote to Stephen A. Douglas, candidate of the northern Democracy, with a pressing question. "What is ment by squatter sovereinty," he asked. "[I]t is Represented here by the democraic party of which I belong in so many diferent ways and I being no politisioner I dont no which to believe." A little clarification, he added, "might make A diference of many votes in your favor." Frustration might well have washed over Douglas as he read these words, for this was a question he could neither escape nor seem to answer to anybody's satisfaction. Nevertheless, he would keep trying up to the election.[1]

Birdsong's letter highlights the dilemmas confronting Douglas and the Democratic Party he loved and wished to lead. The political juggernaut that had dominated national politics for decades reeled with internal strife. So acute were the divisions that the party was fielding two presidential candidates—Douglas, the standard-bearer of the Democrats' northern faction, and John C. Breckinridge of Kentucky, the current vice president and preferred choice of President James Buchanan and many in the South. The main dividing line remained the status of slavery in the territories. Having taken a stand to defend majoritarian rule in Kansas against the underhanded, undemocratic designs of proslavery men and their abettors, Douglas continued to insist on letting the West's white inhabitants decide the issue for themselves. He emerged from the Lecompton controversy with strengthened resolve and popular sovereignty became the centerpiece of his campaign. Slavery proponents, meanwhile, returned to lambasting Douglas's signature doctrine as "squatter sovereignty" and skewering the man himself as "the Squatter King" or, simply, "the Squatter."

Dangerous Ground. John Suval, Oxford University Press. © Oxford University Press 2022.
DOI: 10.1093/oso/9780197531426.003.0010

Douglas stood ready to counterattack. "Call it squatter sovereignty, call it popular sovereignty, call it what you please; it is the great principle of self-government on which this Union was formed, and by the preservation of which alone can it be maintained," he declared at the outset of 1860. "It is the right of the people of every State to govern themselves and make their own laws, and be protected from outside violence or interference, directly or indirectly." No matter how often he tried to explain, the questions about exactly who had the right to exercise sovereignty and when kept coming—the price of having dismantled the Missouri Compromise and handed Congress's authority to squatters. In this most fateful of presidential contests, Douglas faced many foes: southern Democrats, Republicans, Constitutional Unionists, and his own complicated history.[2]

The US Senate race in Illinois two years earlier had foreshadowed the challenges Douglas would encounter in his quest for the White House. His opponent, Abraham Lincoln, relentlessly picked at the scab of squatter sovereignty, emphasizing its essential meaninglessness, especially after the Supreme Court had struck down barriers to slavery expansion. "Under the Dred Scott decision 'squatter sovereignty' squatted out of existence, tumbled down like temporary scaffolding," Lincoln crowed in Springfield on June 17, 1858. In Chicago the next month, he continued to bait Douglas. What did squatter sovereignty mean? "I suppose," Lincoln said, "if it had any significance at all it was the right of the people to govern themselves, to be sovereign in their own affairs . . . while they had squatted on a Territory that did not belong to them. . . . [S]uch right to govern themselves was called 'Squatter Sovereignty.'" Lincoln's definition wedded the physical fact of settlement to the exercise of political authority in the early stages of a community's development. His dig about squatting on land "that did not belong to them" made clear that he, inveterate Whig that he was, accorded no legitimacy to their claims, but he was prepared to play devil's advocate. He was even willing, for the sake of argument, to take seriously the doctrine of popular sovereignty, which granted these usurpers the authority to determine their own institutions in lieu of Congress. He set up these strawmen only to tear them to shreds with the inescapable fact that the *Dred Scott* case had negated the principle of self-determination as related to slavery. The ruling, he noted, "says that there is no such thing as Squatter Sovereignty," despite Douglas's rhetoric about the people's right to self-government.[3]

In response, Douglas positioned popular sovereignty as the foundation of American democracy and the key to the Union's survival. But he struggled to square the circle between the *Dred Scott* ruling, which signaled that slavery could not be barred in territories, and his conviction that settlers had the authority to determine their institutions—a position on which he staked his political fortunes and the country's peace.

In late August, at the debate at Freeport, he found his response, arguing that territorial inhabitants could effectively ban slavery by passing "unfriendly legislation" and using local law enforcement. "It matters not what way the Supreme Court may hereafter decide as to the abstract question whether slavery may or may not go into a Territory under the Constitution," he proclaimed. "[T]he people have the lawful means to introduce it or exclude it as they please, for the reason that slavery cannot exist a day or an hour anywhere, unless it is supported by local police regulations." This "Freeport doctrine" was the ultimate expression of popular sovereignty, giving white men the final say in determining their local institutions. Douglas continued to treat majoritarian democracy as the sine qua non of American political existence, even if it meant parceling out the jurisdictions into smaller and smaller sovereign units. He was, in effect, still dodging his duty to take a principled stand on slavery, and his clever opponent knew it. Lincoln's lawyerly insistence on strict definitions and repeated taunts about the nugatory nature of squatter sovereignty in the wake of Dred Scott kept the pressure on Douglas to explain and defend a doctrine to which he was inextricably bound.[4]

Ultimately Lincoln's taunts proved insufficient to knock Douglas from his Senate perch. The Little Giant fended off his opponent in 1858 but found himself challenged on all sides when he set his sights on the presidency. Still smarting from his stand on Lecompton and angered by his refusal to support a slave code demanded by Jefferson Davis and other southerners, party leaders stripped him of his chairmanship of the Committee on Territories. His most strident critics were the increasingly influential proslavery radicals in the Democratic Party, who found his Freeport Doctrine as loathsome as anything he had said or done. "If the Senator be right," charged Clement C. Clay of Alabama, "squatter sovereignty is superior to the Constitution." Douglas responded, "I do not hold that squatter sovereignty is superior to the Constitution. I hold that no such thing as sovereign power attaches to a Territory while a Territory." Trapped in circular arguments, Democrats continued to clash over squatters' role as arbiters of slavery's fate. Partisans in Texas rued with "the most painful forebodings" a split between "the State Rights Democracy of the South" and "the Douglas or Squatter Democracy of the North and West."[5]

An Indiana newspaper captured the confused state of the Democratic Party in a sketch depicting a conversation between two backcountry settlers.

—Halloo, neighbor, to which branch of the Democracy do you belong?

—Well, friend, to tell the truth, and to be honest, I hardly know myself.—The bosses have got it so tangled up that I can't keep the run of it any longer—they used to call it *Squatter* Democracy, but now I think they call it COPYRIGHT, or some such name. . . . Douglas has taken out a Patent on all us "Squatters." So you see there is no getting away from him now.

—Shaw, neighbor, you ain't posted at all. You see, the Patent Office is at Washington and "Old Buck" is the boss of it, and so Douglas could not get his patent there. Just wait till the Charleston Convention is over and the way we knock the wheels out of the Douglas Patent won't be slow.[6]

Written in the idiom of western humor, the article takes aim at Douglas for hijacking Squatter Democracy and trying to force all squatters to fall in line. This charge was a serious jab at a man whose political survival hinged on the degree to which he could sway voters with his conviction that white Americans enjoyed broad independence and carried fundamental rights with them wherever they ventured. The character in the sketch suggests that there were limits both to Douglas's vision and his actual power. The slavery-friendly Buchanan held command of the Democracy, the character implies, and Douglas, for all his notions of squatter sovereignty, stood on shaky political ground. What is most evident from the exchange is that Jacksonian Squatter Democracy, once a source of party cohesion, was a downright disruptive force.

As forecast by the newspaper squatters, the 1860 Democratic convention in Charleston, South Carolina, was a study in political dysfunction. Douglas enjoyed frontrunner status at the outset, but southerners hammered on the issue of squatter sovereignty throughout ten days that swung from sweltering heat to stretches so overcast and cold that delegates huddled around fires. The taxing work of crafting platform language related to slavery in the territories sucked the oxygen out of the meeting. The Douglasites, predictably, attempted to toe a neutral line, seeking a clear assertion of popular sovereignty. However, the proslavery majority on the platform committee insisted on language barring interference with slavery by territorial governments and demanding federal protection of slaveholder rights. Douglasites signaled a willingness to compromise, approving language declaring it "the duty of the Federal Government, in all its departments, to protect, when necessary, the rights of persons and property in the Territories, and wherever else its constitutional authority extends." This concession failed to appease.[7]

One after another, the southern delegations walked out of the convention. The Florida members railed against "the doctrine of Squatter Sovereignty in the Territories." Texas delegates expressed a nearly identical sentiment as they stormed off. Arkansas made it more personal, attacking Douglas as "the Chief of Squatter Sovereignty." Georgia, Virginia, and Delaware followed suit. The convention was done. When the Douglas forces announced their intention to reconvene in Baltimore in June, an eyewitness to the debacle noted, "There will be two Conventions, the Squatter Sovereignty one at Baltimore, and the Constitutional one, which will assemble at the call of the cotton States." Here was further proof that squatters and cotton did not mix.[8]

The crackup of the Democrats, like the Whig implosion earlier in the decade, created openings for new partisan alignments. The Constitutional Union Party formed and held a convention in Baltimore in early May. Atop their ticket was John Bell of Tennessee, a one-time Jacksonian who had fallen out with the Democrats long before and become a leading Whig in the House and then the Senate. The Constitutional Unionists were small fry compared to the Republican Party, which met in Chicago in mid-May and nominated Abraham Lincoln for president. In their platform, Republicans denounced the Buchanan administration's "subserviency" to the South and explicitly rejected the *Dred Scott* decision, affirming that "the normal condition of all the territory of the United States is that of freedom." It took a swipe at Douglas as well, dismissing "the boasted Democratic principle of Non-Intervention and Popular Sovereignty" as "fraud," spotlighting the repeated meddling by Democrats on behalf of proslavery interests and against the will of the majority in Kansas. While unequivocal in their stance against the spread of slavery, Republicans did not advocate interfering with slavery where it already existed. Party brass understood that an outright abolitionist message would play poorly in many parts of the country, even among their own partisans.[9]

Borrowing a page from the old Squatter Democracy playbook, Republicans turned to public land policies, lauding "actual settlers" while demanding passage of a homestead act, a policy with broad western appeal. Homesteading re-emerged as a significant issue as the presidential canvass gained steam. Lawmakers had debated granting free land off and on since the policy was first introduced in the 1840s. The measure had Democratic backers, not least Douglas, but its embrace by Free Soilers and, later, Republicans killed its chances among most proslavery politicians. There was a handful of exceptions, including Mississippi's Albert G. Brown and Tennessee's Andrew Johnson, perhaps the most persistent homestead proponent in Congress. In April 1860, Johnson introduced a bill "to secure homesteads to actual settlers on the public domain." He tried in vain to convince his fellow southerners that awarding free land was perfectly compatible with slaveholding and born of the same impulses as preemption and graduation—mainstream Democratic policies that many proslavery lawmakers had supported in the past. Louis Wigfall of Texas shot back that much had changed in the politics of land. "The land question presents itself in very different forms from what it did formerly," he argued. "The Senator says that in 1846, when he introduced this measure, it was not a sectional question. It is a sectional question now." Wigfall was right. The issues of land-claiming and slavery extension had become inseparable, driving a wedge between Democrats from the North and South.[10]

Douglas declined to join the rekindled homestead debates, preferring to let his past words and actions speak for themselves. "My opinions have been well known for many years on this question. I have made as many speeches on the subject as I deem it desirable to make," he averred. The Democratic platform in Charleston had made no mention of homesteading, and National Reform Association–inspired crusaders urged Douglas to remedy that defect when the party reconvened in Baltimore, advice he did not heed. He was absent when the Senate and House concurred on a final version of the bill on June 20, sending it to the president for his signature.[11]

Free-land proponents were aghast when James Buchanan vetoed the Homestead Act. In his veto message, dated June 22, the president cited multiple reasons for quashing the legislation: free land for today's settlers would be an injustice to past generations of pioneers who had to pay for their property, the homestead law would undermine "our present admirable land system" that benefited settlers and the government alike, speculators would manipulate the system, and so on. What Buchanan did not say was that his southern base wanted him to kill the measure because it would abet northern family farmers to the detriment of slaveholding planters. Thus, the bill providing for free land—a piece of legislation that in former times would have represented the crowning achievement of Democratic pro-squatterism—got nixed by a veteran Jacksonian unionist allied with the South. The *Dubuque Herald* fumed that "this act fills up the measure of James Buchanan's recreancy to Democratic principles—it is one of the most infamous of his infamous administration." Blasting "the old reprobate," the writer snarled, "The slave propagandists demanded that the Bill should be vetoed, and their pliant tool was swift to obey them."[12]

The veto came as the two branches of the Democracy formalized their platforms and nominated candidates. Douglas won strong support from the northern Democrats. In an attempt to court southerners, his campaign selected Herschel Johnson of Georgia for vice president, a ticket redolent enough of the old planter-plain republican coalition for Martin Van Buren himself to support it. The Democrats' southern wing, meanwhile, nominated John C. Breckinridge for president and Joseph Lane of Oregon as his running mate. Buchanan and his allies threw their support behind Breckinridge, disparaging Douglasites for worshipping the *"brazen calf of Squatterism."* In speeches, cartoons, and songs, the southern Democrats drubbed Douglas with the squatter stick. One Breckinridge campaign ditty, set to the tune of Yankee Doodle, crooned:

The Squatter King should join with us,
Against the nation's foemen,
Instead of kicking up a fuss,
'Bout niggers 'mongst our Yeomen.[13]

The racist song suggested that Douglas's popular sovereignty platform was, at its core, a free-soil contrivance and pined for the days of a unified Democracy, when party faithful did not "kick up a fuss" about slavery. The lyricist clearly saw no incompatibility between the interests of yeomen and large slaveholders—indeed, the yeomen conjured in the ditty may well have been enslavers themselves. Douglas's insistence upon letting local majorities decide the slavery question divided Democrats unnecessarily and only strengthened Republicans ("the nation's foemen"), the song implied. Another verse hailed Breckinridge and Lane for opposing their many enemies like "in the days of Jackson."

Republicans also hammered on the squatter theme, lampooning Douglas as "the squatter giant" who turned a blind eye to the evils of slavery and forsook Congress's responsibilities in favor of mob rule. An Ohioan challenged a Douglas backer to a debate on "the relative merits of Republicanism and squatter Democracy." "I suggest Eden as the place, and the 4th of July as the time for the meeting," he wrote, confident that he occupied the moral high ground and kept faith with the Founders' views of freedom. In August, the *Rail Splitter* newspaper out of Cincinnati ran a cartoon depicting "The Great Political Juggle," in which all four presidential candidates juggle balls inscribed with the names of the states the artist projects they will carry. Lincoln has nearly all of the free states, Breckinridge a significant portion of the South, and

Bell various states in the mid-Atlantic, South, and beyond. Douglas, meanwhile, is sinking under the weight of one extra-large ball labeled "Squat. Sov."
The caption reads: "Poor Douglas has been playing with a large, mysterious,
'Black Pill,' improperly called Squatter Sovereignty, which, owing to the failure
of the people to swallow it, has got him down. He can't carry a single State
next November." Another paper gleefully forecast that when the election for
president came "there will be nothing left of squatter Democracy."[14]

Douglas understood perfectly well that the squatter label had lost all
charm for Democrats and that there was nothing to gain from flirting with
this intensely polarizing symbol. Indeed, he would have preferred for all talk
about squatters and squatter sovereignty to go away as he conducted a national
campaign, with swings through the East, West, North, and even the South.
Wherever he went there were signs reminding him that to many a mind he
was "Stephen A. Douglas, squatter candidate of the Squatter Democracy."[15]

THE GREAT POLITICAL JUGGLE.

WHO IS THE BEST MAN?

"HONEST ABE" has all the Free States, (California excepted,) under perfect control, while the South is
divided between Bell and Breckinridge.

Poor Douglas has been playing with a large, mysterious, "Black Pill," improperly called Squatter
Sovereignty, which, owing to the failure of the people to swallow it, has got him down. He can't carry a single
State next November.

FIGURE 9.1 Stephen A. Douglas sinks under the weight of squatter sovereignty in an
1860 campaign cartoon in the Cincinnati *Rail Splitter*. Courtesy of the Hanna Holborn
Gray Special Collections Research Center, University of Chicago Library.

At a rally in Syracuse in mid-September, Douglas found himself compelled yet again to explain the difference between popular sovereignty and squatter sovereignty. Speaking before a crowd estimated at 50,000—"the largest and most attentive ever held in that portion of New York," according to the *New York Herald*—he traced the origins of the term "squatter sovereignty" to the controversy over Oregon in the 1840s. He recalled how American settlers in the Willamette Valley, vulnerable to Britain's mighty Hudson's Bay Company, had appealed to Congress to establish a territorial government. When Congress failed to act, they formed their own Provisional Government—in Douglas's view a completely warranted course of action under the circumstances. Their constitution banned slavery, triggering southern ire several years later when Douglas introduced the bill to organize Oregon Territory in 1848. John C. Calhoun, he explained to the masses, charged that "the settlers in Oregon were mere trespassers; that they were 'squatters' on the public lands, without title and without the authority of law; that the government which they had established was a squatter government, and had no other validity than that of squatter sovereignty." Douglas rejected that perspective, emphasizing "that every civilized people on earth were entitled to a government" and that when a nation withheld its protection from any part of its population—as the United States had from Oregonians—those people had every right to "protect themselves until the government should extend laws to them." The endorsement of self-government drew cheers from the Syracuse crowd.[16]

Determined to make his position clear, Douglas differentiated between legitimate and illegitimate assertions of authority, which boiled down to a distinction between popular and squatter sovereignty. "Squatter sovereignty is where the people go and seize upon the public domain, and set up a government in violation of law and in defiance of the authority of the government," he declared. Here he positioned squatters as trespassers with no legitimate claim to land or political authority. "Popular sovereignty," by contrast, "is where the people have settled in pursuance of law and are exercising all the rights of self-government according to the Constitution of the United States." He hardly needed to add, "I am in favor of popular sovereignty."

Douglas, who had chaired the Committee on Territories in both the House and Senate, insisted that settlement of the West by white Americans was a blessing, as long as they adhered to basic protocols. The most important involved working with Congress to establish structures of territorial governance and observing formal processes to gain admission into the Union as a state such as procuring authorization to draft a constitution and securing its ratification in a popular referendum. Once the residents of western domains took those steps, it was Congress's sacred obligation to accept them into the US fold, in whatever form the local majority chose. Indeed, Douglas argued, following such protocols was precisely what turned potentially lawless hordes into virtuous citizens. He told the gathering, "I am in favor of either enforcing all the laws of the land against these trespassers and intruders, or of legalizing their settlement by giving them a government according to the Constitution and the laws of the land." Adherence by statesmen and squatters to the niceties of process kept Washington and the West in sync, converting "trespassers and intruders" into the best of Americans.

Back in the heyday of Squatter Democracy, a Jacksonian never would have disparaged squatters to make this point. These settlers, according to the party line, were doing the vital work of nation-building simply by setting down roots in the West. They also formed a solid base of support for Democrats, extending the party's power across the land. By virtue of those contributions they could never be "trespassers and intruders." Stigmatizing them, Douglas sounded like a card-carrying Whig of old. But these were desperate times. The

FIGURE 9.2 George Caleb Bingham, "The Squatters," 1850. Courtesy of the Museum of Fine Arts, Boston.

Little Giant was willing to sacrifice the squatter to save popular sovereignty and his own political skin.

It was not enough. In the general election the vote split along predictable sectional lines. The planters of the South and Southwest overwhelmingly supported Breckinridge, and the plain republicans of the North, Old Northwest, and new western states of California and Oregon by and large backed the Republican Lincoln, while Bell captured his home state of Tennessee and bordering Kentucky and Virginia. Douglas received the second most popular votes but his electoral count was negligible. Defying cartoon predictions, he did however manage to carry one state: Missouri, with its mix of yeoman farmers and slaveholders, Bentonites and Border Ruffians. "Miss Soureye," as the almanac Crockett called it, was where many American minds drifted when imagining squatters, a legacy of writers like John S. Robb who set their boisterous backwoods vignettes there. Sixteen-year-old native son Samuel Langhorne Clemens (aka Mark Twain) arrived on the literary scene in 1854 with a humor sketch about a brawny squatter encountering a riverboat dandy. Missouri artist and Whig politician George Caleb Bingham offered an enduring glimpse of squatter life in his 1850 painting "The Squatters," featuring a pair of men lounging outside their cabin looking a shade mistrustful while a woman does washing in the background. Missouri was a fitting place to give its nine electoral votes to the Squatter King.[17]

Squatters' symbolic presence in American political culture diminished following Douglas's defeat in 1860 and his death at forty-eight a year later. Their physical presence faded too with the passage of the Homestead Act of 1862, which Lincoln signed into law. With public lands widely available for free, these sovereigns of the antebellum frontier were, as Honest Abe might have said, largely "squatted out of existence."

Epilogue

GEORGE BUSH'S AMERICA

ON FEBRUARY 7, 1855, Democratic senator John Pettit of Indiana presented a bill "to confirm the claim of George Bush, to six hundred and forty acres of land, in virtue of his early settlement, and continued residence and cultivation" in Washington Territory. Bush lived in Thurston County, named for Samuel R. Thurston, the young lawmaker who had spent the final months of his life laboring to secure passage of the 1850 Oregon Donation Land Act. Because of his race, George Bush had been unable to avail himself of the act, which provided for a free grant of 320 acres for each white man or "half-breed" Indian, and 320 acres for his wife. Pettit explained:

> In 1845, George Bush, a free mulatto, with his wife and children, emigrated to, and settled, in Thurston county, then in Oregon, but now in Washington Territory, and settled upon, and laid claim to six hundred and forty acres of land. He has continuously occupied the land and cultivated it. He has put upon it a valuable farm-house and other improvements, and now has the tract in a high state of cultivation. Bush having been excluded from the benefits of the law granting donations of land in the Territories, the Territorial Legislature, on the 27th of February, 1854, adopted a memorial to Congress, asking that his case should be made an exception to the general rule, and that an act be passed giving to Bush and his wife title to that section of land so occupied and cultivated by them.

Dangerous Ground. John Suval, Oxford University Press. © Oxford University Press 2022.
DOI: 10.1093/oso/9780197531426.003.0011

Following Pettit's report the Senate passed the bill, securing to George Bush and his wife Isabella lands known for generations to come as "Bush Prairie," just south of downtown Olympia, Washington's capital.[1]

Born in Pennsylvania around 1790, George Bush was indeed "an exception to the general rule" of trying to prevent people of color from becoming landowners in America. He moved to Illinois as a young man and entered the stock-raising trade. He later worked as a trapper based in Missouri, eventually settling in Clay County, where in 1832 he married Isabella James, a white woman with whom he had six sons who survived infancy. Like Free Frank and Lucy McWorter and many other non-whites who prospered in the American West, George Bush and his family had to overcome a gauntlet of exclusionary racist structures.[2]

As part of an emigrant train to Oregon in 1844 the Bushes accounted for six wagons so well-provisioned that they had enough supplies to share with fellow travelers in need. Unlike those other migrants, they faced an uncertain reception in Oregon because of its ban on free blacks, a reality that likely factored in their decision not to end their journey in the Willamette Valley, where the majority of American migrants set down roots. Instead, joined by four other families, they ventured north of the Columbia River and established the first permanent settlement of Americans in what would become Washington Territory. Before heading out for the north country, the band had received a letter from John McLoughlin, chief factor of the Hudson's Bay Company, instructing an associate at Fort Nisqually to provision them on credit. In this way the party obtained wheat, potatoes, cattle, and other goods. The Bushes, however, preferred to pay cash.[3]

As squatters, the Bush family displayed great resourcefulness and their farm and orchards thrived. The value of their livestock alone exceeded $2,000, more than $70,000 today. Isabella was especially adept at raising fowl, including turkeys. Fellow settler Ezra Meeker was struck by their generosity: "George Bush . . . had an abundance of farm produce, but would not sell a pound of anything to a speculator; but to immigrants, for seed or for immediate, pressing wants, to all alike, without money and without price—'return it when you can,'—he would say, and so divided up his whole crop, then worth thousands of dollars." The West, of course, had complicated layers. While the Bushes enjoyed amicable relations with the Nisqually Indians upon whose homelands they had settled, their farm became the site of the fort that they and their white neighbors constructed when war broke out between settlers and the Indians in 1855, leading to further encroachments on Native terrains.[4]

Meeker praised George Bush as "a big-hearted pioneer" and community benefactor, ruing that his "oath could not at that time be taken; neither could he sue in the courts or acquire title to the land upon which he lived, or any land. He had negro blood in his veins, and under the law of this great country, then, was a proscribed outcast." Neighbors recognized this "flagrant wrong" and prevailed upon Washington's territorial legislature to petition Congress to award Bush a patent to his land, resulting in the coveted title that secured the Bushes' place in the community they had helped establish in the far northwest corner of the United States. Through proficiency, resolve, and humanity, George Bush and untold other people of color trumped the narrow racist vision of Squatter Democracy and the barriers set in place to exclude them.[5]

Land for political support formed the beating heart of Squatter Democracy, the marriage of interests between Jacksonian statesmen and white settlers that helped propel the United States across the continent and make Democrats the preeminent force in antebellum politics. The alliance coalesced because North America held tremendous bounty, and Democrats advanced measures like preemption and Indian removal that enabled a wide cross-section of white men to exploit it. The helping hand and tributes to "hardy pioneers" found resonance because they acknowledged the grinding realities of thousands of frontier families and communicated a message that their "friends" in high office valued their toils.

Yet Democrats had to engage in perpetual myth-making to rally partisans across classes and geographical sections and make conquest palatable. For years, the white squatter yeoman was the hero of their narrative, the unsung emblem of American grit and greatness, who converted the lands of Indians, Mexicans, and European rivals into productive American territory. The rhetoric united plain republicans of the North and planters of the South in a program that yielded spoils for all, and sharply distinguished them from their Whig rivals, whom they portrayed as cruel elites out to oppress salt-of-the-earth farmers. Pro-squatterism was pure pandering and it delivered political rewards.

The Democrats' pro-squatter expansionist program faced an existential threat when David Wilmot drew his antislavery line in 1846, forcing a prolonged reckoning about what kind of societies would emerge on conquered lands. The Constitution gave Congress the authority "to dispose of and make all needful Rules and Regulations respecting the Territory or other Property belonging to the United States." Despite that straightforward provision, enslavers resisted any curbs on their capacity to bring human property into western domains that they claimed belonged equally to all the states and their citizens.

Recognizing the dangers of exercising their constitutional mandate to administer the territories, leading Democrats including Lewis Cass and Stephen Douglas doubled down on squatters, vesting these much-mythologized settlers with the authority to solve the explosive slavery question that threatened party cohesion. Popular sovereignty grew from the fiction that the white squatter yeoman was too sensible, too patriotic, and far too busy forging a farm for his family in the western wilds to get overly exercised about slavery one way or the other. The settlement of Oregon and California challenged this theory. Kansas blew it apart. When applied as an actual basis for settlement, "squatter sovereignty" resulted in a destabilizing transfer of authority away from the national government to frontier inhabitants, whose age-old land-taking mechanisms like claim clubs became instruments for waging guerilla war. Squatters ceased to function as agents of US expansion and Democratic hegemony. Instead, they became foot soldiers in clashes to determine whether there was a place for the South's "peculiar institution" in America's future. Each new skirmish added fresh fuel to the agitation engulfing the country, intensified by the sense that national Democrats were not honest brokers but accomplices of the Slave Power who genuflected at the altar of democracy while enabling anti-democratic ruffians to run roughshod over the majority.

Popular sovereignty threw into sharp relief the astonishing degree of moral relativism among Democratic leadership. Prizing power and party unity above all else, they denounced as extremists anyone who took a stand on slavery, strictly avoiding value judgments and treating the institution's expansion or extinction merely as questions of climate, financial bottom lines, or whatever local populations happened to decide for themselves.

Squatter Democracy arose on promises of boundless opportunity for white male partisans and crashed because it sold greed as generosity, peddled violence as virtue, and—blinded by its own spin—failed to recognize the dangerous forces it had unleashed until it was too late. Rhetorically, the shapeshifting squatter yeoman could, for a time, advance the fortunes of the white populations of the North and South. In reality, this mythic figure more closely matched the small family farmer than the slaveholding planter. Squatters could embody sovereignty but not to the benefit of both free farmers and increasingly anti-democratic enslavers, nor to the exclusion of resilient, resourceful non-white people across the continent such as George Bush. By the time men like Robert J. Walker and Stephen A. Douglas acknowledged these truths, the Party of Jackson lay broken in two and the lands to which white Americans staked their sovereign claims had become battlegrounds.

Notes

ABBREVIATIONS

ASP   *American State Papers: Documents Legislative and Executive, of the Congress of the United States.* 38 vols. Washington, DC: Gales and Seaton, 1832–1861

BL   Bancroft Library, University of California, Berkeley

CG   *Congressional Globe*

CLAH   Center for Legislative Archives, Records of the US House of Representatives, Committee on Public Lands, Petitions and Memorials, NARA, Washington, DC

CLAS   Center for Legislative Archives, Records of the US Senate, Committee on Public Lands, Petitions and Memorials, NARA, Washington, DC

CMP   *A Compilation of the Messages and Papers of the Presidents, 1789–1897.* Edited by James D. Richardson. 10 vols. Washington, DC: Government Printing Office, 1896–1899

CRC   Charles Robinson Collection, KSRL

CSH   Center for Sacramento History, Sacramento, CA

EMC   Eleanor McClatchy Collection, CSH

HJ   *Journal of the House of Representatives of the United States*

ISL   Indiana State Library

JBP   James Buchanan Papers, Historical Society of Pennsylvania, Philadelphia

KSHS   Kansas State Historical Society, Topeka

KSRL   Kenneth Spencer Research Library, University of Kansas, Lawrence

LCP   Library Company of Philadelphia

LOC   Library of Congress, Washington, DC

NARA   National Archives and Records Administration, Washington, DC

OHSRL   Oregon Historical Society Research Library, Portland

PAJ   Harold D. Moser et al., eds., *The Papers of Andrew Jackson.* 11 vols. Knoxville: University of Tennessee Press, 1980–

RD   *Register of Debates in Congress*
RJWP   Robert J. Walker Papers, LOC
SADP   Stephen A. Douglas Papers, Special Collections Research Center, University of Chicago Library
SGKN   Records of the US Surveyor General of Kansas and Nebraska, KSHS
SJ   *Journal of the Senate of the United States*
TFP   Thurston Family Papers, OHSRL
TYV   Thomas Hart Benton, *Thirty Years' View; or, A History of the Working of the American Government for Thirty Years, from 1820 to 1850*. 2 vols. New York: D. Appleton and Company, 1854–1856

INTRODUCTION

1. "To the Friends of the South," *Squatter Sovereign* (Atchison, KS Territory), March 27, 1855, 2; "Startling News," *Squatter Sovereign,* June 10, 1856, 3. See also Bill Cecil-Fronsman, "'Death to All Yankees and Traitors in Kansas': The *Squatter Sovereign* and the Defense of Slavery in Kansas," in *Territorial Kansas Reader*, ed. Virgil W. Dean (Topeka: Kansas State Historical Society, 2005), 215–26.

2. Noah Webster, *An American Dictionary of the English Language* (New York: S. Converse, 1828). The Oxford English Dictionary defines "squatter" as "a settler having no formal or legal title to the land occupied by him, *esp.* one thus occupying land in a district not yet surveyed or apportioned by the government." It gives as its earliest example of this usage a 1788 letter from Nathaniel Gorham to James Madison that provided updates on debates at Massachusetts's hotly contested convention to ratify the US Constitution. Referencing resistance to the proposed national charter among representatives from Maine—then a province of Massachusetts—Gorham writes, "Many of them & their Constituents are only squatters upon other Peoples Land, & they are afraid of being brought to account." See "squatter, *n.*" OED Online, http://www.oed.com/ (accessed September 9, 2021).

3. "Republican Principles," *Clermont Courier* (Batavia, OH), December 10, 1857, 2 (emphasis in original).

4. Historian Daniel Walker Howe interprets Jacksonian Democracy—a term he rejects as an oxymoron—as a triumph of white supremacy that left a trail of death, dispossession, and misery for Native Americans and other non-whites. See Howe, *What Hath God Wrought: The Transformation of America, 1815–1848* (New York: Oxford University Press, 2007), 4–5, 356–57. J. M. Opal argues that the "promise of greater sovereignty for white Jacksonians was ... directly tied to the enhanced misery of black and native peoples in antebellum America." See Opal, *Avenging the People: Andrew Jackson, the Rule of Law, and the American Nation* (New York: Oxford University Press, 2017), 225. See also Joshua A. Lynn, *Preserving the White Man's Republic: Jacksonian Democracy, Race, and the Transformation of American Conservatism* (Charlottesville: University of Virginia Press, 2019).

5. Sean Wilentz, *The Rise of American Democracy: Jefferson to Lincoln* (New York: W. W. Norton, 2005), 576, 587, 791.

6. Martin Van Buren to Thomas Ritchie, January 13, 1827, Martin Van Buren Papers, Library of Congress; Michael E. Woods, *Arguing until Doomsday: Stephen Douglas, Jefferson Davis, and the Struggle for American Democracy* (Chapel Hill: University of North Carolina Press, 2020), 46–48.

7. Historians have recognized the prominent position that squatters occupied in antebellum discourse on class. Nancy Isenberg identifies squatters as a dominant Jacksonian-era incarnation of "white trash." See Isenberg, *White Trash: The 400-Year Untold History of Class in America* (New York: Viking, 2016), 105–32. Allan Kulikoff situates squatters in the class struggles that attended capitalist development in the United States. See Kulikoff, *The Agrarian Origins of American Capitalism* (Charlottesville: University of Virginia Press, 1992). Studies exploring squatter politics in the early republic include Alan Taylor, *Liberty Men and Great Proprietors: The Revolutionary Settlement on the Maine Frontier, 1760–1820* (Chapel Hill: University of North Carolina Press, 1990); Stephen Aron, *How the West Was Lost: The Transformation of Kentucky from Daniel Boone to Henry Clay* (Baltimore: Johns Hopkins University Press, 1996); Reeve Huston, "Land Conflict and Land Policy in the United States, 1785–1841," in *The World of the Revolutionary American Republic: Land, Labor, and the Conflict for a Continent,* ed. Andrew Shankman (New York: Routledge, 2014), 324–45; and John R. Van Atta, *Securing the West: Politics, Public Lands, and the Fate of the Old Republic, 1785–1850* (Baltimore: Johns Hopkins University Press, 2014).

8. Daniel Philpott, *Revolutions in Sovereignty: How Ideas Shaped Modern International Relations* (Princeton, NJ: Princeton University Press, 2001), 16–17. John Reda usefully distinguishes between "titular sovereignty acquired by treaty" and "effective sovereignty," observing that sovereignty is a process constructed over time and not "with the stroke of a pen." See Reda, *From Furs to Farms: The Transformation of the Mississippi Valley, 1762–1825* (DeKalb: Northern Illinois University Press, 2016), 41, 148. Anne F. Hyde highlights the fluid state of sovereignty in the North American West in the early decades of the nineteenth century, demonstrating how interracial family networks—not nation-states—wielded a controlling influence and created a degree of order, even as rival nations and empires vied for supremacy. See Hyde, *Empires, Nations, and Families: A New History of the North American West, 1800–1860* (New York: Ecco, 2012). On the relationship between property and sovereignty, see John C. Weaver, *The Great Land Rush and the Making of the Modern World, 1650–1900* (Montreal: McGill-Queen's University Press, 2003), 139–40; and Andro Linklater, *Owning the Earth: The Transforming History of Land Ownership* (New York: Bloomsbury, 2013), 81–82.

9. Under the "doctrine of discovery," purported "discovery" conferred ownership of lands, regardless of the fact that Native peoples had long called them home. "Only the right of occupancy was conceded to the Indians," writes historian Paul

W. Gates, in reference to British and US policies toward Native Americans. "When treaties were made with them for purchase of their land, this right of occupancy was ceded." See Gates, *History of Public Land Law Development* (Washington, DC: Government Printing Office, 1968), 1. The Supreme Court affirmed these principles in *Johnson v. McIntosh* (1823), ruling that Euro-American nations exercised "ultimate dominion" over the Native lands they had discovered or conquered, with the authority to extinguish title to those terrains (21 US 573–74). On the doctrine of discovery, see Robert J. Miller, "American Indians, the Doctrine of Discovery, and Manifest Destiny," *Wyoming Law Review* 11:2 (2011): 329–49; and Gary Lawson and Guy Seidman, *The Constitution of Empire: Territorial Expansion and American Legal History* (New Haven, CT: Yale University Press, 2004).

10. Patrick Wolfe, "Settler Colonialism and the Elimination of the Native," *Journal of Genocide Research* 8:4 (December 2006): 387–409. Walter L. Hixson argues that "American history is the most sweeping, most violent, and most significant example of settler colonialism in world history." See Hixson, *American Settler Colonialism: A History* (New York: Palgrave Macmillan, 2013), 1. See also Jeffrey Ostler and Nancy Shoemaker, "Settler Colonialism in Early American History: Introduction," *William and Mary Quarterly* 76:3 (July 2019): 361–68.

11. Edmund S. Morgan, *Inventing the People: The Rise of Popular Sovereignty in England and America* (New York: W. W. Norton, 1988), 153–54, 169. In a similar vein to Morgan, political scientist Dieter Grimm notes that by vesting sovereignty in the fictive construct of "the people" the framers of the US Constitution curtailed "the autonomy of the individual states for the benefit of the United States." See Grimm, *Sovereignty: The Origin and Future of a Political and Legal Concept* (New York: Columbia University Press, 2015), 37–38, 51.

12. Thomas Jefferson, *Notes on the State of Virginia* (1785; repr., Boston: Lilly and Wait, 1832), 172; Jefferson to George Rogers Clark, December 25, 1780, in *The Works of Thomas Jefferson*, vol. 3, ed. Paul Leicester Ford (New York: G. P. Putnam's Sons, 1904), 103; Walter Johnson, *River of Dark Dreams: Slavery and Empire in the Cotton Kingdom* (Cambridge, MA: Belknap Press of Harvard University Press, 2013), 4. Roger G. Kennedy suggests that for all his stated reverence for yeomen, Jefferson "took no exalted view of the actual yeomen of his acquaintance." See Kennedy, *Mr. Jefferson's Lost Cause: Land, Farmers, Slavery, and the Louisiana Purchase* (New York: Oxford University Press, 2003), 39.

13. For the past century historians have debated the guiding passions and legacies of Jacksonian Democracy. Were Old Hickory and party self-interested elites or champions of the "common man"? Frontier chieftains or eastern sophisticates? For every thesis there is a rebuttal. A tension has long existed between scholars who view Jacksonian Democracy primarily as a sectional phenomenon rooted in the West, and those who style it as a class-driven movement. Frederick Jackson Turner planted the standard for the former view, interpreting Jackson's rise as a "triumph" of rural, agricultural society in the West "over the conservative, industrial, commercial, and manufacturing society of the New England type." See Turner, *The United*

States, 1830–1850: The Nation and its Sections (1935; repr., New York: W. W. Norton, 1963), 30. Arthur M. Schlesinger Jr. challenged this thesis in *The Age of Jackson*, foregrounding economic class over geographical section, while at the same time fixing the nerve center of the Democracy in the cities of the East rather than the farms of the West. See Schlesinger, *The Age of Jackson* (Boston: Little, Brown, 1945). Since Schlesinger, leading scholars have reinforced an eastern-centric perspective, including Lee Benson, *The Concept of Jacksonian Democracy: New York as a Test Case* (Princeton, NJ: Princeton University Press, 1961); Jonathan H. Earle, *Jacksonian Antislavery and the Politics of Free Soil, 1824–1854* (Chapel Hill: University of North Carolina Press, 2004); and Wilentz, *The Rise of American Democracy*. For studies on land in antebellum politics, see Daniel Feller, *The Public Lands in Jacksonian Politics* (Madison: University of Wisconsin Press, 1984); and Reeve Huston, *Land and Freedom: Rural Society, Popular Protest, and Party Politics in Antebellum New York* (New York: Oxford University Press, 2000).

14. For studies that underscore fundamental incompatibilities between North and South, see Charles A. Beard and Mary R. Beard, *The Rise of American Civilization*, vol. 2, *The Industrial Era* (New York: Macmillan, 1927), 3–10; Eugene D. Genovese, *The Political Economy of Slavery: Studies in the Economy and Society of the Slave South* (New York: Pantheon Books, 1965); James McPherson, *Battle Cry of Freedom: The Civil War Era* (New York: Oxford University Press, 1988); and Bruce Levine, *Half Slave and Half Free: The Roots of Civil War* (New York: Hill and Wang, 1992). Marc Egnal analyzes the economic foundations of the sectional conflict in *Clash of Extremes: The Economic Origins of the Civil War* (New York: Hill and Wang, 2009). James L. Huston, *The British Gentry, the Southern Planter, and the Northern Family Farmer: Agriculture and Sectional Antagonism in North America* (Baton Rouge: Louisiana State University Press, 2015). Other works foregrounding the role of competing agricultural systems in the sectional conflict include Eric Foner, *Free Soil, Free Labor, Free Men: The Ideology of the Republican Party Before the Civil War* (1970; repr., New York: Oxford University Press, 1995); and Adam Wesley Dean, *An Agrarian Republic: Farming, Antislavery Politics, and Nature Parks in the Civil War Era* (Chapel Hill: University of North Carolina Press, 2015). "Two agrarianisms" appears in Henry Nash Smith, *Virgin Land: The American West as Symbol and Myth* (New York: Vintage Books, 1950), 151.

CHAPTER 1

1. *Public Dinner, Given in Honor of the Chickasaw and Choctaw Treaties, at Mr. Parker's Hotel, in the City of Natchez, on the 10th Day of October, 1830*, 1–2, Sabin Americana, 1500–1926.

2. Ibid., 5.

3. William Leggett, "The Squatter," in *Tales and Sketches. By a Country Schoolmaster* (New York: J. and J. Harper, 1829), 13–83. Jonathan H. Earle interprets "The

Squatter" as an early articulation of Leggett's antislavery views, noting the sympathetic portrayal of Mungo, a central character described by the narrator as the protagonist's "aged negro domestic." See Earle, *Jacksonian Antislavery and the Politics of Free Soil, 1824–1854* (Chapel Hill: University of North Carolina Press, 2004), 19–27. Author John Neal offered his own tale of a down-on-his-luck squatter in the 1835 short story "The Squatter." See Neal, *The Genius of John Neal: Selections from His Writings*, ed. Benjamin Lease and Hans-Joachim Lang (Frankfurt, Germany: Peter Lang, 1978), 58–66.

4. Benjamin Rush, *Essays, Literary, Moral and Philosophical*, 2nd ed. (Philadelphia: Thomas and William Bradford, 1806), 221; Henry Bradshaw Fearon, *Sketches of America: A Narrative of a Journey of Five Thousand Miles through the Eastern and Western States of America* (London: Longman, Hurst, Rees, Orme, and Brown, 1818), 221–22, 261 (emphasis in original). Alan Taylor explores how the term "white Indian" factored in land disputes in post-Revolutionary Maine in *Liberty Men and Great Proprietors: The Revolutionary Settlement on the Maine Frontier, 1760–1820* (Chapel Hill: University of North Carolina Press, 1990).

5. *Annals of Congress*, 9th Cong., 1st sess., 469; Payson Jackson Treat, *The National Land System: 1785–1820* (New York: E. B. Treat, 1910), 373; Thomas L. Karnes, *William Gilpin: Western Nationalist* (1970; repr., Austin: University of Texas Press, 2014), 4; J. M. Peck, *A New Guide for Emigrants to the West, Containing Sketches of Michigan, Ohio, Indiana, Illinois, Missouri, Arkansas, with the Territory of Wisconsin and the Adjacent Parts*, 2nd ed. (Boston: Gould, Kendall and Lincoln, 1837), 121.

6. James Fenimore Cooper, *The Prairie: A Tale* (Philadelphia: Carey, Lea and Carey, 1827), 19, 106. On Cooper's background and relationship to Jacksonian Democracy, see Alan Taylor, *William Cooper's Town: Power and Persuasion on the Frontier of the Early American Republic* (New York: Vintage Books, 1995); Reeve Huston, *Land and Freedom: Rural Society, Popular Protest, and Party Politics in Antebellum New York* (New York: Oxford University Press, 2000), 73–75; Richard Slotkin, *The Fatal Environment: The Myth of the Frontier in the Age of Industrialization, 1800–1890* (New York: Atheneum, 1985), 81–106; Marvin Meyers, *The Jacksonian Persuasion: Politics and Belief* (1957; repr., Stanford, CA: Stanford University Press, 1960), 57–100; and Joseph L. Blau, ed., *Social Theories of Jacksonian Democracy: Representative Writings of the Period 1825–1850* (New York: Hafner, 1947), xv.

7. Joseph M. White to Thomas Hart Benton, January 12, 1828, *ASP Public Lands*, 5:357. There is a long-running debate among scholars about the pervasiveness of yeomen farmers in the South, their relationship to slavery, and their standing in societies dominated by slaveholding planters. See, for example, Eugene D. Genovese, "Yeomen Farmers in a Slaveholders' Democracy," *Agricultural History* 49:2 (April 1975): 331–42; Steven Hahn, *The Roots of Southern Populism: Yeoman Farmers and the Transformation of the Georgia Upcountry, 1850–1890* (New York: Oxford University Press, 1983); Harry L. Watson, "Conflict and Collaboration: Yeomen,

Slaveholders, and Politics in the Antebellum South," *Social History* 10:3 (October 1985): 273–98; Charles C. Bolton, *Poor Whites of the Antebellum South: Tenants and Laborers in Central North Carolina and Northeast Mississippi* (Durham, NC: Duke University Press, 1994); Stephanie McCurry, *Masters of Small Worlds: Yeoman Households, Gender Relations, and the Political Culture of the Antebellum South Carolina Low Country* (New York: Oxford University Press, 1995); Edward E. Baptist, *Creating an Old South: Middle Florida's Plantation Frontier Before the Civil War* (Chapel Hill: University of North Carolina Press, 2002); Adam Rothman, *Slave Country: American Expansion and the Origins of the Deep South* (Cambridge, MA: Harvard University Press, 2005); Walter Johnson, *River of Dark Dreams: Slavery and Empire in the Cotton Kingdom* (Cambridge, MA: Belknap Press of Harvard University Press, 2013); and James L. Huston, *The British Gentry, the Southern Planter, and the Northern Family Farmer: Agriculture and Sectional Antagonism in North America* (Baton Rouge: Louisiana State University Press, 2015). In his letter to Benton, White observed that the poor farmers of the South were "apt to wither and decay in the proximity to the more wealthy planter," *ASP Public Lands*, 5:358.

8. *RD*, 21st Cong., 2d sess., 470, 474; *CG*, 25th Cong., 2d sess., app., 132, 134; Natchitoches Parish residents to Congress, undated, CLAS, SEN21A-G17, box 34.

9. Robert Baird, *View of the Valley of the Mississippi, or the Emigrant's and Traveller's Guide to the West* (Philadelphia: H. S. Tanner, 1834), 99–101. On the settlement of the Trans-Appalachian frontier, see Andrew R. L. Cayton, *Frontier Indiana* (Bloomington: Indiana University Press, 1996); Thomas D. Clark and John D. W. Guice, *Frontiers in Conflict: The Old Southwest, 1795–1830* (Albuquerque: University of New Mexico Press, 1989); John Mack Faragher, *Sugar Creek: Life on the Illinois Prairie* (New Haven, CT: Yale University Press, 1986); Susan E. Gray, *The Yankee West: Community Life on the Michigan Frontier* (Chapel Hill: University of North Carolina Press, 1996); R. Douglas Hurt, *The Ohio Frontier: Crucible of the Old Northwest, 1720–1830* (Bloomington: Indiana University Press, 1996); and Malcolm J. Rohrbough, *The Trans-Appalachian Frontier: People, Societies, and Institutions, 1775–1850*, 3rd ed. (Bloomington: Indiana University Press, 2008). On patterns of westward settlement, see also D. W. Meinig, *Continental America, 1800–1867*, vol. 2 of *The Shaping of America: A Geographical Perspective on 500 Years of History* (New Haven, CT: Yale University Press, 1993).

10. Conevery Bolton Valenčius, *The Health of the Country: How American Settlers Understood Themselves and Their Land* (New York: Basic Books, 2002), 34–36; Peck, *A New Guide for Emigrants to the West*, 317–18; Baird, *View of the Valley of the Mississippi*. On the labor and costs required to establish a farm, see also Allan G. Bogue, *From Prairie to Corn Belt: Farming on the Illinois and Iowa Prairies in the Nineteenth Century* (Chicago: University of Chicago Press, 1963).

11. Rebecca Burlend, *A True Picture of Emigration* (1848; repr., Chicago: Lakeside Press, 1936), 47–49.

12. Ibid., 59. Reginald Horsman, *The Frontier in the Formative Years, 1783–1815* (New York: Holt, Rinehart and Winston, 1970), 104–25; Faragher, *Sugar Creek*, 4–6; Baptist, *Creating an Old South*, 47; Allan Kulikoff, *The Agrarian Origins of American Capitalism* (Charlottesville: University of Virginia Press, 1992), 264–65.

13. Robert Grant et al. to Congress, undated, CLAS, SEN25A-G18.1, box 118.

14. W. W. Lester, *Decisions of the Interior Department in Public Land Cases, and Land Laws Passed by the Congress of the United States; Together with the Regulations of the General Land Office* (Philadelphia: H. P. and R. H. Small, 1860), 64–65; Paul W. Gates, *History of Public Land Law Development* (Washington, DC: Government Printing Office, 1968), 222–27; *ASP Public Lands*, 3:619.

15. "Alive with Men, Women, Children . . ." quoted in James A. Henretta, Eric Hinderaker, Rebecca Edwards, and Robert O. Self, *America's History*, vol.1, *To 1877*, 8th ed. (Boston: Bedford/St. Martin's, 2011), 142; Richard White, *The Middle Ground: Indians, Empires, and Republics in the Great Lakes Region, 1650–1815* (New York: Cambridge University Press, 1991), 269–314; Colin G. Calloway, *The Scratch of a Pen: 1763 and the Transformation of North America* (New York: Oxford University Press, 2006), 66–111.

16. *The Works of the Right Honourable Edmund Burke*, vol. 1 (London: Henry G. Bohn, 1854), 472–73.

17. The literature on the US public lands is sizable, if somewhat dated. Volumes that remain vital include Paul W. Gates, *History of Public Land Law Development*; Vernon Carstensen, ed., *The Public Lands: Studies in the History of the Public Domain* (Madison: University of Wisconsin Press, 1963); Malcolm J. Rohrbough, *The Land Office Business: The Settlement and Administration of American Public Lands, 1789–1837* (New York: Oxford University Press, 1968); and Roy M. Robbins, *Our Landed Heritage: The Public Domain, 1776–1936* (Princeton, NJ: Princeton University Press, 1942). More recent treatments include Alan Taylor, "Land and Liberty on the Post-Revolutionary Frontier," in *Devising Liberty: Preserving and Creating Freedom in the New American Republic*, ed. David Thomas Konig (Stanford, CA: Stanford University Press, 1995), 81–108; Reeve Huston, "Land Conflict and Land Policy in the United States, 1785–1841," in *The World of the Revolutionary American Republic: Land, Labor and the Conflict for a Continent*, ed. Andrew Shankman (New York: Routledge, 2014), 324–45; and John R. Van Atta, *Securing the West: Politics, Public Lands, and the Fate of the Old Republic, 1785–1850* (Baltimore: Johns Hopkins University Press, 2014).

18. Andrew R. L. Cayton, *The Frontier Republic: Ideology and Politics in the Ohio Country, 1780–1825* (Kent, OH: Kent State University Press, 1986), 7; Gates, *History of Public Land Law Development*, 67–68; "Anything short of a Chinese wall . . ." quoted in Gordon S. Wood, *Empire of Liberty: A History of the Early Republic, 1789–1815* (New York: Oxford University Press, 2009), 120–21; Anne F. Hyde, *Empires, Nations, and Families: A New History of the North American West, 1800–1860* (New York: Ecco, 2012), 242; Henry Knox to George Washington, June 15, 1789, *ASP Indian Affairs*, 1:12–14.

19. Thomas Jefferson, "First Inaugural Address," *CMP*, 1:323.
20. Act of April 24, 1820 (3 Stat. 566).
21. On Jefferson's views on land ownership and political economy, see Christopher Michael Curtis, *Jefferson's Freeholders and the Politics of Ownership in the Old Dominion* (New York: Cambridge University Press, 2012); Drew R. McCoy, *The Elusive Republic: Political Economy in Jeffersonian America* (Chapel Hill: University of North Carolina Press, 1980); and Roger G. Kennedy, *Mr. Jefferson's Lost Cause: Land, Farmers, Slavery, and the Louisiana Purchase* (New York: Oxford University Press, 2003). On the importance of the Louisiana Purchase to US national development, see Peter J. Kastor, *The Nation's Crucible: The Louisiana Purchase and the Creation of America* (New Haven, CT: Yale University Press, 2004). On the advent of Indian trading factories and other federal efforts to manage the lands and people of the Mississippi Valley, see John Reda, *From Furs to Farms: The Transformation of the Mississippi Valley, 1762–1825* (DeKalb: Northern Illinois University Press, 2016), 66–119; and David Andrew Nichols, *Engines of Diplomacy: Indian Trading Factories and the Negotiation of American Empire* (Chapel Hill: University of North Carolina Press, 2016).
22. Act of March 3, 1807 (2 Stat. 445); Jeremy Adelman and Stephen Aron, "From Borderlands to Borders: Empires, Nation-States, and the Peoples in Between in North American History," *American Historical Review* 104:3 (June 1999): 828; Peter J. Kastor, *William Clark's World: Describing America in an Age of Unknowns* (New Haven, CT: Yale University Press, 2011), 194. On US acquisition of Creek territory, see Howe, *What Hath God Wrought: The Transformation of America, 1815–1848* (New York: Oxford University Press, 2007), 125–32. On opposition to Madison's order, see Reda, *From Fur to Farms*, 93–94. "Everyman is an *intruder* . . ." from Harry Toulmin to James Madison, January 20, 1816, in Everett Dick, *The Lure of the Land: A Social History of the Public Lands from the Articles of Confederation to the New Deal* (Lincoln: University of Nebraska Press, 1970), 53.
23. Jackson to Monroe, March 4, 1817, *PAJ*, 4:93–98.
24. Richard Hofstadter, *The American Political Tradition and the Men Who Made It* (1948; repr., New York: Vintage Books, 1989), 65.
25. Historian Gregory H. Nobles makes provocative observations when he writes, "Jackson claimed to be a political descendant of Jefferson, and he was in a sense a coarser second coming of the yeoman president. Jefferson saw the yeoman as an admirable abstraction; Jackson knew him as a fellow soldier from the frontier wars. Jefferson wanted to assimilate Indians; Jackson was willing to kill them." Nobles, *American Frontiers: Cultural Encounters and Continental Conquest* (New York: Hill and Wang, 1997), 126.
26. "Address of Robert J. Walker, Esq. of Natchez, Miss., to the People of Hinds county," *Richmond Enquirer*, October 17, 1834, 1; Elbert B. Smith, *Magnificent Missourian: The Life of Thomas Hart Benton* (Philadelphia: J. B. Lippincott, 1957), 13–58; Sean Wilentz, *The Rise of American Democracy: Jefferson to Lincoln* (New York: W. W. Norton, 2005), 287; James Parton, *The Life of Andrew Jackson*

(New York: Mason Brothers, 1860), 1:386–98; Holly Zumwalt Taylor, "Neither North nor South: Sectionalism, St. Louis Politics, and the Coming of the Civil War, 1846–1861" (PhD diss., University of Texas at Austin, 2004), 30–32.

27. *TYV*, 1:12. On Benton's land program, see Daniel Feller, *The Public Lands in Jacksonian Politics* (Madison: University of Wisconsin Press, 1984), 68–70; Ken S. Mueller, *Senator Benton and the People: Master Race Democracy on the Early American Frontiers* (DeKalb: Northern Illinois University Press, 2014), 149–55; and John Opie, *The Law of the Land: Two Hundred Years of American Farmland Policy* (Lincoln: University of Nebraska Press, 1987), 62. Mary E. Young unpacks the elements of "the Bentonian school of political economy" in "Congress Looks West: Liberal Ideology and Public Land Policy in the Nineteenth Century," in *The Frontier in American Development: Essays in Honor of Paul Wallace Gates*, ed. David M. Ellis (Ithaca, NY: Cornell University Press, 1969), 77–79.

28. Allan Nevins, ed., *The Diary of John Quincy Adams, 1794–1845: American Diplomacy, and Political, Social, and Intellectual Life, from Washington to Polk* (New York: Charles Scribner's Sons, 1951), 365–66, 459–60; *RD*, 21st Cong., 1st sess., 443. For accounts of debates prompted by Foot's resolution, see Christopher Childers, *The Webster-Hayne Debate: Defining Nationhood in the Early American Republic* (Baltimore: Johns Hopkins University Press, 2018); and Van Atta, *Securing the West*, 139–69.

29. On the Indian Removal Act (4 Stat. 411), see Ronald N. Satz, *American Indian Policy in the Jacksonian Era* (Lincoln: University of Nebraska Press, 1975), 9–31; Francis Paul Prucha, *The Great Father: The United States Government and the American Indians*, vol. 1 (Lincoln: University of Nebraska Press, 1984), 200–208; Stuart Banner, *How the Indians Lost Their Land: Law and Power on the Frontier* (Cambridge, MA: Belknap Press of Harvard University Press, 2005), 191–227; and Walter L. Hixson, *American Settler Colonialism: A History* (New York: Palgrave Macmillan, 2013), 80–83.

30. *SJ*, 21st Cong., 1st sess., 83; *HJ*, 21st Cong., 1st sess., 778–79. Historians have found evidence in the preemption roll calls of a fleeting alliance between politicians from the South and West. See, for example, Feller, *The Public Lands in Jacksonian Politics*, 129–31; and Gates, *History of Public Land Law Development*, 224–25. Political scientists Sean Gailmard and Jeffery A. Jenkins question the existence of such an alliance in "Distributive Politics and Congressional Voting: Public Lands Reform in the Jacksonian Era," *Public Choice* 175 (2018): 259, 272.

31. *SJ*, 21st Cong., 1st sess., 268; *HJ*, 21st Cong., 1st sess., 729–30; Leonard A. Carlson and Mark A. Roberts, "Indian Lands, 'Squatterism,' and Slavery: Economic Interests and the Passage of the Indian Removal Act of 1830," *Explorations in Economic History* 43 (2006): 488.

32. On the Preemption Act of May 29, 1830 (4 Stat. 420), see Gates, *History of Public Land Law Development*, 224–28; Rohrbough, *The Land Office Business*, 205–12; and Feller, *The Public Lands in Jacksonian Politics*, 129–31.

33. Memorial of Mississippi legislature to US Congress, December 15, 1831, and memorial of Illinois legislature to US Congress, undated, CLAH, HR22A-G19.4 (emphasis in original).

34. George B. Willis et al. to Congress, undated, CLAH, HR22A-G19.4; Moses Finch et al. to Congress, December 25, 1834, CLAS, SEN23A-G15, box 126; William Matheson to Congress, December 14, 1830, HR21A-G18.5. On Matheson, see also "Petition 20184710," Race & Slavery Petitions Project, Digital Library on American Slavery, University of North Carolina at Greensboro, https://library.uncg.edu/slavery/petitions/details.aspx?pid=3181 (accessed on April 27, 2021).

35. O. P. Lacey et al. to US Congress and Isaac Darneille et al. to Congress, 1836, CLAS, SEN24A-G15, box 93. On land speculation, see Ray Allen Billington, "The Origin of the Land Speculator as a Frontier Type," *Agricultural History* 19:4 (October 1945): 204–12; Gates, *History of Public Land Law Development*, 62–63n7; John C. Weaver, *The Great Land Rush and the Making of the Modern World, 1650–1900* (Montreal: McGill-Queen's University Press, 2003), 195–202; Robert P. Swierenga, *Pioneers and Profits: Land Speculation on the Iowa Frontier* (Ames: Iowa State University, 1968); Swierenga, "Land Speculation and Its Impact on American Economic Growth and Welfare: A Historiographical Review," *Western Historical Quarterly* 8:3 (July 1977): 283–302; Leslie E. Decker, "The Great Speculation: An Interpretation of Mid-Continent Pioneering," in *The Frontier in American Development: Essays in Honor of Paul Wallace Gates*, ed. David M. Ellis (Ithaca, NY: Cornell University Press, 1969), 357–80.

36. L. H. T. Maxson et al. to Congress, December 6, 1834, CLAS, SEN23A-G15, box 126; "Cherokee Country" residents to Congress, December 24, 1836, CLAS, SEN24A-G15, box 93.

37. Darneille et al. to Congress, ibid. (emphasis in original).

38. "On the Purchase of Texas," *Arkansas Gazette* (Little Rock, AR), February 23, 1830, 3; J. L. McConnel, *Western Characters; or, Types of Border Life in the Western States* (New York: Redfield, 1853), 137.

39. William H. Smith to Congress, undated, CLAS, SEN26A-G17, box 102; Joel Barnett et al. to Andrew Jackson, May 22, 1834, NARA, RG 75, M234, reel 188; Mary W. Robison to Congress, January 25, 1841, CLAS, SEN26A-G16, box 102.

40. Northern Illinois residents to Congress, undated, CLAS, SEN24A-G15, box 93; Illinois/Michigan Territory border residents to Congress, undated, SEN22A-G16.1, box 68; "Cherokee Country" residents to Congress, December 24, 1836, CLAS, SEN24A-G15, box 93. For an examination of the rhetoric used to justify and abet conquests, see James Joseph Buss, *Winning the West with Words: Language and Conquest in the Lower Great Lakes* (Norman: University of Oklahoma Press, 2011), 42–70.

41. Catharine Cheike to Congress, undated, CLAS, SEN22A-G16.1, box 68.

42. Isaac Darneille et al. to US Congress, undated, CLAS, SEN24A-G15, box 93.

43. Ibid.; Isaac Darneille to Ambrose H. Sevier and William S. Fulton, November 15, 1836; *RD*, 23d Cong., 2d sess., 1352.

44. Glen O. Burnett to Thomas Hart Benton, December 18, 1839, CLAS, SEN26A-G17, box 102; *RD*, 21st Cong., 2d sess., 407; *HJ*, 23d Cong., 1st sess., 67, 387, 447; William M. Stewart to Joseph Duncan, December 20, 1832, CLAH, HR22A-G19.4.

45. Ibid.; Andrew Jackson, "Fourth Annual Message," *CMP*, 2:600–602.

46. *RD*, 22d Cong., 1st sess., 3529.

47. Major L. Wilson, *Space, Time, and Freedom: The Quest for Nationality and the Irrepressible Conflict, 1815–1861* (Westport, CT: Greenwood Press, 1974), 4–12; Thomas R. Hietala, *Manifest Design: Anxious Aggrandizement in Late Jacksonian America* (Ithaca, NY: Cornell University Press, 1985), 4–5; Feller, *The Public Lands in Jacksonian Politics*, 189–94.

48. Michael F. Holt, *The Rise and Fall of the American Whig Party: Jacksonian Politics and the Onset of the Civil War* (New York: Oxford University Press, 1999); Daniel Walker Howe, *The Political Culture of the American Whigs* (Chicago: University of Chicago Press, 1979), 18–19. For a short, well-drawn biography of Clay, see Howe, *The Political Culture of the American Whigs*, 123–49. On Henry Clay's early career as a legislator in Kentucky and architect of the "Bluegrass System"—a precursor to his American System—see Aron, *How the West Was Lost*, 92–101; 124–49.

49. *RD*, 23d Cong., 1st sess., 4473; *RD*, 22d Cong., 1st sess., 3527.

50. Ibid., 3528; ibid., 23d Cong., 1st sess., 4539. For analysis of how "squatter demands" played a pivotal role in advancing preemption legislation, see Mark T. Kanazawa, "Possession Is Nine Points of the Law: The Political Economy of Early Public Land Disposal," *Explorations in Economic History* 33 (1996): 227–49.

51. *ASP Public Lands*, 8:701; Benjamin Horace Hibbard, *A History of the Public Land Policies* (1924; repr., Madison: University of Wisconsin Press, 1965), 103.

52. Scholars have attributed far-reaching influence to squatter associations. In his pathbreaking work of legal history, James Willard Hurst argued that claim clubs helped establish the foundations of legal order in frontier regions. See Hurst, *Law and the Conditions of Freedom in the Nineteenth-Century United States* (Madison: University of Wisconsin Press, 1956). Paul W. Gates argued that by thwarting the designs of speculators and "loan sharks" (who loaned money to cash-strapped squatters "at extortionate rates"), squatter associations "made the land system more democratic in its operation." See Gates, *Landlords and Tenants on the Prairie Frontier: Studies in American Land Policy* (Ithaca, NY: Cornell University Press, 1973), 112. See also Ilia Murtazashvili, *The Political Economy of the American Frontier* (New York: Cambridge University Press, 2013); and Allan G. Bogue, "The Iowa Claim Clubs: Symbol and Substance," in *The Public Lands: Studies in the History of the Public Domain*, ed. Vernon Carstensen (Madison: University of Wisconsin Press, 1963), 47–69.

53. No Headline (Letter to William Lloyd Garrison), *The Liberator*, March 29, 1834, 2.

54. Henry Watterson Heggie, *Indians and Pioneers of Old Eliot: A Grenada County, Mississippi, Community* (Grenada, MS: Tuscahoma Press, 1989), 179–81; Rohrbough, *The Land Office Business*, 221–49.

55. Charles J. Kappler, *Indian Affairs: Laws and Treaties*, vol. 2 (Washington, DC: Government Printing Office, 1904), 310–19; Satz, *American Indian Policy in the Jacksonian Era*, 64–87; Richard White, *The Roots of Dependency: Subsistence, Environment, and Social Change Among the Choctaws, Pawnees, and Navajos* (Lincoln: University of Nebraska Press, 1983), 139–44; Robert V. Remini, *The Life of Andrew Jackson* (New York: Harper and Row, 1988), 215–16; Heggie, *Indians and Pioneers of Old Eliot*, 181, 240.

56. *ASP Public Lands*, 7:608–22, 8:711–88; *SDoc* 22, 23d Cong., 2d sess., 10–18, 42–69, 86–119, Serial 267.

57. Lewis Cecil Gray, *History of Agriculture in the Southern United States to 1860*, vol. 2 (1933; repr., New York: Peter Smith, 1941), 697.

58. *SDoc* 22, 23d Cong., 2d sess., 91, 95–96, 102–3, 113–14, Serial 267; *SDoc* 461, 23d Cong., 1st sess., 22–26, Serial 243; *ASP Public Lands*, 8:745. Under the company's terms, squatters could acquire a quarter section (160 acres) at cost if their improvements extended beyond an eighth section (80 acres).

59. *ASP Public Lands*, 8:739–45.

60. William Dusinberre, *Slavemaster President: The Double Career of James Polk* (New York: Oxford University Press, 2003), 14. A report by Mississippi's state auditor published in January 1836—scarcely two years after the creation of the "Choctaw counties"—shows enslaved people outnumbering taxable whites three to one in Yalobusha County and five to one in Carroll County, both in the heart of Chocchuma country. See *Journal of the Senate of the State of Mississippi*, 14th sess. (Jackson, MS: G. R. and J. S. Fall, 1837), 25–26.

61. William M. Gwin to Andrew Jackson, August 9, 1834, Library of Congress, Papers of Andrew Jackson (emphasis in original); Edwin A. Miles, *Jacksonian Democracy in Mississippi* (New York: Da Capo Press, 1970) 95–96; James P. Shenton, *Robert John Walker: A Politician from Jackson to Lincoln* (New York: Columbia University Press, 1961), 19–20.

62. *SDoc* 151, 23d Cong., 2d sess., 4–5, Serial 269 (emphasis in original).

63. *SDoc* 22, 23d Cong., 2d sess., 108, Serial 267; "State of Mississippi," *Richmond Enquirer*, November 28, 1834, 3; Shenton, *Robert John Walker*, 17–21; Henry S. Foote, *Casket of Reminiscences* (Washington, DC: Chronicle Publishing, 1874), 218–19; *Journal of the Senate of the State of Mississippi*, January 1836 session, 71–76.

64. *SJ*, 24th Cong., 1st sess., 254; *RD*, 24th Cong., 1st sess., 1029.

65. Ibid.

66. Ibid., 1029–30.

67. "Fraud! fraud!! fraud!!!," *Commercial Advertiser* (New York, NY), April 2, 1836, 2; "Correspondence of the Courier," *Boston Courier*, May 30, 1836, 3; "Correspondence of the Courier," *Boston Courier*, May 31, 1836, 1; "From Our

Washington Correspondent," *Daily Evening Advertiser* (Portland, ME), April 29, 1836, 2.

68. *SDoc* 401, 24th Cong., 1st sess., 1, Serial 283; *CG*, 24th Cong., 2d sess., app., 289.

69. Northern Illinois residents to Congress, undated, CLAS, SEN24A-G15, box 93.

70. Racine residents to Congress, August 24, 1837, SEN25A-G18.1, box 118.

71. *SJ*, 25th Cong., 2d sess., 70; *CG*, 25th Cong., 2d sess., app., 132, 134, 139. On Clay, squatters, and preemption, see Van Atta, *Securing the West*, 205–31; and Gates, *History of Public Land Law Development*, 233.

72. *CG*, 25th Cong., 2d sess., app., 137; Jackson to Joel R. Poinsett, January 24, 1833, *PAJ*, 11:67.

73. *CG*, 25th Cong., 2d sess., app., 142 (emphasis in original).

74. Act of June 22, 1838 (5 Stat. 251); *SJ*, 25th Cong., 2d sess., 191; *HJ*, 25th Cong., 2d sess., 1101. For a breakdown of the 1838 preemption roll calls in the Senate and House, see Van Atta, *Securing the West*, 222–24.

CHAPTER 2

1. NARA-RG 75, T494, reel 3.

2. Ibid.

3. Patrick Wolfe, "Settler Colonialism and the Elimination of the Native," *Journal of Genocide Research* 8:4 (December 2006): 396; Benjamin F. Currey to Andrew Jackson, November 10, 1834, NARA-RG 75, M234, reel 76.

4. Andrew Jackson, "Second Annual Message," *CMP*, 2:519–23.

5. 30 US 1 (1831); 31 US 515 (1832); Stuart Banner, *How the Indians Lost Their Land: Law and Power on the Frontier* (Cambridge, MA: Belknap Press of Harvard University Press, 2005), 217–24; Ronald N. Satz, *American Indian Policy in the Jacksonian Era* (Lincoln: University of Nebraska Press, 1975), 11–13, 43–53; Charles Sellers, *The Market Revolution: Jacksonian America, 1815–1846* (New York: Oxford University Press, 1991), 309–12; Daniel Walker Howe, *What Hath God Wrought: The Transformation of America, 1815–1848* (New York: Oxford University Press, 2007), 346–57.

6. John Ross et al. to Andrew Jackson, January 23, 1835, in *The Papers of Chief John Ross*, vol. 1, ed. Gary Moulton (Norman: University of Oklahoma Press, 1985), 317–19; John Ross et al. to Lewis Cass, February 14, 1835, ibid., 321–23; Cass to Ross et al., February 16, 1835, NARA-RG 75, M21, reel 15.

7. Andrew Jackson to the Seminoles, February 16, 1835, *ASP Military Affairs*, 6:524.

8. Act of August 4, 1842 (5 Stat. 502); Benton quoted in Theodore Roosevelt, *Thomas Hart Benton* (1886; repr. Boston: Houghton, Mifflin, 1900), 216. Julius Wilm provides insightful analysis of the Armed Occupation Act and other efforts to conquer new lands through government-supported settlement schemes in *Settlers as Conquerors: Free Land Policy in Antebellum America* (Stuttgart, Germany: Franz Steiner Verlag, 2018).

9. Memorial of Mississippi legislature to Congress, December 19, 1831, and memorial of Indiana legislature to Congress, January 16, 1832, CLAS, SEN22A-G16.1, box 68; Paul Frymer, *Building an American Empire: The Era of Territorial and Political Expansion* (Princeton, NJ: Princeton University Press, 2017), 10.

10. Putnam County residents to Congress, December 12, 1832, CLAH, HR22A-G19.4; Solon Robinson et al. to Congress, undated, CLAS, SEN24A-G15, box 92; Zadoc Martin to US Congress, undated, ibid., SEN26A-G17, box 102; Charles J. Kappler, *Indian Affairs: Laws and Treaties*, vol. 2 (Washington, DC: Government Printing Office, 1904), 353.

11. "Constitution of the Squatters Union in Lake County, Indiana," Squatters' Union of Lake County Papers, 1836–1838, ISL (emphasis in original). On Solon Robinson, see Herbert Anthony Kellar, ed., *Solon Robinson: Pioneer and Agriculturalist*, 2 vols. (Indianapolis: Indiana Historical Bureau, 1936); William Frederick Howat, *A Standard History of Lake County, Indiana, and the Calumet Region*, vol. 1 (Chicago: Lewis Publishing, 1915), 36–37; and James Joseph Buss, *Winning the West with Words: Language and Conquest in the Lower Great Lakes* (Norman: University of Oklahoma Press, 2011), 64–68.

12. *CG*, 24th Cong., 2d sess., app., 339; Buss, *Winning the West with Words*, 62; Allan Kulikoff, *The Agrarian Origins of American Capitalism* (Charlottesville: University of Virginia Press, 1992), 88.

13. Juliet E. K. Walker, *Free Frank: A Black Pioneer on the Antebellum Frontier* (Lexington: University of Kentucky Press, 1983), 7–25.

14. Ibid., 33–66.

15. Ibid., 68–77, 100–101; John Reda, *From Furs to Farms: The Transformation of the Mississippi Valley, 1762–1825* (DeKalb: Northern Illinois University Press, 2016), 137–41; Eugene H. Berwanger, *The Frontier Against Slavery: Western Anti-Negro Prejudice and the Slavery Extension Controversy* (1967; repr., Urbana: University of Illinois Press, 2002), 14, 32; James Simeone, *Democracy and Slavery in Frontier Illinois: The Bottomland Republic* (DeKalb: Northern Illinois University Press, 2000), 31; *The Revised Code of Laws, of Illinois* (Shawneetown, IL: Alexander F. Grant, 1829), 109–11.

16. Walker, *Free Frank*, 67–70.

17. Ibid., 3–4, 125, 154–55.

18. James A. Clifton, *The Pokagons, 1683–1983: Catholic Potawatomi Indians of the St. Joseph River Valley* (Lanham, MD: University Press of America, 1984), 56, 68.

19. NARA-RG 75, T494, reel 3 (emphasis in original); John P. Bowes, *Land Too Good for Indians: Northern Indian Removal* (Norman: University of Oklahoma Press, 2016), 155–57.

20. NARA-RG 75, T494, reel 3; John W. Hall, *Uncommon Defense: Indian Allies in the Black Hawk War* (Cambridge, MA: Harvard University Press, 2009), 203–8.

21. Kappler, *Indian Affairs: Laws and Treaties*, 2:402–14.

22. Ibid., 413; NARA-RG 75, T494, reel 3; Bowes, *Land Too Good for Indians*, 160–61; Stephen Aron, *American Confluence: The Missouri Frontier from Borderland to Border State* (Bloomington: Indiana University Press, 2006), 230.

23. NARA-RG 75, M234, reel 777.

24. Clifton, *The Pokagons*, 69–71; Bowes, *Land Too Good for Indians,* 177–81; Gregory Evans Dowd, "Custom, Text, and Property: Indians, Squatters, and Political Authority in Jacksonian Michigan," *Early American Studies: An Interdisciplinary Journal* 18:2 (Spring 2020): 195–228.

CHAPTER 3

1. "Colonel Crockett's Celebrated Squatter Speech," *Crockett's Yaller Flower Almanac, for '36* (New York: Elton, 1835), 4–6 (emphasis in original).

2. On the Crockett almanacs, see Franklin J. Meine, ed., *The Crockett Almanacks: Nashville Series, 1835–1838* (Chicago: Caxton Club, 1955); John Seelye, "A Well-Wrought Crockett: Or, How the Fakelorists Passed through the Credibility Gap and Discovered Kentucky," in *Davy Crockett: The Man, the Legend, the Legacy, 1786–1986*, ed. Michael A. Lofaro (Knoxville: University of Tennessee Press, 1985), 21–45; and Richard Boyd Hauck, "The Man in the Buckskin Hunting Shirt: Fact and Fiction in the Crockett Story," in *Davy Crockett: The Man, the Legend, the Legacy, 1786–1986*, 3–20. On Elton, see Helen Lefkowitz Horowitz, "Another 'American Cruikshank' Found: John H. Manning and the New York Sporting Weeklies," *Proceedings of the American Antiquarian Society* 112:1 (April 2002): 93–126; and Michael Joseph, "Old Comic Elton and the Age of Fun: Robert H. Elton and the Picture Book," *Children's Literature Association Quarterly* 28:3 (Fall 2003): 158–170.

3. *HJ*, 21st Cong., 1st sess., 729–30; Hauck, "The Man in the Buckskin Hunting Shirt," 9–14.

4. James Joseph Buss astutely observes that the "popular vision of pioneering helped western politicians pass preemption measures, but stories about the frontier squatter also began to gain the folksy characteristics of the vernacular hero." See Buss, *Winning the West with Words: Language and Conquest in the Lower Great Lakes* (Norman: University of Oklahoma Press, 2011), 58. On the evolution of the Crockett myth, see Richard Slotkin, *The Fatal Environment: The Myth of the Frontier in the Age of Industrialization, 1800–1890* (New York: Atheneum, 1985), 162–73; Slotkin, *Regeneration Through Violence: The Mythology of the American Frontier, 1600–1860* (Middletown, CT: Wesleyan University Press, 1973), 414–17; and Meine, *The Crockett Almanacks*, vi.

5. Biographers question Crockett's claims about his role in the abortive insurrection. See, for example, James Atkins Shackford, *David Crockett: The Man and the Legend* (1956; repr., Chapel Hill: University of North Carolina Press, 1986), 26–28; and Michael Wallis, *David Crockett: The Lion of the West* (New York: W. W. Norton, 2011), 117–18.

6. Shackford, *David Crockett*, 51–52, 67–68.

7. *RD*, 20th Cong., 2d sess., 162–63; Shackford, *David Crockett*, 87–107.

8. *RD*, 20th Cong., 2d sess., 162–63. The speech appears to have become an iconic piece of oration. In addition to its presence—in spiced-up form—in the almanacs, Crockett's "celebrated defense of the Squatters" formed part of the lineup of famous political addresses performed during a "night of imitations and improvisations" at a New York theater in December 1834. See Advertisement, *New-York American* (New York, NY), December 16, 1834, 3.

9. Hauck, "The Man in the Buckskin Hunting Shirt," 10–11; *RD*, 23d Cong., 2d sess., 1354.

10. Catherine L. Albanese, "King Crockett: Nature and Civility on the American Frontier," *Proceedings of the American Antiquarian Society* 88:2 (October 1979): 227.

11. "Davy Crockett," *Crockett's Yaller Flower Almanac, for '36*, 19–20 (emphasis in original). For an example of the use of "half horse, half alligator," see "A Man of Enlarged Ideas," *Public Ledger* (Philadelphia, PA), May 14, 1838, 1. The short vignette runs as follows: " 'Mister, where is your house?' asked a curious traveller [*sic*] of a 'half horse and half alligator' squatter. 'House, eh?' do you think I'm one of them sort, stranger? I sleeps in the Government purchase—I eats raw bear and buffalo, and drinks out of the Mississippi!' " On the revolution in printing, see Daniel Walker Howe, *What Hath God Wrought: The Transformation of America, 1815–1848* (New York: Oxford University Press, 2007), 626–27.

12. "Clay and the Occupants," *Piney Woods Planter* (Liberty, MS), December 21, 1839, 2; No Headline, *Bellows Falls Gazette* (Bellows Falls, VT), February 2, 1839, 1.

13. Martin Van Buren, "First Annual Message," *CMP*, 3:388–89; Christina Snyder, *Great Crossings: Indians, Settlers, and Slaves in the Age of Jackson* (New York: Oxford University Press, 2017), 44–47, 197–201.

14. "To the Farmers of Michigan," *Kalamazoo Gazette* (Kalamazoo, MI), October, 26, 1839, 2. On the Specie Circular and the economy, see *TYV* 1:676–78; James Parton, *The Life of Andrew Jackson* (New York: Mason Brothers, 1860), 3:592–93, 623–24; Howe, *What Hath God Wrought*, 503–508; and Paul W. Gates, *The Jeffersonian Dream: Studies in the History of American Land Policy and Development* (Albuquerque: University of New Mexico Press, 1996), 102–3. On the "flush times," see Joseph G. Baldwin, *The Flush Times of Alabama and Mississippi: A Series of Sketches* (New York: D. Appleton, 1853); and Joshua D. Rothman, *Flush Times and Fever Dreams: A Story of Capitalism and Slavery in the Age of Jackson* (Athens: University of Georgia Press, 2012).

15. Harry L. Watson, *Liberty and Power: The Politics of Jacksonian America*, rev. ed. (New York: Hill and Wang, 2006), 215.

16. "General Harrison," *Southern Argus* (Columbus, MS), March 24, 1840, 1 (emphasis in original); Solon Robinson to John B. Niles, August 1841, John B. Niles Papers, ISL; *The Harrison and Log Cabin Song Book* (Columbus, OH: I. N. Whiting, 1840), 1, 8, LCP.

17. "Speech of Mr. Profitt," *The Madisonian* (Washington, DC), April 2, 1840, 1. The *Courant's* reportage appears in No Headline, *The North Bend* (Worcester, MA), July 25, 1840, 4.

18. Ronald P. Formisano, "The New Political History and the Election of 1840," *Journal of Interdisciplinary History* 23:4 (Spring 1993): 661–82; Michael F. Holt, "The Election of 1840, Voter Mobilization, and the Emergence of the Second American Party System: A Reappraisal of Jacksonian Voting Behavior," in Holt, *Political Parties and American Political Development from the Age of Jackson to the Age of Lincoln* (Baton Rouge: Louisiana State University, 1992), 151–91.

19. *CG*, 29th Cong., 1st sess., app., 777.

20. *CG*, 26th Cong., 2d sess., app., 35.

21. Ibid.

22. *HJ*, 27th Cong., 1st sess., 221–23; *SJ*, 27th Cong., 1st sess., 216. When the House returned the bill after rejecting certain amendments, twenty-five senators voted to recede from the amendments while eighteen declined, enabling the measure to pass. *SJ*, 27th Cong., 1st sess., 221–222. On the Preemption Act of 1841 (5 Stat. 453), see Roy M. Robbins, *Our Landed Heritage: The Public Domain, 1776–1936* (Princeton, NJ: Princeton University Press, 1942), 85–91; Benjamin Horace Hibbard, *A History of the Public Land Policies* (1924; repr., Madison: University of Wisconsin Press, 1965), 156–58; and John R. Van Atta, *Securing the West: Politics, Public Lands, and the Fate of the Old Republic, 1785–1850* (Baltimore: Johns Hopkins University Press, 2014), 228.

CHAPTER 4

1. "The Greatest American Author," *Boston Semi-Weekly Advertiser* (Boston, MA), March 30, 1844, 1.

2. "Who Is Seatsfield?—The Great Question Answered!" *Centinel of Freedom* (Newark, NJ), April, 16, 1844, 2; "Who Is 'Seatsfield?'" *Daily National Intelligencer* (Washington, DC), April 17, 1844, 3; "Seatsfield," *New World* (New York, NY), April 20, 1844, 493.

3. "The New Era in American Literature—Seatsfield," *New York Herald*, May 1, 1844, 2.

4. Charles Sealsfield, *Life in the New World; or, Sketches of American Society* (New York: J. Winchester, 1844). Biographical sketches indicate that Karl Anton Postl, whose pen name was Charles Sealsfield, was born in 1793 into an Austrian farming family. He took up the robes of a monastic as a young man before quitting the cloistered life. He arrived in the United States in the 1820s and became an admirer of Andrew Jackson, heartily embracing the white egalitarianism of the rising Democratic Party. When he returned to Europe a decade later, he carried these affinities with him and gave expression to them in his fiction. See Walter Grünzweig, *Charles Sealsfield* (Boise, ID: Boise State University, 1985); and Jeffrey L. Sammons, "Charles Sealsfield: A Case of Non-Canonicity," in *Autoren Damals*

und Heute: Literaturgeschichtliche Beispiele Veranderter Wirkungshorizonte, ed. Gerhard P. Knapp (Amsterdam: Rodopi, 1991), 155–72.

5. William Paul Dallmann argues that for the pro-Jackson Sealsfield, squatters "were the true carriers of the American tradition . . . of the equality of all citizens." See Dallmann, "The Spirit of America as Interpreted in the Works of Charles Sealsfield" (PhD diss., Washington University, 1935), 48.

6. Sealsfield, *Life in the New World*, 312.

7. Ibid., 297–98, 323–24.

8. Ibid., 343.

9. Raúl A. Ramos, *Beyond the Alamo: Forging Mexican Ethnicity in San Antonio, 1821–1861* (Chapel Hill: University of North Carolina Press, 2008), 112; David J. Weber, *The Mexican Frontier, 1821–1846: The American Southwest Under Mexico* (Albuquerque: University of New Mexico Press, 1982), 177.

10. "House of Commons," *New-York Evening Post* (New York, NY), July 8, 1830, 1; Andrés Reséndez, *Changing National Identities at the Frontier: Texas and New Mexico, 1800–1850* (New York: Cambridge University Press, 2005), 87; Terán to Francisco Moctezuma, November 24, 1829, in *Texas by Terán: The Diary Kept by General Manuel de Mier y Terán on His 1828 Inspection of Texas*, ed. Jack Jackson (Austin: University of Texas Press, 2000), 178–79. On Terán's observation about Texas, see also Brian DeLay, *War of a Thousand Deserts: Indian Raids and the U.S.-Mexican War* (New Haven, CT: Yale University Press, 2008), 21–29.

11. Weber, *The Mexican Frontier*, 170–74; Ramos, *Beyond the Alamo*, 122–25.

12. *SJ*, 24th Cong., 2d sess., 110; *CG*, 24th Cong., 1st sess., 378, 461. Walker carried into the Senate a personal grievance against Mexico stemming from the 1834 arrest by Mexican authorities of his brother Duncan, who died soon after his release. See Henry Stuart Foote, *Texas and the Texans; or, Advance of the Anglo-Americans to the South-West*, vol. 2 (Philadelphia: Thomas, Cowperthwait, 1841), 356–57; and M. W. Cook, "Memoirs of Robert J. Walker (1873)," 5–6, RJWP.

13. William Ellery Channing, *The Works of William E. Channing*, vol. 2 (Boston: James Munroe, 1848), 200, 205, 238.

14. Robert J. Walker, *Letter of Mr. Walker, of Mississippi, Relative to the Annexation of Texas: In Reply to the Call of the People of Carroll County, Kentucky, to Communicate His Views on that Subject* (Washington, DC: Globe, 1844), 3.

15. Walker, *Letter of Mr. Walker*, 9, 18, 25.

16. Ibid., 14–15. Whether Walker himself truly believed the "safety-valve" theory is impossible to know. A few months after publication of the Texas letter, he and fellow managers of the Democrats' 1844 campaign circulated throughout the South an anonymous tract, *The South in Danger*, discussing the urgency of annexation to slaveholding interests. On Walker's Texas letter, see Frederick Merk, *Fruits of Propaganda in the Tyler Administration* (Cambridge, MA: Harvard University Press, 1971), 95–128; William W. Freehling, *The Road to Disunion*, vol. 1, *Secessionists at Bay, 1776–1854* (New York: Oxford University Press, 1990), 418–20; Thomas R. Hietala, *Manifest Design: Anxious Aggrandizement in Late Jacksonian*

America (Ithaca, NY: Cornell University Press, 1985), 26–34, 50–52; and Stephen John Hartnett, *Democratic Dissent and the Cultural Fictions of Antebellum America* (Urbana: University of Illinois Press, 2002), 93–131. On the 1840 census, see Daniel Walker Howe, *What Hath God Wrought: The Transformation of America, 1815–1848* (New York: Oxford University Press, 2007), 481.

17. Merk, *Fruits of Propaganda*, 123–26; James P. Shenton, *Robert John Walker: A Politician from Jackson to Lincoln* (New York: Columbia University Press, 1961), 38–39. Walker's Texas letter, likened by one leading newspaper to Thomas Paine's *Common Sense*, became the "textbook" for annexation boosters, especially those in the North seeking to convince skeptical constituents. See Joel H. Silbey, *Storm over Texas: The Annexation Controversy and the Road to Civil War* (New York: Oxford University Press, 2005), 35; and Hietala, *Manifest Design*, 51. To blunt the influence of Walker's letter, anti-annexationists raised questions about his motivations, charging that he owned extensive property in Texas and simply wanted to cash in when land values shot up after Texas came into the US fold. Walker roundly denied those accusations. Scholar Magdalen Eichert located a copy of a deed for sixteen square leagues (roughly 74,000 acres) that Walker purchased in Texas in 1835 as well as records indicating that he had acquired title to his deceased brother's Texas properties. See Eichert, "Some Implications Arising from Robert J. Walker's Participation in Land Ventures," *Journal of Mississippi History* 13:1 (January 1951): 45. See also Edwin A. Miles, "Robert J. Walker—His Mississippi Years" (Master's thesis, University of North Carolina, 1949), 109; and David M. Pletcher, *The Diplomacy of Annexation: Texas, Oregon, and the Mexican War* (Columbia: University of Missouri Press, 1973), 139–44. On the 1844 campaign, see Sean Wilentz, "The Bombshell of 1844," in *America at the Ballot Box: Elections and Political History*, ed. Gareth Davies and Julian E. Zelizer (Philadelphia: University of Pennsylvania Press, 2015), 36–58; Howe, *What Hath God Wrought*, 680–90; Michael Holt, *Political Parties and American Political Development from the Age of Jackson to the Age of Lincoln*, 59–63; and David M. Potter, *The Impending Crisis, 1848–1861* (New York: Harper and Row, 1976), 23–27.

18. "1844 Democratic Party Platform," May 27, 1844, American Presidency Project, University of California, Santa Barbara, https://www.presidency.ucsb.edu/documents/1844-democratic-party-platform (accessed September 27, 2021).

19. "Whig Party Platform of 1844," American Presidency Project, University of California, Santa Barbara, https://www.presidency.ucsb.edu/documents/whig-party-platform-1844 (accessed September 28, 2021); "Who Is James K. Polk?" *Pennsylvania Telegraph* (Harrisburg, PA), May 29, 1844, 2; "The Nomination at Baltimore," *New-Hampshire Sentinel* (Keene, NH), June 5, 1844, 3.

20. "Who Is James K. Polk?" *Pittsfield Sun* (Pittsfield, MA), June 6, 1844, 3 (emphasis in original).

21. "Henry Clay Against the Frontier Settlers," *Kendall's Expositor for 1844* (Washington, DC: William Greer, 1844), 4: 115–22 (emphasis in original). Thanks

to Cornelia King at the Library Company of Philadelphia for guiding me to this tract.

22. William M. Gwin, "The Preemption System," September 8, 1844, 4, Mississippi Department of Archives and History. Thanks to Brian Hamilton for procuring this document on site at MDAH.

23. "Political Dishonesty," *Boon's Lick Times* (Fayette, MO), April 20, 1844, 2.

24. "Democratic Barbecue in the Parish of Carroll—Great Rally of the New Settlers in Louisiana,—Boundless Enthusiasm for the Cause," *Mississippi Free Trader* (Natchez, MS), October 18, 1844, 3.

25. Ibid.; Freehling, *The Road to Disunion*, 1:438; and Michael F. Holt, *The Rise and Fall of the American Whig Party: Jacksonian Politics and the Onset of the Civil War* (New York: Oxford University Press, 1999), 194.

26. Sealsfield, *Life in the New World*, 340; Sammons, "Charles Sealsfield," 171.

27. William Gilmore Simms, *Border Beagles; A Tale of Mississippi*, vol. 1 (Philadelphia: Carey and Hart, 1840), 6, 37, 159. On Simms, see John Caldwell Guilds and Caroline Collins, eds., *William Gilmore Simms and the American Frontier* (Athens: University of Georgia Press, 1997); Masahiro Nakamura, *Visions of Order in William Gilmore Simms: Southern Conservatism and the Other American Romance* (Columbia: University of South Carolina Press, 2009); Charles S. Watson, *From Nationalism to Secessionism: The Changing Fiction of William Gilmore Simms* (Westport, CT: Greenwood Press, 1993); and Jon L. Wakelyn, *The Politics of a Literary Man: William Gilmore Simms* (Westport, CT: Greenwood Press, 1973).

28. Wallis, *David Crockett*, 174–75; "Crockett's Opinion of Oregon, and the Annexation of Texas to the US," *The Squatter's Almanac, 1845* (New York: Turner and Fisher, 1844); "Diving into It; or, the Crocodile Kidnapping," *The Squatter's Almanac, 1845,* 13. Henry Nash Smith observes that southwestern humor "dealt with slavery only incidentally and had no case to make for the institution. The boisterous mood of this writing veers toward satire rather than toward apologetics; it makes no appeal to sentiment, which proved to be the most powerful weapon of both defenders and attackers of slavery." See Smith, *Virgin Land: The American West as Symbol and Myth* (New York: Vintage Books, 1950), 173. For a collection of southwestern humor, see Hennig Cohen and William B. Dillingham, eds., *Humor of the Old Southwest*, 3rd ed. (Athens: University of Georgia Press, 1994).

29. John S. Robb ("Solitaire"), *Streaks of Squatter Life, and Far-West Scenes* (Philadelphia: Carey and Hart, 1847), ix.

30. Ibid., 73, 76.

31. Ibid., 92–97 (emphasis in original). For an examination of political, cultural, and class aspects of "The Standing Candidate," see Nancy Isenberg, *White Trash: The 400-Year Untold History of Class in America* (New York: Viking, 2016), 129–31.

32. "Solitaire," *Streaks of Squatter Life*, 117, 132.

CHAPTER 5

1. Jesse Applegate to Lisbon Applegate, April 11, 1843, in Leta Lovelace Neiderheiser, *Jesse Applegate: A Dialogue with Destiny* (Mustang, OK: Tate, 2010), 45; Jesse Applegate, "Views of Oregon History," Yoncalla, Oregon, 1878, 31, OHSRL.

2. "Annexation," *United States Magazine and Democratic Review* 17 (July/August 1845): 7.

3. Ibid., 5, 9. Julius W. Pratt, "The Origin of 'Manifest Destiny,'" *American Historical Review* 32:4 (July 1927): 795–98. Pratt credits O'Sullivan with coining the phrase "manifest destiny," and historians have followed his lead for decades. However, scholar Linda S. Hudson attributes the term to Jane Cazneau, a contributor to the *Democratic Review* and an ardent expansionist. See Hudson, *Mistress of Manifest Destiny: A Biography of Jane McManus Storm Cazneau, 1807–1878* (Austin: Texas State Historical Association, 2001), 60–62.

4. *CG*, 26th Cong., 1st sess., app., 191.

5. On the Treaty of 1818, see Frederick Merk, *The Oregon Question: Essays in Anglo-American Diplomacy and Politics* (Cambridge, MA: Belknap Press of Harvard University Press, 1967), 171–78; and Dorothy O. Johansen and Charles M. Gates, *Empire of the Columbia: A History of the Pacific Northwest*, 2nd ed. (New York: Harper and Row, 1967), 112–21.

6. On the HBC and Fort Vancouver, see Merk, *The Oregon Question*, 175; David Alan Johnson, *Founding the Far West: California, Oregon, and Nevada, 1840–1890* (Berkeley: University of California Press, 1992), 49; Anne F. Hyde, *Empires, Nations, and Families: A New History of the North American West, 1800–1860* (New York: Ecco, 2012), 92–104; Earl Pomeroy, *The Pacific Slope: A History of California, Oregon, Washington, Idaho, Utah, and Nevada* (1965; repr., Reno: University of Nevada Press, 2003), 18–19; and Gregory P. Shine, "Fort Vancouver," *The Oregon Encyclopedia*, https://oregonencyclopedia.org/articles/for t_vancouver/#.WUnSlmjysdU (accessed October 4, 2021).

7. A. Atwood, *The Conquerors: Historical Sketches of the American Settlement of the Oregon Country, Embracing Facts in the Life and Work of Rev. Jason Lee, the Pioneer and Founder of American Institutions on the Western Coast of North America* (Glendale, CA: Arthur H. Clark, 1907), 65–66; Elwood Evans, "Annual Address," *Transactions of the Fifth Annual Re-union of the Oregon Pioneer Association; for 1877* (Salem, OR: E. M. Waite, 1878), 26.

8. "Oregon. American Protection to American Pioneers; or, Shall Oregon be Surrendered to Great Britain?" Published by Order of a Committee of the Democratic Members of Congress, Washington, DC, 1844, 2, Henry D. Gilpin Collection, LCP.

9. Atwood, *The Conquerors*, 65.

10. *SDoc* 514, 26th Cong., 1st sess., 1–2, Serial 360.

11. For detailed information about the provenance of settlers, see William A. Bowen, *The Willamette Valley: Migration and Settlement on the Oregon Frontier* (Seattle: University of Washington Press, 1978).

12. Robert J. Loewenberg, *Equality on the Oregon Frontier: Jason Lee and the Methodist Mission, 1834–43* (Seattle: University of Washington Press, 1976), 184–94; Johnson, *Founding the Far West*, 50–51; Samuel R. Thurston, "Letter of the Delegate from Oregon, to the Members of the House of Representatives, in Behalf of His Constituents, Touching the Oregon Land Bill," 6, in TFP, box 1, folder 11; "Copy of a Document Found Among the Private Papers of the Late Dr. John McLoughlin," *Constitution and Quotations from the Register of the Oregon Pioneer Association* (Salem, OR: E. M. Waite: 1875), 52 [hereafter "McLoughlin Document"]. Historian Robert J. Loewenberg writes that McLoughlin made his claim at the behest of HBC Governor George Simpson in 1828. See Loewenberg, *Equality on the Oregon Frontier*, 18.

13. Johnson, *Founding the Far West*, 50–51; Loewenberg, *Equality on the Oregon Frontier*, 192.

14. "McLoughlin Document," 52; Charles H. Carey, *A General History of Oregon Prior to 1861* (Portland, OR: Metropolitan Press, 1935), 1:287–89; Neiderheiser, *Jesse Applegate*, 83–84; Jason Lee to Elijah White, April 25, 1843, in Loewenberg, *Equality on the Oregon Frontier*, 191.

15. *SDoc* 105, 28th Cong., 1st sess., 1–4, Serial 433. On Robert Shortess, see Carey, *A General History*, 1:332; and Jesse Applegate, "Views of Oregon History," 40.

16. *SJ*, 26th Cong., 1st Sess., 12; Michael B. Husband, "Senator Lewis F. Linn and the Oregon Question," *Missouri Historical Review* 66:1 (October 1971): 10.

17. Thurston, "Letter of the Delegate from Oregon," 5; John Mack Faragher, *Women and Men on the Overland Trail* (New Haven, CT: Yale University Press, 1979), 192–93; Johansen and Gates, *Empire of the Columbia*, 154; *CG*, 27th Cong., 3rd Sess., app., 74.

18. *CG*, 27th Cong., 3d Sess., 134; *CG*, 27th Cong., 3rd Sess., app., 117; Husband, "Senator Lewis F. Linn and the Oregon Question," 16; *SJ*, 27th Cong., 3d sess., 148.

19. Neiderheiser, *Jesse Applegate*, 45; Husband, "Senator Lewis F. Linn and the Oregon Question," 18.

20. Carey, *A General History*, 1:329–38; Evans, "Annual Address," 33.

21. Provisional and Territorial Documents, MSS 1226, reel 76, item 12187, OHSRL.

22. James K. Polk, "First Inaugural Address," *CMP*, 4:381.

23. Evans, "Annual Address," 26; Carey, *A General History*, 1:353; The *London Morning Chronicle* quoted in "England and the United States," *The Sun* (Baltimore, MD), April 30, 1846, 1.

24. The *New York Morning News* quoted in "The True Title," *Republican Herald* (Providence, RI), January 7, 1846, 2. See also Frederick Merk, *Manifest Destiny and Mission in American History: A Reinterpretation* (1963; repr., New York: Vintage Books, 1966), 31–32.

25. "True Policy of the West," *Cleveland Plain Dealer* (Cleveland, OH), June 24, 1846, 2; David M. Potter, *The Impending Crisis, 1848–1861* (New York: Harper and Row, 1976), 25–26. On the lead-up to the US-Mexican War, see Amy S. Greenberg, *A Wicked War: Polk, Clay, Lincoln, and the 1846 U.S. Invasion of Mexico* (New York: Vintage Books, 2012), 84–121; and Brian DeLay, *War of a Thousand Deserts: Indian Raids and the U.S.-Mexican War* (New Haven, CT: Yale University Press, 2008), 247–49.

26. The *London Spectator* quoted in "English Views of the Mexican War," *Scioto Gazette* (Chillicothe, OH), November 4, 1846, 1.

27. "Major Jack Downing," *Lancaster Gazette* (Lancaster, OH), February 4, 1848, 2.

28. *HJ*, 29th Cong., 1st sess., 1272; *CG*, 29th Cong., 1st sess., 1217; *CG*, 29th Cong., 2d sess., app., 317. On David Wilmot and the proviso, see Jonathan H. Earle, *Jacksonian Antislavery and the Politics of Free Soil, 1824–1854* (Chapel Hill: University of North Carolina Press, 2004), 123–43; James McPherson, *Battle Cry of Freedom: The Civil War Era* (New York: Oxford University Press, 1988), 52–53; and Charles Sellers, *The Market Revolution: Jacksonian America, 1815–1846* (New York: Oxford University Press, 1991), 426–27.

29. *TYV*, 2:695.

30. *HJ*, 26th Cong., 1st sess., 165; George M. Stephenson, *The Political History of the Public Lands from 1840 to 1862: From Pre-emption to Homestead* (Boston: Richard G. Badger, 1917), 116. On Evans and the NRA, see Mark A. Lause, *Young America: Land, Labor, and the Republican Community* (Urbana: University of Illinois Press, 2005), 9–20; Helene Sara Zahler, *Eastern Workingmen and National Land Policy, 1829–1862* (New York: Columbia University Press, 1941), 41–56; Earle, *Jacksonian Antislavery*, 27–37, 58–62; Sean Wilentz, *Chants Democratic: New York City and the Rise of the American Working Class, 1788–1850* (New York: Oxford University Press, 1984), 340–43; and Reeve Huston, *Land and Freedom: Rural Society, Popular Protest, and Party Politics in Antebellum New York* (New York: Oxford University Press, 2000), 158–59. The widely circulated "Vote Yourself a Farm" broadside queried, "Are you an American citizen? Then you are a joint owner of the public lands. Why not take enough of your property to provide yourself a home? Why not vote yourself a farm?" See Stephenson, *The Political History of the Public Lands from 1840 to 1862*, 109; and Zahler, *Eastern Workingmen and National Land Policy*, 207–8.

31. "Passage of the Land Graduation Bill Through the Senate," *New-York Daily Tribune*, July 10, 1846, 2. On Greeley and land reform, see Daniel Walker Howe, *The Political Culture of the American Whigs* (Chicago: University of Chicago Press, 1979), 195–96; and Adam-Max Tuchinsky, "'The Bourgeoisie Will Fall and Fall Forever': The *New-York Tribune*, the 1848 French Revolution, and American Social Democratic Discourse," *Journal of American History* 92:2 (September 2005): 470–97.

32. Lewis Cass to Alfred O. P. Nicholson, December 24, 1847, published in "A Letter from Gen. Cass in relation to the War and the Wilmot Proviso," *The Union*

(Washington, DC), January 1, 1848, 1; Willard Carl Klunder, *Lewis Cass and the Politics of Moderation* (Kent, OH: Kent State University Press, 1996), 162–63; James L. Huston, *Calculating the Value of the Union: Slavery, Property Rights, and the Economic Origins of the Civil War* (Chapel Hill: University of North Carolina Press, 2003), 170–71.

33. On the promises and pitfalls of popular sovereignty, see Christopher Childers, *The Failure of Popular Sovereignty: Slavery, Manifest Destiny, and the Radicalization of Southern Politics* (Lawrence: University Press of Kansas, 2012); and Potter, *The Impending Crisis*, 58–59.

34. R. Gregory Nokes, *Breaking Chains: Slavery on Trial in the Oregon Territory* (Corvallis: Oregon State University Press, 2013); Johansen and Gates, *Empire of the Columbia*, 260–61.

35. "Message of the Governor of Oregon Territory," Provisional and Territorial Documents, MSS 1226, reel 77, item 12189, OHSRL; Daniel McKissick to Congress, undated, CLAS, SEN30A-H17.2, box 108.

36. *SDoc* 143 (Misc.), 30th Cong., 1st sess., 1–24, Serial 511.

37. *CG*, 30th Cong., 1st sess., app., 657.

38. Ibid., 657–59.

39. *CG*, 30th Cong., 1st sess., 813; "Navy Bill—Slavery," *Weekly National Intelligencer* (Washington, DC), June 10, 1848, 6.

40. *CG*, 30th Cong., 1st sess., 812.

41. Ibid., 813.

42. *SJ*, 30th Cong., 1st sess., 101, 155; Robert W. Johannsen, *Stephen A. Douglas* (1973; repr., Urbana: University of Illinois Press, 1997), 221–22; *Niles' National Register* 74 (July 1848–January 1849): 151.

43. *SJ*, 29th Cong., 2d sess., 209–10; John C. Calhoun, "Speech on the Oregon Bill, delivered in the Senate, June 27th, 1848," in *The Works of John C. Calhoun*, vol. 4 (New York: D. Appleton, 1854), 498; *TYV*, 2:723. On Calhoun's defense of slavery, see Childers, *The Failure of Popular Sovereignty*, 115–18.

44. *SJ*, 30th Cong., 1st sess., 563, 590; *HJ*, 30th Cong., 1st sess., 1245.

45. Potter, *The Impending Crisis*, 75–76; Milo Milton Quaife, ed., *The Diary of James K. Polk During His Presidency, 1845 to 1849*, vol. 4 (Chicago: A. C. McClurg, 1910), 63–74.

46. Ibid., 67.

47. No Headline, *Jefferson Inquirer* (Jefferson City, MO), February 26, 1848, 2; "Ratification of the Democratic Nominees," *Mississippi Free Trader* (Natchez, MS), June 14, 1848, 2.

48. "Gen. Taylor and the South Carolina Democracy!" *Green Mountain Freeman* (Montpelier, VT), August 31, 1848, 1.

49. "From the Country," *Richmond Whig and Public Advertiser,* June 23, 1848, 1.

50. The *St. Louis Weekly Reveille* sketch was reprinted in various newspapers in September and October 1848. See, for example, "Taking the Mississippi," *Daily*

Sanduskian (Sandusky, OH), October 10, 1848, 3. This encounter appears to have been inspired by an 1848 excursion by Robb down the Mississippi in the "sketching boat" of artist Henry Lewis. See John Francis McDermott's introduction to John S. Robb, *Streaks of Squatter Life, and Far-West Scene* (Gainesville, FL: Scholars' Facsimiles and Reprints, 1962), vii. On Robb and the *Reveille*, see Nicholas Joost, "Reveille in the West: Western Travelers in the St. Louis *Weekly Reveille*, 1844–50," in *Travelers on the Western Frontier*, ed. John Francis McDermott (Urbana: University of Illinois, 1970), 209–14.

51. Joseph G. Rayback, *Free Soil: The Election of 1848* (Lexington: University of Kentucky Press, 1970), 279–87.

52. Michael E. Woods, *Arguing until Doomsday: Stephen Douglas, Jefferson Davis, and the Struggle for American Democracy* (Chapel Hill: University of North Carolina Press, 2020), 96; Wilentz, *The Rise of American Democracy*, 631–32.

53. The *Tribune* article appears in "Mr. Calhoun Right and Wrong," *Anti-Slavery Bugle* (Salem, OH), March 30, 1850, 1. Historian Jonathan H. Earle astutely notes that the Free Soilers garnered significant support by making a material case for stopping slavery—specifically, reserving land for poor whites—as opposed to a moral case like abolitionists. See Earle, *Jacksonian Antislavery*, 7.

54. Jerry A. O'Callaghan, *The Disposition of the Public Domain in Oregon* (Washington, DC: Government Printing Office, 1960), 8.

55. "Diary of Samuel Royal Thurston" (transcribed copy), 12–13, TFP, box 1, folder 12.

56. Mrs. W. H. Odell, "Biography of Samuel R. Thurston" (1879), 11–12, TFP, box 1, folder 16, OHSRL; Samuel R. Thurston, "To the Electors and People of the Territory of Oregon," 1, TFP, box 1, folder 13 (emphasis in original).

57. *SJ*, 31st Cong., 1st sess., 36.

58. *CG*, 32d Cong., 1st sess., app., 512; *CG*, 31st Cong., 1st sess., 258. On Brown's father and slavery, see James Byrne Ranck, *Albert Gallatin Brown: Radical Southern Nationalist* (1937; repr., Philadelphia: Porcupine Press, 1974), 1.

59. Odell, "Biography of Samuel R. Thurston," 15; *HJ*, 31st Cong., 1st sess., 821; "Diary of Samuel Royal Thurston," 55.

60. *Congressional Globe*, 31st Cong., 1st sess., 1090; Kenneth R. Coleman, "'We'll All Start Even': White Egalitarianism and the Oregon Donation Land Claim Act," *Oregon Historical Quarterly* 120:4 (Winter 2019): 424–26; Peggy Pascoe, *What Comes Naturally: Miscegenation Law and the Making of Race in America* (New York: Oxford University Press, 2009), 66.

61. Thurston, "To the Electors and People," 6 (emphasis in original).

62. Joseph Lane to Samuel R. Thurston, January 27, 1850, TFP, box 1, folder 5. For the development of political parties in Oregon, see Johnson, *Founding the Far West*; Robert W. Johannsen, *Frontier Politics and the Sectional Conflict: The Pacific Northwest on the Eve of the Civil War* (Seattle: University of Washington Press, 1955); and Walter Carleton Woodward, *The Rise and Early History of Political Parties in Oregon, 1843–1868* (Portland, OR: J. K. Gill, 1913).

63. William P. Bryant to W. J. Brown, January 6, 1851, TFP, box 1, folder 2; Thurston, "To the Electors and People," 9; "McLoughlin Document," 54.

64. Wesley Shannon to Samuel R. Thurston, August 15, 1850, TFP, box 1, folder 6 (emphasis in original); William P. Bryant to Samuel R. Thurston, August 17, 1850, TFP, box 1, folder 2.

65. Jesse Applegate to Samuel R. Thurston, undated (1850), TFP, box 1, folder 2 (emphasis in original).

66. Jesse Applegate, "A Day with the Cow Column in 1843," *Transactions of the Fourth Annual Re-union of the Oregon Pioneer Association; for 1876* (Salem, OR: E. M. Waite, 1877), 57–65; Neiderheiser, *Jesse Applegate*, 24–25; Jesse Applegate to Samuel R. Thurston, undated (1850).

67. Applegate, "Views of Oregon History," 32; Neiderheiser, *Jesse Applegate*, 34–35.

68. "Diary of Samuel Royal Thurston," 62; *CG*, 31st Cong., 1st sess., 1741; "Hairbreadth Escapes" in Thurston, "To the Electors and People," 6; *SJ*, 31st Cong., 1st sess., 650. The *Senate Journal* does not include the roll call for the vote on the Oregon Donation Land Act. President Millard Fillmore signed the measure into law on September 27, 1850 (9 Stat. 496).

69. "Squatter's Rights in Oregon," *Daily Ohio Statesman* (Columbus, OH), October 10, 1850, 2; "Squatter's Rights in Oregon," *Portage Sentinel* (Ravenna, OH), October 21, 1850, 1; Thurston, "To the Electors and People," 6; O'Callaghan, *The Disposition of the Public Domain in Oregon*, 34; "Autobiography of Joseph Lane," 57, Joseph Lane Papers, OHSRL; No Headline, *Daily National Intelligencer* (Washington, DC), May 8, 1851, 3.

CHAPTER 6

1. Charles Robinson et al. v. Noble C. Cunningham et al., Court of First Magistrate, Civil #310, CSH; Will Bagley, ed., *Scoundrel's Tale: The Samuel Brannan Papers*, vol. 3 of *Kingdom in the West: The Mormons and the American Frontier* (Spokane, WA: Arthur H. Clark, 1999). Tamara Venit Shelton's indispensable monograph on nineteenth-century squatter politics in California served as a valuable guide to events examined and sources consulted in developing this chapter. See Shelton, *A Squatter's Republic: Land and the Politics of Monopoly in California, 1850–1900* (San Marino, CA: Huntington Library, 2013).

2. John A. Sutter et al. to Murray Morrison, December 7, 1849, Court of First Magistrate, Civil #310, CSH; Sacramento City Council Minutes, December 7, 1849, 51, box 1, folder 6, CSH; John A. Sutter, "Personal Reminiscences of General John Augustus Sutter" (transcribed copy), 85–86, BL.

3. "The Late Dr. Robinson," *The Bee* (Sacramento, CA), August 18, 1894, 4.

4. Zachary Taylor, "First Annual Message," *CMP*, 5:18.

5. Ibid., 19.

6. *CG,* 31st Cong., 1st sess., app., 200; "The President on the Territorial Question," *Anti-Slavery Bugle* (Salem, OH), February 2, 1850, 2.

7. For a textured examination of the convergence of cultures in Gold Rush-era California, see Susan Lee Johnson, *Roaring Camp: The Social World of the California Gold Rush* (New York: W. W. Norton, 2000).

8. "Annexation," *United States Magazine and Democratic Review* 17 (July/August 1845): 9.

9. "Some kind of meddle . . ." from the diary of Henry W. Bigler, appears in "The Discovery of Gold in California," *Century Illustrated Monthly Magazine* 19:41 (November 1890 to April 1891), 528–29; John Umbeck, "The California Gold Rush: A Study of Emerging Property Rights," *Explorations in Economic History* 14 (1977): 214; Gary D. Libecap, "The Assignment of Property Rights on the Western Frontier: Lessons for Contemporary Environmental and Resource Policy," *Journal of Economic History* 67:2 (June 2007): 266–67.

10. Thomas W. Streeter, *Alta California: Embracing Notices of the Climate, Soil, and Agricultural Products of Northern Mexico and the Pacific Seaboard* (Philadelphia: H. Packer, 1847), 11.

11. "Letter from Senator Benton to the People of California," *Wisconsin Argus* (Madison, WI), October 17, 1848, 3.

12. Albert L. Hurtado, *John Sutter: A Life on the North American Frontier* (Norman: University of Oklahoma Press, 2006), 65, 91; Sutter, "Personal Reminiscences," 13–21.

13. Ibid. 92–93; Land Case Files, 319 ND, box B, 1393–96, BL; Tomás Almaguer, *Racial Fault Lines: The Historical Origins of White Supremacy in California,* 2nd ed. (Berkeley: University of California Press, 2009), 50–51.

14. Anne F. Hyde, *Empires, Nations, and Families: A New History of the North American West, 1800–1860* (New York: Ecco, 2012), 391–94; Hurtado, *John Sutter,* 195–96.

15. William R. Prince to Charlotte Prince, August 18, 1850, William Robert Prince Letters, folder 4, BL.

16. "Notice to Squatters," *Placer Times* (Sacramento, CA), July 28, 1849, 4 (emphasis in original); William R. Prince to Charlotte Prince, August 18, 1850.

17. Charles Robinson, *The Kansas Conflict* (New York: Harper and Brothers, 1892), 27.

18. Ibid., 36–37.

19. Ibid., 37–38; "California," *New-York Daily Tribune,* May 22, 1850, 2; "California Correspondence," *Daily Picayune* (New Orleans, LA), evening edition, February 15, 1850, 1.

20. Charles Robinson et al. v. Noble C. Cunningham et al., Court of First Magistrate, Civil #310, CSH; *"For every hut . . ."* in "California," *New-York Daily Tribune,* May 22, 1850, 2 (emphasis in original).

21. "The Sacramento City Settlers' Association," Broadside, December 1849, BL; "California Correspondence," *Daily Picayune* (New Orleans, LA), evening edition, February 15, 1850, 1.

22. "Sutter's Grant," *Settlers and Miners Tribune* (Sacramento, CA), November 14, 1850, 1; William R. Prince to Charlotte Prince, August 18, 1850.

23. On dynamics of "squatter law in California," see Donald J. Pisani, *Water, Land, and Law in the West: The Limits of Public Policy, 1850–1920* (Lawrence: University Press of Kansas, 1996), 57–85; Paul W. Gates, *Land and Law in California: Essays on Land Policies* (Ames: Iowa State University Press, 1991), 156–84; and W. W. Robinson, *Land in California: The Story of Mission Lands, Ranchos, Squatters, Mining Claims, Railroad Grants, Land Scrip, Homesteads* (Berkeley: University of California Press, 1948).

24. "The Squatter Claims," *Daily Alta California*, May 24, 1850, 2.

25. Robinson, *The Kansas Conflict*, 63; "Free Soil in California," *Young America* (New York, NY), March 2, 1850, 2. On links between McClatchy and the National Reform Association, see Shelton, *A Squatter's Republic*, 23–24; and Mark A. Lause, *Young America: Land, Labor, and the Republican Community* (Urbana: University of Illinois Press, 2005), 113.

26. William R. Prince to Charlotte Prince, August 18, 1850; Sacramento City Council Minutes, March 4, 1850, 80, box 1, folder 8, CSH.

27. Samuel W. Brown to wife, August 14, 1850, Samuel W. Brown Diary and Letters, California Historical Society (emphasis in original).

28. "California Correspondence," *Daily Picayune* (New Orleans, LA), evening edition, February 15, 1850, 1; "California—The Other Side of the Picture," *Texian Advocate* (Victoria, TX), March 8, 1850, 1.

29. *CG*, 31st Cong., 1st sess., 451–55.

30. On Douglas, see Robert W. Johannsen, *Stephen A. Douglas* (1973; repr., Urbana: University of Illinois Press, 1997); Michael E. Woods, *Arguing until Doomsday: Stephen Douglas, Jefferson Davis, and the Struggle for American Democracy* (Chapel Hill: University of North Carolina Press, 2020); and James L. Huston, *Stephen A. Douglas and the Dilemmas of Democratic Equality* (Lanham, MD: Rowman and Littlefield, 2007).

31. *CG*, 31st Cong., 1st sess., app., 373–74.

32. "Parties at Washington—The Compromise," *Georgia Telegraph* (Macon, GA), May 14, 1850, 2 (emphasis in original); Woods, *Arguing until Doomsday*, 92, 102.

33. "California," *New-York Tribune*; May 22, 1850; Hurtado, *John Sutter*, 283–85; "Dangerous Ground," *Placer Times* (Sacramento, CA), June 3, 1850, 2; Pisani, *Water, Land, and Law*, 61.

34. "The Sacramento Troubles," *New-York Daily Tribune*, October 15, 1850, 6; "Squatter Meeting on the Levee," *Sacramento Transcript* (Sacramento, CA), August 12, 1850, 2; Robinson, *The Kansas Conflict*, 43–48; Josiah Royce, "The Squatter Riot of '50 in Sacramento," *Overland Monthly* 6:33 (September 1885): 240; Hubert Howe Bancroft, *History of California*, vol. 6, *1848–1859* (San Francisco: History Company, 1888), 330–31.

35. Robinson, *The Kansas Conflict*, 46–47.

36. Ibid., 49–53; Bancroft, *History of California*, 6:332; Samuel W. Brown to wife, August 14, 1850.

37. Robinson, *The Kansas Conflict*, 49–52; "Yesterday," *Placer Times* (Sacramento, CA), August 15, 1850, transcribed in John F. Morse, *The Sacramento Directory for the Year 1853–54* (Sacramento, CA: Samuel Colville, 1853), 29; *Sacramento Transcript*, (Sacramento, CA), "Tremendous Excitement!!," August 15, 1850, 2.

38. Robinson, *The Kansas Conflict*, 52–53; Shelton, *A Squatter's Republic*, 31; "Insure the defense" in Sacramento City Council Minutes, August 14, 1850, 87, box 1, book B, CHS; Samuel W. Brown to wife, August 14, 1850.

39. Untitled *Placer Times* article from August 16, 1850, transcribed in Winfield J. Davis, *An Illustrated History of Sacramento County, California* (Chicago: Lewis , 1890), 30; William R. Prince to Charlotte Prince, August 18, 1850.

40. *SJ*, 31st Cong., 1st sess., 530, 557; *HJ*, 31st Cong., 1st sess., 1423; "Passage of the California Bill," *Daily Morning News* (Savannah, GA), August 19, 1850, 2; Woods, *Arguing until Doomsday*, 104–5.

41. "Later from California," *Maine Farmer* (Augusta, ME), October 10, 1850, 2; Robinson, *The Kansas Conflict*, 61–62; "Squatterism," *Settlers and Miners Tribune* (Sacramento, CA), October 30, 1850, 2.

42. "Sacramento Intelligence," *Alta California* (San Francisco, CA), November 30, 1850, 3.

43. Sara Tappan Doolittle Lawrence to Phebe Stone, February, 11, 1851, folder 1, Sara Tappan Doolittle Robinson Letters, KSRL. In this missive, Lawrence transcribes contents of a letter from Charles Robinson.

44. "Who Are 'the Settlers,'" *Alta California* (San Francisco, CA), September 15, 1851, 6.

45. "Speech of Mr. Gwin, of California, on Land Claims in California, delivered in the Senate of the United States, August 2, 1852" (Washington, DC: Congressional Globe Office, 1852), 8, LCP; Shelton, *A Squatter's Republic*, 40–46.

46. *CG*, 31st Cong., 2d sess., app., 283–84.

47. "Letter from Jefferson Davis," *Weekly Union* (Washington, DC), March 20, 1852, 1.

CHAPTER 7

1. John Baldwin to Charles Robinson, October 6, 1854, box 1, folder 24, CRC.

2. William G. Cutler, *History of the State of Kansas* (Chicago: A. T. Andreas, 1883), 314–16; Charles Robinson, *The Kansas Conflict* (New York: Harper and Brothers, 1892), 72; Ibid., 80–81.

3. See, for example, William W. Freehling, *The Road to Disunion*, vol. 2, *Secessionists Triumphant, 1854–1861* (New York: Oxford University Press, 2007); Michael F. Holt, *The Fate of Their Country: Politicians, Slavery Extension, and the Coming of the Civil War* (New York: Hill and Wang, 2004); James McPherson, *Battle Cry of Freedom: The Civil War Era* (New York: Oxford University Press, 1988); and David M. Potter, *The Impending Crisis, 1848–1861* (New York: Harper and Row, 1976). On the overlapping issues of land and slavery in Kansas, see ibid., 202–3; Everett

Dick, *The Lure of the Land: A Social History of the Public Lands from the Articles of Confederation to the New Deal* (Lincoln: University of Nebraska Press, 1970), 109–11; Richard Slotkin, *The Fatal Environment: The Myth of the Frontier in the Age of Industrialization, 1800–1890* (New York: Atheneum, 1985), 263–64; and Allan Kulikoff, *The Agrarian Origins of American Capitalism* (Charlottesville: University of Virginia Press, 1992), 93.

4. "Joseph Savage's Recollections of 1854," no. 6, Kansas Memory, KSHS, https://www.kshs.org/km/items/view/90813 (accessed May 2, 2021).

5. Cutler, *History of the State of Kansas*, 314; Robinson, *The Kansas Conflict*, 79.

6. Robert W. Johannsen, *Stephen A. Douglas* (1973; repr., Urbana: University of Illinois Press, 1997), 395–400; James L. Huston, *Calculating the Value of the Union: Slavery, Property Rights, and the Economic Origins of the Civil War* (Chapel Hill: University of North Carolina Press, 2003), 195.

7. Holt, *The Fate of their Country*, 92–127; Potter, *The Impending Crisis*, 160–77; Johannsen, *Stephen A. Douglas*, 395–434; Sean Wilentz, *The Rise of American Democracy: Jefferson to Lincoln* (New York: W. W. Norton, 2005), 671–72.

8. *CG*, 33d Cong., 1st sess., app., 337; *CG*, 33d Cong., 1st sess., 280; "Squatter Sovereignty," *Evening Post* (New York, NY) February 1, 1854, 2.

9. *CG*, 33d Cong., 1st sess., app., 714, 788; Salmon P. Chase et al., "Appeal of the Independent Democrats in Congress, to the People of the United States" (Washington, DC: Towers, 1854), 7. On Chase and colleagues' "Appeal," see Eric Foner, *Free Soil, Free Labor, Free Men: The Ideology of the Republican Party Before the Civil War* (1970; repr., New York: Oxford University Press, 1995), 94–95); Jonathan H. Earle, *Jacksonian Antislavery and the Politics of Free Soil, 1824–1854* (Chapel Hill: University of North Carolina Press, 2004), 193; and Sean Wilentz, *The Rise of American Democracy*, 673.

10. Foner, *Free Soil, Free Labor, Free Men*, 158; *CG*, 33d Cong., 1st sess., app., 714–16.

11. *CG*, 33d Cong., 1st sess., 1876; "Mr. Benton on the Nebraska Bill," *Daily National Era* (Washington, DC), April 25, 1854, 2. On Benton's Senate reelection loss, see William Nisbet Chambers, *Old Bullion Benton: Senator from the New West* (Boston: Little, Brown, 1956), 370. On Benton and Kansas, see Dick, *The Lure of the Land*, 115–16.

12. *CG*, 33d Cong., 1st sess., app. 557–61; *CG*, 33d Cong., 1st sess., 1232.

13. *CG*, 33d Cong., 1st sess., app., 772.

14. Foner, *Free Soil, Free Labor, Free Men*, 193–95.

15. 10 Stat. 277; *SJ*, 33rd Cong., 1st sess., 236; *HJ*, 33rd Cong., 1st sess., 923–24; Johannsen, *Stephen A. Douglas*, 451; Michael E. Woods, *Arguing until Doomsday: Stephen Douglas, Jefferson Davis, and the Struggle for American Democracy* (Chapel Hill: University of North Carolina Press, 2020), 135–36.

16. *CG*, 33d Cong., 1st sess., app., 769; "Citizens of the West" quoted from the *Platte Argus* without a date in Robinson, *The Kansas Conflict*, 76–77; T. H. Gladstone, *The Englishman in Kansas: or, Squatter Life and Border Warfare* (New York: Miller, 1857), 227.

17. Andrew Reeder to Stephen A. Douglas, July 10, 1854, box 4, folder 8, SADP; Nicole Etcheson, *Bleeding Kansas: Contested Liberty in the Civil War Era* (Lawrence: University Press of Kansas, 2004), 29. A definitive work on federal land policies in Kansas is Paul Wallace Gates, *Fifty Million Acres: Conflicts over Kansas Land Policy, 1854–1890* (1954; repr., Norman: University of Oklahoma Press, 1997). On Native Americans in the region of Kansas, see John P. Bowes, *Exiles and Pioneers: Eastern Indians in the Trans-Mississippi West* (New York: Cambridge University Press, 2007); and Craig Miner and William E. Unrau, *The End of Indian Kansas: A Study of Cultural Revolution, 1854–1871* (1978; repr., Lawrence: University Press of Kansas, 1990).

18. J. H. Smith to John Calhoun, September 6, 1854, box 6, folder 5, Correspondence, SGKN; Gladstone, *The Englishman in Kansas*, 165.

19. Martha Caldwell, ed., "Records of the Squatter Association of Whitehead District," *Kansas Historical Quarterly* 13:1 (February 1944): 21–22; digitized at https://www.kshs.org/p/records-of-the-squatter-association-of-whitehead-district/12956 (accessed October 9, 2021); Survey of T3S, R22E, vol. 589, Land Survey Field Notes, SGKN. On squatter associations in Kansas, see Gladstone, *The Englishman in Kansas*, 166–72; and Ilia Murtazashvili, *The Political Economy of the American Frontier* (New York: Cambridge University Press, 2013), 71–72.

20. Caldwell, ed., "Records of the Squatter Association of Whitehead District," 22–32.

21. Ibid., 23; James R. Whitehead to John Calhoun, December 15, 1854, box 6, folder 5, Correspondence, SGKN.

22. Caldwell, ed., "Records of the Squatter Association of Whitehead District," 22–23.

23. Historian Scott Reynolds Nelson describes how proslavery US senator David R. Atchison of Missouri helped create a squatter association near Leavenworth to claim lands in defiance of the New England capitalists who had gained control of the Hannibal & St. Joseph Railroad. See Nelson, *A Nation of Deadbeats: An Uncommon History of America's Financial Disasters* (New York: Alfred A. Knopf, 2012), 140–41.

24. Samuel A. Johnson, *The Battle Cry of Freedom: The New England Emigrant Aid Company in the Kansas Crusade* (Westport, CT: Greenwood Press, 1954) 9–15; Wilentz, *The Rise of American Democracy*, 677–78.

25. Robinson, *The Kansas Conflict*, 67.

26. Ibid., 34 (emphasis in original); Don W. Wilson, *Governor Charles Robinson of Kansas* (Lawrence: University Press of Kansas, 1975), 13.

27. Survey of T12S, R20E, vol. 491, Land Survey Field Notes, SGKN; Robinson, *The Kansas Conflict*, 79; "Joseph Savage's Recollections of 1854," no. 3.

28. "Joseph Savage's Recollections of 1854," no. 8; Robinson, *The Kansas Conflict*, 86.

29. Wilson, *Governor Charles Robinson*, 15; Robinson, *The Kansas Conflict*, 77; Achilles Wade to Charles Robinson, undated, box 1, folder 24, CRC.

30. W. H. T. Wakefield, "Squatter Courts in Kansas," *Transactions of the Kansas State Historical Society*, vol. 5, *1889–96* (Topeka: J. K. Hudson, 1896) 71–74; "Joseph Savage's Recollections of 1854," no. 8; "Plain-spoken and thorough Free-soiler"

Notes to pages 151–157

239

quoted in Gladstone, *The Englishman in Kansas*, 248; Robinson, *The Kansas Conflict*, 78.

31. Ibid., 82. Frank W. Blackmar, *The Life of Charles Robinson, the First State Governor of Kansas* (Topeka: Crane, 1902), 119.

32. Horace Greeley, *An Overland Journey, from New York to San Francisco, in the Summer of 1859* (New York: C. M. Saxton, Barker, 1860), 68–69.

33. Dick, *Lure of the Land,* 109–11; Robinson, *The Kansas Conflict*, 75, 77.

34. William E. Treadway, *Cyrus K. Holliday: A Documentary Biography* (Topeka: Kansas State Historical Society, 1979), 9–15, 19, 23.

35. Ibid.; Cyrus K. Holliday Diary, KSRL (emphasis in original).

36. Gladstone, *The Englishman in Kansas*, 171–72.

37. Mary A. Humphrey, *The Squatter Sovereign, or Kansas in the '50's: A Life Picture of the Early Settlement of the Debatable Ground* (Chicago: Coburn and Newman, 1883), 102–3; Robinson, *The Kansas Conflict*, 87.

38. *Kansas Herald of Freedom* (Lawrence, KS), January 27, 1855, 2; Jonathan Earle, "The Making of the North's 'Stark Mad Abolitionists': Antislavery Conversion in the United States, 1824–1854," *Slavery and Abolition* 25:3 (December 2004): 54–72.

39. Sheffield Ingalls, *History of Atchison County, Kansas* (Lawrence, KS: Standard Publishing, 1916), 67; Bill Cecil-Fronsman, "'Death to All Yankees and Traitors in Kansas': The *Squatter Sovereign* and the Defense of Slavery in Kansas," in *Territorial Kansas Reader,* ed. Virgil W. Dean (Topeka: Kansas State Historical Society, 2005), 215–26; John H. Stringfellow to James Buchanan, January 5, 1858, box 35, folder 9, JBP.

40. "Prospectus of the 'Squatter Sovereign,'" *Squatter Sovereign* (Atchison, KS Territory), February 3, 1855, 4.

41. "Negro Slavery, No Evil," February 20, 1855, *Squatter Sovereign*, 1.

42. "Advocates with power and ability . . ." quoted in "Notices of the Press," *Squatter Sovereign*, February 20, 1855, 2; Ingalls, *A History of Atchison County*, 334–35.

43. "To the Friends of the South," *Squatter Sovereign,* March 27, 1855, 2; "Proclamation," Ibid., March 13, 1855, 2 (emphasis in original).

44. "Emigrant Aid Society," *Squatter Sovereign*, March 6, 1855, 2; Andrew Reeder to Stephen A. Douglas, February 12, 1855, box 4, folder 12, SADP.

45. On voting irregularities, see Sara T. L. Robinson, *Kansas: Its Interior and Exterior Life* (Boston: Crosby, Nichols, 1856), 362; Gladstone, *The Englishman in Kansas*, 82–85; and George W. Brown, *Reminiscences of Gov. R. J. Walker; with the True Story of the Rescue of Kansas from Slavery* (Rockford, IL: George W. Brown, 1902), 12–13.

46. Charles Robinson to Edward Everett Hale, April 9, 1855, Kansas Memory, KSHS, http://www.kansasmemory.org/item/1785 (accessed October 13, 2021).

47. Sara T. L. Robinson, *Kansas,* 360; *Collections of the Kansas State Historical Society, 1913–14,* vol. 13 (Topeka: W. R. Smith, 1915), 185; Etcheson, *Bleeding Kansas,* 71–72; Wilson, *Governor Charles Robinson of Kansas,* 19, 29–30; Eugene H. Berwanger, *The Frontier Against Slavery: Western Anti-Negro Prejudice and the*

Slavery Extension Controversy (1967; repr., Urbana: University of Illinois Press, 2002), 111–12.

48. On Calhoun, see Robert W. Johannsen, "John Calhoun: The Villain of Territorial Kansas?" *Trail Guide* 3:3 (September 1958): 1–19.

49. John Calhoun to Stephen A. Douglas, November 27, 1855, box 4, folder 14, SADP.

50. "The Kansas War!" *Squatter Sovereign*, January 1, 1856, 1; Robinson, *The Kansas Conflict*, 183; Etcheson, *Bleeding Kansas,* 79–87.

51. "The Kansas War!" *Squatter Sovereign*, January 1, 1856, 1; Cyrus K. Holliday to Mary Holliday, December 13, 1855, Cyrus Kurtz Holliday letters, KSHS, https://www.kshs.org/p/letters-of-cyrus-kurtz-holliday-1854-1859/12717 (accessed October 10, 2021).

52. Charles Robinson and George W. Deitzler to A. Guthrie, December 5, 1855, Kansas Memory, KSHS, http://www.kansasmemory.org/item/225115 (accessed October 10, 2021); Cyrus K. Holliday to Mary Holliday, December 6, 1855, Cyrus Kurtz Holliday letters, KSHS, https://www.kshs.org/p/letters-of-cyrus-kurtz-holliday-1854-1859/12717 (accessed October 10, 2021).

53. "A Full and Accurate Account of the Invasion of Kansas Ter.," *Kansas Herald of Freedom* (Lawrence, KS Territory), December 15, 1855, 1–2; Etcheson, *Bleeding Kansas,* 85.

54. "Address of Governor Walker at Topeka," June 6, 1857, *Transactions of the Kansas State Historical Society* 5:293; Wilson, *Governor Charles Robinson*, 35; Johnson, *The Battle Cry of Freedom*, 145.

55. No Headline, *Squatter Sovereign*, March 11, 1856, 2; "Missourians Going over in Crowds," *Squatter Sovereign*, July 1, 1856, 2.

56. "Republicanism in Kansas," *Kansas Herald of Freedom* (Lawrence, KS Territory), January 19, 1856, 2.

57. Ibid.

58. Franklin Pierce to Congress, January 24, 1856, *CMP*, 5:352–60.

59. Franklin Pierce, "A Proclamation," ibid., 390–91.

60. *CG*, 34th Cong., 1st sess., app., 288.

61. "Message from the Governor," *Collections of the Kansas State Historical Society* 13:178–88.

62. Ibid., 180, 183, 185.

63. John C. Frémont to Charles Robinson, March 17, 1856, box 1, folder 1, CRC.

64. "A Kansas Patriot," *Squatter Sovereign*, April 1, 1856, 2.

65. Johnson, *The Battle Cry of Freedom,* 157; Robinson, *The Kansas Conflict,* 237; "Got Him Fast," *Squatter Sovereign*, May 13, 1856, 2; William Phillips to Sara Robinson, May 26, 1856, box 1, folder 1, CRC; Charles Robinson to Sara Robinson, May 29, 1856, ibid.; Stringfellow quoted in Sara T. L. Robinson, *Kansas*, 247.

66. *CG*, 34th Cong., 1st sess., app., 629; Wilentz, *The Rise of American Democracy*, 689–91.

67. Robinson's letter to Brown appears in Oswald Garrison Villard, *John Brown, 1800–1859: A Biography Fifty Years After* (London: Constable, 1910), 262–63; Charles Robinson to James McClatchy, May 29, 1856, box 15, folder 4, EMC.

CHAPTER 8

1. Robert J. Walker to James Buchanan, April 28, 1856, box 28, folder 12, JBP; James P. Shenton, *Robert John Walker: A Politician from Jackson to Lincoln* (New York: Columbia University Press, 1961), 127–31; Roy Franklin Nichols, *Franklin Pierce: Young Hickory of the Granite Hills* (Philadelphia: University of Pennsylvania Press, 1931), 309.

2. Walker to Buchanan, April 28, 1856; Arthur M. Schlesinger Jr., *The Age of Jackson* (Boston: Little, Brown, 1945), 481.

3. "1856 Democratic Party Platform," June 2, 1856, American Presidency Project, University of California, Santa Barbara, https://www.presidency.ucsb.edu/node/273169 (accessed October 13, 2021); Douglas to William A. Richardson, June 5, 1856, box 42, folder 6, SADP.

4. Robert J. Walker, *An Appeal for the Union: Letter from the Hon. Robert J. Walker* (New York: John F. Trow, 1856); "Republican Party Platform of 1856," American Presidency Project, University of California, Santa Barbara, https://www.presidency.ucsb.edu/node/273293 (accessed October 13, 2021).

5. Michael E. Woods, *Arguing until Doomsday: Stephen Douglas, Jefferson Davis, and the Struggle for American Democracy* (Chapel Hill: University of North Carolina Press, 2020), 148.

6. "Communications," *St. Albans Messenger* (St. Albans, VT), December 18, 1856, 2.

7. James Buchanan, "Inaugural Address," *CMP*, 5:431; William W. Freehling, *The Road to Disunion*, vol. 2, *Secessionists Triumphant, 1854–1861* (New York: Oxford University Press, 2007), 115–18.

8. 60 US 393 (1856). On the Dred Scott decision, see Stephen Kantrowitz, *More than Freedom: Fighting for Black Citizenship in a White Republic, 1829–1889* (New York: Penguin, 2012), 223–24; Don E. Fehrenbacher, *The Dred Scott Case: Its Significance in Law* (1978; repr., New York: Oxford University Press, 2001); Christopher Childers, *The Failure of Popular Sovereignty: Slavery, Manifest Destiny, and the Radicalization of Southern Politics* (Lawrence: University Press of Kansas, 2012), 5; and David M. Potter, *The Impending Crisis, 1848–1861* (New York: Harper and Row, 1976), 287–89.

9. Thomas Hart Benton, "Historical and Legal Examination of that Part of the Decision of the Supreme Court of the United States in the Dred Scott Case, which Declares the Unconstitutionality of the Missouri Compromise Act, and the Self-Extension of the Constitution to Territories, Carrying Slavery Along with It" (New York: D. Appleton, 1857), 123.

10. "Governor Walker's Letter of Acceptance," March 26, 1857, *Transactions of the Kansas State Historical Society*, vol. 5, *1889–96* (Topeka: Kansas State Printing Company, 1896), 290; Robert W. Johannsen, *Stephen A. Douglas* (1973; repr., Urbana: University of Illinois Press, 1997), 564–65.

11. Robert J. Walker to M. E. Cook, April 6, 1857, RJWP (emphasis in original).

12. Schlesinger, *The Age of Jackson*, 484; James L. Huston, *Calculating the Value of the Union: Slavery, Property Rights, and the Economic Origins of the Civil War* (Chapel Hill: University of North Carolina Press, 2003), 219; Philip Shriver Klein, *President James Buchanan: A Biography* (University Park: Pennsylvania State University Press, 1962), 292.

13. "Highly Important from Washington. Walker's Plan for the Pacification of Kansas," *New York Herald*, April 4, 1857, 1; *Harper's Weekly* quoted by Dunbar Rowland, ed., *Encyclopedia of Mississippi History, Comprising Sketches of Counties, Towns, Events, Institutions and Persons*, vol. 2 (Madison, WI: Selwyn A. Brant, 1907), 893.

14. Johannsen, *Stephen A. Douglas*, 564–65; Charles Robinson, *The Kansas Conflict* (New York: Harper and Brothers, 1892), 351.

15. "Meeting of the Citizens of Lawrence and Governor Walker [Correspondence of the Quindaro Chindowan]," *New York Herald*, June 7, 1857, 2.

16. "Governor Walker's Inaugural Address," *Transactions of the Kansas State Historical Society*, 5:328.

17. Ibid., 331–32.

18. Ibid., 335–36.

19. Ibid., 336.

20. Ibid., 339–40.

21. Ibid., 337–38, 341.

22. "Governor Walker in Kansas," *New York Sun*, June 4, 1857, RJWP, clipped in a way that does not show the page number; "He openly allies himself . . ." quoted from the *Richmond South* without a date in Robinson, *The Kansas Conflict*, 352; Charles Robinson to James McClatchy, June 28, 1857, box 15, folder 4, EMC. On southern dismay at Walker's interactions with Robinson and other Free State partisans, see Fehrenbacher, *The Dred Scott Case*, 459.

23. Robert J. Walker to James Buchanan, June 28, 1857, box 34, folder 9, JBP.

24. Ibid. (emphasis in original).

25. Ibid.

26. *HRRep* 648, 36th Cong., 1st sess., 112–13, Serial 1071.

27. "Mr. Walker to Mr. Cass," July 15, 1857, *Transactions of the Kansas State Historical Society*, 5:346; Robert J. Walker to James Buchanan, June 28, 1857.

28. "The Land Sales," *New-York Daily Tribune*, July 4, 1857, 3.

29. "Mr. Walker to Mr. Cass," July 15, 1857, 347.

30. "To the People of Lawrence.—Proclamation," *Transactions of the Kansas State Historical Society*, 5:357; *Leavenworth Times* article reprinted in *Transactions of the Kansas State Historical Society*, vol. 6, *1897–1900* (Topeka: W. Y. Morgan, 1900), 302–3.

31. Samuel Pomeroy to Thaddeus Hyatt, July 24, 1857, box 1, folder 1, Samuel Clark Pomeroy Papers, KSHS; John B. Floyd to James Buchanan, July 31, 1857 (emphasis in original), and Floyd to Robert J. Walker, July 31, 1857, box 33, folder 13, JBP.

32. Robert J. Walker to James Buchanan, August 3, 1857, box 34, folder 14, JBP.

33. Stephen A. Douglas to Robert J. Walker, July 21, 1857, Robert J. Walker Correspondence, New-York Historical Society.

34. Amos Lawrence to Charles Robinson, August 16, 1857, box 1, folder 3, CRC.

35. Robert J. Walker, "Proclamation to the People of Kansas," October 19, 1857, and Ibid., October 22, 1857, *Transactions of the Kansas State Historical Society,* 5:403–408; Robinson, *The Kansas Conflict,* 365; Robert W. Johannsen, "John Calhoun: The Villain of Territorial Kansas?" *Trail Guide* 3:3 (September 1958): 10–11; James McPherson, *Battle Cry of Freedom: The Civil War Era* (New York: Oxford University Press, 1988), 164; Nicole Etcheson, *Bleeding Kansas: Contested Liberty in the Civil War Era* (Lawrence: University Press of Kansas, 2004), 153–55.

36. Ibid., 156; Potter, *The Impending Crisis,* 307–310; Johannsen, "John Calhoun," 11–13.

37. "The infamous manner . . ." in *HRRep* 648, 36th Cong., 1st sess., 114, Serial 1071; Johannsen, "John Calhoun," 13; Michael F. Holt, *The Fate of Their Country: Politicians, Slavery Extension, and the Coming of the Civil War* (New York: Hill and Wang, 2004), 121; "Lessons," *Lawrence Republican* (Lawrence, KS Territory), November 12, 1857, 2.

38. "Gov. Walker Ill," *Kansas National Democrat* (Lecompton, KS Territory), November 12, 1857, RJWP, 2; Robert J. Walker, Unpublished autobiography, 34, RJWP.

39. Robert J. Walker, unpublished autobiography, 13–30, RJWP. Walker could have added that he was also an innovative administrator. As treasury secretary he successfully led efforts to create the US Department of the Interior.

40. Walker, Unpublished autobiography, 31, RJWP.

41. Jeriah Bonham, *Fifty Years' Recollections; with Observations and Reflections on Historical Events* (Peoria, IL: J. W. Franks, 1883), 195–96; Sean Wilentz, *The Rise of American Democracy: Jefferson to Lincoln* (New York: W. W. Norton, 2005), 717–18.

42. "Republican Principles," *Clermont Courier* (Batavia, OH), December 10, 1857, 2 (emphasis in original).

43. Willard Carl Klunder, *Lewis Cass and the Politics of Moderation* (Kent, OH: Kent State University Press, 1996), 162–63, 299–300; James L. Huston, *Stephen A. Douglas and the Dilemmas of Democratic Equality* (Lanham, MD: Rowman and Littlefield, 2007), 131; Michael F. Holt, *Political Parties and American Political Development from the Age of Jackson to the Age of Lincoln* (Baton Rouge: Louisiana State University, 1992), 83.

44. John H. Stringfellow to James Buchanan, January 5, 1858, box 35, folder 9, JBP.

45. Ibid.

CHAPTER 9

1. M. H. Birdsong to Stephen A. Douglas, July 12, 1860, box 35, folder 17, SADP. Thanks to Michael Woods for bringing this item to my attention.

2. *CG,* 36th Cong. 1st sess., 559.

3. *Political Debates between Hon. Abraham Lincoln and Hon. Stephen A. Douglas, in the Celebrated Campaign of 1858, in Illinois* (Columbus, OH: Follett, Foster, 1860), 2, 15–16.

4. Ibid., 95; Robert W. Johannsen, *Stephen A. Douglas* (1973; repr., Urbana: University of Illinois Press, 1997), 670.

5. *CG*, 35th Cong., 2d sess., 1246; "The New Political Organization," *Dallas Herald*, June 15, 1859, 1; Johannsen, *Stephen A. Douglas*, 693–97.

6. No Headline, *Randolph County Journal* (Winchester, IN), September 8, 1859, 2.

7. *Official Proceedings of the Democratic National Convention, Held in 1860* (Cleveland, OH: Nevins', 1860), 58; M. Halstead, *Caucuses of 1860. A History of the National Political Conventions of the Current Presidential Campaign* (Columbus, OH: Follett, Foster, 1860), 98; Roy Franklin Nichols, *The Disruption of American Democracy* (New York: Macmillan, 1948), 296–304; Michael E. Woods, *Arguing until Doomsday: Stephen Douglas, Jefferson Davis, and the Struggle for American Democracy* (Chapel Hill: University of North Carolina Press, 2020), 198.

8. *Official Proceedings of the Democratic National Convention*, 61, 65; Halstead, *Caucuses of 1860*, 92–93.

9. "Republican Party Platform of 1860," American Presidency Project, University of California, Santa Barbara, https://www.presidency.ucsb.edu/node/273296 (accessed October 15, 2021).

10. *SJ*, 36th Cong., 1st sess., 407; *CG*, 36th Cong., 1st sess., 1658.

11. Douglas quote in ibid., 1660; Benjamin Price to Stephen A. Douglas, June 5, 1860, box 34, folder 25, SADP.

12. *SJ*, 36th Cong., 1st sess., 747–53; *Dubuque Herald* quoted in George M. Stephenson, *The Political History of the Public Lands from 1840 to 1862: From Pre-emption to Homestead* (Boston: Richard G. Badger, 1917), 217.

13. J. C. Spencer to James Buchanan, July 4, 1860, box 40, folder 1, JBP (emphasis in original); "Breckinridge & Lane campaign song" (Philadelphia: Johnson's, 1860), American Song Sheets, Rare Books and Special Collections, LOC, https://www.loc.gov/item/amss.cw200320 (accessed on October 15, 2021).

14. Letter to the Editor, *Delaware Gazette* (Delaware, OH), June 29, 1860, 2; Cartoonist unknown, "The Great Political Juggle," *Rail Splitter* (Cincinnati, OH), August 1, 1860, 3; "Republican Thunder from Maine," *Delaware Gazette* (Delaware, OH), September 14, 1860, 2.

15. "Keep It Before the People," *Wabash Express* (Terre Haute, IN), September 19, 1860, 1.

16. "The Difference Between Squatter Sovereignty and Popular Sovereignty. Speech of Hon. Stephen A. Douglas, at Syracuse, N.Y." *Virginia Weekly* (Morgantown, VA), undated, box 43, folder 11, SADP. This article appears among the sundry newspaper clippings in Douglas's papers. The opening paragraph attributes the contents to the *New York Herald*. It is clipped in a manner that does not give the article's date.

Douglas delivered the address in Syracuse on September 17, 1860, and subsequently distributed it in pamphlet form.

17. "Colonel Crockett's Celebrated Squatter Speech," *Crockett's Yaller Flower Almanac, for '36* (New York: Elton, 1835), 6; S.L.C., "The Dandy Frightening the Squatter," *The Carpet-Bag* (Boston, MA), May 1, 1852.

EPILOGUE

1. *CG*, 33d Cong., 2d sess., 604.

2. Paul F. Thomas, "George Bush" (Master's thesis, University of Washington, 1965), 2–25; Shirley Ann Wilson Moore, *Sweet Freedom's Plains: African Americans on the Overland Trails, 1841–1869* (Norman: University of Oklahoma Press, 2016), 30, 67, 230.

3. Thomas, "George Bush," 23–25; Darrell Millner, "George Bush of Tumwater: Founder of the First American Colony on Puget Sound," *Columbia Magazine* 8:4 (Winter 1994–95): 14–19; Quintard Taylor, *In Search of the Racial Frontier: African Americans in the American West, 1528–1990* (New York: W. W. Norton, 1998), 82.

4. Millner, "George Bush of Tumwater," 18; Ezra Meeker, *Pioneer Reminiscences of Puget Sound: The Tragedy of Leschi* (Seattle: Lowman and Hanford, 1905), 82; Thomas, "George Bush," 59–63.

5. Meeker, *Pioneer Reminiscences*, 82.

Bibliography

MANUSCRIPT COLLECTIONS

Bancroft Library, University of California, Berkeley
    John A. Sutter, "Personal Reminiscences of General John Augustus Sutter"
    Land Case Files, 1852–1892
    Sacramento County Land Papers
    William Robert Prince Letters
    William McKendree Gwin Papers
California Historical Society
    William M. Gwin Correspondence
    Samuel W. Brown Diary and Letters
Center for Sacramento History
    Court of First Magistrate
    Eleanor McClatchy Collection
    Sacramento City Council Minutes
Historical Society of Pennsylvania
    George Mifflin Dallas Collection
    James Buchanan Papers
    Salmon P. Chase Papers
Indiana State Library
    Squatters' Union of Lake County Papers, 1836–1838
    John B. Niles Papers
Kansas State Historical Society
    Amos Lawrence Papers
    Cyrus Kurtz Holliday Papers
    Records of the US Surveyor General of Kansas and Nebraska
    Samuel Clark Pomeroy Papers
    Transactions of the Kansas State Historical Society

Library Company of Philadelphia
    Henry D. Gilpin Pamphlet Collection
    Chew Family Collection
Library of Congress
    Caleb Cushing Papers
    Andrew Jackson Papers
    Martin Van Buren Papers
    Robert J. Walker Papers
National Archives and Records Administration (NARA)
    RG 75, Records of the Bureau of Indian Affairs
        M21, Letters Sent by the Office of Indian Affairs, 1824–1881
        M234, Letters Received by the Office of Indian Affairs, 1824–1881
        T494, Documents Relating to the Negotiation of Ratified and Unratified
        Treaties with Various Indian Tribes, 1801–1869
Center for Legislative Archives, NARA
    RG46, Records of the US Senate, Committee on Public Lands, Petitions and
        Memorials
    Records of the US House of Representatives, Committee on Public Lands, Petitions
        and Memorials
New-York Historical Society
    Robert J. Walker Correspondence
Oregon Historical Society Research Library
    Applegate Family Papers
    Joseph Lane Papers
    Provisional and Territorial Documents
    Thurston Family Papers
Kenneth Spencer Research Library, University of Kansas, Lawrence
    Cyrus K. Holliday Diary
    Charles Robinson Collection
    Sara Tappan Doolittle Robinson Letters
University of Chicago Library, Special Collections Research Center
    Stephen A. Douglas Papers

                        DIGITAL COLLECTIONS

    The American Presidency Project, University of California, Santa Barbara, https://
        www.presidency.ucsb.edu/
    Digital Library on American Slavery, University of North Carolina at Greensboro,
        https://library.uncg.edu/slavery/
    Kansas Memory, Kansas State Historical Society, https://www.kansasmemory.org/
    The Oregon Encyclopedia, https://www.oregonencyclopedia.org/
    Sabin Americana, 1500–1926, Gale Digital Collections, https://www.gale.com/c/
        sabin-americana-history-of-the-americas-1500-1926

NEWSPAPERS AND PERIODICALS

Alta California (San Francisco, CA)
Anti-Slavery Bugle (Salem, OH)
Arkansas Gazette (Little Rock, AR)
The Bee (Sacramento, CA)
Bellows Falls Gazette (Bellows Falls, VT)
Boon's Lick Times (Fayette, MO)
Boston Courier (Boston, MA)
Boston Semi-Weekly Advertiser (Boston, MA)
The Carpet-Bag (Boston, MA)
Centinel of Freedom (Newark, NJ)
The Century Illustrated Monthly Magazine (New York, NY)
Cherokee Phoenix, and Indians' Advocate (New Echota, GA)
Clermont Courier (Batavia, OH)
Cleveland Plain Dealer (Cleveland, OH)
Commercial Advertiser (New York, NY)
Daily Atlas (Boston, MA)
Daily Evening Advertiser (Portland, ME)
Daily Evening Transcript (Boston, MA)
Daily Morning News (Savannah, GA)
Daily National Era (Washington, DC)
Daily Ohio Statesman (Columbus, OH)
Daily Picayune (New Orleans, LA)
Daily Sanduskian (Sandusky, OH)
Dallas Herald (Dallas, TX)
Delaware Gazette (Delaware, OH)
Georgia Telegraph (Macon, GA)
Green Mountain Freeman (Montpelier, VT)
Illinois State Register (Springfield, IL)
Jefferson Inquirer (Jefferson City, MO)
Kalamazoo Gazette (Kalamazoo, MI)
Kansas Herald of Freedom (Lawrence, KS Territory)
Kansas National Democrat (Lecompton, KS Territory)
Kanzas News (Emporia, KS Territory)
Kendall's Expositor (Washington, DC)
Lancaster Gazette (Lancaster, OH)
Lawrence Republican (Lawrence, KS Territory)
The Liberator (Boston, MA)
The Madisonian (Washington, DC)
Maine Farmer (Augusta, ME)
Mississippi Free Trader (Natchez, MS)
National Intelligencer (Washington, DC)

New-Hampshire Sentinel (Keene, NH)
New-York American (New York, NY)
New-York Evening Post (New York, NY)
New York Herald (New York, NY)
New York Sun (New York, NY)
New-York Tribune (New York, NY)
The New World (New York, NY)
Niles' National Register
The North Bend (Worcester, MA)
Pennsylvania Telegraph (Harrisburg, PA)
Piney Woods Planter (Liberty, MS)
Pittsfield Sun (Pittsfield, MA)
Placer Times (Sacramento, CA)
Portage Sentinel (Ravenna, OH)
Public Ledger (Philadelphia, PA)
Rail Splitter (Cincinnati, OH)
Randolph County Journal (Winchester, IN)
Republican Herald (Providence, RI)
Richmond Enquirer (Richmond, VA)
Richmond Whig (Richmond, VA)
St. Albans Messenger (St. Albans, VT)
Scioto Gazette (Chillicothe, OH)
Settlers and Miners Tribune (Sacramento, CA)
Southern Argus (Columbus, MS)
The Squatter (St. Louis, MO)
Squatter Sovereign (Atchison, KS Territory)
The Sun (Baltimore, MD)
Texian Advocate (Victoria, TX)
The Torch Light (Hagerstown, MD)
The Union (Washington, DC)
United States Magazine and Democratic Review (New York, NY)
Virginia Weekly (Morgantown, VA)
Wabash Express (Terre Haute, IN)
Wisconsin Argus (Madison, WI)

GOVERNMENT DOCUMENTS

American State Papers: Documents Legislative and Executive, of the Congress of the United States. 38 vols. Washington, DC: Gales and Seaton, 1832–1861.
The Congressional Globe. 46 vols. Washington, DC, 1833–1873.
The Debates and Proceedings in the Congress of the United States. 42 vols. Washington, DC, 1834–1856.

Journal of the House of Representatives of the United States.

Journal of the Senate of the State of Mississippi.

Journal of the Senate of the United States.

Kappler, Charles J. *Indian Affairs: Laws and Treaties.* Vol. 2. Washington, DC: Government Printing Office, 1904.

Peters, Richard et al., eds., *The Public Statutes at Large of the United States of America.* 12 vols. Boston, 1845–1863.

Register of Debates in Congress. 14 vols. Washington, DC, 1825–1837.

Reports of Decisions in the Supreme Court of the United States. 569 vols. Boston, New York, and Washington, DC, 1875–.

The Revised Code of Laws, of Illinois. Shawneetown, IL: Alexander F. Grant, 1829.

Richardson, James D., ed. *A Compilation of the Messages and Papers of the Presidents, 1789–1897.* 10 vols. Washington, DC: Government Printing Office, 1896–1899.

United States Congressional Serial Set.

PUBLISHED PRIMARY SOURCES

Benton, Thomas Hart. "Historical and Legal Examination of that Part of the Decision of the Supreme Court of the United States in the Dred Scott Case, which Declares the Unconstitutionality of the Missouri Compromise Act, and the Self-Extension of the Constitution to Territories, Carrying Slavery along with It." New York: D. Appleton and Company, 1857.

Benton, Thomas Hart. *Thirty Years' View; or, A History of the Working of the American Government for Thirty Years, from 1820 to 1850.* 2 vols. New York: D. Appleton and Company, 1854–1856.

Bonham, Jeriah. *Fifty Years' Recollections; with Observations and Reflections on Historical Events.* Peoria, IL: J. W. Franks and Sons, 1883.

Brown, Albert G. *Speeches, Messages, and Other Writings of the Hon. Albert G. Brown, a Senator in Congress from the State of Mississippi.* New Orleans: H. D. Maginnis, 1859.

Burlend, Rebecca. *A True Picture of Emigration.* 1848. Reprint, Chicago: Lakeside Press, 1936.

Burke, Edmund. *The Works of the Right Honourable Edmund Burke.* Vol. 1. London: Henry G. Bohn, 1854.

Calhoun, John C. *The Works of John C. Calhoun.* Vol. 4. New York: D. Appleton, 1854.

Channing, William Ellery. *The Works of William E. Channing.* Vol. 2. Boston: James Munroe, 1848.

Chase, Salmon P. et al., "Appeal of the Independent Democrats in Congress to the People of the United States." Washington, DC: Towers, 1854.

Claiborne, J. F. H. *Mississippi, as a Province, Territory and State; with Biographical Notices of Eminent Citizens.* Jackson: Power and Barksdale, 1880.

Clayton, John M. "Speech of Mr. Clayton, of Delaware, Delivered at the Whig Mass Meeting Held in Wilmington on the 15th of June, 1844." Washington, DC: Gales and Seaton, 1844.

Cooper, James Fenimore. *The Prairie: A Tale*. Philadelphia: Carey, Lea and Carey, 1827.

Cutler, William G. *History of the State of Kansas*. Chicago: A. T. Andreas, 1883.

Democratic Party. "Oregon. American Protection to American Pioneers; or, Shall Oregon be Surrendered to Great Britain?" Washington, DC: Published by Order of a Committee of the Democratic Members of Congress, 1844.

Elton, Robert H. *Crockett's Yaller Flower Almanac, for '36*. New York: Elton, 1835.

Evans, Elwood. "Annual Address." *Transactions of the Fifth Annual Re-union of the Oregon Pioneer Association; for 1877*. Salem, OR: E. M. Waite, 1878.

Fearon, Henry Bradshaw. *Sketches of America: A Narrative of a Journey of Five Thousand Miles through the Eastern and Western States of America*. London: Longman, Hurst, Rees, Orme, and Brown, 1818.

Fisher, James. *The Squatter's Almanac, 1845*. New York: Turner and Fisher, 1844.

Foote, Henry S. *Casket of Reminiscences*. Washington, DC: Chronicle Publishing, 1874.

Foote, Henry S. *Texas and the Texans; or, Advance of the Anglo-Americans to the South-West*. Vol. 2. Philadelphia: Thomas, Cowperthwait, 1841.

Ford, Paul Leicester, ed. *The Works of Thomas Jefferson*. Vol. 3. New York: G. P. Putnam's Sons, 1904.

Gladstone, T. H. *The Englishman in Kansas: or, Squatter Life and Border Warfare*. New York: Miller, 1857.

Greeley, Horace. *An Overland Journey, from New York to San Francisco, in the Summer of 1859*. New York: C. M. Saxton, Barker, 1860.

Gwin, William M. "The Preemption System." September 8, 1844. Mississippi Department of Archives and History.

Gwin, William M. "Speech of Mr. Gwin, of California, on Land Claims in California, delivered in the Senate of the United States, August 2, 1852." Washington, DC: Congressional Globe Office, 1852.

Hall, John E. *The American Law Journal*. Vol. 5. Baltimore: William Fry, 1814.

Halstead, M. *Caucuses of 1860. A History of the National Political Conventions of the Current Presidential Campaign*. Columbus, OH: Follett, Foster, 1860.

The Harrison and Log Cabin Song Book. Columbus, OH: I. N. Whiting, 1840.

Humphrey, Mary A. *The Squatter Sovereign, or Kansas in the '50's: A Life Picture of the Early Settlement of the Debatable Ground*. Chicago: Coburn and Newman, 1883.

Jackson, Jack, ed. *Texas by Terán: The Diary Kept by General Manuel de Mier y Terán on His 1828 Inspection of Texas*. Austin: University of Texas Press, 2000.

Jefferson, Thomas. *Notes on the State of Virginia*. 1785. Reprint, Boston: Lilly and Wait, 1832.

Kellar, Herbert Anthony, ed., *Solon Robinson, Pioneer and Agriculturalist*. 2 vols. Indianapolis: Indiana Historical Bureau, 1936.

Leggett, William. *Tales and Sketches. By a Country Schoolmaster*. New York: J. and J. Harper, 1829.

Lincoln, Abraham and Stephen A. Douglas. *Political Debates between Hon. Abraham Lincoln and Hon. Stephen A. Douglas, in the Celebrated Campaign of 1858, in Illinois*. Columbus, OH: Follett, Foster, 1860.

Martineau, Harriet. *Retrospect of Western Travel*. Vol. 1. New York: Charles Lohman, 1838.

McConnel, J. L. *Western Characters; or, Types of Border Life in the Western States.* New York: Redfield, 1853.

McLoughlin, John. "Copy of a Document Found among the Private Papers of the Late Dr. John McLoughlin," 46–55. In *Constitution and Quotations from the Register of the Oregon Pioneer Association*. Salem: E. M. Waite: 1875.

Meeker, Ezra. *Pioneer Reminiscences of Puget Sound: The Tragedy of Leschi*. Seattle: Lowman and Hanford, 1905.

Meine, Franklin J., ed. *The Crockett Almanacks: Nashville Series, 1835–1838*. Chicago: Caxton Club, 1955.

Morse, John F. *The Sacramento Directory for the Year 1853–54*. Sacramento: Samuel Colville, 1853.

Moser, Harold D. et al., eds. *The Papers of Andrew Jackson*. 13 vols. Knoxville: University of Tennessee Press, 1980–.

Moulton, Gary E., ed. *The Papers of Chief John Ross*. Vol. 1. Norman, Okla., 1985.

Neal, John. "The Squatter." In *The Genius of John Neal: Selections from His Writings*, edited by Benjamin Lease and Hans-Joachim Lang, 58–66. Frankfurt: Peter Lang, 1978.

Nevins, Allan, ed. *The Diary of John Quincy Adams, 1794–1845: American Diplomacy, and Political, Social, and Intellectual Life, from Washington to Polk*. New York: Charles Scribner's Sons, 1951.

Official Proceedings of the Democratic National Convention, Held in 1860. Cleveland, OH: Nevins', 1860.

Peck, J. M. *A New Guide for Emigrants to the West, Containing Sketches of Michigan, Ohio, Indiana, Illinois, Missouri, Arkansas, with the Territory of Wisconsin and the Adjacent Parts*. 2nd ed. Boston: Gould, Kendall, and Lincoln, 1837.

Peterson, Merrill, ed. *Thomas Jefferson: Writings*. New York: Library of America, 1984.

Quaife, Milo Milton, ed. *The Diary of James K. Polk During His Presidency, 1845 to 1849*. Vol. 4. Chicago: A. C. McClurg, 1910.

Robb, John S. ("Solitaire"). *Streaks of Squatter Life, and Far-West Scenes*. Philadelphia: Carey and Hart, 1847.

Robinson, Charles. *The Kansas Conflict*. New York: Harper and Brothers, 1892.

Robinson, Sara T. L. *Kansas; Its Interior and Exterior Life*. Boston: Crosby, Nichols, 1856.

Rush, Benjamin. *Essays, Literary, Moral and Philosophical*. 2nd ed. Philadelphia: Thomas and William Bradford, 1806.

Savage, Joseph. "Joseph Savage's Recollections of 1854." Kansas Memory, Kansas State Historical Society, https://www.kshs.org/km/items/view/90813.

Sealsfield, Charles. "The Squatter Chief; or, The First American in Texas." In Sealsfield, *Life in the New World; or, Sketches of American Society*, 269–349. New York: J. Winchester, 1844.

Simms, William Gilmore. *Border Beagles: A Tale of Mississippi*. Vol. 1. Philadelphia: Carey and Hart, 1840.

Streeter, Thomas W. *Alta California: Embracing Notices of the Climate, Soil, and Agricultural Products of Northern Mexico and the Pacific Seaboard.* Philadelphia: H. Packer, 1847.

Walker, Robert J. *An Appeal for the Union: Letter from the Hon. Robert J. Walker.* New York: John F. Trow, 1856.

Walker, Robert J. *Letter of Mr. Walker, of Mississippi, Relative to the Annexation of Texas: In Reply to the Call of the People of Carroll County, Kentucky, to Communicate His Views on that Subject.* Washington, DC: Washington Globe, 1844.

Walker, Robert J. *Public Dinner, Given in Honor of the Chickasaw and Choctaw Treaties, at Mr. Parker's Hotel, in the City of Natchez, on the 10th Day of October, 1830.* Sabin Americana, 1500–1926.

Webster, Noah. *An American Dictionary of the English Language.* New York: S. Converse, 1828.

SECONDARY SOURCES

Adelman, Jeremy and Stephen Aron. "From Borderlands to Borders: Empires, Nation-States, and the Peoples in Between in North American History." *American Historical Review* 104, no. 3 (June 1999): 814–41.

Albanese, Catherine L. "King Crockett: Nature and Civility on the American Frontier." *Proceedings of the American Antiquarian Society* 88, no. 2 (October 1979): 225–49.

Almaguer, Tomás. *Racial Fault Lines: The Historical Origins of White Supremacy in California.* 2nd ed. Berkeley: University of California Press, 2009.

Aron, Stephen. *American Confluence: The Missouri Frontier from Borderland to Border State.* Bloomington: Indiana University Press, 2006.

Aron, Stephen. *How the West Was Lost: The Transformation of Kentucky from Daniel Boone to Henry Clay.* Baltimore: Johns Hopkins University Press, 1996.

Atwood, A. *The Conquerors: Historical Sketches of the American Settlement of the Oregon Country, Embracing Facts in the Life and Work of Rev. Jason Lee, the Pioneer and Founder of American Institutions on the Western Coast of North America.* Glendale, CA: Arthur H. Clark, 1907.

Auchampaugh, Philip Gerald. *James Buchanan and His Cabinet on the Eve of Secession.* Lancaster, PA: Lancaster Press, 1926.

Bagley, Will, ed. *Scoundrel's Tale: The Samuel Brannan Papers,* vol. 3 of *Kingdom in the West: The Mormons and the American Frontier.* Spokane, WA: Arthur H. Clark, 1999.

Balogh, Brian. *A Government Out of Sight: The Mystery of National Authority in Nineteenth-Century America.* New York: Cambridge University Press, 2009.

Bancroft, Hubert Howe. *History of California.* Vol. 6, *1848–1859.* San Francisco: History Company, 1888.

Banner, Stuart. *How the Indians Lost Their Land: Law and Power on the Frontier.* Cambridge, MA: Belknap Press of Harvard University Press, 2005.

Baptist, Edward E. *Creating an Old South: Middle Florida's Plantation Frontier Before the Civil War*. Chapel Hill: University of North Carolina Press, 2002.

Beard, Charles A. and Mary R. Beard. *The Rise of American Civilization*. Vol. 2, *The Industrial Era*. New York: Macmillan, 1927.

Benson, Lee. *The Concept of Jacksonian Democracy: New York as a Test Case*. Princeton, NJ: Princeton University Press, 1961.

Berwanger, Eugene H. *The Frontier Against Slavery: Western Anti-Negro Prejudice and the Slavery Extension Controversy*. 1967. Reprint, Urbana: University of Illinois Press, 2002.

Billington, Ray Allen. "The Origin of the Land Speculator as a Frontier Type." *Agricultural History* 19, no. 4 (October 1945): 204–12.

Blackmar, Frank W. *The Life of Charles Robinson, the First State Governor of Kansas*. Topeka: Crane, 1902.

Blau, Joseph L., ed. *Social Theories of Jacksonian Democracy: Representative Writings of the Period 1825–1850*. New York: Hafner, 1947.

Bogue, Allan G. *From Prairie to Corn Belt: Farming on the Illinois and Iowa Prairies in the Nineteenth Century*. Chicago: University of Chicago Press, 1963.

Bogue, Allan G. "The Iowa Claim Clubs: Symbol and Substance." In *The Public Lands: Studies in the History of the Public Domain*, edited by Vernon Carstensen, 47–69. Madison: University of Wisconsin Press, 1963.

Bolton, Charles C. *Poor Whites of the Antebellum South: Tenants and Laborers in Central North Carolina and Northeast Mississippi*. Durham, NC: Duke University Press, 1994.

Bowen, William A. *The Willamette Valley: Migration and Settlement on the Oregon Frontier*. Seattle: University of Washington Press, 1978.

Bowes, John P. *Exiles and Pioneers: Eastern Indians in the Trans-Mississippi West*. New York: Cambridge University Press, 2007.

Bowes, John P. *Land Too Good for Indians: Northern Indian Removal*. Norman: University of Oklahoma Press, 2016.

Brown, George W. *Reminiscences of Gov. R. J. Walker; with the True Story of the Rescue of Kansas from Slavery*. Rockford, IL: George W. Brown, 1902.

Buss, James Joseph. *Winning the West with Words: Language and Conquest in the Lower Great Lakes*. Norman: University of Oklahoma Press, 2011.

Caldwell, Martha, ed. "Records of the Squatter Association of Whitehead District." *Kansas Historical Quarterly* 13, no. 1 (February 1944): 16–35.

Calloway, Colin G. *The Scratch of a Pen: 1763 and the Transformation of North America*. New York: Oxford University Press, 2006.

Carey, Charles H. *A General History of Oregon Prior to 1861*. 2 vols. Portland, OR: Metropolitan Press, 1935–1936.

Carlson, Leonard A. and Mark A. Roberts. "Indian Lands, 'Squatterism,' and Slavery: Economic Interests and the Passage of the Indian Removal Act of 1830." *Explorations in Economic History* 43 (2006): 486–504.

Carstensen, Vernon, ed. *The Public Lands: Studies in the History of the Public Domain.* Madison: University of Wisconsin Press, 1963.

Cayton, Andrew R. L. *Frontier Indiana.* Bloomington: Indiana University Press, 1996.

Cayton, Andrew R. L. *The Frontier Republic: Ideology and Politics in the Ohio Country, 1780–1825.* Kent, OH: Kent State University Press, 1986.

Cecil-Fronsman, Bill. "'Death to All Yankees and Traitors in Kansas': The *Squatter Sovereign* and the Defense of Slavery in Kansas." In *Territorial Kansas Reader*, edited by Virgil W. Dean, 215–26. Topeka: Kansas State Historical Society, 2005.

Chambers, William Nisbet. *Old Bullion Benton: Senator from the New West.* Boston: Little, Brown, 1956.

Childers, Christopher. *The Failure of Popular Sovereignty: Slavery, Manifest Destiny, and the Radicalization of Southern Politics.* Lawrence: University Press of Kansas, 2012.

Childers, Christopher. *The Webster-Hayne Debate: Defining Nationhood in the Early American Republic.* Baltimore: Johns Hopkins University Press, 2018.

Clark, Thomas D. and John D. W. Guice. *Frontiers in Conflict: The Old Southwest, 1795–1830.* Albuquerque: University of New Mexico Press, 1989.

Clifton, James A. *The Pokagons, 1683–1983: Catholic Potawatomi Indians of the St. Joseph River Valley.* Lanham, MD: University Press of America, 1984.

Cohen, Hennig and William B. Dillingham, eds. *Humor of the Old Southwest.* 3rd ed. Athens: University of Georgia Press, 1994.

Coleman, Kenneth R. "'We'll All Start Even': White Egalitarianism and the Oregon Donation Land Claim Act." *Oregon Historical Quarterly* 120, no. 4 (Winter 2019): 414–37.

Cronon, William. *Nature's Metropolis: Chicago and the Great West.* New York: W. W. Norton, 1991.

Cronon, William, George Miles, and Jay Gitlin, "Becoming West: Toward a New Meaning for Western History." In *Under an Open Sky: Rethinking America's Western Past,* edited by William Cronon, George Miles, and Jay Gitlin, 3–27. New York: W. W. Norton, 1992.

Curtis, Christopher Michael. *Jefferson's Freeholders and the Politics of Ownership in the Old Dominion.* New York: Cambridge University Press, 2012.

Davis, Winfield J. *An Illustrated History of Sacramento County, California.* Chicago: Lewis, 1890.

Dean, Adam Wesley. *An Agrarian Republic: Farming, Antislavery Politics, and Nature Parks in the Civil War Era.* Chapel Hill: University of North Carolina Press, 2015.

Decker, Leslie E. "The Great Speculation: An Interpretation of Mid-Continent Pioneering." In *The Frontier in American Development: Essays in Honor of Paul Wallace Gates,* edited by David M. Ellis, 357–80. Ithaca, NY: Cornell University Press, 1969.

DeLay, Brian. *War of a Thousand Deserts: Indian Raids and the U.S.-Mexican War.* New Haven, CT: Yale University Press, 2008.

Dick, Everett. *The Lure of the Land: A Social History of the Public Lands from the Articles of Confederation to the New Deal.* Lincoln: University of Nebraska Press, 1970.

Dodd, William Edward. *Robert J. Walker, Imperialist.* Chicago: Chicago Literary Club, 1914.

Dowd, Gregory Evans. "Custom, Text, and Property: Indians, Squatters, and Political Authority in Jacksonian Michigan." *Early American Studies: An Interdisciplinary Journal* 18, no. 2 (Spring 2020): 195–228.

Dusinberre, William. *Slavemaster President: The Double Career of James Polk.* New York: Oxford University Press, 2003.

Earle, Jonathan H. *Jacksonian Antislavery and the Politics of Free Soil, 1824–1854.* Chapel Hill: University of North Carolina Press, 2004.

Earle, Jonathan H. "The Making of the North's 'Stark Mad Abolitionists': Antislavery Conversion in the United States, 1824–1854." *Slavery and Abolition* 25, no. 3 (December 2004): 54–72.

Edelman, Murray. *The Symbolic Uses of Politics.* 1964. Reprint, Urbana: University of Illinois Press, 1985.

Egnal, Marc. *Clash of Extremes: The Economic Origins of the Civil War.* New York: Hill and Wang, 2009.

Eichert, Magdalen. "Some Implications Arising from Robert J. Walker's Participation in Land Ventures." *Journal of Mississippi History* 13, no. 1 (January 1951): 41–46.

Etcheson, Nicole. *Bleeding Kansas: Contested Liberty in the Civil War Era.* Lawrence: University Press of Kansas, 2004.

Faragher, John Mack. *Sugar Creek: Life on the Illinois Prairie.* New Haven, CT: Yale University Press, 1986.

Faragher, John Mack. *Women and Men on the Overland Trail.* New Haven, CT: Yale University Press, 1979.

Fehrenbacher, Don E. *The Dred Scott Case: Its Significance in Law.* 1978. Reprint, New York: Oxford University Press, 2001.

Feller, Daniel. *The Public Lands in Jacksonian Politics.* Madison: University of Wisconsin Press, 1984.

Foner, Eric. *Free Soil, Free Labor, Free Men: The Ideology of the Republican Party Before the Civil War.* 1970. Reprint, New York: Oxford University Press, 1995.

Formisano Ronald P. "The New Political History and the Election of 1840." *Journal of Interdisciplinary History* 23, no. 4 (Spring 1993): 661–82.

Freehling William W. *The Road to Disunion.* 2 vols. New York: Oxford University Press, 1990–2007.

Frymer, Paul. *Building an American Empire: The Era of Territorial and Political Expansion.* Princeton, NJ: Princeton University Press, 2017.

Gailmard, Sean and Jeffery A. Jenkins. "Distributive Politics and Congressional Voting: Public Lands Reform in the Jacksonian Era." *Public Choice* 175 (2018): 259–75.

Gates, Paul W. *Fifty Million Acres: Conflicts over Kansas Land Policy, 1854–1890.* 1954. Reprint, Norman: University of Oklahoma Press, 1997.

Gates, Paul W. *History of Public Land Law Development.* Washington, DC: Government Printing Office, 1968.

Gates, Paul W. *The Jeffersonian Dream: Studies in the History of American Land Policy and Development*. Albuquerque: University of New Mexico Press, 1996.

Gates, Paul W. *Land and Law in California: Essays on Land Policies*. Ames: Iowa State University Press, 1991.

Gates, Paul W. *Landlords and Tenants on the Prairie Frontier: Studies in American Land Policy*. Ithaca, NY: Cornell University Press, 1973.

Genovese, Eugene D. *The Political Economy of Slavery: Studies in the Economy and Society of the Slave South*. New York: Pantheon Books, 1965.

Genovese, Eugene D. "Yeoman Farmers in a Slaveholders' Democracy," *Agricultural History* 49, no. 2 (April 1975): 331–42.

Gray, Lewis Cecil. *History of Agriculture in the Southern United States to 1860*. Vol. 2. 1933. Reprint, New York: Peter Smith, 1941.

Gray, Susan E. *The Yankee West: Community Life on the Michigan Frontier*. Chapel Hill: University of North Carolina Press, 1996.

Greenberg, Amy S. *A Wicked War: Polk, Clay, Lincoln, and the 1846 U.S. Invasion of Mexico*. New York: Vintage Books, 2012.

Grimm, Dieter. *Sovereignty: The Origin and Future of a Political and Legal Concept*. New York: Columbia University Press, 2015.

Guilds, John Caldwell and Caroline Collins, eds. *William Gilmore Simms and the American Frontier*. Athens: University of Georgia Press, 1997.

Hahn, Steven. *A Nation Without Borders: The United States and Its World in An Age of Civil Wars, 1830–1910*. New York: Viking, 2016.

Hahn, Steven. *The Roots of Southern Populism: Yeoman Farmers and the Transformation of the Georgia Upcountry, 1850–1890*. New York: Oxford University Press, 1983.

Hall, John W. *Uncommon Defense: Indian Allies in the Black Hawk War*. Cambridge, MA: Harvard University Press, 2009.

Hämäläinen, Pekka and Samuel Truett, "On Borderlands." *Journal of American History* 98, no.2 (September 2011): 338–61.

Hartnett, Stephen John. *Democratic Dissent and the Cultural Fictions of Antebellum America*. Urbana: University of Illinois Press, 2002.

Hauck, Richard Boyd. "The Man in the Buckskin Hunting Shirt: Fact and Fiction in the Crockett Story." In *Davy Crockett: The Man, the Legend, the Legacy, 1786–1986*, edited by Michael A. Lofaro, 3–20. Knoxville: University of Tennessee Press, 1985.

Heggie, Henry Watterson. *Indians and Pioneers of Old Eliot: A Grenada County, Mississippi, Community*. Grenada, MS: Tuscahoma Press, 1989.

Henretta, James A., Eric Hinderaker, Rebecca Edwards, and Robert O. Self. *America's History*. Vol. 1, *To 1877*. 8th ed., Boston: Bedford/St. Martin's, 2011.

Hibbard, Benjamin Horace. *A History of the Public Land Policies*. 1924. Reprint, Madison: University of Wisconsin Press, 1965.

Hietala, Thomas R. *Manifest Design: Anxious Aggrandizement in Late Jacksonian America*. Ithaca, NY: Cornell University Press, 1985.

Hixson, Walter L. *American Settler Colonialism: A History*. New York: Palgrave Macmillan, 2013.

Hofstadter, Richard. *The American Political Tradition and the Men Who Made It*. 1948. Reprint, New York: Vintage Books, 1989.

Hofstadter, Richard. "William Leggett, Spokesman of Jacksonian Democracy." *Political Science Quarterly* 58, no. 4 (December 1943): 581–94.

Holt, Michael F. *The Fate of Their Country: Politicians, Slavery Extension, and the Coming of the Civil War*. New York: Hill and Wang, 2004.

Holt, Michael F. *Political Parties and American Political Development from the Age of Jackson to the Age of Lincoln*. Baton Rouge: Louisiana State University, 1992.

Holt, Michael F. *The Rise and Fall of the American Whig Party: Jacksonian Politics and the Onset of the Civil War*. New York: Oxford University Press, 1999.

Horowitz, Helen Lefkowitz. "Another 'American Cruikshank' Found: John H. Manning and the New York Sporting Weeklies." *Proceedings of the American Antiquarian Society* 112, no. 1 (April 2002): 93–126

Horsman, Reginald. *The Frontier in the Formative Years, 1783–1815*. New York: Holt, Rinehart and Winston, 1970.

Horsman, Reginald. *Race and Manifest Destiny: The Origins of American Racial Anglo-Saxonism*. Cambridge, MA: Harvard University Press, 1981.

Howat, William Frederick. *A Standard History of Lake County, Indiana, and the Calumet Region*. Vol. 1. Chicago: Lewis, 1915.

Howe, Daniel Walker. *The Political Culture of the American Whigs*. Chicago: University of Chicago Press, 1979.

Howe, Daniel Walker. *What Hath God Wrought: The Transformation of America, 1815–1848*. New York: Oxford University Press, 2007.

Hudson, Linda S. *Mistress of Manifest Destiny: A Biography of Jane McManus Storm Cazneau, 1807–1878*. Austin: Texas State Historical Association, 2001.

Hurst, James Willard. *Law and the Conditions of Freedom in the Nineteenth-Century United States*. Madison: University of Wisconsin Press, 1956.

Hurt, R. Douglas. *The Ohio Frontier: Crucible of the Old Northwest, 1720–1830*. Bloomington: Indiana University Press, 1996.

Hurtado, Albert L. *John Sutter: A Life on the North American Frontier*. Norman: University of Oklahoma Press, 2006.

Husband, Michael B. "Senator Lewis F. Linn and the Oregon Question." *Missouri Historical Review* 66, no. 1 (October 1971): 1–19.

Huston James L. *The British Gentry, the Southern Planter, and the Northern Family Farmer: Agriculture and Sectional Antagonism in North America*. Baton Rouge: Louisiana State University Press, 2015.

Huston James L. *Calculating the Value of the Union: Slavery, Property Rights, and the Economic Origins of the Civil War*. Chapel Hill: University of North Carolina Press, 2003.

Huston James L. *Stephen A. Douglas and the Dilemmas of Democratic Equality*. Lanham, MD: Rowman and Littlefield, 2007.

Huston, Reeve. *Land and Freedom: Rural Society, Popular Protest, and Party Politics in Antebellum New York*. New York: Oxford University Press, 2000.

Huston, Reeve. "Land Conflict and Land Policy in the United States, 1785–1841." In *The World of the Revolutionary American Republic: Land, Labor, and the Conflict for a Continent*, edited by Andrew Shankman, 324–45. New York: Routledge, 2014.

Hyde, Anne F. *Empires, Nations, and Families: A New History of the North American West, 1800–1860*. New York: Ecco, 2012.

Ingalls, Sheffield. *History of Atchison County, Kansas*. Lawrence: Standard Publishing, 1916.

Isenberg, Nancy. *White Trash: The 400-Year Untold History of Class in America*. New York: Viking, 2016.

James, D. Clayton. *Antebellum Natchez*. Baton Rouge: Louisiana State University, 1968.

Johannsen, Robert W. *Frontier Politics and the Sectional Conflict: The Pacific Northwest on the Eve of the Civil War*. Seattle: University of Washington Press, 1955.

Johannsen, Robert W. "John Calhoun: The Villain of Territorial Kansas?" *Trail Guide* 3, no. 3 (September 1958): 1–19.

Johannsen, Robert W. *Stephen A. Douglas*. 1973. Reprint, Urbana: University of Illinois Press, 1997.

Johansen, Dorothy O. and Charles M. Gates. *Empire of the Columbia: A History of the Pacific Northwest*. 2nd ed. New York: Harper and Row, 1967.

Johnson, David Alan. *Founding the Far West: California, Oregon, and Nevada, 1840–1890*. Berkeley: University of California Press, 1992.

Johnson, Samuel A. *The Battle Cry of Freedom: The New England Emigrant Aid Company in the Kansas Crusade*. Westport, CT: Greenwood Press, 1954.

Johnson, Susan Lee. *Roaring Camp: The Social World of the California Gold Rush*. New York: W. W. Norton, 2000.

Johnson, Walter. *River of Dark Dreams: Slavery and Empire in the Cotton Kingdom*. Cambridge, MA: Belknap Press of Harvard University Press, 2013.

Joost, Nicholas. "Reveille in the West: Western Travelers in the St. Louis *Weekly Reveille*, 1844–50." In *Travelers on the Western Frontier*, edited by John Francis McDermott, 203–40. Urbana: University of Illinois, 1970.

Joseph, Michael. "Old Comic Elton and the Age of Fun: Robert H. Elton and the Picture Book." *Children's Literature Association Quarterly* 28, no. 3 (Fall 2003): 158–70.

Kaine, David. *Jonathan Hoge Walker: The First Judge of the United States District Court for the Western District of Pennsylvania: A Sketch*. Pittsburgh: Joseph Eichbaum, 1882.

Kanazawa, Mark T. "Possession Is Nine Points of the Law: The Political Economy of Early Public Land Disposal." *Explorations in Economic History* 33 (1996): 227–49.

Kantrowitz, Stephen. *More than Freedom: Fighting for Black Citizenship in a White Republic, 1829–1889*. New York: Penguin, 2012.

Karnes, Thomas L. *William Gilpin: Western Nationalist*. 1970. Reprint, Austin: University of Texas Press, 2014.

Kastor, Peter J. *The Nation's Crucible: The Louisiana Purchase and the Creation of America.* New Haven, CT: Yale University Press, 2004.

Kastor, Peter J. *William Clark's World: Describing America in an Age of Unknowns.* New Haven, CT: Yale University Press, 2011.

Kennedy, Roger G. *Mr. Jefferson's Lost Cause: Land, Farmers, Slavery, and the Louisiana Purchase.* New York: Oxford University Press, 2003.

Klein, Philip Shriver. *President James Buchanan: A Biography.* University Park: Pennsylvania State University Press, 1962.

Klunder, Willard Carl. *Lewis Cass and the Politics of Moderation.* Kent, OH: Kent State University Press, 1996.

Kulikoff, Allan. *The Agrarian Origins of American Capitalism.* Charlottesville: University of Virginia Press, 1992.

Lause, Mark A. *Young America: Land, Labor, and the Republican Community.* Urbana: University of Illinois Press, 2005.

Lawson, Gary and Guy Seidman. *The Constitution of Empire: Territorial Expansion and American Legal History.* New Haven, CT: Yale University Press, 2004.

Lester, W. W. *Decisions of the Interior Department in Public Land Cases, and Land Laws Passed by the Congress of the United States; Together with the Regulations of the General Land Office.* Philadelphia: H. P. and R. H. Small, 1860.

Levine, Bruce. *Half Slave and Half Free: The Roots of Civil War.* New York: Hill and Wang, 1992.

Libecap, Gary D. "The Assignment of Property Rights on the Western Frontier: Lessons for Contemporary Environmental and Resource Policy." *Journal of Economic History* 67, no. 2 (June 2007): 257–91.

Limerick, Patricia Nelson. *The Legacy of Conquest: The Unbroken Past of the American West.* New York: W. W. Norton, 1987.

Linklater, Andro. *Owning the Earth: The Transforming History of Land Ownership.* New York: Bloomsbury, 2013.

Loewenberg, Robert J. *Equality on the Oregon Frontier: Jason Lee and the Methodist Mission, 1834–43.* Seattle: University of Washington Press, 1976.

Lynn, Joshua A. *Preserving the White Man's Republic: Jacksonian Democracy, Race, and the Transformation of American Conservatism.* Charlottesville: University of Virginia Press, 2019.

McCoy, Drew R. *The Elusive Republic: Political Economy in Jeffersonian America.* Chapel Hill: University of North Carolina Press, 1980.

McCurry, Stephanie. *Masters of Small Worlds: Yeoman Households, Gender Relations, and the Political Culture of the Antebellum South Carolina Low Country.* New York: Oxford University Press, 1995.

McPherson, James. *Battle Cry of Freedom: The Civil War Era.* New York: Oxford University Press, 1988.

Meinig, D. W. *Continental America, 1800–1867.* Vol. 2 of *The Shaping of America: A Geographical Perspective on 500 Years of History.* New Haven, CT: Yale University Press, 1993.

Merk, Frederick. *Fruits of Propaganda in the Tyler Administration.* Cambridge, MA: Harvard University Press, 1971.

Merk, Frederick. *Manifest Destiny and Mission in American History: A Reinterpretation.* 1963. Reprint, New York: Vintage Books, 1966.

Merk, Frederick. *The Oregon Question: Essays in Anglo-American Diplomacy and Politics.* Cambridge, MA: Belknap Press of Harvard University Press, 1967.

Meyers, Marvin. *The Jacksonian Persuasion: Politics and Belief.* 1957. Reprint, Stanford, CA: Stanford University Press, 1957.

Miles, Edwin A. *Jacksonian Democracy in Mississippi.* New York: Da Capo Press, 1970.

Miles, Tiya. *Ties That Bind: The Story of an Afro-Cherokee Family in Slavery and Freedom.* Berkeley: University of California Press, 2005.

Miller, Robert J. "American Indians, the Doctrine of Discovery, and Manifest Destiny." *Wyoming Law Review* 11, no. 2 (2011): 329–49.

Millner, Darrell. "George Bush of Tumwater: Founder of the First American Colony on Puget Sound." *Columbia Magazine* 8, no. 4 (Winter 1994–95): 14–19.

Miner, Craig and William E. Unrau. *The End of Indian Kansas: A Study of Cultural Revolution, 1854–1871.* 1978. Reprint, Lawrence: University Press of Kansas, 1990.

Moore, Shirley Ann Wilson. *Sweet Freedom's Plains: African Americans on the Overland Trails, 1841–1869.* Norman: University of Oklahoma Press, 2016.

Morgan, Edmund S. *Inventing the People: The Rise of Popular Sovereignty in England and America.* New York: W. W. Norton, 1988.

Morrison, Michael A. *Slavery and the American West: The Eclipse of Manifest Destiny and the Coming of the Civil War.* Chapel Hill: University of North Carolina Press, 1997.

Mueller, Ken S. *Senator Benton and the People: Master Race Democracy on the Early American Frontiers.* DeKalb: Northern Illinois University Press, 2014.

Murtazashvili, Ilia. *The Political Economy of the American Frontier.* New York: Cambridge University Press, 2013.

Nakamura, Masahiro. *Visions of Order in William Gilmore Simms: Southern Conservatism and the Other American Romance.* Columbia: University of South Carolina Press, 2009.

Neiderheiser, Leta Lovelace. *Jesse Applegate: A Dialogue with Destiny.* Mustang, OK: Tate Publishing, 2010.

Nelson, Scott Reynolds. *A Nation of Deadbeats: An Uncommon History of America's Financial Disasters.* New York: Alfred A. Knopf, 2012.

Nichols, David Andrew. *Engines of Diplomacy: Indian Trading Factories and the Negotiation of American Empire.* Chapel Hill: University of North Carolina Press, 2016.

Nichols, Roy Franklin. *The Disruption of American Democracy.* New York: Macmillan, 1948.

Nichols, Roy Franklin. *Franklin Pierce: Young Hickory of the Granite Hills.* Philadelphia: University of Pennsylvania Press, 1931.

Nobles, Gregory H. *American Frontiers: Cultural Encounters and Continental Conquest.* New York: Hill and Wang, 1997.

Nokes, R. Gregory. *Breaking Chains: Slavery on Trial in the Oregon Territory.* Corvallis: Oregon State University Press, 2013.

O'Callaghan, Jerry A. *The Disposition of the Public Domain in Oregon.* Washington, DC: Government Printing Office, 1960.

Opal, J. M. *Avenging the People: Andrew Jackson, the Rule of Law, and the American Nation.* New York: Oxford University Press, 2017.

Opie, John. *The Law of the Land: Two Hundred Years of American Farmland Policy.* Lincoln: University of Nebraska Press, 1987.

Ostler, Jeffrey and Nancy Shoemaker. "Settler Colonialism in Early American History: Introduction." *William and Mary Quarterly* 76, no. 3 (July 2019): 361–68.

Parton, James. *The Life of Andrew Jackson.* 3 vols. New York: Mason Brothers, 1860.

Pascoe, Peggy. *What Comes Naturally: Miscegenation Law and the Making of Race in America.* New York: Oxford University Press, 2009.

Philpott, Daniel. *Revolutions in Sovereignty: How Ideas Shaped Modern International Relations.* Princeton, NJ: Princeton University Press, 2001.

Pisani, Donald J. *Water, Land, and Law in the West: The Limits of Public Policy, 1850– 1920.* Lawrence: University Press of Kansas, 1996.

Pomeroy, Earl. *The Pacific Slope: A History of California, Oregon, Washington, Idaho, Utah, and Nevada.* 1965. Reprint, Reno: University of Nevada Press, 2003.

Potter, David M. *The Impending Crisis, 1848–1861.* New York: Harper and Row, 1976.

Pratt, Julius W. "The Origin of 'Manifest Destiny.'" *American Historical Review* 32, no. 4 (July 1927): 795–98.

Prucha, Francis Paul. *The Great Father: The United States Government and the American Indians.* Vol. 1. Lincoln: University of Nebraska Press, 1984.

Quinn, Arthur. *The Rivals: William Gwin, David Broderick, and the Birth of California.* New York: Crown, 1994.

Ramos, Raúl A. *Beyond the Alamo: Forging Mexican Ethnicity in San Antonio, 1821– 1861.* Chapel Hill: University of North Carolina Press, 2008.

Ranck, James Byrne. *Albert Gallatin Brown: Radical Southern Nationalist.* 1937. Reprint, Philadelphia: Porcupine Press, 1974.

Rayback, Joseph G. *Free Soil: The Election of 1848.* Lexington: University of Kentucky Press, 1970.

Reda, John. *From Furs to Farms: The Transformation of the Mississippi Valley, 1762–1825.* DeKalb: Northern Illinois University Press, 2016.

Remini, Robert V. *The Life of Andrew Jackson.* New York: Harper and Row, 1988.

Reséndez, Andrés. *Changing National Identities at the Frontier: Texas and New Mexico, 1800–1850.* New York: Cambridge University Press, 2005.

Robbins, Roy M. *Our Landed Heritage: The Public Domain, 1776–1936*. Princeton, NJ: Princeton University Press, 1942.

Robinson, W. W. *Land in California: The Story of Mission Lands, Ranchos, Squatters, Mining Claims, Railroad Grants, Land Scrip, Homesteads*. Berkeley: University of California Press, 1948.

Rohrbough, Malcolm J. *The Land Office Business: The Settlement and Administration of American Public Lands, 1789–1837*. New York: Oxford University Press, 1968.

Rohrbough, Malcolm J. *The Trans-Appalachian Frontier: People, Societies, and Institutions, 1775–1850*. 3rd ed. Bloomington: Indiana University Press, 2008.

Roosevelt, Theodore. *Thomas Hart Benton*. 1886. Reprint, Boston: Houghton, Mifflin and Company, 1900.

Rothman, Adam. *Slave Country: American Expansion and the Origins of the Deep South*. Cambridge, MA: Harvard University Press, 2005.

Rowland, Dunbar, ed. *Encyclopedia of Mississippi History, Comprising Sketches of Counties, Towns, Events, Institutions and Persons*. Vol. 2. Madison, WI: Selwyn A. Brant, 1907.

Saler, Bethel. *The Settlers' Empire: Colonialism and State Formation in America's Old Northwest*. Philadelphia: University of Pennsylvania Press, 2014.

Sammons, Jeffrey L. "Charles Sealsfield: A Case of Non-Canonicity." In *Autoren Damals und Heute: Literaturgeschichtliche Beispiele Veranderter Wirkungshorizonte*, edited by Gerhard P. Knapp, 155–72. Amsterdam: Rodopi, 1991.

Satz, Ronald N. *American Indian Policy in the Jacksonian Era*. Lincoln: University of Nebraska Press, 1975.

Schlesinger, Arthur M. Jr. *The Age of Jackson*. Boston: Little, Brown, 1945.

Seelye, John. "A Well-Wrought Crockett: Or, How the Fakelorists Passed Through the Credibility Gap and Discovered Kentucky." In *Davy Crockett: The Man, the Legend, the Legacy, 1786–1986*, edited by Michael A. Lofaro, 21–45. Knoxville: University of Tennessee Press, 1985.

Sellers, Charles. *The Market Revolution: Jacksonian America, 1815–1846*. New York: Oxford University Press, 1991.

Shackford, James Atkins. *David Crockett: The Man and the Legend*. 1956. Reprint, Chapel Hill: University of North Carolina Press, 1986.

Shelton, Tamara Venit. *A Squatter's Republic: Land and the Politics of Monopoly in California, 1850–1900*. San Marino, CA: Huntington Library, 2013.

Shenton, James P. *Robert John Walker: A Politician from Jackson to Lincoln*. New York: Columbia University Press, 1961.

Silbey, Joel H. *Storm over Texas: The Annexation Controversy and the Road to Civil War*. New York: Oxford University Press, 2005.

Simeone, James. *Democracy and Slavery in Frontier Illinois: The Bottomland Republic*. DeKalb: Northern Illinois University Press, 2000.

Slotkin, Richard. *The Fatal Environment: The Myth of the Frontier in the Age of Industrialization, 1800–1890*. New York: Atheneum, 1985.

Slotkin, Richard. *Regeneration Through Violence: The Mythology of the American Frontier, 1600–1860.* Middletown, CT: Wesleyan University Press, 1973.

Smith, Elbert B. *Magnificent Missourian: The Life of Thomas Hart Benton.* Philadelphia: J. B. Lippincott, 1957.

Smith, Henry Nash. *Virgin Land: The American West as Symbol and Myth.* New York: Vintage Books, 1950.

Snyder, Christina. *Great Crossings: Indians, Settlers, and Slaves in the Age of Jackson.* New York: Oxford University Press, 2017.

Stephenson, George M. *The Political History of the Public Lands from 1840 to 1862: From Pre-emption to Homestead.* Boston: Richard G. Badger, 1917.

Swierenga, Robert P. "Land Speculation and Its Impact on American Economic Growth and Welfare: A Historiographical Review." *Western Historical Quarterly* 8, no. 3 (July 1977): 283–302.

Swierenga, Robert P. *Pioneers and Profits: Land Speculation on the Iowa Frontier.* Ames: Iowa State University Press, 1968.

Taylor, Alan. "Land and Liberty on the Post-Revolutionary Frontier." In *Devising Liberty: Preserving and Creating Freedom in the New American Republic*, edited by David Thomas Konig, 81–108. Stanford, CA: Stanford University Press, 1995.

Taylor, Alan. *Liberty Men and Great Proprietors: The Revolutionary Settlement on the Maine Frontier, 1760–1820.* Chapel Hill: University of North Carolina Press, 1990.

Taylor, Alan. *William Cooper's Town: Power and Persuasion on the Frontier of the Early American Republic.* New York: Vintage Books, 1995.

Taylor, Quintard. *In Search of the Racial Frontier: African Americans in the American West, 1528–1990.* New York: W. W. Norton, 1998.

Treadway, William E. *Cyrus K. Holliday: A Documentary Biography.* Topeka: Kansas State Historical Society, 1979.

Treat, Payson Jackson. *The National Land System, 1785–1820.* New York: E. B. Treat, 1910.

Tuchinsky, Adam-Max. "'The Bourgeoisie Will Fall and Fall Forever': The *New-York Tribune*, the 1848 French Revolution, and American Social Democratic Discourse." *Journal of American History* 92, no. 2 (September 2005): 470–97.

Turner, Frederick Jackson. "The Significance of the Frontier in American History." In *The Early Writings of Frederick Jackson Turner*, 185–229. Madison: University of Wisconsin Press, 1938.

Turner, Frederick Jackson. *The United States, 1830–1850: The Nation and Its Sections.* 1935. Reprint, New York: W. W. Norton, 1963.

Umbeck, John. "The California Gold Rush: A Study of Emerging Property Rights." *Explorations in Economic History* 14 (1977): 197–226.

Valenčius, Conevery Bolton. *The Health of the Country: How American Settlers Understood Themselves and Their Land.* New York: Basic Books, 2002.

Van Atta, John R. *Securing the West: Politics, Public Lands, and the Fate of the Old Republic, 1785–1850.* Baltimore: Johns Hopkins University Press, 2014.

Villard, Oswald Garrison. *John Brown, 1800–1859: A Biography Fifty Years After.* London: Constable, 1910.

Wakelyn, Jon L. *The Politics of a Literary Man: William Gilmore Simms.* Westport, CT: Greenwood Press, 1973.

Walker, Juliet E. K. *Free Frank: A Black Pioneer on the Antebellum Frontier.* Lexington: University of Kentucky Press, 1983.

Wallis, Michael. *David Crockett: The Lion of the West.* New York: W. W. Norton, 2011.

Watson, Charles S. *From Nationalism to Secessionism: The Changing Fiction of William Gilmore Simms.* Westport, CT: Greenwood Press, 1993.

Watson, Harry L. "Conflict and Collaboration: Yeomen, Slaveholders, and Politics in the Antebellum South." *Social History* 10, no. 3 (October 1985): 273–98.

Watson, Harry L. *Liberty and Power: The Politics of Jacksonian America.* Rev. ed. New York: Hill and Wang, 2006.

Weaver, John C. *The Great Land Rush and the Making of the Modern World, 1650–1900.* Montreal: McGill-Queen's University Press, 2003.

Weber, David J. *The Mexican Frontier, 1821–1846: The American Southwest Under Mexico.* Albuquerque: University of New Mexico Press, 1982.

White, Richard. *The Middle Ground: Indians, Empires, and Republics in the Great Lakes Region, 1650–1815.* New York: Cambridge University Press, 1991.

White, Richard. *The Roots of Dependency: Subsistence, Environment, and Social Change Among the Choctaws, Pawnees, and Navajos.* Lincoln: University of Nebraska Press, 1983.

Wilentz, Sean. *Chants Democratic: New York City and the Rise of the American Working Class, 1788–1850.* New York: Oxford University Press, 1984.

Wilentz, Sean. *The Rise of American Democracy: Jefferson to Lincoln.* New York: W. W. Norton, 2005.

Wilm, Julius. *Settlers as Conquerors: Free Land Policy in Antebellum America.* Stuttgart, Germany: Franz Steiner Verlag, 2018.

Wilson, Don W. *Governor Charles Robinson of Kansas.* Lawrence: University Press of Kansas, 1975.

Wilson, Major L. *Space, Time, and Freedom: The Quest for Nationality and the Irrepressible Conflict, 1815–1861.* Westport, CT: Greenwood Press, 1974.

Wolfe, Patrick. "Settler Colonialism and the Elimination of the Native." *Journal of Genocide Research* 8, no. 4 (December 2006): 387–409.

Wood, Gordon S. *Empire of Liberty: A History of the Early Republic, 1789–1815.* New York: Oxford University Press, 2009.

Woods, Michael E. *Arguing until Doomsday: Stephen Douglas, Jefferson, Davis, and the Struggle for American Democracy.* Chapel Hill: University of North Carolina Press, 2020.

Woodward, Walter Carleton. *The Rise and Early History of Political Parties in Oregon, 1843–1868.* Portland, OR: J. K. Gill, 1913.

Young, Mary E. "Congress Looks West: Liberal Ideology and Public Land Policy in the Nineteenth Century." In *The Frontier in American Development: Essays in Honor of Paul Wallace Gates*, edited by David M. Ellis, 74–112. Ithaca, NY: Cornell University Press, 1969.

Zahler, Helene Sara. *Eastern Workingmen and National Land Policy, 1829–1862.* New York: Columbia University Press, 1941.

DISSERTATIONS AND THESES

Dallmann, William Paul. "The Spirit of America as Interpreted in the Works of Charles Sealsfield." PhD diss., Washington University, 1935.

Miles, Edwin A. "Robert J. Walker—His Mississippi Years." Master's thesis, University of North Carolina, 1949.

Taylor, Holly Zumwalt. "Neither North nor South: Sectionalism, St. Louis Politics, and the Coming of the Civil War, 1846–1861." PhD diss., University of Texas at Austin, 2004.

Thomas, Paul F. "George Bush." Master's thesis, University of Washington, 1965.

Index

For the benefit of digital users, indexed terms that span two pages (e.g., 52–53) may, on occasion, appear on only one of those pages.